HENRY JAMES

LETTERS

Volume II
1875–1883

The Thayer drawing of Henry James

HENRY JAMES LETTERS

Edited by

Leon Edel

Volume II

1875-1883

First published in Great Britain 1978 by
MACMILLAN LONDON LIMITED
4 Little Essex Street London WC2R 3LF
and Basingstoke
Associated companies in Delhi, Dublin,
Hong Kong, Johannesburg, Lagos, Melbourne,
New York, Singapore and Tokyo

Printed in Hong Kong

Acknowledgments

The letters in this volume come from a variety of institutions and sources; and I want to express my thanks to those who have helped me assemble them. The brief guide-words at the beginning of each letter certify not only the location of the document but imply also my gratitude. The abbreviations refer to the following collections:

Barrett—C. Waller Barrett collection at the University of Virginia
BM—British Museum, Manuscript Division
Brown—John Hay Library, Brown University
Colby—Colby College Library
Congress—Library of Congress, Manuscript Division
Cornell—Cornell University Library
Duke—Duke University Library
Gardner—Isabella Stewart Gardner Museum, Boston
Harvard—Houghton Library, Harvard College
Louvenjoul—Louvenjoul Collection, Chantilly, France
Mass. Historical—Massachusetts Historical Society, Boston
Morgan—Morgan Library, New York
N.Y. Public Library—New York Public Library, Astor, Lenox and Tilden Foundations, Manuscript Division
Scotland—The National Library, Edinburgh
Trinity—Library of Trinity College, Cambridge, England
Vaux—Robertson James Archive
Yale—Beinecke Library, American Collection, Yale University

As in the previous volume, Ts signifies typescript; Mf microfilm; and Ms holograph.

I am indebted to the following for letters designated as "Ms Private"—Robert Taylor, Richard L. Purdy, Mrs. Paul Hammond, H. Livingston Schwartz III, the late Katharine Lewis, Count Bernardo Rucellai, the Marchesa Fossi, and Phyllis Wheelock. I

want to mention in especial the kindness of C. Waller Barrett who
made available to me his collection long before he moved it into
the Barrett Wing of the University Library at Charlottesville. I
have often thanked, and do so again, Dr. W. H. Bond, the director
of the Houghton Library, and its librarian, Carolyn E. Jakeman.
Alan S. Bell, of the Department of Manuscripts in the National
Library of Scotland, has shown a very particular interest, as have
Professors Donald Gallup of Yale and Henry James Vaux of
Berkeley.

L. E.

Honolulu
1975

Contents

Illustrations

Introduction

"I take possession of the old world—I inhale it—I appropriate it!" Henry James wrote these exultant words to his family (as we have seen) on his arrival in London in 1875. His was indeed an act of taking possession and of appropriation, as if he were a foreign conqueror, planting a standard—an American standard—in the midst of European civilization. The letters that follow show Henry James in the act of carrying out his conquests. First he lays siege to Paris; and then, after a sudden change of direction, a swift crossing of the Channel, he establishes the center and focus of his art in London, that "great grey Babylon" which became for him the center of the Western world.

His earlier letters showed us a small boy, a precocious adolescent, a young novice in letters. His letters of the 1870's, in their abundance as weekly chronicles, sent by packet across three thousand miles of ocean, show the simple strategies by which James moved toward his long-planned goals. He wanted fame, he wanted "society," he wanted money—but the synthesis of these ambitions was personal freedom: freedom to be an artist, to pursue his art in relative security. He had no illusions about the extent of his fame; he was aware of the limitations of his "popularity." The silver cord stretched these many miles across the sea has provided posterity with a weekly record, long and continuous, of Quincy Street's ambitious son. In no other years of Henry James's career is his life documented so fully or consistently. He is sensitively attuned to parental expectations and family myths. Nevertheless, a great deal of information is to be found within the record of a complex American temperament seeking to impose itself on a foreign environment.

From the first there is the stance of the "professional." He believes in himself; he believes in his art; he believes that he deserves proper rewards for literary endeavor, for the works of his long-prepared skill and such genius as he possesses. Above all we can discern James's enormous capacity for work. He has an almost Balzacian prodigality and fertility; he is determined to find glory and to bestow it on his family, and with it the proper pecuniary position that will ease financial stresses in Quincy Street. He is the first "earner" among the five James children.

We see in the letters an equable temperament: Henry James is on candid terms with himself. He follows his bent and his feelings rather than cutting himself to the family mold and the family's demands. His letters to his friends show the same kind of candor, as well as the abundance of his wit and his sophistication—this son of New York and Boston who seems to have been a cosmopolitan without ever passing through the stage of being "provincial." He finds Flaubert and his *cénacle* insular; he can meet them on the ground of their own language—and with great fluency—while they know not a word of his. Perhaps this was why the cosmopolitan Ivan Turgenev, among his other qualities, had so potent an appeal for the cosmopolitan Henry James. Both novelists came to France, Europe's crossroads of culture, as finished cosmopolites out of great sleeping continents just beginning to stir before assuming a role in the world.

If the present volume offers many details in the building of James's personal career, it takes us also intimately into the Victorian world of England, its drawing rooms, its dinners, its country houses. We see this world through the critical and perceptive eyes of a man who calls himself an "observant stranger." Such an American view of the England of that time is unique in our literary annals. Henry Adams had an analogous view during his London years, but he was weighed down by history, by politics, by the vicissitudes of the Civil War—and then he was an Adams! James's vision is always that of the objective artist for whom the changing human scene is a constant answer to curiosity, observation, search for the foundation materials of all novels: how humans organize and live their lives. He moves through the London world with a kind "sweet reasonableness" and good nature which strongly appeals to his hosts.

As we have noted, James went to Paris first, stopping in London only long enough to complete his wardrobe. The letters of his year in the French capital document for us a series of fertile intellectual and artistic adventures. No other American came as close to the Flaubert circle; no other American acquired so warm an intimacy with one of the great Russians. But James, who studied the French closely, and seems to have tried to see as much of Parisian and country life as was possible to him, found himself a stranger in that land. The French were not organized for the kind of hospitality which the English, with their larger social ease and their greater wealth, could offer to an American steeped in the English tradition and deeply saturated in its imagination—that is, its literature. France was stimulating to James's intellect. But the French simply were not *accueillant* to an American stranger; and after a year in the French capital, the American followed his intuitions and settled in the heart of London, a few minutes' walk from Piccadilly Circus. There, in dusky lodgings, with a sooty blank wall facing the window at which he wrote—there was nothing to distract his imagination— he created those early tales of Americans in England, of the Old World and the New, of outraged innocence and provincial ig- norance, which established him as one of the most civilized writers in the English-speaking world.

England speedily opened its arms to him, as it does to anyone who is at ease with the world. It is recorded that diners-out paused on the great stairways of London's houses to look at the brown- bearded keen-eyed American—then thirty-three—who reminded them of the intensity and passion of Elizabethan sea captains. London's clubs, its literary salons, its elderly dowagers, received the genial American bachelor with warmth and even enthusiasm, and its codes, even its rudenesses, provided a great deal for the play of his benign and "accepting" American mind. He entered heartily into the English social game, as his volume *Portraits of Places* shows. This book contains many of his early impressions of England as well as later-recorded memories; in a sense it represents the public distillation of the private opinions contained in his long letters home, as well as his appetite for life and the probity of his judgments.

The letters here selected from great masses of correspondence in many archives take us to the end of the first phase of James's career—his discovery of the "international" theme, his growing literary success arising out of "Daisy Miller"—and continue to his first large masterpiece, *The Portrait of a Lady*. At the end of the volume, with the death of his parents, the silver cord is cut. We come then to a new kind of correspondence: that of the artist in the world of his art.

As in the first volume, I have continued to edit these letters with a modicum of footnotes and to correct silently the slips of the pen resulting from James's rapid scrawl. His letters speak to us with such directness and eloquence that only the lightest editorial hand should be interposed between James and his readers.

Brief Chronology

1875: Settles at 29 rue de Luxembourg. Meets Turgenev, Flaubert, Edmond de Goncourt, Renan, Daudet, Zola.

1876: Writes series of Paris letters for New York *Tribune*. Serializes *The American*. Visits Paris salons and studies French theater. Summer in south of France, glimpse of Spain. In autumn decides to move to London.

1876–1877: Establishes himself at 3 Bolton Street, Piccadilly. Begins extensive English social life.

1877: Writes series of essays on English life. Visits Paris and Rome; starts country visits in England.

1878: Achieves fame with "Daisy Miller" and "An International Episode."

1879–1880: *The Europeans, Washington Square, Confidence.*

1880–1881: Travels in Italy and Switzerland. Completes *Portrait of a Lady.*

1881: Revisits United States.

1882: Death of mother. Dramatizes "Daisy Miller." Returns to England. Makes "little tour" of France. Returns to United States in December on death of father.

1883: Discharges duties as father's executor and returns to England.

I
The Siege of Paris

1875-1876

1
The Siege of Paris

Henry James began his permanent expatriation by a series of visits to his London tailor. With a well-organized English wardrobe, he crossed the Channel and took up residence in Paris, in the rue de Luxembourg. All his life he would seek to live in the center of cities, and always with a park at the end of the given street. The particular street, today called the rue Cambon, leads from the Boulevards to the Tuileries. The record of his year in the French capital—a year that cast a light on his entire future—is sufficiently told in his family letters: his meetings with Ivan Turgenev and assorted Russian émigrés; the entrée given him by the Russian to Flaubert and his circle—Zola, Daudet, Edmond de Goncourt, and the then unpublished Maupassant. James also moved in royalist circles, introduced by French journalists to whom he had letters from the *Nation*. The American studied the waning aristocracy with fascination; he felt he was in Balzac's world—but only on its periphery.

Having committed himself to write letters on the arts and Paris society for the New York *Tribune,* he struggled to find the journalistic idiom and the journalistic subject: but he had no flair for reportage; his interests were transcendently literary for so popular a journal. The record of his writings for that paper has been told in the collection of his various contributions titled *Parisian Sketches* (1957) and it shows him attending sessions of the Assembly at Versailles, noting the progess of the emerging Third Republic, and his casual encounters with various French public figures. At the same time he must write a novel in order to support himself, and the result is *The American,* intended for the *Galaxy* but serialized in the *Atlantic Monthly*—a novel James always felt he had written in too great a hurry but whose melodrama made it almost a best-seller.

Only his refusal to give it a happy ending kept it from being a popular success. He wrote steadily in Paris. He had formed, by now, regular habits of work and relaxation. He gave himself, as we can see, only a month's holiday, during August of 1874, when he visited an American friend who had made a French marriage and lived in a toy chateau (as it appears today), that of Varennes near Montargis. He got to know the American colony in Paris intimately and certain revolutionary as well as aristocratic foreign exiles, who provided him with material he would incorporate later in *The Princess Casamassima*. He had arrived in Paris in November 1875; he stayed until December 1876 and then, quite suddenly, decided he had had enough. He made a straight crossing of the Channel into the heart of the English winter, into the thick fogs of smoke-smudged London. He found rooms in Bolton Street where he had a view, by leaning out of his window, of the Green Park. Here he became, in a very short time, the well-known bachelor of Bolton Street, the darling of certain London hostesses. And here he achieved a certain "show" of fame of which he later spoke.

To His Parents

Ms Harvard

London
Nov. 9*th* [1875]

Dearest dears—

I am still in London you see, and I drop you this line to make things comfortable for you until I am able to write from Paris that I am in some way settled—for you shall not hear from me until I do. I have been waiting here these ten days for my clothes to be made. At last they have arrived—and very handsome they are—and I depart tomorrow *via* Calais. I have little to relate and my stay here has not been eventful. I have seen but two persons. I called for half an hour, on Sunday on Leslie Stephen, who was good and friendly as before; and I went out to a place near Richmond to see my old friend Coulson of Homburg—he being laid up with a lame leg. I found him married to a Miss Unwin, great-granddaughter, of Cowper's Mrs. U., and living in a charming old house—his mother-in-law's—on the Thames, in a lovely neighborhood. He hobbled out with me to Ham House, near by, which belongs to Lord Dysart, his wife's uncle, and of which enchanting spot I enclose to Alice a most ineffectual photograph. She would have enjoyed my lunch in the bosom of the Unwin family, who would have reminded her of the jealous lady of Lausanne.[1]—For the rest, I have scribbled somewhat during the day and gone to the play in the evening. Of course I have seen Henry Irving, who is clever, but by no means a genius.[2] I enclose his photo. London is as usual; I should like living here if I belonged to a club and were in society. I think on the whole it strikes me as stuffier and duskier indoors and smuttier and damper out than ever before. As you sit in your room you seem to taste the very coal in the great clumsy fires, and when you open your windows for fresh air you admit upon your book, your linen and your skin, a rain of sootflakes. I am impatient for glittering Paris—especially as I expect letters there. Peace be with you all!

Your affectionate
H. James Jr.

1. An allusion to HJ's European trip of 1872.
2. Irving was playing Macbeth. HJ's note on his acting appeared in the *Nation,* unsigned, on 25 November 1875.

To Henry James Sr.

Ms Harvard

Paris. Rue de Luxembourg. 29.
Nov. 18th [1875]

Dear Father:

I received a couple of days since your letter of Oct. 31st with its account of your sudden return from Milwaukee, and Aunt Kate's serious illness. I have waited till today to answer it, because I was but just settled in my lodging and I wished to leave myself time to look about me and tell you how I found myself. I am greatly grieved to hear of Aunt Kate's downfall from her high estate of vigor. It shakes one's faith in human nature. I am afraid, from what you say, that she suffered much and that her convalescence must be slow. Give her all my love and sympathy. I shall write to her the next time—she will then be completely able, I hope, to do justice to letters. Nurse her well and make her better than ever! Of all the things that occurred to me as possibly transpiring at home, in the night watches of the dismal voyage, that was the last I thought of.

I have been exactly a week in Paris; but it seems a long week, so permanently and comfortably am I established. I spent my first two or three days knocking about, looking for rooms; which I found wearisome and annoying work. At last, when I was on the point of collapsing upon something that only half suited me, I stumbled by accident into this place, which completely suits me, and where behold me installed for five months. Do you remember the Rue de Luxembourg? It runs from the Rue de Rivoli to the Boulevard des Capucines, and has the advantage of being both central and noiseless. If you were to see me I think you would pronounce me well off: a snug little *troisième* with the eastern sun, two bedrooms, a parlor, an antechamber and a kitchen. Furniture clean and pretty, house irreproachable, and a gem of a *portier,* who waits upon me. I am near everything it is convenient, in winter weather, to be near; and altogether the material basis for existence is comfortably assured. You will be interested in my figures: I pay for my apartment 325 frs. a month. Considering how nice it is it isn't dear, and when I reflect upon my last winter's disbursements in New York it is remarkably cheap. I pay the porter 30 frs. a month for all conceivable service, and I pay nine frs. a month for the hire of washing of linen, in abundance. I have a kitchen full of copper *casseroles,* and a cupboard full of glass and china (my *antichambre* being at need a dining room); I have mirrors and clocks and curtains and lamps and picturesque candlesticks in plenty; and for a large monthly wood-pile in my kitchen I pay about 25 frs. more. You can now enter sympathetically into my situation.

I find Paris the same old Paris—a city of shop-fronts, a great fancy bazaar. I would give fifty of it for that great interesting old

6

London; but if one can't be in London, this is next best. —*Apropos* of London I had a horrid time on the channel-crossing from Dover to Calais, where the boats are mere squalid little cockles. I stayed, I think, a day or two in London after I last wrote, and just before leaving (don't tell this last to Aunt Mary Tweedy) saw Lady Rose[1] —a very agreeable embodiment of good manners, good sense and good humor. I also saw her daughter Mrs. Clarke, whom I liked, and who sent a very particular—in fact very tender—message to Willy, whom she had once associated with at Newport and of whom she seemed to have retained a very high opinion.—Here I have seen but two people—Mrs. Mason (Sumner) who is spending the autumn here to be near a doctor, and with whom I have fraternized greatly (she is a most comfortable creature, especially for so handsome a woman). I wish she were going to be here all winter: but she leaves Dec. 1st for Rome. Yesterday A.M. appeared Charles Peirce, who is wintering here and who had heard of me from William.[2] He took me up very vigorously, made me dine with him at the Maison Dorée, and spend the evening at his rooms, which are very charming. He seems quite a swell (at least from the point of view of that little house on the car-track where I last knew him)—has a secretary, etc.—The weather is mild, but like Paris autumn, too rainy for comfort.—I think I have told you everything. Tell me everything in turn. I took much pleasure in your favorable mention of the boys, and in Bob's changes. May it yield him all prosperity. I have not seen the *Academy's* notice, but have sent for it. I infer, from what you say, that Aunt Kate will be still in Cambridge. If she has recovered sufficiently to go to New York send her this. Love to everyone; I perish for Dido.[3] Address everything as above. Love to all. Think kindly, dear Dad, of your affectionate son.

H. J. Jr.

1. Lady Rose, before her marriage to Sir John Rose, was Charlotte Temple, an aunt to HJ's Temple cousins and sister of Mrs. Edmund Tweedy.
2. Charles Sanders Peirce (1839–1914), physicist, mathematician, and one of America's foremost philosophers. His philosophy of pragmatism profoundly influenced William James.
3. The family dog.

To Whitelaw Reid

Ms Brown

29 Rue de Luxembourg
November 22*nd* [1875]

My dear Sir:[1]

I enclose herewith my first attempt at a letter to the *Tribune*. I
hope it will pass muster. I have been here but a few days and feel
by no means *au courant* or wound up to the writing pitch. This is
a thing which will have to come little by little; the lapse of time will
help me more and more to do as I desire. Meanwhile I will do what
I can. I have unfortunately had no *Tribune* at hand, and have not
been able to take a very accurate measure of my copy. I am afraid
there will be rather too much than too little. I hope, however, that
there will be about just enough. Let me also hope that any heading
prefixed to the letter will be as brief and simple as possible. The above
is my permanent address. I beg you, if Mr. Hay is in New York, to
commend me very kindly to him.

Yours very truly
H. James Jr.

1. HJ's correspondence with Reid, publisher of the New York *Tribune,*
and the letters the novelist wrote for that journal are contained in *Parisian
Sketches,* edited by Leon Edel and Ilse Dusoir Lind (1957).

To F. P. Church

Ms N.Y. Public Library

Paris, Rue de Luxembourg 29
Dec. 1*st* [1875]

My dear Mr. Church[1]
[the first page of this letter is missing]
. . . this before I left N.Y.

I propose to take for granted, as soon as I can, that you will be
ready to publish, on receipt of them, the opening chapters of a
novel. I have got at work upon one sooner than I expected, and

particularly desire it to come out without delay. The title of the thing is *The American*. I hope you will not consider that it will interfere with such other serials as you may have under way, nor deem it a drawback if it runs over into next year. I will send you as promptly as possible the first of the MS.

Yours very truly,
H. James Jr.

1. Editor of the *Galaxy*.

To Catharine Walsh

Ms Harvard

Rue de Luxembourg 29.
Dec. 3d [1875]

Dearest Aunt Kate

I would have written to you before this, to condole with you in your sufferings and congratulate you on your recovery if my time had not been particularly occupied in working to make up the lost days which my travels etc the last month have made so numerous. I wrote to father about a fortnight since so you know that I am in Paris, and housed for the winter. Yesterday came a letter from William of Nov. 14th., in which to my grief he speaks of my first letter from London not having arrived. What an age it seems since it was posted! But he speaks of your being still in Cambridge and I trust you will be there when this comes. I shall tell them to open it if you are not, and then forward it to you. I am afraid you have suffered much, for every one says that you have behaved so sweetly. (By every one I mean father, mother and William. I think I acknowledged in my last the receipt of mother's letter). It was only fair you should at last be laid low yourself, to let the rest of us return some of your past favors. But now that the account is a little more "square," I trust that neither you nor anyone else will ever be ill again. But I won't talk to you about this; you would rather hear about myself and my circumstances. My chief "circumstance" is the

vicious Paris cold which has set in in all its fury. The cold in itself
is not so bad (it has been snowing these three days), but the draughts
thro' windows and doors, the ineffectual fires and the black darkness.
But I sit muffled in rugs, cardigans and strange cloth shoes and I get
on. I have had a very quiet fortnight since I wrote, and nothing
momentous has befallen me. I have an extremely comfortable, convenient and agreeable apartment, with a jewel of a servant (the
portier) and in this respect am thoroughly well off. It was a very
happy find. I have seen three or four people—all, save one, old
stories: Mrs. Mason, the poor Crafts, Mrs. Von Hoffmann etc.[1]
The former have left Paris—the Crafts going to Cannes. James Crafts
gives a poor account of himself, but he looked well and seemed
cheerful. They are all in a poor way—Mrs. Annie Shaw having
developed some cruel malady (a tumor) and their means being
narrower than heretofore. So at least says Mrs. Mason. Mrs. Von
H. lives in a species of Palace along side the Arc de Triomphe, and
is hospitable but unattractive. But my new acquaintance was interesting—none other than the great Muscovite novelist—the immortal
Ivan Petrowitch [Sergeitch]! I wrote to Turgénieff and asked per-
mission to come and see him. He answered most cordially, and
appointed an hour, in the morning.[2] He lives in an out of the way
street, in the Montmartre direction, in the hôtel of M. and Mme.
Viardot, who are apparently his nearest and dearest. I saw them both
for a moment. Turgénieff made me very welcome and I took an
unprecedented fancy to him. He is a magnificent creature, and much
handsomer than his portraits. I sat and talked with him for two hours
upon a great variety of topics. We got on very well; I think he
liked me, and that if opportunity served we might become intimate.
But opportunity will not serve, for he goes shortly to St. Petersburg
for the winter. Besides, I have an idea that his residence with the
Viardots makes him rather inaccessible, and they keep him much to
themselves—the brutes! But I shall keep hold of him as far as I can,
and see him again before he leaves. He said he was coming to see
me, but he has not turned up. I remember nothing particular that he
said. He speaks English well, though stiffly, from want of practice,
and said no language was comparable to the Russian. He seemed

very simple and kind etc; his face and shoulders are hugely broad, his stature very high, and his whole aspect and temperament of a larger and manlier kind than I have ever yet encountered in a scribbler. I should think acquaintance with him would be a mine of satisfaction. He told me that, after the Viardots, his most intimate friend was Gustave Flaubert, to whom he offered to introduce me. He is also intimate with Mme. Sand, and said he would make me know her. Unfortunately, she is very rarely in Paris. I have seen no other foreigners of distinction except Charles Peirce. Godkin sent me two or three days ago a letter to Auguste Laugel,[3] which I left yesterday, with my card, at his door. I see Charles Peirce quite often, at the dinner hour, and we have several times dined together and gone to the theatre. I don't find him of thrilling interest, but he seems so much more gentle and urbane than I remembered him in Cambridge—that I think well of him. I should doubtless think better still if I were an astronomer or a logician. He is impatient to get out of Paris, which he dislikes. I have been pretty often to the theatre, having, as yet, after scribbling days, no other resource for the evening. The Francais is, as ever, much better than anything else, and I won't torment you by saying how much, in spite of my *blasé* perceptions, I still enjoy it. Mrs. Kemble has very kindly sent me a letter to Mme Mohl,[4] a famous old lady here who keeps the last of the saloons and has many celebrities. I have seen W. H. Huntington, a forlorn old womanish but amiable individual.[5] He has lived here twenty two years, and speaks no French, and knows no one whatever. As a social or "worldly" acquaintance he is of no value. But he seemed a kindly old fellow. I have left myself no space for commentaries on home news; but I will enclose a line to William. Farewell dearest aunt. I devoutly hope that when this reaches you you will be all your wondrous self again.

Ever your loving nephew
H. J. Jr.

1. James Mason Crafts (1839–1917) was a renowned chemist, later to be president of M.I.T., who lived much abroad. HJ had met Mrs. Mason and Mrs. Von Hoffmann during his stay in Rome in 1873–74.

2. HJ here uses the French transliteration for Turgenev. The Russian nove-

list had received James at his apartment in the rue de Douai house of the Viardots on 22 November 1875.

3. Auguste Laugel (1830–1914), a French authority on British and American history. He wrote on French affairs for the *Nation*.

4. Mme Jules Mohl (1793–1883), born Mary Clarke, had married the German-orientalist and had a famous salon. Her home and garden at 120 rue du Bac is described by HJ in his scenario for *The Ambassadors*. (*Notebooks*, p. 373. See also Kathleen O'Meare, *Mme Mohl, Her Salon and Her Friends,* 1886.)

5. W. H. Huntington (1820–1885), a Paris correspondent of the New York *Tribune*.

To William James

Ms Harvard

Rue de Luxembourg 29.
Dec. 3d [1875]

Dear William.

I have safely received your letter of Nov. 14th. My own from London must have come immediately after it left. Since then I have written three times (including letter just sent to Aunt Kate). This last, which if she has left Quincy Street you had better open and read, will give you some gossip about myself. I am very comfortable and have every ground for contentment and as Uncle Robertson would say, for "gratitude." I am very well lodged, and bating the dismal prospect of the Paris winter weather and the in-door cold, have nothing but good to say of everything. The improvement in my physical condition which I hoped would ensue upon a return to this climate, gave from the first of my arrival, very marked symtoms of setting in. The difficulty of keeping warm is against me, but if they continue I will let you know more about it. In such of your news as was good—your own condition etc.—I much rejoiced. May it daily increase! Thanks also for the note from Bob, about his farm. I hope he will thrive mightily; but from the point of view of the Rue de Luxembourg it is hard to enter into his situation. I have seen few people—chiefly Turgénieff of whom I descanted to Aunt Kate. He is a most attractive man and I took a great shine to him. I saw a couple of times J. Crafts who had heard from you and has gone to Cannes. His countenance seemed healthy and his conversation cheerful, but he said he was poorly. Also Charles Peirce, who wears beautiful clothes etc. He is busy swinging pendulums at the Observatory and thinks himself indifferently treated by the Paris scientists. We meet every two or three days to dine together; but tho' we get on very well, our sympathy is economical rather than intellectual.—I have plenty of work here, and shall be able to do it comfortably. I can think of nothing in life to put into the *Tribune:* it is quite appalling. But I suppose it will come. I see *Roderick Hudson* is out. Send me any notices you see of it. You will of course allow for all the misprints in the *Balzac;*[1] in one quotation there is a whole line left out. That is the bane of my present situation. I suppose you will have twigged the translation of my tale in the *Revue* of Nov. 15th.[2] I don't know by whom it was done —I suppose by Mme Bentzon; whom, if it was, I shall know. It was copied into the *Indépendance Belge!* Write me what you (and others) think of the close of *Roderick Hudson*. I shall speedily begin, in the *Galaxy,* another novel: it is the best I can do. Thank you for sending Shephard's letter, about my bill. You don't mention what the amount was; and I am glad on the whole not to know. It must have been hideously large. Father will know all I feel about his paying it. Please to tell him also that I have been obliged to use my letter of credit rather more than I expected. My ten days in London, purchases of clothes, etc., and journey, and first expenses of installation here made it necessary. But before very long this will stop, I trust. Meanwhile I hope Osgood[3] has paid him the money he owes me and concerning which I solemnly enjoined him. I also make over to the family the full profits, such as they may be, of *Roderick Hudson,* in return for its advances. May they be something decent! Farewell. (The call upon Laugel has just been followed by an invitation to dinner.) Love to all and especial compliments to Alice on her heroics as a nurse.

Yours always

H. J. Jr.

1. HJ's essay on Balzac appeared in the December 1875 *Galaxy* (XX, 814–836).
2. "The Last of the Valerii," translated by Lucien Biart, appeared in the *Revue des Deux Mondes,* XII, 431–455.
3. James Ripley Osgood (1836–1892) of Boston, publisher of *Roderick Hudson* and other early works by HJ.

To Henry James Sr.

Ms Harvard

Rue de Luxembourg 29.
Dec. 20*th* [1875]

Dear father.

I received a long time since a letter from William of Nov. 14th; but weeks elapsed without my getting anything more until last two days since when there came a too brief note from you (inclosing a letter from New York) without any date, and not mentioning the receipt of any of my letters. But I suppose they have all reached you. I am sorry to say I can write but little today, as I am afflicted with a species of felon on my right hand; I hasten to scribble a few lines before it gets worse—tho' I imagine it will not be very bad. So excuse calligraphy. The principal fact you mentioned was that Aunt Kate and Alice had gone to New York. This implies that the former is quite restored and, I hope, that the latter was going to have a "good time." The days roll over my head, without bringing anything very new. I am very comfortable and do a good deal of work, but I don't make hordes of acquaintances. I wrote you that I had seen Turgénieff and liked him much. Since then I have seen him again several times, with unabated regard. He seems rather older and drowsier than I at first thought him, but he is the best of men. He has twice called on me, and last Sunday he took me and introduced me to Gustave Flaubert. I took a mighty fancy to F. as well; he is not at all what his books led me to expect. "*C'est un naïf,*" as Tourgénieff says—a great, stout, handsome, simple, kindly, elderly fellow, rather embarrassed at having a stranger presented to him, and bothering himself over what he can say and do. He is about the

14

style of figure of old Dumas, but with a serious, sober face, a big moustache, and a mottled red complexion. He looks like some weather beaten old military man. There were present Edmond de Goncourt (*type du gentilhomme français*), Charpentier the publisher, Emile Zola, the novelist (a very common fellow), Catulle Mendès, son-in-law of T. Gautier, a sort of Parisian B. G. Hosmer, etc. I suppose I shall see Flaubert again once or twice. The only other people I have seen have been the Laugels, who asked me to dine. There were none but obscure Americans at the dinner. Laugel is polite, but he is not (to me) particularly *simpatico* (*au contraire*). (Don't tell this to Godkin, who introduced me to him.) He has a deadly melancholy tone and manner which depress and distance one. Very likely indeed, though, he will improve on acquaintance; and it is very natural he should be long-faced, as his party have just received a complete and to my mind most merited defeat. I find the political situation here very interesting and devour the newspapers. The great matter for the last fortnight has been the election of the seventy-five life-members of the new Senate, by the Assembly, in which the coalition of the Republicans, Legitimists and Bonapartists (which the attitude of the Orléanists has made necessary) had entirely routed the latter. The Left has carried through the whole thing with great skill and good sense, and there is a prospect of there being a very well composed Senate.[1] But you will have read about all this;—only read Laugel's letters in the *Nation cum grano*. Mme Laugel is very well, and she has a very agreeable youthful elderly sister or cousin, Miss Weston by name. The winter is turning out extremely mild, and to me most delightful. There was at first a little scare of cold weather (tho' nothing that we should call cold); but for three weeks, now, all has been soft and moist and grey, with no complain [*sic*] to complain of. Everyone assures me that it is the regular winter weather, and I conclude that the Paris winter has been greatly maligned. To me it is eminently satisfactory, but I am eating my heart out with longing for Italy. It is a crime to be in Europe and not to be there. I have seen two or three times W. H. Huntington, a kindly long-haired hermit. I met the other day in the street Mrs. Dorr, on her way to Rome; more fantastic and "intellectual" than ever.[2] I meant to add about poor Turgénieff that there [are] insuperable limits to seeing much of him, for the poor man is a slave—the slave of Mme Viardot.[3] She has made him her property, is excessively jealous, keeps him to herself etc. She, her husband and her children (of one of whom T. is supposed to be papa,) keep him as a sort of *vache à lait,* use him, spend his money etc. Such is the tale and I am told his friends greatly deplore his situation, and it is certainly an odd one all round. Mme V. is old and ugly, but, I believe, very agreeable. T. strikes me as a man with something pressing upon him and making him unhappy, more than he knows. I have written three letters to the *Tribune*[4]—tho' I am afraid the first was a failure from excessive length and being pitched in too vague and diffuse a key. I like the work and am sure I can do it easily and well, if providence only furnishes subjects. I wish Alice would cut them out and keep them for me: I should like to have duplicates. Send any notices of *Roderick Hudson,* which (the book) I have not yet seen, and don't seem likely to, as Trübner is deaf to all appeals to send it to me, as Osgood wrote me to bid him do. William's notice of Saintsbury was excellent; of course the editorial note was also his. Have there been any notice or remarks on my *Balzac*? Send anything you have seen. The letter you enclosed was from Mrs. Charles Peirce, about that and "R. H." I continue to see C. Peirce himself, who turns out quite a "sweet" fellow. Osgood tells me he sent you a cheque for $200 on my *Transatlantic Sketches* which pray keep. It ought to have [been] about $260, and I have written about it. You don't mention the receipt of it, but I suppose it had come. I received the other cheque from Uncle Robertson, which I also wish you had kept. If I had known Shelton was going to send it to you, I would have notified you to do so. My request had been that it should be sent to me. Let me add *à propos* of this, that they owe me $125 for another article which they will probably send you; this you will please to keep. I think you would hardly find it pay to *subscribe* either to the *Débats* or the *Temps* and would find that seven numbers a week would overwhelm you. They are both now so exclusively political that you would be glutted with discussions which are interesting mainly if you are here. If you took either, however, it should be the *Débats*, as that has much oftener a literary article. The *Temps* almost never does. Schérer[5] (who has just been elected for life to the Senate) still writes for the latter, but only on politics. Mme Laugel tells me that he is an abandoned gambler—has "gambled away two or three fortunes." I don't know where he got them; it may be only inimical scandal. But it will help you to allow for the Laugel point of view that they consider the moderate and sagacious *Temps* too radical. I see both the *Débats* and the *Temps* every day and can easily mail you two or three a week. In this way you can judge for yourself, and to see them so will perhaps content you.—You say nothing of Bob and Wilky. I suppose B. has bought the farm spoken of in his letter (enclosed to me.) Good luck to him. I am waiting anxiously for the letter William was to write me on the Sunday after yours. But make mother write too; I have heard from her but once since I left home; it seems an age. I invite Alice also to let me know of her "New York life." I suppose the [*word illegible*] has been put by— I still hanker for Dido, in spite of all her unladylikeisms. Much love to the Bootts—and tell Lizzie I will answer a letter I lately received from her at the earliest possible moment.

Your loving
H.

1. The Third Republic, which lasted until the German invasion of France in 1940, had been officially proclaimed in 1870 following the collapse of Napoleon III. It had functioned provisionally without government structure, but the constitutional groundwork was now being laid.

2. Julia C. R. Dorr (1825–1913) contributed prose and poetry to various American journals.

3. Pauline Viardot (1821–1910), the celebrated singer beloved of Turgenev; Mme. Viardot had accepted Turgenev in her household after he became one of her devoted admirers. HJ repeats the gossip of the time about the two.

4. See footnote to letter of 22 November 1875.

5. Edmund Schérer (1815–1889), the French critic.

To Mrs. Henry James Sr.

Ms Harvard

Rue de Luxembourg 29.

Jan. *24th* [1876]

Dearest mother:

I have just received a letter from you, of January 11th; and a week ago I got one from William of Jan. 1st. I answer yours first as most becoming, and most urgent. Thank William meanwhile for his, which was a great blessing, and every way agreeable and comfortable.

I passed a wretched hour this morning over that part of your letter which mentioned that my drafts of money had been excessive and inconvenient. I am very sorry to learn that father's income has been disturbed, and I shall be very careful to do nothing more to disturb it. Of course I know I had drawn more largely and at shorter intervals than could be at all agreeable to you; but it seemed, for the moment, a necessity of my situation. Not that, as you seem to suppose, I was "living extravagantly." On the contrary; I have hardly had my expenses off my mind an hour since I have been abroad, and I had arranged my life here, in Paris, well within my means. It was my stay in England, my tailor's bill etc, there and my journey hither and first *frais d'installation,* that made necessary—or helped to make necessary—what seemed so large a sum of money. I am living comfortably, but nothing more. Paris is of course not cheap—far from it; but it is not so dear as New York; and once under way, as I am now, I am in for nothing that I cannot face. I knew you would be somewhat bothered by my drafts, and I have already written to you about it—a letter which you seemed not yet to have received: but I had no idea that father's resources were curtailed, or I should have been doubly and triply careful. This I was not; but it is only in that sense that I have been extravagant. I *am* to receive my moneys for my writing myself as you suppose; which accounts for father's receiving nothing. I am sorry to say that the mistake which I supposed to exist in Osgood's account and which would have made him owe me (on the sum paid to father) somewhat more was a mistake of mine. The sum was correct. I cannot say how soon any returns from *Roderick Hudson* will come in; but of course as they do they are all father's, to whom they will be sent. I strongly hope, and have reason to expect, that the three drafts you mention are all I shall, for the present, have had need to make. I have made none since, and have no prospect of making any for some time. If I make none for three months to come, I shall probably be so far ahead of my expenses that I shall not need to make any more at all—unless in case of sickness; which is not probable, happily. Of this at any rate, I am sure; that by the end of the year I shall have a balance in my favor and I shall be able to refund and compensate inconveniences. I tend, all the while, to work more smoothly and abundantly. I heartily subscribe to what you say about poor Bob's dues in the way of assistance, and I should feel like a profligate monster, if I in any way obstructed them. I hope your Syracuse trouble will be short-lived, and shall do nothing in the world to increase your embarrassment. But let me add that I beg you to banish from your mind your visions of my extravagance. I am living simply as well as physical well-being, and decent mental cheerfulness (so far as it depends on circumstances) seem, in a lonely life, to demand. Unquestionably, the mere daily process of life in Paris is a conspiracy against one's purse, but I repeat that all things considered, it is cheaper than home. The money in question does not simply cover two months, but has covered me up for the future.

But enough of this, which doubtless you do not wish too much descanted on. It is nine o'clock in the evening; and I am going in three quarters of an hour—where do you think?—to a reception of the Duc d'Aumale's,[1] for which Mme Laugel has very kindly sent me an invitation—as well as to another, which follows in a fortnight hence. She has also invited me tomorrow to dine, to meet M. and Mme Ernest Renan:[2] so you see that she does at the least her duty. I must go and dress, in five minutes, for the Duke, but I shall finish my letter when I come in, as we are invited but from 9 to 11.—I wrote you a short time since, giving you an impression, I am afraid, that I was not seeing much of the world. This was true enough at the time: but since then I have seen more. I have taken a desperate plunge into the American world, and have lately been to two balls and a dinner party: one of the former given by Mrs. Harrison Ritchie of Boston (a very nice woman) and the other by Mrs. Kernachan, who I believe is chiefly celebrated for having, as Miss Winthrop, been engaged to George Curtis. The dinner was given by some very good people named Reubell, whom I know thro' Mrs. Crafts, and who have always lived in Paris. I sat next a very nice Mme Autrey, formerly Miss Helen Russell of Newport. *12 p.m.* I have just come back from the Duc d'Aumale's, where I spent an entertaining hour, in the bosom of the Orléans family, assisted by a few Ambassadors and their wives. All the Orléans family was there, except the Comte de Paris; and I was presented to the Duke and to a Princess of Saxe Coburg—the latter old, corpulent and deaf, and ignorant of my literary fame, and yet in spite of these drawbacks so gracious and "chatty" as to give me a realising sense of what princesses are trained to. The Orléans people are a great collection of ugly women—and indeed there was not a beauty in the assembly. Laugel introduced me also to John Lemoinne, and Louis de Loménée.[3] The former is a dwarfish man with a glittering eye: the other began to talk to me immediately about American anti-slavery orators!—and their *"style biblique."* I also renewed acquaintance with Mme Autrey, whom I mentioned above, and with the Nortons' friend Edward Lee Childe,[4] who called upon me the other day, struck me as a good fellow, and invited me to dine on Saturday.—I saw Tourgénieff the other day—he being laid up with gout, from which he is a great sufferer. He was on his sofa, and I sat with him an hour. I returned a few days later, but he was too unwell to see me, and sent word that as soon as he went out he would come to my house. I continue to like him as much as ever: all his talk is full of sense and feeling and *justesse*. I also spent a Sunday afternoon again at Flaubert's with his *cénacle:* E. de Goncourt, Alphonse Daudet etc. They are a queer lot, and intellectually very remote from my own sympathies. They are extremely narrow and it makes me rather scorn them that not a mother's son of them can read English. But this hardly matters, for they couldn't really understand it if they did. If I'd gone the Sunday before I should have found Taine, who is a frequenter, and a great friend of Turguéneff and Flaubert. I was surprised to learn from T. that he has a very bad convergent squint. I have further made the acquaintance of an amiable family named Turguéneff, remote relations of Ivan, at whose house I have been twice, and who seem amicably inclined.[5] This is all the amusing gossip I can think of; I will give you more when I gather it. A lady some time since sent me a particular message to father—her *warmest love*. She is by name Mrs. Albert Gallatin,[6] who said she knew him at Fort Hamilton twenty years ago, and that he used to sit with her on the piazza and delight and edify her with his conversation. She is an elderly widow, very pretty, and rather silly, and has lived in Paris ever since. But father must acknowledge her message, for she affirmed that it is her belief that he is *the best man in the world!* He must send her something very handsome.—I am glad, dear mother, that your own parties succeed, that the little dog flourishes, and that your winter is comfortable. I wish I could contribute to your social pleasure, but I can't—save by scribbling you thus what I see and hear. I would gladly give Alice and William my chance at the theatre here, of which I am extremely tired. I have given up everything but the Théâtre Français. I am sorry poor Wilky suffers still: I hope Aunt Kate continues well. Tell William I will answer his letter, but this is for all of you. I enclose a pair of gloves for Alice, which were meant to go with the other pair. Love to father who I hope will soon write.

Ever, dearest M. your
H.——

1. The Duc d'Aumale (1822–1891) wrote articles on politics and military subjects.
2. Joseph Ernest Renan (1823–1892), philologist and historian.
3. John Lemoinne (1815–1892) journalist and critic. HJ dealt with his election to the French Academy in a letter to the *Tribune* (1 April 1876). Louis de Loménie (1815–1878) was the author of many biographical works.
4. Edward Lee Childe (1836–1911), a nephew of General Robert E. Lee, spent the greater part of his life in France.
5. The family of Nicholas Turgenev, political exiles, at whose home HJ was often received.
6. The former Louisa Bedford Ewing (1842–1922).

To William Dean Howells

Ms Harvard

Paris, Rue de Luxembourg 29
Feb. 3rd [1876]

Dear Howells—

Ambiguous tho' it sounds, I was sorry to get your letter of the 16th ult. Shortly after coming to Paris, finding it a matter of prime necessity to get a novel on the stocks immediately, I wrote to F. P. Church, offering him one for the *Galaxy,* to begin in March, and I was just sending off my first instalment of MS. when your letter arrived. (The thing has been delayed to April.) It did not even occur to me to write to you about it, as I took for granted that the *Atlantic* would begin nothing till June or *July,* and it was the money question solely that had to determine me. If I had received your letter some weeks before I think my extreme preference to have the thing appear in the *Atlantic* might have induced me to wait till the time you mention. But even of this I am not sure, as by beginning in April my story, making nine long numbers, may terminate and appear in a volume by next Christmas. This, with the prompter monthly income (I have demanded $150 a number), is a momentous consideration. The story is *The American*—the one I spoke to you about (but which, by the way, runs a little differently from your memory of it). It was the only subject mature enough in my mind to use immediately. It has in fact perhaps been used somewhat prematurely; and I hope you find enough faults in it to console you for not having it in the *Atlantic.* There are two things to add. One is that the insufferable *nonchalance,* neglect and ill-manners of the Churches have left me very much in the dark as to whether my conditions are acceptable to them: and I have written to them that if they are not satisfied they are immediately to forward my parcel to you. The other is that I would, at any rate, rather give a novel to the *Atlantic* next year, (beginning, that is, in January) than this.[1] So far as one party can make a bargain, I hereby covenant to do so. I expect to have the last half of the summer and the autumn to work on such a tale; for I shall have obviously to settle down and produce my yearly romance. I am sorry, on many accounts, that the thing

22

for the present, stands as it does, but I couldn't wait. I hope you will find something that will serve your turn.

Why didn't you tell me the name of the author of the very charming notice of *Roderick Hudson* in the last *Atlantic,* which I saw today at Galignani's? I don't recognize you, and I don't suspect Mrs. Wister. Was it Lathrop? If so please assure him of my gratitude. I am doing as I would be done by and not reading your story in pieces.[2] Will you mail me the volume when it appears? I should like to notice it.

Yes, I see a good deal of Tourguéneff and am excellent friends with him. He has been very kind to me and has inspired me with an extreme regard. He is everything that one could desire—robust, sympathetic, modest, simple, profound, intelligent, naif—in fine angelic. He has also made me acquainted with G. Flaubert, to whom I have likewise taken a great fancy, and at whose house I have seen the little *coterie* of the young realists in fiction. They are all charming talkers—though as editor of the austere *Atlantic* it would startle you to hear some of their projected subjects. The other day Edmond de Goncourt (the best of them) said he had been lately working very well on his novel—he had got upon an episode that greatly interested him, and into which he was going very far. *Flaubert:* "What is it?" *E. de G.* "A whore-house *de province.*"

I oughtn't to give you any news—you yourself were so brief. Indeed I have no news to give: I lead a quiet life, and find Paris more like Cambridge than you probably enviously suppose. I like it—(Paris)—much, and find it an excellent place to work.—I am glad my *Tribune* letters amuse you.—They are most impudently light-weighted, but that was part of the bargain. I find as I grow older, that the only serious work I can do is in story-spinning.—Farewell. With a friendly memory of your wife and children

Yours very truly

H. James Jr.

1. *The American* was published in the *Atlantic Monthly* from June through December 1876 and January through May 1877.
2. HJ seems to allude here to *Private Theatricals* by Howells, published in the *Atlantic* from November 1875 through May 1876.

To Thomas Sergeant Perry

Ms Duke

Rue de Luxembourg, 29
Feb. *3rd* [1876]

Dear Tom.

I am very sorry you have had any trouble with the *Academy,* or about it—especially on my account. Don't fear that I have been perplexed or annoyed by anything. Haven't I your private friendship, *mon vieux?* "Jane" is indeed ineffably vulgar: it is the triple extract of "cheapness." How does she do it? It is stuff for the gods to blush over—but it is stuff that succeeds in this base earth.

Aussi j'ai vu le grand Ivan Petrovitch! et j'ai conçu pour lui la plus vive affection. Je le vois assez souvent et pas plus tard qu'hier j'ai passé deux grosses heures chez lui, à l'entendre discourir sur l'original de Bazarof, sur les procédés de conception et de travail, sur Flaubert, Dickens, etc., etc. C'est un causeur admirable—très tranquille et très simple, mais trouvant toujours, comme disait l'autre jour Flaubert, l'expression à la fois étrange et juste. *Daudet:* "Il me rappelle un peu Ste. Beuve!!!" *Edmond de Goncourt:* "Ste. Beuve trouvait bien l'expression juste, mais . . . . . . pas étrange!" Tu vois que je suis dans les conseils des dieux—que je suis lancé en plein Olympe. J'ai vu deux ou trois fois Flaubert (par Tourguéneff avec lequel il est très lié)—et il m'a fait un accueil fort gracieux. C'est un grand gaillard à visage sanguin, à l'encolure d'athlète, mais très simple et très doux de manières, très naïf et très sincère de caractère et pas du tout pétillant d'esprit. Depuis que je le connais j'envisage ses livres tout autrement que je n'ai fait jusqu'ici. Nous causerons un jour de ça. J'ai rencontré chez lui deux fois sa petite *école*—Zola, Goncourt, Daudet et etc. Cela m'a intéressé bien qu'évidemment je ne pousserai pas bien loin dans leur intimité. Ce sont des garçons d'un grand talent, mais je les trouve affreusement bornés. Ils sont pourtant bien amusants, et la première fois que je me trouvai parmi eux il me sembla que j'entendais *causer* pour la 1ere fois.—Je ne voulais te parler que de Tourguéneff, mais me voici au bout de mon griffonage. Sauras-tu le déchiffrer? L'ami T. n'a pas publié de roman en Russe, comme on nous le disait, mais il en a un sur le métier dans ce moment-ci qu'il ne compte pas terminer avant un an. Il retourne en Russie au printemps pour y travailler. Cependant il a fait un petit conte qui va paraître sans peu dans le *Temps*, en feuilleton. Je ne manquerai pas de t'envoyer cela en numéros, pour que tu puisses travailler a ta traduction bien. promptement. Tu devrais entendre le ton que prennent ces messieurs (chez Flaubert) à l'égard de Cherbuliez et de Gustave Droz.[1] Ils n'en font pas plus de cas que tu ne fais de Dr. Holland. Mais je termine. 1000 amitiés à Madame!

Tout à toi
H. J. Jr.

1. HJ speaks of this in his sixth letter to the *Tribune* (5 February 1876) as follows: "You ask a writer whose productions you admire some questions about any other writer, for whose works you have also a relish. 'Oh, he is of the School of This or That; he is of the *Queue* of So and So,' he answers. 'We think nothing of him: you mustn't talk of him here; for us he doesn't exist.' And you turn away, meditative, and perhaps with a little private elation at being yourself an unconsolidated American and able to enjoy both Mr. A. and Mr. X. who enjoy each other so little."

To William James

Ms Harvard

29 Rue de Luxembourg.
Feb. 8th [1876]

Dear William.

I am in your debt for many letters—for all of which I have been devoutly grateful. The last, arrived yesterday, was of Feb. [January] 22d. I wrote home, last, I think, about a fortnight ago. Today I could believe I am at home. The snow is falling from a leaden sky, and the opposite house tops are piled thick with it. But the winter is drifting rapidly away and the European spring is not very far off. The days bring me nothing much to relate, and I am ashamed of myself that, living in Paris, I have not more rich and rare things to tell you. I do my best to collect such material, and it is not my fault if I haven't more of it.—I keep seeing a little of the few people I know. I dined a while since at the Laugels' with Renan and his wife, and am invited there tomorrow evening to encounter the Duc d'Aumale, who is their great social card. Renan is hideous and charming—more hideous even than his photos, and more charming even than his writing. His talk at table was really exquisite for urbanity, fineness and wit—all quite without show-off. I talked with him for three quarters of an hour, in the corner, after dinner, told him that I couldn't measure his writings on the side of erudition, but that they had always been for me (and all my family!!) "*la plus haute perfection de l'expression*," and he treated me as if I were a distinguished savant.—I saw Tourguénieff the other day, again—he having written me a charming note (I enclose it, if I can find it, for Alice) telling me he was still ill, and asking me to come and see him. So I went and passed almost the whole of a rainy afternoon with him. He is an *amour d'homme*. He talked more about his own writings etc. than before, and said he had never *invented* anything or any one. Everything in his stories comes from some figure he has seen—tho' often the figure from whom the story has started may turn out to be a secondary figure.[1] He said moreover that he never consciously *puts anything into* his people and things. To his sense all the interest, the beauty, the poetry, the strangeness, etc., are there, *in* the people and things (the definite ones, whom he has seen) in much larger measure than he can get out and that (what strikes him himself as a limitation of his genius) touches that are too *raffiné*, words and phrases that are too striking, or too complete, inspire him with an instinctive *méfiance*; it seems to him that they *can't* be true—for to be true to a given individual type is the utmost he is able to strive for. In short, he gave me a sort of definition of his own mental process, which was admirably intelligent and limpidly honest. This last is the whole man; and it is written in his face. He also talked much about Flaubert, with regard to whom he thinks that the great trouble is that he has never known a decent woman—or even a woman who was a little interesting. He has passed his life exclusively *"avec des courtisanes et des rien-du-tout."*[2] In poor old Flaubert there is something almost tragic: his big intellectual temperament, machinery, etc., and vainly colossal attempts to press out the least little drop of *passion*. So much talent, and so much naïveté and honesty, and yet so much dryness and coldness.—I have seen a little of the Lee Childes, the Nortons' friends, who seem agreeable and kindly people, tho' a trifle superfine and *poseurs*. I dined there the other day with a large and gorgeous party—all American; and I call in the afternoon and find Mme Lee Childe in black velvet by her fire (she is a very graceful, elegant and clever Frenchwoman), with old decorated counts and generals leaning against the mantlepiece. Mme Viardot has invited me to a *bal costume* on the 19th, to which I shall probably go, if I find a domino doesn't cost too much. There are some amiable Boston people here, the Harrison Ritchies by name, with whom I dined a couple of days since, and took in Mme Bonaparte—an American with beautiful eyes. She was a Mrs. Edgar, I believe, and is now wife of the American-born grandson of old Gérôme. He is now recognised by the Empress and Prince Imperial as against Prince Napoléon; and the ci-devant Mrs. Edgar (she is a grand-daughter of Daniel Webster, whom she strikingly resembles) is moving heaven and earth in the Bonapartist cause, as if it ever comes up again she will be a princess, or a great swell. She is very charming, very clever, and quite capable of playing a part. Bonaparte is a *bel homme,* but stupid.—

Que vous dirai-je encore? I keep on scribbling—sending stuff to the *Nation* and the *Tribune* (whose headings and editorial remarks over my letters sicken me to the soul) and working at the novel I have begun for the *Galaxy*. The *Galaxy's* printing is as usual. I write (in that last thing) "a quiet and peaceful *nun*"—and it stands "a quiet and peaceful man"! Little Henry Mason ("Sonny") came the other day to see me—a very nice, gentle, sweet-faced youth of twenty-two —living in the Latin Quarter and working at painting in Gérôme's studio. I believe he has been summoned home by his father.—It was true, in Laugel's letter, that the Right and Left combined to exclude the Right Centre (the Orléanists). But this was only after the O's had refused with much arrogance to admit a single Left or Extreme Right name to their Senatorial list. "It must be all ours or nothing!" they said. "It shall be nothing, then!" said the others, and clubbed together to make it so. It was a regular chopping off of their own head by the O's. But they have lost nothing, because they have nothing to lose; they have no hold on the country—partly because they are too good for it. *"Ils n'ont pas de prestige"* I heard a Frenchman say the other day—and they haven't—a grain. And yet they are the only party in France who hasn't proscribed, murdered, burnt etc. That is "prestige."—But I think there is a very fair chance now for the conservative republicans. In the elections, just over, the Bonapartists have been heavily beaten.—Love to all, and blessings on yourself.

Yours ever
H. James Jr.

1. HJ embodied his memories of this conversation many years later in his New York Edition preface to *The Portrait of a Lady*.
2. Flaubert's affair with Louise Colet was not known to Turgenev at the time.

To Alice James

Ms Harvard

29 Rue de Luxembourg.
Feb. 22*d* [1876]

Dearest Sister—

I write you a line today in preference to keeping you waiting longer for a longer letter. I am not in good writing case, but I am afraid to alarm you by a longer silence. Yours of January 30th was received promptly and with pleasure. I have been laid up for a week with a bad head, from which I still suffer, as it is complicated with a detestable attack of neuralgia. I hope each day for its departure, as it is fatal to work or comfort; but it hangs on doggedly, though I am in the doctor's hands. Speedily, I trust, it will take its flight; and meantime I mention it as an excuse for the brevity and the stupidity of my letter.

I have no other recent news but this. I have seen no one in almost ten days, which I have spent in my room. I have declined two or three invitations to dinner, but that is as near as I have come to any gayety. I have received Mrs. Perkins's letters: one of them is to some people I know—the Tourguéneffs with whom I went to dine the day her letter came. They are Russians of a pleasant kind—a mother, two sons and a more or less deformed daughter—family of the political exile Tourguéneff. They have a very pleasant house in the Faubourg St. Germain, but their dinner party was exclusively Russian, and I was a fish out of water—not being introduced (according to the rigorous custom here) even to the lady I sat next to at table.—I had a visit a couple of days since from Jean [Ivan] Tourguéneff, *qui me raconta merveille* of Mme Viardot's fancy-ball, to which I had meant to go in the simple equipment of a *marmiton*— a white cap and apron, like a cook. (This was supplied on the premises.) But my head was too bad. Jean himself was as good as ever, but one sees, as one knows him more, that there is something weak about him. I can't stand, or understand, his consorting so with the little rabble of Flaubert's satellites, fellows not worthy to unlace his shoe-ties. I went for an hour last Sunday afternoon to Flaubert's, and while I was there in came M. Benedetti, the author of the Prussian war—the little French diplomat who insulted the Emperor William at Ems. A polite, harmless little man, in aspect. They were talking at Flaubert's about the great theatrical event, Alex. Dumas's *Étrangère*.[1] I haven't seen it yet—I had taken a ticket for last night but couldn't use it. They all detest Dumas—very properly, and predict for him a great fiasco before long. But they generate poor stuff, themselves. Alphonse Daudet has just produced a novel called *Jack, qui se vend comme du pain,* which I recommend to you who admired *Fromont et Risler* (his other one) so much. It made me sick to hear Tourguéneff seriously discussing *Jack* with Flaubert.—Of course you have read *Daniel Deronda,* and I hope you have enjoyed it a tenth as much as I. It was disappointing, and it brings out strongly the defects of later growth, of the author's style. But I enjoyed it more than anything of hers—or any other novelist's almost—I have ever read. Partly for reading it in this beastly Paris, and realizing the superiority of English culture and the English mind to the French. The English richness of George Eliot beggars everything else, everywhere, that one might compare with her.—I met some fortnight since at the Laugels' Emile Montégut, the critic—a little black man, with an abnormally shaped head and a crooked face—a Frenchman of the intense, unhumorous type, *abondant dans son propre sens* and spinning out his shallow ingeniosities with a complacency to make the angels howl. He is a case of the writer in the flesh killing one's mental image of him.

I don't think, *chère sœur*, that I can scrape together anything more in the ways of *"causerie parisienne."* The weather is delightfully mild and soft, a west wind (which, however, I have to thank for my neuralgia) blowing, beneath a cloudy sky, for a week, and fires all but superfluous. The elections for the Assembly have just come off, with a large majority for the republicans and a great defeat for the diabolical M. Buffet.[2] The Republic will now be in republican hands (till now it has been managed altogether by the conservatives) and we shall see how it will behave. I hope for the best. I see none but ardent monarchists and hear everything vile said about the Republic but I incline to believe in it, nevertheless. A type I have little esteem for is the American Orléanist of whom I have seen several specimens. Of all the superfluous and ridiculous mixtures it is the most so. But I must close, *chère sœur*. I hope that all things are well and comfortable with you. My blessings on all.

Your loving
H. J. Jr.

I *beseech* you to send me a couple of my card-photos, in a letter. Imagine me on my knees, with streaming hair, and flaming eyes. I *entreat* you. Please do it without loss of time. This is the third request.

1. An account of this appears in HJ's ninth letter to the *Tribune* (25 March 1876).
2. Louis-Joseph Buffet (1818–1898), later Minister of the Interior. HJ

discusses the political developments in his eighth letter to the *Tribune* (4 March 1876).

To F. P. Church

Ms N.Y. Public Library

29 Rue de Luxembourg.
March 3d [1876]

My dear Mr. Church—

I have just received your letter of Feb. 18th. acknowledging the receipt of Ms.

I hasten to assure you that it is of the very greatest importance to me that the publication of my novel should begin immediately. I thought I made it clear in my letter—I certainly intended to—that I sent you the Ms. only on the understanding that the publication might proceed without delay. This is not only of importance to me, but it is an absolute necessity on pecuniary grounds. If, therefore, you are unable to begin *The American* at the latest in the May *Galaxy,* I must forego the pleasure of having the story appear in the Magazine. I decided it should be plain that this and the price I fixed per number ($150) were the only terms on which I offered it. I greatly hoped you would be able to put it forward in April, and the delay, save for a month, is perforce a matter of regret to me. If these conditions are impossible or inconvenient to you, I beg you to forward the Ms. to my father, 20 Quincy St. Cambridge, *as soon as* you decide such to be the case. Let me repeat with all possible emphasis that the May number is the latest moment to which I can afford to wait, and let me also add that I shall be obliged to you in case you relinquish the Ms., for despatching it, as above without even a day's delay. These then are my terms—$150 a number—to commence in *May*—and failing this to send the copy instantly to Cambridge. But I hope you will be able to accede to them, and I am sorry that this time has been lost in discussion through any ambiguity in my former letter.

Yours very truly
H. James Jr.

To William James

Ms Harvard

29 Rue de Luxembourg.
March 14*th* [1876]

Dear William

I am afraid that I have neglected writing home longer than has been agreeable to you: but the delay has been inevitable. When I last wrote I was unwell, and this may have increased your impatience of my silence. I have nothing but good news however, and it is not illness that has kept me from writing. I was pretty poorly for up-wards of a fortnight, but since then I have been quite myself. Since then, too, have come two letters from mother (of Feb. 12th and 13th) and yours of Feb. 21st. I can't say how much I thank you for the frequency of your letters. They are a balm and blessing, and I beg you to persevere, so far as you can, in your noble work. I write to you, rather than to mother; but tell her that I was overcome by the loveliness of hers of Feb. 13th, and am most grieved for any pain she had in writing it.

I have not much to show for my silence, nothing of moment having befallen me. It has been a month of detestable weather, but I am expecting a great charm when the spring really shows itself. Already, when the wind and rain stop the air is soft and lovely. There is something very amiable in Paris in these coming weeks, and I expect to enjoy them. I keep along seeing a little of a few people, but I form no intimacies and never have a visitor. *Apropos* of "intimacies," Charles Peirce departed a week since for Berlin—my intimacy with whom mother says "greatly amuses" you. It was no intimacy, for during the last two months of his stay I saw almost nothing of him. He is a very good fellow, and one must appreciate his mental ability; but he has too little social talent, too little art of making himself agreeable. He had however a very lonely and dreary winter here and I should think would detest Paris. I did what I could to give him society—introduced him to Mrs. Von Hoffmann (who was very civil to him and to whom he took a fancy) and to Mrs. Harrison Ritchie; but I think he believed I could have done more. I couldn't! I have seen no one very new or strange. I had another talk with Renan at Mme Tourguéneff's the widow of the Russian emancipationist (the William L. Garrison of Russia) who has lived here in exile for so many years. (She had given a party to keep the anniversary of the emancipation and Renan and I were the only non-Muscovites.) He is a most *ameno* little man, and essentially good and gentle, but I of course am too entirely profane, as regards his interests and occupations, to go very far with him. His conversation, equally of course, has a perfume of the highest intelligence. He thinks very ill of the prospects of France. *"Je voyais tout en noir avant les élections, je vois tout en noir depuis."* I don't think *that* is thoroughly intelligent, but *enfin* I like Renan—*bien qu'il soit d'une laideur vraiment repoussante.* His wife is a plain and excellent person, niece of Ary Scheffer[1] and initiated into all his work, in which she assists him. The Tourguéneffs are of a virtue worthy of Cambridge —especially the plain high-shouldered Mlle. T.—*le dévouement même.* I am sorry to say I have seen nothing, of late, of Ivan Sergeitch, nor of Flaubert; but I expect to see them both soon.—The Childes continue civil to me and I dined there the other day in company with Dr. Guéneau de Mussey, the great Orléanist medical man (who shared the exile of the princess)—a very pleasant fellow—and a certain Mrs. Mansfield, an Englishwoman steeped in diplomacy, and the most extraordinary, clever and entertaining woman I ever met. I can't describe her, but some day I shall clap her into a novel. Trollope, with a finer genius, might have invented her. Mrs. Childe is a very charming woman—charming to look at too, and extremely intelligent. Childe strikes me as taking himself rather more *au sérieux* than one sees warrant for; but he is a good fellow. I have seen something of late of one Baron Holstein, German *secrétaire d'ambassade*—one of the most acute and intelligent men I have ever met.[2] We occasionally dine together—he being the only detached male that I know. (He is by the way the gentleman whose attentions to Mrs. Sumner—he was then secretary in Washington—were the prime cause of the explosion of the Hon. Charles, and the consequent separation.)—I went the other evening with Mrs. Von Hoffmann, who shows to much better advantage in Paris, as a Frenchwoman,

33

than in New York, to the salon of an old Marquise de Blocqueville— the daughter of Marshal Davout.[3] She is a literary dowager and the patroness of Émile Montégut, who is her *commensal* or pensioner, like the literati of the last century.[4] *C'est un type* very *curieux* and a very gracious and caressing woman. She is a great invalid, very corpulent, never leaves the house and has her head swathed in long veils and laces *à la sultane*—but with the remains of beauty. She had a lot of people about her, none of whom of course I knew, and as I was not introduced of course it was not exhilarating. But I shall go again (she receives every Monday) and by keeping it up long enough shall perhaps get something out of it.—I have found as yet poor old Mme Mohl more remunerative. She is much flattened out by the recent death of her husband and of her best friend Lady Augusta Stanley,[5] but she is a little battered old stoic, and she is still entertaining. Imagine a little old woman of ninety with her grey hair in her eyes, precisely like a Skye terrier, a grotesque cap and a shabby black dress. It is hard to imagine her as the quondam rival of Mme Récamier and the intimate friend of the Queen of Holland and other potentates. She was very kind and friendly with me, and I shall have no trouble in seeing her as often as I wish. Unfortunately she appears somewhat to have lost her memory.

These are all my anecdotes, and I have no more *intimes* experiences to relate. I scribble along week by week—though I am afraid I don't appear to you at home to accomplish much. I would do more for the *Nation* but I have no English books. This however, I don't regret, as I am weary of reviewing. I sent sometime since the beginning of a novel to the *Galaxy;* but there is a hitch thro' their threatening delay of publication. In case they delay, I have given straight orders to have it sent to father, who, if he receives it, will make it straight over to Howells. I don't know how it will turn out and meanwhile it annoys me.—I hope your short vacation passed agreeably away and that you are working comfortably again. My heart goes forth to you all and I wish you every blessing. I have just got a letter from Wilky, speaking sadly of his foot. Is it true that there is peril of his losing it? What a strange and sad consummation. I depend upon its being his loose way of talking. *Tell Alice to send me (what she believes to be)* Carrie's *number in gloves.* I want to send her a pair or two. *Pray attend to this.* I hope that by the time you get this the softness of spring will rest on you. Infinite love to parents and sister. Exhort father to write—he hasn't in an age. I have heard nothing about Aunt Kate in an age. *Send her this.* Is she keeping well in New York? Farewell, sweet brother.

Your faithful
H. James Jr.

1. Mrs. Renan was the niece and adopted daughter of Arry Scheffer (1785–1858), the painter.
2. Baron Friedrich von Holstein (1837–1909), the German diplomat whose journals document the diplomatic history of this time.
3. Marquise de Blocqueville (1815–1892), a French *femme de lettres,* who wrote a work on her distinguished military father.
4. Émile Montégut (1825–1895), critic and translator.
5. Lady Augusta Stanley (1822–1876), wife of Dean A.P. Stanley, and formerly Woman of the Bedchamber to Queen Victoria, had died a fortnight earlier.

To William Dean Howells

Ms Harvard

29 Rue de Luxembourg.
April 4th [1876]

Dear Howells—

I am very glad now that you have got hold of my story, and I wish you all prosperity and satisfaction with it. I am very well pleased that you should have made your proposal to Church—whose own conduct, however, remains to me a mystery. *Enfin,* all's well that end's well. I hope you will think my story does, since the beginning pleases you. I have been suspending work upon it while its fate was in the balance, but I shall now send you another instalment in a very few days and the following ones as regularly and speedily as possible.

What shall I tell you? My windows are open, the spring is becoming serious, and the soft hum of this good old Paris comes into my sunny rooms, whence, thro' an open door, I see my porter, the virtuous Adrien, making up my bed in an alcove of voluminous blue chintz. I like Paris, I like alcoves, I like even porters—abhorred race as they generally are. In these simple likings my life flows gently on. I see a good many people, but no one intimately. I saw Tourguéneff a couple of days since, since receiving your letter, but I had no chance to give him your message, as 'twas in a crowd; but I shall do so. He is a most worthy man, and purely a genius. I don't remember what I told you about the "realists" to make you thank God you are not a Frenchman[1]—the only one I really know is Flaubert, to whom I have taken a great fancy. He is a very solid old fellow—quite a *man*. But I like the man better than the artist. The other day came to see me C. D. Warner, from Munich—very amiable and diffusing into the Parisian air a sensible savor of Hartford. We dined together, and I shall see him again. I have heard several times from home that your story is extremely *brilliant*: that is the word that is always used. It is a very good one, methinks. Your list of your other achievements and projects almost takes my breath away—*comme vous y allez!* But I shall be in my single person a crowded audience to your comedy. Farewell. My love to your wife and children. Say a word of friendship for me to Lathrop and believe me always yours

H. James Jr.

1. See HJ to Howells, 3 February 1876, on the conversation with Edmond de Goncourt.

To Henry James Sr.

Ms Harvard

29 Rue de Luxembourg.

April 11*th* [1876]

Dear father:

Since last writing home I have received from you all no less than *four* letters: was ever a man so blessed. I assure you that they have been a pure blessing, and I beg you not to rest on your laurels. One from you, of March 12th; one from Alice of the 5th (they came almost together); one from mother of the 19th, and yesterday one from Willy, of the 26th. In so far as this profuse devotion was called forth by my mention of my illness of six weeks ago and by my rather indiscreet silence afterward, I greatly regret it, inasmuch as you appear to have been uncomfortably anxious about me. I was not conscious of having written in a way to make you so, and that was why I did not write again, more promptly. But you will long ago have heard that I am better; for several weeks, now. I have been very comfortable. I am not so well as I should like to be; but if my maximum is lower than might be, my minimum is also much higher. In fine I do very well. I beg each of you to thank the other for me *dans les termes les plus choisis. Je n'ai rien de bien neuf à vous raconter. Nous avons enfin le printemps dans toute sa pureté. Le ciel et la verdure résplendissent à l'envi; je n'avais pas encore vu Paris aussi brillant et aussi gai. Nous en avons encore pour deux mois de cette animation chaque jour croissant: je voudrais bien en faire parvenir jusqu'à vous tous, dans votre séjour rustique, quelque faible écho!* All this month the weather has been delicious, and the particular external gaiety and entertainingness of Paris has come out very strong. But nothing very personal has happened to me. The very slender thread of my few personal relations hangs on, without snapping, but it doesn't grow very stout. You crave chiefly news, I suppose, about Ivan Sergeitch, whom I have lately seen several times. I spent a couple of hours with him at his room, some time since, and I have seen him otherwise at Mme. Viardot's. The latter has invited me to her musical parties (Thursdays), and to her Sundays *en famille.* I have been to a couple of the former and (as yet only) one of the latter. She herself is a most fascinating and interesting woman, as ugly as eyes in the sides of her head and an interminable upper lip can make her, and yet also very handsome or, at least, in the French sense, *très-belle.* Her musical parties are rigidly musical and to me, therefore, rigidly boresome, especially as she herself sings very little. I stood the other night on my legs for three hours (from 11 to 2) in a suffocating room, listening to an interminable fiddling, with the only consolation that Gustave Doré, standing beside me, seemed as bored as myself.—But when Mme. Viardot does sing, it is superb.

She sang last time a scene from Glück's *Alcestis,* which was the finest piece of musical declamation, of a grandly tragic sort, that I can conceive. Her Sundays seem rather dingy and calculated to remind one of Concord—"historical games" etc. But it was both strange and sweet to see poor old Tourguéneff acting charades of the most extravagant description, dressed out in old shawls and masks, going on all fours etc. The charades are their usual Sunday evening occupation and the good faith with which Tourguéneff, at his age and with his glories, can go into them is a striking and I think a very pleasant example of that spontaneity which Europeans have and we have not. Fancy Longfellow, Lowell, or Charles Norton doing the like, and every Sunday evening!—I am likewise gorged with music at Mme. de Blocqueville's, where I continue to meet Émile Montégut, whom I don't like so well as his writing, and don't forgive for having, *à l'avenir,* spoiled his writing a little for me. Calling the other day on Mme. de B. I found her with M. Caro, the philosopher, a man in the expression of whose mouth you would discover depths of dishonesty, but a most witty and agreeable personage and apparently much addicted to flirting with pretty women.—I had also the other day a very pleasant call upon Flaubert, whom I like personally more and more each time I see him. But I think I easily—more than easily—see all round him intellectually. There is something wonderfully simple, honest, kindly, and touchingly inarticulate about him. He talked of many things, of Théophile Gautier among others, who was his intimate friend. He said nothing new or rare about him, except that he thought him after the Père Hugo the greatest of French poets, much above Alfred de Musset. He said, very justly, that other nations had the equivalent of de Musset; but Gautier in his extreme perfection was unique. And he recited some of his sonnets in a way to make them seem the most beautiful things in the world. Find in especial (in the volume I left at home) one called *Les Portraits Ovales.*[1]

This is the sum of my recent observations. My friend Mrs. Lockwood has lately been passing thro' Paris on her way home from Italy and I had the pleasure of being able to render her a number of services. Charles Dudley Warner, the "humorist" has also called upon me, and is a very amiable and, in a mild way, intelligent personage. I am to lose the acquaintance of Holstein (of whom I spoke) thro' his leaving the German embassy here for the foreign office in Berlin. I shall regret him, but he is *ex officio* too invidious toward every [thing] French to be fully sympathetic. He has been here four years, he is keenly intelligent and he immitigably despises and mistrusts the French. This however is a natural result of the social proscription which, as a German, he labors under. But it has kept him from approaching and really knowing them. I have seen of late little of the Laugels, tho' I call upon them at regular intervals. They are very *mondains.* I went down to Chartres the other day and had a charming time—but I won't speak of it as I have done it in the *Tribune.*[2]—The American papers, over here, are *accablants,* and the vulgarity and repulsiveness of the *Tribune* whenever I see it, strikes me so violently that I feel tempted to stop my letter. But I shall not, though of late there has been a painful dearth of topics to write about. But soon comes the *Salon.* (May 1st). It is not a thing, probably, however, that I shall keep up forever—though at present it is a welcome resource. Apropos of such things, I suppose you reflected, yourselves, that I had not sent that thing on Mme Geoffrin to the *Galaxy* as an article.[3] I sent it to the *Nation,* but Laugel had noticed the work, and Garrison made it over to Church, who used it so very disagreeably to me. I have lately sent two short tales to Scribner, which you will see when they are printed, and I trust judge according to their pretensions, which are small.[4] One by the way (much the best) is on the history of your friend Webster in Albany, according to the account of it that you gave me three years ago. I had had it in mind ever since, and had thoughts of using it for a longer story; but then I decided it was too lugubrious to be spun out. As it is, however, you will probably think I have been brutally curt.—I am very glad indeed that Howells is pleased with my new tale; I am now actively at work upon it. I am well pleased that the *Atlantic* has obtained it. His own novel I have not read, but he is to send it to me. I am very curious to see it.—Your home news has all been duly digested, and I am delighted Wilky's foot is better. Has he come to Cambridge? Tell Willy that I will answer his most interesting letter specifically; and say to my dearest sister that if she will tell me which—*black* or *white*—she prefers I will send her gratis a *fichu* of *écru* lace, which I am told is the proper thing for her to have. The answer is a design. The little black *fichu* [here James draws a caricature of a female wearing one]: it ties [*word illegible*] is the behind. Also make her tell me the number of Carrie's gloves. So the Bootts are coming out so soon! I suppose I must prepare for a *rencontre* with Frank here, in June. You never say anything about the Tweedies. Don't you see them: are they well? I hope you often show my letters to Aunt Kate, and give her a great deal of love. Be patient with my intervals of silence: you see I break them to good purpose, and it seems to me I do nothing but write letters. Ever, dearest daddy,

your loving son,
H. James Jr.

1. HJ recalls this conversation in his *Notebooks,* 25 November 1881, when he sums up his year in Paris. In this passage he speaks of the Gautier poem as *Les Vieux Portraits.* The poem was actually the well-known "Pastel."

2. *Tribune,* 29 April 1876.

3. "The King of Poland and Madame Geoffrin," a review of *Correspondance inédite du Roi Stanislas Auguste Poniatowski et de Mme Geoffrin (1764–1797),* ed. Charles de Mouy, *Galaxy,* XXI (April), 548–550.

4. The tales were "Crawford's Consistency," *Scribner's Monthly,* XII (August 1876), 569–584, and "The Ghostly Rental," XII (September), 664–679.

To William James

Ms Harvard

29 Rue de Luxembourg.
April 25th [1876]

My dear William.

I received a letter from you some little time ago, which I acknowledged thro' father, in my last letter. It was peculiarly welcome, as all your letters are. Yesterday came one from mother without a date, which was peculiarly lovely, as all *hers* are.—Let me say immediately I have just (half an hour since) received the two *coupes de*

Brücke which you asked me some time ago to get. I delayed going for them for a little while, because I was for the moment short of money. Then I received a handsome cheque from the *Tribune* for my winter's letters, and felt rich. I ordered them but they have been some time sending them. (The address is *1 Rue Bonaparte.*) They are very heavy to send by post but I will try it.—In my last letter written not long since I gave you all possible news and gossip and I have little of interest today. The spring is now quite settled and very lovely. It makes me feel extremely fond of Paris and confirms my feeling of being at home here. My life runs on in an even current, very rapidly, but brings forth nothing very important. I scribble along with a good deal of regularity (tho' I imagine I don't seem to you to be very productive). But I don't aspire to do more, in quantity, than I am forced to. What I am doing gains me enough money to live comfortably and I rest content with that. The *Tribune* publishes my letters at longer intervals than it bargained to, though I send them regularly enough. I am rather sick of them, but I shall keep it up. Politics now are very quiet and not nearly so interesting as they were earlier in the winter. The most interesting thing is to watch the gradual extreme conservatization of Gambetta.[1] —I have heard of late a quantity of music—music at Mme Viardot's, music at Mme de Blocqueville's, music at the Baronne de Hoffmann's (late Mrs. L. W. of New York) music a couple of nights since at Miss Reid's (the American singer whom you saw in Rome) where I heard a certain Mme Conneau, wife of the late Emperor's doctor, whose singing was the finest thing possible. On this same occasion I sat in a corner all the evening with the very handsome Mrs. Wadsworth, (once famous, I believe, as Miss Peters,) of whom I had heard a great deal and whose conversation disappointed me somewhat. *Mais elle est diablement belle*—especially as she is rather ugly. In the little American crowd that I see something of here no figures detach themselves with any relief. Those that come nearest to it are two very amiable women—Mrs. Charles Strong, whom I like much and have seen lately pretty often.[2] She has a spark of *feu sacré*, and ability to interest herself and *s'enthousiasmer* which is sincere and pleasing. The other is a certain Miss Reubell, who has lived here always, is twenty-seven or twenty-eight years old and extremely ugly, but with something very frank, intelligent and agreeable about her.[3] If I wanted to desire to marry an ugly Parisian-American, with money and *toutes les élégances*, and a very considerable capacity for development if transported into a favoring medium, Miss R would be a very good objective. But I don't— *j'en suis à 1000 lieues.*—These are the only women—except poor Miss Julia Tucker—and the men are complete nullities. I have been several times of late to the [Nicholas] Tourguéneff's' who are very friendly, and of a literally more than Bostonian virtue. They are an oasis of purity and goodness in the midst of this Parisian Babylon, and I like much to be with them. They and Ivan Sergéitch, and a young man whose acquaintance I have lately made, give me a high idea of the Russian nature—at least in some of its forms. The young man, Paul Joukowsky, is a great friend of Ivan S's, and has told me some interesting things about him. He says his absolute goodness and tenderness cannot be exaggerated, but that also neither can his *mollesse* and want of will. He can't even choose a pair of trousers for himself. (Don't repeat this promiscuously.) He also told me that Ivan Sergéitch spoke to him of me with an appreciation *"qui alla jusqu'à l'attendrissement"* and in a way that he had rarely spoken to him of anyone!! At the risk of seeming fatuous I repeat this for the entertainment of the family.—Joukowsky himself is a very amiable fellow, of about my own age, and we have quite sworn an eternal friendship.[4] He is a painter (amateurish, as he has money) has lived many years in Italy, adores it etc. and tho' endowed I suspect also with a great deal of *mollesse* and want of will, has something very sweet and *distingué* about him. He was brought up at court as an orphan by the Empress (wife of Nicholas), his father having been tutor of the present Emperor; so you see that I don't love beneath my station. He is to dine with me tomorrow, and I will make him tell me something more about Ivan Sergéitch. The latter I have not seen myself, I think, since I last wrote. I *have* however seen the divine Smalley (of the *Tribune*).[5] He was in Paris some time since and called upon me, and now is here again. He is a singular specimen of a successfully anglicised Yankee, and, to me, very civil and friendly. His letters seem to me the one redeeming feature of the *Tribune,* when I see it.—I sometimes see Huntington—the most amiable, loosely-knit optimist on the planet; a very good creature, but an extreme Bohemian.—These are about all the stories I can tell you. Your own remarks about Cabot Lodge, and the frequency of the type here were excellent. I can fancy that if one were much in society here it would often be very exasperating. Indeed its mere physiognomy which one recognises, is often annoying. I hope your fatigue is ebbing away. Guard yourself on your return to health, against expecting to be without fatigue. When it comes one regards it as belonging to one's old invalidism, but often it is quite normal and one would have had it if one had never been ill. These reflections, at least, I have often made for myself. I am very sorry to hear from mother of Uncle Robertson's troubles; I hope they will remain within reasonable bounds. Please give father a message *en attendant* that I can write to him Osgood is to send him (May 1st) the account of the sales of *Roderick Hudson;* with the money he owes me. Tell him that he is not to forward to me, but to keep it. I will write him. I have almost finished reading one or two books which I will send to Alice. I sent her one some weeks ago. I am very curious to see the notice of *R. H.* in the *North American Review.* Send it, and tell me who wrote it. I know who did the *Nation's.* Farewell, sweet brother.

Yours ever

H. James Jr.

1. Léon Gambetta (1838–1882), leader of the Republican party, whose political sense HJ admired. He was largely responsible for maneuvering adoption of the Third Republic's constitution of February 1875.
2. The former Eleanor Fearing had gone to live abroad after a scandal in Newport. See Louis Auchincloss, *Reflections of a Jacobite* (1961), pp. 173–207.
3. Henrietta Reubell, of American-French descent, became one of HJ's closest Parisian friends, and he regularly visited her salon in the Avenue Gabriel. It was frequented by Oscar Wilde, John Singer Sargent, William Rothenstein, and others. She was the original of Miss Barrace in *The Ambassadors.*
4. Paul Joukowsky, whose name would be transliterated today Zhukovski, was a Russian painter and amateur of the arts.
5. George W. Smalley (1833–1916), European correspondent of the *Tribune.*

To Thomas Sergeant Perry

Ms Colby

[Postmarked Paris, 2 Mai 1876]

Dear Thomas—

I have just received your postal card, and will with pleasure look up the photos. I have little doubt I can find them. I got from you a note some fortnight since which I have had at heart to answer, but a glut of writing—especially a terrible *encombrement* of letters—must be my excuse for delay.—So Miss Bessie Lee marries? What a lovely thought for F. Shattuck! I remember her with a quite intense and peculiar admiration and should like to make bold to tell her so. (Excuse me: I have just discovered that the rear of my sheet is bescribbled.)—Yes, I have seen Daudet several times. He is a little fellow (very little) with a refined and picturesque head, of a Jewish type. Former private secretary of the Duc de Morny. A brilliant talker and *raconteur*. A Bohemian. An extreme imitator of Dickens— but a *froid,* without D.'s real exuberance. *Jack* has had immense success here—*ça se vend comme du pain.* Mme Sand *en raffole.* The stepfather is a portrait—Pierre Véron, editor of the *Charivari.* The book to me was dreary and disagreeable, and in spite of cleverness intrinsically weak. I prefer an inch of Gustave Droz to a mile of Daudet. Why the Flaubert circle don't like him is their own affair. I don't care. I heard Émile Zola characterize his manner sometime since as *merde à la vanille.* I send you by post Zola's own last—*merde au naturel.* Simply hideous.

Yours ever in extreme haste
H. James Jr.

To Mrs. Henry James Sr.

Ms Harvard

29 Rue de Luxembourg.

May 8*th* [1876]

Beloved mammy

I received this A.M. your letter of April 24th, deploring my not writing oftener. I grieve that my letters should have seemed too rare and in especial that I should have seemed to neglect you for other correspondents. I remember no period at which letter-writing, in the gross, has taken up more of my time (often too much) than this winter and I have seemed to myself to write you generally a good deal. But I have made the mistake of wishing to wait till I could write a long and graphic letter (you must admit that my letters have been long). I will adopt a new system and write oftener and more briefly.—I am sorry—or rather glad—to hear of poor Margaret Gourlay's death—and I suppose that, except for Libby's sake, it is not to be regretted that Janet should seem likely to follow her. Your other news was duly noted—from T. Bancroft's marriage to Dido's infamy. The last is, as Carlyle says, too terrible for tears. As regards Miss James I should think that she might make a very good wife—the worst thing that she was ever accused of was wanting to become one. The days go on here, but the spring is playing detestable tricks—the cold for ten days has been intolerable. I pine for weather in which one can comfortably sit out of doors. My life retains its mildly-rosy complexion. In the way of work I am doing nothing but my novel, and my letters to the *Tribune*—it is enough. I wish to get the former off my hands. As regards the latter, the Salon, just opened, is a godsend.—I have written two letters upon it. I needn't, therefore, speak of it now. The most agreeable social episode that has lately happened to me was dining the other day, "au cabaret," with Ivan Sergéitch, my friend Paul Joukowsky (whom I have mentioned to you) and the Princess Ouroussoff.[1] It was Joukowsky who invited us and it was charming—I have never seen Tourguénieff so jovial, prattlesome and entertaining. His mixture of the wit of the artist and the naïveté of the infant is adorable.

But Mme. Viardot does not let him stay out later than 9.30 o'clock, so our party broke up rather too early. He is indeed, as he ingenuously relates that Flaubert calls him, a *poire molle*. But Joukowsky and I went home with the Princess and finished the evening, with the further assistance of Prince Hohenlohe, the German ambassador. The Princess Ourousoff I must explain is a very agreeable Russian lady (an intimate friend of Joukowsky) with whom I have laid, for next winter, I hope, the foundation of an intimacy. (She leaves Paris, in a few days, unfortunately, for the summer.) She is very intelligent, poor and without princely splendor, and as easy as an old glove. Her only fault is that she smokes too much. Joukowsky and I have become bosom friends—he is a very sweet fellow. He lacks vigor, but has a very amiable and interesting nature, and, on the artistic side, very fine perceptions. He has two large pictures in the Salon, but I am afraid will never be anything but a rather curious and delicate dilettante. He is one of the flowers of civilization, and has had more pretty things happen to him, in the way of being dandled by Empresses and living, all alone, in Venetian palaces, than any one I have encountered. He has here a most enchanting studio and apartment, a treasury of Italian relics, drawings (awful) by Goethe who was an intimate friend of his father—who begot him at the age of sixty-five etc.—The other day I was at the house of a dreadful old lion huntress, Mme. Blaze de Bury—an Englishwoman with a French husband and daughter. She invited me, unsolicited, from having read my threadbare tales in the *Revue des Deux Mondes* (you noticed, I suppose, that they have lately translated a third). Such is fame! These last days I have had the Englishman Rutson, who was in America, on my hands. He came bringing a letter from Gurney (tho' I had seen him in London). I took him to the Salon, explained him the pictures, and gave him a very good dinner. He is as amiable as an angel and as unparisian.—I have been reading Macaulay's Life with extreme interest and entertainment, and admiration of the intellectual robustness of the man. I suppose Alice has read it—if not she must. She *must* also read Klaczko, whom I lately sent her—the wittiest little hunchbacked Pole whom I dined with awhile ago at Laugel's. None of you speak of *Daniel*

Deronda—tho' you must be reading it. With what effect? It disappoints me as it goes on—the analysing and the sapience—to say nothing of the tortuosity of the style—are overdone. Gwendolen, too, is too thin and mean for a rich tragic interest.—I continue to see poor old Mme Mohl occasionally, and the last time I called there I found her sitting with M. Mignet, the historian, a handsome-faced old man, of extreme urbanity. I enclose for the entertainment of Alice, especially, a note I lately got from her. Would you suppose it had emanated from one *"qui a hérité du salon de Mme Récamier"?* *Burn it immediately without showing it to any one.* (Mind this.)

Father told me in his last letter that he had received a letter for me from Bob Temple and would inclose it. He didn't, and it has never come. I desire particularly to see it—pray ask him to not fail to send it forwith. Please tell him also that he is to keep the money that Osgood sent him for the sale [of] *Roderick Hudson.* (I have given O. directions.) I have no idea how much it will amount to; but whatever it is, it will do something toward cancelling the heavy draft I made upon you in the autumn. You will recognise the high propriety of this and believe that I will listen to [no] demurs.— With this, dearest mammy, haven't I sufficiently bescribbled and begossiped you? I can think of nothing more. Love to all, in superabundance. Why too don't you send the article on *Roderick Hudson* out of the *North American Review?* Cut it out and envelope it. Have you learned the authorship? Farewell, sweet mammy.

Your loving child
H. James Jr.

1. Daughter of a Russian industrialist, she had married Prince Serge Ouroussov. Her salon was frequented by notables in the artist-life of Europe: Brahms, when she lived in Germany, Turgenev and Tolstoy in Russia, Maupassant and Gide in France, and the young Maurice Baring.

To Alice James

Ms Harvard

29 Rue de Luxembourg.
May 24*th* [1876]

My dearest sister—

When I last wrote home I remember I announced a new programme, and said that I would write oftener, even if I had to write shorter letters. I am afraid you will think I am not keeping my promise, particularly, for some time has elapsed since my letter departed. But I find justification for my silence in the fact that since then I have received no news from home. I am growing impatient, and if no letter comes tomorrow (I often get them on Thursdays) I shall grow anxious. During these days I have not been fabricating news with any especial speed and have no great accumulation of history on my hands. We have had a fleeting touch of summer, but it has vanished and rain and cold are *à l'ordre du jour*. My life has become quieter than ever and the mild gaieties of my winter are quite subsiding. I went last night to the theatre for the first time in many weeks—a confession of dull days. (The insupportably bad air of the theatres as the cold weather disappears, makes it a heavy penalty to enter them.) I suppose you will think me strangely blasé, or cynically dead to my opportunities, if I tell you that (except to take Mrs. Lockwood, when she was here, some time since) I have not been to the Théâtre Français in nearly three months. *Que veux-tu, ma chère? Tout lasse, tout passe, tout casse.* Besides it's a great economy. I *did* go the other night, though to the Italiens to hear Verdi's *Aida* (admirably given) by invitation of Mrs. Strong, the most amiable of women; and I am to go again, three nights hence, by invitation of Madame Jameson, a charming Frenchwoman whose acquaintance I have made through Mrs. Childe;—she is the spouse of a Frenchman of British parentage. I breakfasted the other day with Mrs. Childe and Mme J., and Childe being absent (a moderate loss, in strict verity) had these two accomplished Parisiennes to myself. I was doubtless not *à la hauteur de la situation,* but I enjoyed it. Mme J. and Mme C. are intimate friends, and afterwards, calling on each of them, I had her version of the other. But they are both very nice women, and Mrs. C. has invited me to dine on Friday, and to come and stay with her in July at her moated chateau near Montargis.—Ivan Sergéitch has left Paris—he goes to Russia for a couple of months to try and finish the long novel he has for some time been busy with. He works very little here, I suspect. I saw him three times before he left and he sent you the photo, which I enclose (with his name, and yours, on the back.) It is horribly bad. I saw him, one night at Mme Viardot's where he again played charades—he has not a gram of dramatic talent—and where, decidedly, the whole entourage is much beneath him. Then I went a few days later and paid him a morning visit—he was more charming than I had ever seen him—his naïveté and softness, gentleness and sweetness—and at the same time extreme sense of *justesse,* in his great Cossack body, make me want to embrace him. While I was there came in M. Henri Martin, to look at some of his pictures, and displayed a very fine head and pure physiognomy of French radical-idealist—*républicain-illuminé:* a type which, when it is not very odious, has something to me very touching and even noble. Then a day or two later Tourguénieff dined with my friend Joukowsky and me and was again adorable: but, he had, as usual, to rejoin Mme Viardot at a very early hour. I am trying to think whom else I have seen, to talk about it. Mme Mohl, the other afternoon, who is more than ever *de l'autre monde.* I saw her for the first time alone and made her talk about her early memories—Madame Récamier, Chateaubriand etc. They are, of course her *chevaux de bataille,* but to me her stories were fresh. Chateaubriand spent his last years, and died, in the house which she inhabits (120 Rue du Bac). When he had gone Madame Récamier, blind, eighty years old and *désolée,* took to her bed. Mme Mohl, sitting with her, asked her what she could do for her now—what she wished. She replied— "with adorable grace" (at eighty in bed!)—*Je ne voudrais pas avoir l'air pédant; mais je ne souhaite que la vertu."*—The person I have seen altogether most of, of late, is my dear young friend Joukowsky, for whom I entertain a most tender affection. He is one of the pure flowers of civilization and Ivan Sergéitch says of him—*"C'est l'épicurien le plus naïf que j'aie rencontré.*" (I. S. likes him extremely.) A sense of "human fellowship" is not his forte; but he is the most— or one of the most—refined specimens of human nature that I have ever known, a very delicate and interesting mind with a valuable background of Germanism (his mother was a German) and a great deal of amiability and elevation of disposition—a considerable *dévergondage* of imagination and an extreme purity of life. His life has been too picturesque, felicitous (with small exceptions) to have formed a positive character for him: but as a figure, taken altogether, he is much to my taste, and we have sworn an eternal friendship. He asks nothing better than to make me acquainted with all sorts of interesting Russians, as they come along; and a couple of days since asked me to dine with him and the young Duke of Leuchtenberg— nephew of the Czar, grandson of Eugène Beauharnais, great-grandson of Josephine, etc.—as you see a sufficiently picturesque *convive*. Unfortunately I was engaged and the Duke of L. was only passing thro' Paris. The Princess Ourousoff has departed, and so has Holstein—which latter I shall not miss incurably: for intelligent as he is, he is *peu sympathique, en somme,* and as dry as Mr. Boott. With this, sweet child, I have scraped together all the local color I can think of: may I not have labored in vain. I hope your silence portends no evil, and that you are all well and happy. Do you get comfortable news from the boys? I have sent you two or three books of late, and will send you tomorrow Renan's new volume. I suppose the Bootts will soon loom above my horizon—they will perhaps even hasten to Paris, to be near me! *Cela c'est vu.* I will do my best for them. I expect to be here late—till July 15th and to spend the summer quietly, economically, and industriously—perhaps, if it doesn't prove too hot, at Fontainebleau. And you, *chère sœur?* You have no Fontainebleau, but I hope you may find a reasonable substitute. *Je vous embrasse bien tous et je salue tous ceux qui demanderaient de mes nouvelles*—especially Sara Sedgwick. I have found here a person very much like her in loveliness of character—Mlle Fanny Tourguéneff. I must close—I am going to dine with Mrs. Strong— I believe all alone!—and 'tis 7 o'clock. Don't think that I adore Mrs. S. or have *velléités* of flirtation with her: *j'en suis à 1000 lieues.*

She is a poor sick woman with an amiability and natural sweetness unspoiled—and apparently quite untouched—by an excess of very silly Catholicism—of which, however, she never speaks. I will keep this till tomorrow and if a letter comes, add a word.—

May 25th No letters! Yours, dearest sister, affectionately and disconsolately

H. James Jr.

To William Dean Howells

Ms Harvard

29 Rue de Luxembourg, Paris.
May 28*th* [1876]

Dear Howells—

I have just received (an hour ago) your letter of May 14th. I shall be very glad to do my best to divide my story so that it will make twelve numbers, and I think I shall probably succeed. Of course 26 pp. is an impossible instalment for the magazine. I had no idea the second number would make so much, though I half expected your remonstrance. I shall endeavour to give you about 14 pp., and to keep doing it for seven or eight months more. I sent you the other day a fourth part, a portion of which, I suppose, you will allot to the fifth.

My heart was touched by your regret that I hadn't given you "a great deal of my news"—though my reason suggested that I couldn't have given you what there was not to give. "*La plus belle fille du monde ne peut donner que ce qu'elle a.*" I turn out news in very small quantities—it is impossible to imagine an existence less pervaded with any sort of *chiaroscuro*. I am turning into an old, and very contented, Parisian: I feel as if I had struck roots into the Parisian soil, and were likely to let them grow tangled and tenacious there. It is a very comfortable and profitable place, on the whole—I mean, especially, on its general and cosmopolitan side. Of pure Parisianism I see absolutely nothing. The great merit of the place is that one can arrange one's life here exactly as one pleases—that there are facilities for every kind of habit and taste, and that everything is accepted and understood. Paris itself meanwhile is a sort of painted background which keeps shifting and changing, and which is always there, to be looked at when you please, and to be most easily and comfortably ignored when you don't. All this, if you were only here, you would feel much better than I can tell you—and you would write some happy piece of your prose about it which would make me feel it better, afresh. *Ergo,* come—when you can! I shall probably be here still. Of course every good thing is still better in spring, and in spite of much mean weather I have been liking Paris these last weeks more than ever. In fact I have accepted destiny here, under the vernal influence. If you sometimes read my poor letters in the *Tribune,* you get a notion of some of the things I see and do. I suppose also you get some gossip about me from Quincy Street. Besides this there is not a great deal to tell. I have seen a certain number of people all winter who have helped to pass the time, but I have formed but one or two relations of permanent value, and which I desire to perpetuate. I have seen almost nothing of the literary fraternity, and there are fifty reasons why I should not become intimate with them. I don't like their wares, and they don't like any others; and besides, they are not *accueillants.* Tourguéneff is worth the whole heap of them, and yet he himself swallows them down in a manner that excites my extreme wonder. But he is the most loveable of men and takes all things easily. He is so pure and strong a genius that he doesn't need to be on the defensive as regards his opinions and enjoyments. The mistakes he may make don't hurt him. His modesty and naïveté are simply infantine. I gave him some time since the message you sent him, and he bade me to thank you very kindly and to say that he had the most agreeable memory of your two books. He has just gone to Russia to bury himself for two or three months on his estate, and try and finish a long novel he has for three or four years been working upon. I hope to heaven he may. I suspect he works little here.

I interrupted this a couple of hours since to go out and pay a visit to Gustave Flaubert, it being his time of receiving, and his last Sunday in Paris, and I owing him a farewell. *He* is a very fine old fellow, and the most interesting man and strongest artist of his circle. I had him for an hour alone, and then came in his "following," talking much of Émile Zola's catastrophe—Zola having just had a serial novel for which he was being handsomely paid interrupted on account of protests from provincial subscribers against its indecency. The opinion apparently was that it was a bore, but that it could only do the book good on its appearance in a volume. Among your tribulations as editor, I take it that this particular one at least is not in store for you. On my [way] down from Flaubert's I met poor Zola climbing the staircase, looking very pale and sombre, and I saluted him with the flourish natural to a contributor who has just been invited to make his novel last longer yet.

Warner has come back to Paris, after an apparently rapturous fortnight in London, and the other morning breakfasted with me—but I have not seen him since, and I imagine he has reverted to London. He is conspicuously amiable. I have seen no other Americans all winter—men at least. There are no men here to see but horribly effeminate and empty-pated little *crevés*. But there are some very nice women.—I went yesterday to see a lady whom and whose *intérieur* it is a vast pity you shouldn't behold for professional purposes: a certain Baroness Blaze de Bury—a (supposed) illegitimate daughter of Lord Brougham. She lives in a queer old mouldy, musty *rez de chaussée* in the depths of the Faubourg St. Germain, is the grossest and most audacious lion-huntress in all creation and has the two most extraordinary little French, emancipated daughters. One of these, wearing a Spanish mantilla, and got up apparently to dance the cachacha, presently asked me what I thought of *incest* as a subject for a novel—adding that it had against it that it was getting, in families, so terribly common. *Basta!* But both figures and setting are a curious picture.—I rejoice in the dawning of your dramatic day, and wish I might be at the *première* of your piece at Daly's. I give it my tenderest good wishes—but I wish you had told me more about it, and about your comedy. Why (since the dramatic door stands so wide open to you) do you print the latter before having it acted? This, from a Parisian point of view, seems quite monstrous.—

Your inquiry "Why I don't go to Spain?" is sublime—is what Philip Van Artevelde says of the Lake of Como, "softly sublime, profusely fair!" I shall spend my summer in the most tranquil and frugal hole I can unearth in France, and I have no prospect of travelling for some time to come. The Waverley Oaks seem strangely far away—yet I remember them well, and the day we went there. I am sorry I am not to see your novel sooner, but I applaud your energy in proposing to change it. The printed thing always seems to me dead and done with. I suppose you will write something about Philadelphia—I hope so, as otherwise I am afraid I shall know nothing about it. I salute your wife and children a thousand times and wish you an easy and happy summer and abundant inspiration.

Yours very faithfully,
H. James Jr.

To William James

Ms Harvard

Paris, 29 Rue de Luxembourg.
June 22d [1876]

Dear William—

Your letter from Newport came safe to hand (with a couple of very brief notes from Alice and Mother) and gave me great pleasure, 1st by its good account of Father's convalescence; 2d by its cheerful report of your beginning of your vacation. I trust both of these things have been going on well. Give all my love to father and tell him that I wish greatly I too were there to glide about his couch and chair, in offices of tenderness. But with such ministrants as he has he can lack nothing, and I hope he will very soon cease to need the ministrations of anyone. Your picture of Newport filled me with a gentle melancholy, but did not make me wish to be there; I hope greatly to hear of your subsequent adventures. Tell me about Philadelphia and H. Temple's marriage. Apropos of the latter I received also Bob Temple's letter at last—a most extraordinarily interesting, and to me, touching, performance. I answered it immediately, but I feared that the address he gave me being so old my letter will not reach him.—This must be but a hasty scrawl, dear William as I am very busy. I have had a very idle and demoralized month, and must make up for lost time. A great lot of people I know have been assembling in Paris and infringing upon my once quiet hours. But it has not been without its agreeable and even profitable side. The Bootts have departed for Villiers-le-Bel, in very good spirits. The day before they went I bade them to a modest repast, and had my friend Joukowsky to meet them. As he found Boott *"extrêmement sympathique"* and thought he looked like one of Titian's men and as Lizzie, among her unsuspected accomplishments, reveals a complete mastery of the French tongue, I suppose it was a success. A few days afterward I went out with my Russian to dine etc. at the good and patriarchal Tourgéneffs (Nicholas) who have a most enchanting place about three-quarters of an hour from Paris, adjoining the Malmaison, the Empress Josephine's old place. The T's are all kindness, naiveté and mutually doting family life. I also spent a day (rather drearily) at Fontainebleau with a "party"— a sort of thing I loathe—the Kings, Mmes Wadsworth and Strong and so forth. But Fontainebleau is enchanting. Then Mme Laugel drove me very kindly to the annual review at Longchamps, where I stood for four hours in the sun on a rickety straw-bottomed chair craning my neck over the crowd toward the glittering squadrons. Then she invited me to a party (dull) where I was introduced to the Duc de Broglie, the Comte Duchatel, the famous Mme de Villeneuve etc. So much for base gossip. Your remarks about G. Eliot were excellent—but *Daniel Deronda* strikes me as (in proportion to its elaborate ability) a great failure compared with her other books. Gwendolen, to me, *lives* a little; but not the others: D. D. least of all. But the episode with Mordecai is fine. I send Alice Fromentin's book, *Les Maîtres d'Autrefois*, worth reading for its charm, even tho' it is rather special. I don't send her the two big volumes of M. Doudan which I have noticed in the *Tribune*,[1] because they are so heavy and on the whole not worth it, in spite of my praise of them. I remember not at all your Darlington-Johnson friends in Rome—

je ne les remets pas: but I will none the less, should they appear, treat them with all possible civility.—It is summer here, *en plein,* and at moments, very hot. But Paris is still charming. I shall be (I have just been interrupted by a young woman from M. Julian Klaczko (of the "Two Chancellors") to know whether I didn't steal his overcoat the other night at the Laugel's. I didn't).—I shall be here to July 15th, and shall between then and August 1st pay a short visit to the Childes, at Montargis. In August and September I don't know what I shall do. I trust you will arrange your summer comfortably, and the rest of them too. I infer from your letter that Aunt Kate is returned to Cambridge. Give her much love and embrace every one. What is thought (outside of the *Nation*) of the nomination of Hayes? *Je n'y comprends rien.* What is heard from Bob and Wilky? *What is B's address?* I wish you rest and joy.

Yours
H. J. Jr.

1. New York *Tribune,* 1 July 1876, a review of Ximenes Doudan's post-humous *Mélanges et lettres.*

To Arthur George Sedgwick

Ms Private

29 Rue de Luxembourg.
July *6th* [1876]

Dear Arthur—

I send you herewith another *note,* which if rather long I hope you will find, seeing the importance of the topic (the late G. Sand,) divisible into two paragraphs.[1] I would have sent you an article *à propos* of G. Sand's death had not I taken for granted that Laugel would treat of it.

I go back in memory to those days of last summer when in the hot eventide you used to come to me in Irving place to fetch me to dinner. I might be expecting you now. I am sitting *en chemise,* as you used to find me then, and it is very little less hot. I am in Paris till July 20th, when I shall betake myself to some ocean-cave—that is, some quiet and frugal spot by the sea-side. And what are you doing, thinking, planning? I suppose you think of nothing but the Campaign. May you help to win in it—in such way as you most desire, or least object to! Here the air is filled with the cannon smoke of the East, with which some people expect very soon to see that of Russia and England mingle. Are you still living in that princely way of the winter? Where do you dine, and with whom? What do you do "evenings?" Are you going to spend the summer in New York? Have you been to Philadelphia and what do you think of it? If I mistake not you were at Cincinnati—but I suppose you don't write the letters upon the Centennial in the *Pall Mall* signed *B. H.* Have you been lately to Cambridge and how are your sisters? How is Godkin and does he think of returning to New York? Give him a tender message from me when you next see him. This is a letter of questions and not of answers; but I have little personal news. I lead a quiet life but I feel quite Parisianized—I have taken root. It's a most satisfactory place. Come and try it some day. Commend me very kindly to Garrison and believe me yours

H. J. Jr.

1. The unsigned note on George Sand appeared in the *Nation*, XXIII (27 July), 61.

To William James

Ms Harvard

Etretat
July 29th [1876]

Dear William,

Your long and charming letter of July 5th came to me just before I left Paris—some ten days since. Since then, directly after my arrival here, I wrote a few words to Alice by which you will know where I am "located." Your letter, with its superior criticism of so many things, the Philadelphia Exhibition especially, interested me extremely and quickened my frequent desire to converse with you. What you said of the good effect of the American pictures there gave me great pleasure; and I have no doubt you are right about our artistic spontaneity and sensibility. My chief impression of the Salon was that four-fifths of it were purely mechanical, (and *de plus,* vile). I bolted from Paris on the 20th, feeling a real need of a change of air. I found it with a vengeance here, where as I write I have just had to shut my window, for the cold. I made a mistake in not getting a room with sun, strange, and even loathesome, as it may appear to you! The quality of the air is delicious—the only trouble is indeed that it has too shipboard and mid-ocean a savor. The little place is picturesque, with noble cliffs, a little Casino, and your French bathing going on all day long on the little pebbly beach. But as I am to do it in the *Tribune,* I won't steal my own thunder.[1] The company is rather low, and I have no one save Edward Boit and his wife (of Boston and Rome)[2] who have taken a most charming old country house for the summer. Before I left Paris, I spent an afternoon with the Bootts, who are in Paradise— though with Ernest Longfellow and lady as fellow-seraphs. They have a delightful old villa, with immense garden and all sorts of picturesque qualities, and their place is (as I found by taking a walk with Boott) much prettier than I supposed—in fact very charming, and with the air of being 500 miles from Paris. Lizzie and Longfellow are working with *acharnement,* and both, I ween, much improving. I have little to tell you of myself. I shall be here till August 15–20, and shall then go and spend the rest of the month with the Childes, near Orléans (an ugly country I believe), and after that try to devise some frugal scheme for keeping out of Paris till as late as possible in the Autumn. The winter there always begins soon enough. I am much obliged to you for your literary encouragement and advice— glad especially you like my novel. I can't judge it. Your remarks on my French tricks in my letters are doubtless most just, and shall be heeded. But it's an odd thing that such tricks should grow at a time when my last layers of resistance to a long-encroaching weariness and satiety with the French mind and its utterance has fallen from me like a garment. I have done with 'em, forever and am turning English all over. I desire only to feed on English life and the contact of English minds—I wish greatly I knew some. Easy and smooth-flowing as life is in Paris, I would throw it over tomorrow for an even very small chance to plant myself for a while in England. If I had but a single good friend in London I would go thither. I have got nothing important out of Paris nor am likely to. My life there makes a much more succulent figure in your letters, as my mention of its thin ingredients, comes back to me, than in my own consciousness. A good deal of Boulevard and third rate Americanism: few retributive relations otherwise. I know the Théâtre Français by heart!—Daniel Deronda (Dan'l himself) is indeed a dead, though amiable failure. But the book is a large affair; I shall write an article of some sort about it. All desire is dead within me to produce something on George Sand; though perhaps I shall, all the same, mercenarily and mechanically—though only if I am forced.[3] *Please make a point of mentioning,* by the way, whether a letter of mine, upon her, exclusively, *did* appear lately in the *Tribune.*[4] I don't see the *Tribune* regularly and have missed it. They misprint sadly. I never said e.g. in announcing her death, that she was "*fearfully* shy": I used no such vile adverb, but another—I forget which.—I am hoping, from day to day, for another letter from home, as the period has come round. I hope father is getting on smoothly and growing able to enjoy life a little more. I am afraid the extreme heat does not help him and I fear also that your common sufferings from it have been great—though you, in your letter, didn't speak of it. I hope Alice will have invented some plan of going out of town. Is there any one left in Cambridge whom the family sees? I am glad you went to Mattapoissett, which I remember kindly, tho' its meagre nature seems in memory doubly meagre beside the rich picturesqueness of this fine old Normandy. What you say of nature putting Wendell Holmes and his wife under a lens there is very true. I see no one here; a common and lowish lot; and the American institution of "ringing in" is as regards the French impossible. I hope your own plans for the summer will prosper, and health and happiness etc. be your portion. Give much love to father and to the ladies.—

Yours always—
H. James Jr.

1. "A French Watering Place" appeared on 26 August 1876 and was reprinted in *Portraits of Places* (1883).

2. HJ had met Edward Boit, the painter, and his wife in Rome three years before.

3. An unsigned note on *Daniel Deronda* had already appeared in the *Nation* in the issue of 24 February 1876; in December of that year HJ published in the *Atlantic* (XXXVIII, 684–694) "Daniel Deronda: A Conversation," later reprinted in *Partial Portraits* (1888).

4. It had appeared on 22 July 1876.

To Mrs. Henry James Sr.

Ms Harvard

Varennes
Amilly par Montargis
Loiret
Aug. 24*th* [1876]

Dearest Mother:

I received this a.m. your letter of August 7th speaking of Janet Gourlay's death, and enclosing the duplicate of William's cheque, and etc. I was much distressed by your further mention of your resentment at my failure to acknowledge the draft from Houghton some weeks since. It was certainly a most culpable omission and I cannot think how it came about. The draft reached me so as a matter of course that I treated acknowledging it too much as a matter of course. I didn't appreciate, either, that *you*, sweet mother, had had all the trouble of procuring it. I am covered with shame, I thank you most tenderly and I assure you that I will never sin in the same way again! I had not heard of poor Jeanette's death and am very sorry for Libby. Still, one can't desire that Jeanette should have lived in suffering to give Libby occupation or companionship. If Libby should by chance come to stay with you give her my love.—I am especially delighted to hear that your terrible temperature had cooled—it was high time—your sufferings must have been extreme. For your good account of father I am also grateful: I wrote to him just leaving Etretat. I hope his days are brightening more and more.—I have been at this place for four days, having come hither directly from Etretat, *via* Paris where I spent the night. I shall never forget the whole journey; the heat was colossal, sickening (even Etretat had become a prey to it)—and travelling in such a temperature was a torture. But on my arrival here the weather changed, with the help of a little terribly needed rain, and I have had nothing but quiet enjoyment. (I am staying, as I suppose you divine, with the Childes—who are perfect hosts and hospitality and *prévenance* incarnate.) It is a very entertaining little glimpse of French *vie de château*. The little chateau itself I wish you could see, with its rare and striking picturesqueness—(unfortunately it isn't photographed). It stands on a little island in a charming little river which makes a wide clear moat all around it, directly washes its base, and with its tower, its turret, its walls three feet thick (it's of the 15th century!) and its originality of construction, it is as pretty as a *décor d'opéra*. The estate[1] is a very large one and contains two other chateaux, one occupied by the old Baronne de Triqueti, Mrs. Childe's aunt (Mrs. Childe inherits the property from her uncle[2] and the aunt has a life-interest in it) and the other by the Comte de Bréssieux, nephew of the hideous and amusing old baronne. Both of these places are also delightfully picturesque and characteristic, and the estate, with meadows and streams and woods, is of the prettiest (tho' the country in general, the ancient Gâtinais, I believe, is rather dull and tame). Here, I am in clover of the deepest sort, the house being as luxurious and elegant within as it is quaint without. I dwell all alone in a detached pavillion, in a charming Blue Room, with a *cabinet de toilette* in a turret, and a valet detailed to do my peculiar bidding. I find everything agreeable and even interesting, and am very glad that I mustered energy to come;—for I had a real wrench in leaving Etretat, of which I had become most fond, and which seemed up to the last, delightfully safe, serene and salubrious. The *châtelaine* is decidedly the most agreeable and accomplished of women, and Childe shines as a country gentleman. They propose every day some pleasant little excursion. Yesterday I went with Madame to make a *tournée* among the peasants in two or three villages, where she plays Lady Bountiful. It

was as good as a chapter in *La Petite Fadette* or the *Maîtres Sonneurs*.[3]
We made a dozen visits, in a dozen queer little smoke-blackened
big-bedded, big-clocked kitchens, and every where I was charmed
with the nature of the people—their good manners, quaintness
and *bonhomie* and the way they did the honors of their little
huts. This morning Mrs. Childe drove me first over to Changy
(one of the other chateaux) to call on Mme de Bressieux, a nice
little woman, in such a perfect French *entourage,* and then further
on to see the curé of the neighboring village, who is a particular
friend of hers and whom she wished to ask to breakfast. This
little visit was delicious—the old curé, charming, candid and
polite, in his queer little rustic *presbytère,* was like a figure out of
Balzac. Another time I went to the Perthuis to see old Mme de
Triqueti, who is an old lady quite *à la Balzac* also; tomorrow
Mrs. Childe is to drive me to Montargis (five miles off) and the
next day she is to give a large dinner-party to certain Montargeois
and others, which will probably be, to an observant mind, something of a collection of types. So you see I am entertained. Among
the attractions of the house is a lovely infant of about six years—
a little orphan nephew of Mrs. Childe whom she has adopted. He
is by name Paul Harvey, has eyelashes six inches long and is a
source of much delectation to me, at the rare moments when the
superior discipline of the house permits him to appear.[4] I shall
probably remain here to September 1st, when I shall return to
Paris for a day or two. But I have no desire to face (for the winter)
either its pleasures or its pains (i.e. its expenses) so early in the
season; though where I shall descend I don't yet know. (My address is always 29 Rue de Luxembourg.—I have taken the rooms
for next winter again.)—I am very glad you answered my question as to how father's affairs are affected by the financial troubles at home, but I am sorry you had to answer it so unfavorably.
I hope you are not too sensibly incommoded. The sight of the
troubles of the more unfortunate classes must indeed be distressing.
I am glad I don't see them—that I see only this strange, thrifty,
grasping, saving, prospering France, where alone the commercial
disasters of the day are not felt. (Some of the "peasants" we saw
yesterday are worth sixty and eighty thousand dollars—made franc

by franc.) You say nothing of William's or Alice's movements; so I suppose they were at home. But I hope they have moved about a little and are well. Tell Alice that this letter was to have been for her, but the receipt of yours this morning makes me address you. 'Tis all one. Did Alice ever receive two photos (large) of Dubois' statues that I sent her some time before leaving Paris? You shall have no more trouble about the *Century*, dear, dear mother; I wish to hold on to the club, for national sentiment's sake, but I will deal with the undertaking directly.[5] I am sorry about the poor boys' troubles—I trust they are waning. Great love to father, sister, aunt and brother. I embrace you, dearest mammy and remain yours ever

H.J. Jr.

1. The estate was known as Le Perthuis, and the Baron Eugène de Triqueti had acquired in 1833 the small Château de Varennes nearby. It had been restored a few years before James stayed there. HJ gives a charming account of this visit in his essay "From Normandy to the Pyrenées" in *Portraits of Places* (1883), pp. 165–173.

2. Mrs. Edward Lee Childe, the former Blanche de Triqueti, had inherited Le Perthuis in 1866. The Childes usually spent their summers at the Château de Varennes and their winters in Paris. James would use certain aspects of this Franco-American family in his short novel *The Reverberator* (1888).

3. Novels by George Sand, published respectively in 1848 and 1852.

4. Harvey was the son of Mrs. Childe's brother, Edward. He was to become a diplomat, a knight, and erudite compiler of the Oxford "Companions" to English and French literature.

5. HJ had been elected to the Century Association, New York's famous club of the arts, just before his departure for Europe. He resigned in 1878 when he recognized that his expatriation was more or less permanent.

To Whitelaw Reid

Ms Brown

Château De Varennes (near Montargis)
August 30, 1876.

Dear Mr. Reid:

I have just received your letter of August 10th. I quite appreciate what you say about the character of my letters, and about their not being the right sort of thing for a newspaper. I have been half expecting to hear from you to that effect. I myself had wondered whether you could make room for them during the present and coming time at home, and I can easily imagine that the general reader should feel indisposed to give the time requisite for reading them. They would, as you say, be more in place in a magazine. But I am afraid I can't assent to your proposal that I should try and write otherwise. I know the sort of letter you mean—it is doubtless the proper sort of thing for the *Tribune* to have. But I can't produce it—I don't know how and I couldn't learn how. It would cost me really more trouble than to write as I have been doing (which comes tolerably easy to me) and it would be poor economy for me to try and become "newsy" and gossipy. I am too finical a writer and I should be constantly becoming more "literary" than is desirable. To resist this tendency would be rowing upstream and would take much time and pains. If my letters have been "too good" I am honestly afraid that they are the poorest I can do, especially for the money! I had better, therefore, suspend them altogether. I have enjoyed writing them, however, and if the *Tribune* has not been the better for them I hope it has not been too much the worse.[1] I shall doubtless have sooner or later a discreet successor. Believe me, with the best wishes,

Yours very truly
Henry James Jr.

1. See *Notebooks*, p. 180, for HJ's memory of this experience with the *Tribune*, which he used in his story "The Next Time" published in the *Yellow Book* (July 1895).

To Henry James Sr.

Ms Harvard

Paris
Sept. 16*th* [1876]

Dear Father—

I wrote to you—or at least to Alice, not many days since from the South—that is from Biarritz. Yesterday I arrived in Paris, hoping to find letters from home and was deeply grieved at having handed me, in response to my much-deferred longing, nothing but the circular of my wood-merchant of last winter. My last letter is still mother's note of August 16th, enclosing William's letter of distress from Saratoga. So that I don't know the end of that episode—or of anything else. A longer time than is usual between your letters has now elapsed, but there is little possibility that anything has miscarried. I suppose that you have simply all been too weary and exhausted with your hot summer to write. But I hope your first cool breezes will have wafted me a letter or two.

I arrived in Paris yesterday, as I say, and was much annoyed and disappointed at finding that my apartment of last winter, which I expected to take possession of again, and which I considered that I had engaged by letter, had been let to another "party." Meanwhile I have gone to a quiet inn on the dusky side of the river. (Rue de Beaune) and am looking up new quarters. I shall perhaps end by taking an inferior apartment in the same house—where, as I have still relations with the concierge, I beg you to continue to address me. I was so disgusted yesterday in looking over a series of vile holes which offered themselves as small furnished apartments that if I do not do this I shall perhaps take an unfurnished apartment on a lease and put in some tables and chairs. Granting one has some money at first to spend on these articles this is much the cheapest and most agreeable course. *Mais rien ne presse.*—It was from Biarritz I wrote last from which moderately attractive spot I departed soon after my letter. I retreated to Bayonne (half an hour's drive away) with the intention of simply seeing the place before the train left, but was so enchanted with it that I halted and stopped a week. If the horrid rain with which we have been deluged for three weeks had not persisted I would gladly have stopped a month. We are evidently in for one of those vile European wet autumns. It is pouring as I write, and I groan at the prospect. But Bayonne is delightful—the prettiest little town in France; extremely picturesque, half Spanish in character, with a most entertaining population and a lovely country all around it. I found there again my friends the Childes, who were staying at a wondrous château above the town, Casa Caradoc, by name, which belongs to some friends of theirs, who inherited it by a strange concatenation—too long to relate—from an eccentric Englishman, the late Lord Howden, long English minister in Spain.[1] These friends, the Bôchers, were very civil to me, had me to dinner and took me with them to a bullfight, at San Sebastian, over the Spanish frontier.[2] The house (Casa Caradoc) is the most splendid I ever was in—or at least ever dined in, and I enjoyed the dinner in spite of my taking it hard to see a depressed English governess sitting in servitude to French people. But the expedition to San Sebastian—M. and Mme Bôcher—the former a perfect model of an amiably humorous Frenchman *de bonne race*—the Childes and a couple of charming young officers from the garrison at Bayonne—B. being tremendously fortified—this was very entertaining. I am ashamed to say I took more kindly to the bullfight than virtue, or even decency, allows. It is beastly, of course, but it is redeemed by an extreme picturesqueness and a by good deal of gallantry and grace on the part of the *espada*—the gorgeous being who at last kills the bull with a sharp sword. I had a plan of seeing a little more of the South of France, but (fortunately, probably, for my finances) the bad weather frustrated it. I took very kindly to gentle Gascony, both as regards man and nature. The latter is charming and the former impressed me as a much softer, kinder Frenchman than the Parisians and northerners. Bordeaux in especial attracted me as a delightful city—nestling in its myriad acres of Médoc—with quite the look and the gayety of a little capital.—And you, dear father, I trust this will find you well and sound again. My late news of your health has all been very satisfying and I hope the next will cap the climax. Your summer's tribulations will by this time be quite over—for long, I hope. I suppose you are by this time reunited at home, William with his valise, I trust. I bless you all. I think I mentioned in my last that Whitelaw Reid had stopped off my letters to the *Tribune*—practically at last—by demanding that they should be of a flimsier sort.[3] I thought in all conscience they had been flimsy enough. I am a little sorry to stop, but much glad. I can use the material more remuneratively otherwise. Love to all, in abundance.

Your affectionate son—
H. James Jr.

Tell William I promised the "duel-girl" absolute secrecy.[4] It was a great farce—very puerile.—

1. The second Lord Howden, originally Sir John Hobart Caradoc (1799–1873).
2. HJ's sole visit to Spain, described in "From Normandy to the Pyrenées" in *Portraits of Places* (1885), pp. 177–182.
3. It is to be noted that HJ here attributes the termination to Reid rather than to his own resignation; see the previous letter.
4. HJ had been asked by one of his readers, an American girl, to intervene in a duel about to be fought over her between an American and an Englishman. See Edel, *The Conquest of London*, p. 261.

To Arthur George Sedgwick

Ms Private

29 Rue de Luxembourg.
Sept. 29*th* [1876]

My dear Arthur—

I received from you a short time since a message about "that letter," which moved me to a certain sort of wonder. I have a general impression of having written you a certain number of notes during the last few months, the aggregate of which might be considered to form a very goodly epistle. But I won't stickle, and I gladly address you once more—embracing the occasion offered by the despatch of a few pages, herewith enclosed, which may serve the *Nation* as a Note. Pray let me hear from you in return and give me *de vos nouvelles*. I get a few of them once in a while, by some vague and roundabout channel—but this offers me but an attenuated echo of your robust personality. I should relish a more vivid picture of your situation, moral, journalistic, domestico-economical, etc.—of your actual opinion, habits and projects. I am told you have been all Summer in New York, but refuse to credit the horrid—or torrid—tale. I am also told you have become a democrat. I think I should do the same (were I at home) if the Democrats were not such a bad lot. But explain to me all this. I am very far away from the Campaign, in the rue de Luxembourg, and the sound of it comes to me simply as a huge confusion of tongues. Of late (for six weeks) even my *Nation* has failed me, and I am without pilot or compass. (Would you kindly add your efforts to Garrison's, by the way, to ensure the *Nation's* again being sent me.) Over here, politics are very interesting, and it's long since England was in such a flurry and ferment. One hardly knows her for the country which but a couple of months ago was so enchanted at Disraeli's sending the fleet to protect Constantinople. *Delenda* Constantinople now. I must say she deserves it. I must say too that my own sentiment in the matter is one of satisfaction at seeing England being, and counting for, something in European politics. I back her, in the long run. —But I haven't gone thither, yet, as you see. I have just come back to Paris (this A.M.) after a summer of various wanderings, none of which took me out of France. It has been very pleasant and I know several things about France I didn't know before. I return to Paris not enthusiastically, but resignedly enough; it is so comfortable and agreeable that I forget that *au fond* it isn't (to me) really interesting. But I have gained a feeling of being at home here, and that goes for much. I am not yet, therefore, in a position to execute your commands in London, but I don't despair of doing so, still. I am unlikely to go there however, until I go there to remain. I have stopped scribbling for the *Tribune,* which wrote me some time since to ask for something more loose and gossipy. I thought the request low and resigned my post. It appears that my stuff has been over the heads of the readers. Imagine their stature!

—But write me, you, something "loose and gossipy" about New York—a city for which I have retained a sneaking affection. How are all the "old set?" How and where do you live, and how do you eat? That last is the supreme question. Restaurants become a burden even in Paris, and one must either starve or marry. I, for my part, shall starve? Does the *Nation* prosper? I suppose the weeks give you heavy loads of work. May you pull through it handsomely! Give my friendliest regards both to Godkin and to Garrison, and please consider *this* letter "that letter," and something more. Answer me liberally and believe me

> very truly yours
> Henry James Jr.

To Louise Chandler Moulton

Ms Congress

29 Rue de Luxembourg.
Oct. 20*th* [1876]

My dear Mrs. Moulton,[1]

I am glad you have found a dwelling that suits you and hope it will prove agreeable and comfortable. I will soon give myself the pleasure of calling upon you. The names of the two best volumes of tales by Mérimée are *Colomba* and *Carmen*. The former is the best, but both are good; though they may not please you especially. They are not in the least sentimental. There are a great many good short stories, or *nouvelles* in French, though not so many I think, as is supposed. Those of Alfred de Musset are very charming, and consist of two volumes entitled respectively simply *Contes* and *Nouvelles*. The latter are the best, and are admirable. They, on the contrary, are very sentimental. Extremely good also are the tales of Henry Murger—tales and short novels. Of these there are several volumes (published by Michel Lévy and costing but 1 franc 25). The *Scènes de la Vie de Bohème*, the *Pays Latin* and two or three others, are all charming. Some of the short tales of Balzac are also excellent— though always disagreeable. Tourgénieff's short stories—*Nouvelles Moscovites, Étranges Histoires* and etc. I suppose you know.—I am almost forgetting two charming collections of *Nouvelles* and *Contes* by Théophile Gautier. These are wonderfully picturesque. I had all these books in America but haven't them here, I am sorry to say, or they would be quite at your service.

Yours very truly,
Henry James

1. Louise Chandler Moulton (1835–1908), Connecticut author, best known for her *Poems and Sonnets* (1909).

To William Dean Howells

Ms Harvard

29 Rue de Luxembourg
Oct. 24*th* [1876]

Dear Howells—

Many thanks for your letter and the promise of *Hayes*, which I shall expect.[1] Thanks also for your good opinion of the notice of *Daniel Deronda*, which charmed and reassured me.[2] I was rather afraid that you would think its form beneath the majesty of the theme. Many thanks, furthermore, for your continuing to like the *American*, of which I shall send you by the next mail another installment. (I sent you one by the last, and I shall very soon send you the closing pages.) Your appeal on the subject of the *dénouement* fairly set me trembling, and I have to take my courage in both hands to answer you. In a word Mme de Cintré doesn't marry Newman, and I couldn't possibly, possibly, have made her do it. The whole point of the *dénouement* was, in the conception of the tale, in his losing her: I am pretty sure this will make itself clear to you when you read the last quarter of the book. My subject was: an American letting the insolent foreigner go, out of his good nature, after the insolent foreigner had wronged him and *he* had held him in his power. To show the good nature I must show the wrong and the wrong of course is that the American is cheated out of Mme de Cintré. That he should only have been scared, and made to fear, for a while, he was going to lose her, would have been insufficient—*non è vero?* The subject is sad certainly but it all holds together. But in my next novel I promise you there shall be much marrying. *Apropos* of this I have it on my conscience to mention that I am in correspondence with Scribner about a serial to begin in this magazine in June next.[3] Nothing is yet settled, but I suppose something will be. The vision of a serial in Scribner does not, I may frankly say, aesthetically delight me; but it is the best thing I can do, so long as having a perpetual serial running has defined itself as a financial necessity for me. When my novels (if they ever do) bring me enough money to carry me over the intervals

William Dean Howells

I shall be very glad to stick to the *Atlantic*. Or I would undertake to do this if I could simply have money down for my MS., leaving the Magazine to publish at its leisure. My novel is to be an *Americana*[4]—the adventures in Europe of a female Newman, who of course equally triumphs over the insolent foreigner.—Yes, I couldn't help translating those [*illegible*]—verses[5] of Turgénieff, tho' I don't share the Russian eagerness for War. T. himself is full of it, and I suspect it is coming. The air is full of it and all the world here expects it.—I think I shall thrive more effectually than here in London, to which city I propose before long to emigrate—if I don't go to Italy. But I shan't, at any rate, winter here. You managed to tell me very little about yourself. What are you writing?

Yours very truly, with love at your fire-side,

H. James Jr.

1. Howells had just written a campaign biography of Rutherford B. Hayes, his wife's cousin, who was elected to the American presidency that autumn.
2. See note 3, 29 July 1876.
3. Nothing came of this plan.
4. Here HJ foreshadows *The Portrait of a Lady*.
5. HJ's prose rendering of Turgenev's verses appeared in the *Nation*, XXIII (5 October), 213.

To Henry James Sr.

Ms Harvard

29 Rue de Luxembourg.
Nov. 11*th* [1876]

Dear father—

I have not received a letter from home for so long that I almost forget when the last one came; but I am hoping that each successive day will take pity on me. Meantime I return good for evil. I think it is about a fortnight since I last wrote home. The days go on, winter has begun in earnest and my stay in Paris draws to a close. I wrote you, in my last, that I had decided to emigrate to London:

and the interval has only fortified this decision. (Excuse my half sheet of paper.) Evidently, another winter in Paris will not be worth the candle. I shall try and fix myself in London in such a way that it may become my permanent headquarters (while I dwell in Europe) if not my constant residence. I don't suppose it will be very amusing at first, and I shall miss and regret acutely many of the satisfactions and *agréments* of Paris: but I shall put it through and I suspect, prosper by it. I hope to find it convenient to get off by December 1st. If not I shall go as soon afterwards as I can. I am sorry to be going to a shadier rather than a sunnier clime; but now that I have begun to shiver over a stingy Paris fireplace I shall find compensation in a London grate.—There are no great things to tell you from here. The Gurneys have been here for a month, after a very charming tour thro' some old French towns, and are of course excellent and amiable. I see them now and then, though the intended invitation to dinner which Mrs. Gurney announced on the first occasion has not yet dropped from the tree. They seem but moderately interested in Paris, and indeed, here, the out-in-the-cold existence of Americans who have been having a very "good time" in England must rather take them down—they fall from country-houses to restaurants. The lovely Mrs. Mason is here for the winter, handsome but ill, and upon her I shall be sorry to turn my back. I have not, of late, seen or done anything remarkable. I was present last night (this deserves the name of remarkable) at a musical séance at my friend Joukowsky's which lasted from 9 to 2 A.M. A young French pianist of great talent played to a small Russian circle a lot of selections from Wagner's Bayreuth operas. I was bored, but the rest were in ecstasy. I have renewed acquaintance with my friend the Princess Ourousoff who has lately returned, and who is a woman of such a liberal understanding and culture that conversation with her is a real pleasure. But she is eclipsed by her lovely sister, the Countess Panin, a ravishing young widow, and one of the sweetest, freest, charmingest women I have ever met. Unfortunately she has gone to Nice. My few Russian friends here are what I shall most regret. They are quite the most (to me) fascinating people one can see; with their personal ease and *désinvolture* and that atmosphere of general culture and curiosity which they owe to having (through their possession of many languages) windows open all round the horizon. My friend Joukowsky is a most *attachant* human creature, but a lightweight and a perfect failure. To my regret Ivan Sergéitch has not yet returned to town and I am afraid that I shall see little of him before I go. It was with infinite disgust I learned that he had lately written to Joukowsky and me a letter proposing to come in and dine with us which never reached us and which, getting no answer, he couldn't act upon. It is a charming chance missed. I can think of no other gossip that will amuse you. But *il s'agit bien de gossip!*—with the strange news that is coming to us about the Tilden and Hayes contested election. By the time this reaches you it is to be supposed that it will be settled; meanwhile you must be much worked up at home. Apparently, from the accounts Tilden is really the man, and I hope to hear what is thought of the matter at 20 Quincy Street, and what light is projected upon it from the glowing atmosphere of the lunch table.—Here there is a rift in the big war-cloud, and with the armistice the excitement has subsided. *Reste à voir si c'est pour toujours.*—I didn't mention just now what will interest you—that poor James Crafts and his wife have lately been here for a fortnight. He sent for me to come and see him, and I went often, it being a kindness. He is in a poor way and spends most of his time in bed; but looks, talks, eats, digests and sleeps perfectly well, and has no pain. He only grows constantly weaker. His wife was even more intelligent, and better company, than usual, and asked very affectionately about you. They have gone to London to consult a quack doctor, and if they remain to be treated I shall see them again there. Otherwise they go straight to Cannes. Crafts can't find out what is the matter with him.—Meanwhile I have asked no questions. How are you, dear dad? I am afraid you won't be able to tell me yourself. But the others will tell me, I trust, that you are in excellent order. And how are the others? Is mother rosy—is Alice happy—is William active, and quite well again? I take for granted that Aunt Kate is in New York? And what about the boys? I feel too far from poor Bob even to write to him; but I *must*. Is it true that business is looking up?—The Bootts write me in enchantment from Rome. Has Alice safely received the Mrs. Winslow parcel (with *brother's love*) and William the books? 1000 *amitiés* from your

H. J. Jr.

2
The Bachelor of Bolton Street

1876-1878

2

The Bachelor of Bolton Street

By the time Henry James had settled into London and found a wide circle of friends, he had made up his mind that he would never marry. Marriage, as he argued in his tale "The Lesson of the Master," hinders the "addicted" artist and makes life difficult for his wife and family. Responsible only to himself, he felt that he was, as an "adjunct" to society, one of its high ornaments and a useful extra man for dinner tables. He was a distinctly eligible bachelor and enjoyed the role. Rumors of his engagement often flew back and forth across the Atlantic. James laughed at them and shrugged his shoulders. Certainly London hostesses agreed that he was an ornament. One British member of parliament, in his memoirs, has left an account of James at Victorian dinner tables:

> No man is more popular in London dining-rooms and drawing-rooms than Henry James . . . He is a delightful talker, and in his talk can develop views and ideas about every passing subject which can clothe even the trivial topics of the day with intellectual grace and meaning. Every now and then some vivid saying or some sparkling epigram comes in, and indeed there is only, so far as I know, one thing which Henry James could never do in conversation—he never could be commonplace.

Thus the Irish parliamentarian and journalist, Justin McCarthy.

James dined out in London with increasing momentum. Counting more than one-hundred engagements in a given season, he marveled at his endurance, the strength of his digestion, and the way in which, in his memory, much of the talk seemed to float away and vanish in the bubbles of the champagne. His recital of his adventures in clubs and at Victorian dinners, his endless gossip for the pleasure of his mother and sister, which fills so many of the letters, has with time become highly "documentary." We can see, in these months of his adaptation to England, how James steadfastly worked as well as played. He collected his French essays—it seemed a way of establishing himself as a serious critic in England. But once that book (*French Poets and Novelists*) appeared, his English publishers asked for the two novels which had already been published in America, and with his turning hand he continued to write for American journals, while finding a foothold in English periodicals. Never a popular novelist, James managed the economy of his literary career with consummate skill. By publishing both in the United States and in England he provided himself with a double source of revenue for the same piece of writing; and, indeed, finally he was able to run entire novels through both the English and American journals. The payment from each gave him the equivalent of a substantial monthly salary. Being a well-organized and industrious writer he delivered copy punctually, and raised his prices as his fame grew.

The pattern of his expatriate life is clearly marked out for us in his correspondence. When the fogs and cold became too dreary, or when he wanted to escape the pressures of the London social season, James would go off to the Continent. All he needed was his writing portfolio. He could set up shop anywhere. He could also fall back on travel articles, then fashionable, for extra revenue over and above his novels and tales. In 1877 he made a foray into Italy with a stopover in Paris. He spent seven happy weeks renewing his sense of Italy, mainly in Florence and Rome, and in Rome took to horseback again in the Campagna as he had done in his early twenties. The Campagna was carpeted with daisies— the flower that he chose as name for an anecdote he picked up during this trip, that of a young American girl whose provincial manners collided with the social snobberies of the expatriates in Rome. Shortly after his return to England he wrote "Daisy Miller," without realizing that he was creating a little masterpiece. In fact he thought it so "thin" that he called it "A Study"—as if it were something in an artist's sketchbook. Leslie Stephen accepted it with excitement for the *Cornhill Magazine,* but James did not trouble to seek immediate American publication. The result was that he lost the American copyright on what was to prove, as he later said, the "ultimately most prosperous child of my invention." To his brother William he wrote, "If I keep along here patiently for a certain time I rather think I shall become a (sufficiently) great man." By mid–1878 "Daisy Miller" had made him the most talked-of American writer in England, and a pirated version of the story was widely read in the United States—he was having his "reasonable show of fame," after twenty years of modest writing and publishing. But the son of Quincy Street did not allow himself to stop, however much he enjoyed the fruits of his success. "Daisy" made him only more industrious, and he began to plan a "great" novel—a work he would write with much deliberation and care. This was *The Portrait of a Lady*.

To Alice James
Ms Harvard

Address regularly:—
3 Bolton St. Piccadilly W.
Dec. 13*th* [1876]

Dearest Sister—

Quincy Street will have been without a letter from me for some time, but you will doubtless have sagely reflected that the mighty cares of a *déménagement* from the rue de Luxembourg to Bolton Street have been the cause of my silence. This tremendous move made, I am once more at liberty to speak. I am sorry that the first thing I have to say is a sad one. I am afraid I have lost—temporarily—a letter from you, sent after the 15th of last month—to Brown and Shipley. They turn out to have stupidly sent such a letter (received on the 27th) to a person of my name in Baltimore, who had just left London and ordered his letters to follow him. They, however, at my behest, immediately wrote in pursuit of it, and I shall before long recover it. I have an idea that the document in question was from your too-rarely-exercised hand and on this assumption put a *high* price upon it. If it was not, so much the better, and I shall still hear from you. If it was, I must possess my soul in patience for two or three weeks longer. The letter will of course return.

—Meanwhile I am in London, having crossed over on the 10th ult., very agreeably, on a Channel as smooth as this paper: a wondrous sensation.[1] I lost no time *à me caser,* which I did yesterday morning in the most satisfactory manner. I have an excellent lodging in this excellent quarter—a lodging whose dusky charm—including a housemaid with a fuliginous complexion, but a divine expression and the voice of a duchess—are too numerous to repeat. I have just risen from my first breakfast of occasional tea, eggs, bacon, and the exquisite English loaf, and you may imagine the voluptuous glow in which such a repast has left me. *Chez moi* I am really very well off—and it is a rare pleasure to feel warm, in my room, as I sit scribbling—a pleasure I never knew in Paris. But after that charming city London seems—superficially—almost horrible; with its darkness, dirt, poverty and general unaesthetic *cachet.* I am extremely glad however to have come here and feel completely that everything will improve on acquaintance. I am moreover much pleased with the economical character of my move. I shall evidently live here much more cheaply than in Paris, where I had fallen into expensive ruts. My rooms, which are highly genteel, are very much cheaper than my habitation in the rue de Luxembourg. I have seen no one here as yet, of course,—save James Crafts and his wife who have been here for some time doctoring, greatly to the advantage of the former, in consequence of the advice of a physician who has made him walk willy-nilly and drink coffee ditto. He is so much better that his wife is going to leave him in England, alone, to visit at country-houses while she joins her poor more and more suffering sister at Cannes. And only a month ago in Paris, Crafts was living almost entirely in bed! It remains to be seen, of course, whether his improvement continues.—Paris was Paris up to the last; the weather was beautiful and it was hard to come away. Before doing so I spent a last morning with Tourguéneff—beside his gouty couch —and parted with him in the most affectionate manner. He expressed a flattering desire to correspond with me even frequently, and gave me an "*adieu, cher ami*" which went to my heart. My last impression of him is as good as my first, which is saying much. —I likewise became strangely intimate with Mrs. Tappan, who apparently desired to have me to dinner every day, and on my praising a very clever picture in Goupil's window, went off and bought it on the spot for 7000 frs. (It is a Russian snow-scene, with superb horses, by Chelmanski.) I am afraid she and Mary (who has greatly "improved") will have a dullish winter in Paris. They scan the horizon vainly for people to dine with them; and when one thinks of all the clever people there are there who would be glad to eat their excellent dinners it seems a pity they shouldn't be put *en rapport.*—All this while I have been a long time without letters, and don't know how you are feeling and thinking about the dreadfully mixed matter of Tilden and Hayes.[2] I won't hazard the expression of conjectures derived solely from the London *Times,* but await private information. Is the "agitation" so great as is here supposed?—are you alarmed, depressed, impoverished? Write me all about it. Here the conference at Constantinople occupies all men's thoughts, and the wind seems turning a little to peace: very little though.—I have written a longer letter than I deemed I had time for, and can only add my blessings on all of you. I hope father grows more and more lusty and that in general your winter *s'annonce bien.* I have of course seen the news of the Brooklyn theatre: but it is too horrible to allude to. Farewell dear child. I send you herein *one* pair of gloves, and will follow it by others, sent individually. I brought them from Paris, purposely, to post here, as I have heard of French letters with soft contents being confiscated by the New York Custom House. These gloves are *not* Bon Marché, but a very superior article. Farewell—farewell from your affectionate brother

H. James Jr.

1. HJ described his move between the two capitals in "An English Easter," *Lippincott's Magazine,* XX (July 1877), 50–60, reprinted in *Portraits of Places* (1883).
2. Tilden had 184 electoral votes and Hayes 165; another 20 were in

dispute. A bipartisan committee of 15 members consisting of 8 Republicans and 7 Democrats ultimately voted along straight party lines, which gave all 20 votes to Hayes. The election was described as the "most deeply corrupt" of that time.

To William Dean Howells

Ms Harvard

3, Bolton St., Piccadilly W.
Dec. 18*th* [1876]

Dear Howells.

Your letter of Nov. 10th lies opened before me, and as I glance over it I derive new satisfaction from your good opinion of my tale. I send you herewith the 11th part, which I have been keeping to post in England, as I never feel that I can take precautions enough. It is shorter than any: and the 12th which will soon follow, will likewise be brief. I trust that, to the end, the thing will seem to you to carry itself properly. I received a few days since a letter from my brother William, in which he speaks of some phrases (on Newman's part) as being so shocking as to make the "reader's flesh creep." Two or three that he quotes are indeed infelicitous, as I perceive as soon as my attention is called to them. He mentioned having persuaded you to omit one or two of the same sort. I am very glad you have done so, and would give you *carte blanche.* It is all along of my not seeing a proof—which is a great disadvantage. There are many things, which, as they stand printed, I should have changed. *Ma che vuole?* Here I have no one to try anything on, or to ask how things sound.—

Àpropos of my Scribner project, let me say now that it is abandoned. They lately wrote me that my novel could begin not in June, but only in November, and then conditionally. So I have retreated. Once I wait so long as that, I prefer to wait for the *Atlantic,* and hereby bestow on you my next-generated romance. Only I should like you to let me know as far in advance as possible when you should be able to begin it.—

You see I have changed my sky: as far as sky goes, for the worse.

But as regards other things, I imagine, for the better. I like London, in so far as thro' the present fog-blanket I can puzzle it out, and I suspect that in the long run I shall prosper here. Just now it is rather lugubrious, as I know few people, and the change from glittering, charming, civilized Paris is rude. But I shall scribble better here, which you will agree with me is everything. I hope that *you* are scribbling well in spite of the political turmoil. I am so much out of it here that I don't pretend to understand the rights and wrongs and don't risk an opinion. I can imagine that the suspense is very wearisome and depressing.—What are you doing? I'm sorry you haven't sent me Hayes, anyhow. I heard from my mother that poor Lathrop's wife has been very ill, and at Somerville. Pray give him my friendliest regards and assure him of my sympathy. I hope by this time she is restored to health and to her home. I trust your own fireside is tranquil and Mrs. Howells reasonably vigorous. Give my love to her and believe me

always faithfully yours
H. James Jr.

To Mrs. Henry James Sr.

Ms Harvard

3 Bolton St., Piccadilly. W.
Christmas eve [1876]

Dearest mammy—

I lately received your two letters: the one involving William's, and the note enclosing Bob's verses. William will forgive me for addressing my answer to you, rather than to him; but it is meant for both of you. Many thanks for all. I have already written to you since my arrival here, and you know that I am fairly established. It is only a fortnight today, but it seems a long time—which I don't mean in an invidious sense. This is rather a combination of two drearinesses—a London Sunday afternoon and a London detached Christmas eve. The weather is, and has been, beyond expression vile—a drizzle of sleet upon a background of absolutely *glutinous* fog, and the deadly darkness of a London holiday brooding over all. To relieve the monotony of the situation I could do nothing better than commune a bit with the mammy of my love. You are not to suppose from this that I am in low spirits. Oh no; my spirits never were higher. I take very kindly indeed to London, and am immensely contented at having come here. I must be a born Londoner, for the place to withstand the very severe test to which I am putting it: leaving Paris and its brilliancies and familiarities, the easy resources and the abundant society I had there, to plunge into darkness, solitude and sleet, in mid-winter—to say nothing of the sooty, woolsy desolation of a London lodging—to do this, and to like this murky Babylon really all the better, is to feel that one is likely to get on here. I like the place, I like feeling in the midst of the English world, however lost in it I may be; I find it interesting, inspiring, even exhilarating. As yet, no great things have happened to me; but I have not objected to being quiet: on the contrary. I have been glad to do some quiet work. I have besides, seen two or three people. I breakfasted only this morning, at the Arts Club, with a very pleasant young Englishman whom I met last summer at Etretat, and have renewed my acquaintance with here. He is a journalist and you may read him in the "Occasional Notes" of the Pall Mall Gazette, many of which he does. He is likewise a Jew and has a nose, but is handsome and looks very much like Daniel Deronda.[1] Gurney gave me a letter to a young Benson who was in America while I was away and who a couple of days since invited me to dine with him very kindly, at the Oxford and Cambridge Club, where two other men, one of them Andrew Lang, who writes in the *Academy* and who, though a Scotchman, seemed a quite delightful fellow. Benson is not exciting, but most gentle and *bon comme du pain*. That is the only introduction I have brought with me to England: but I have written home to two or three persons for two or three more, which I suppose in the course of time will arrive and fructify. As Henry Adams had sent me a message through William I wrote to him; and also to Mrs. Wister, who had made me offers of that sort of old. I have also called upon G. W. Smalley, who had called upon me in Paris; and who has a very pretty house and wife, and is very civil.—That is as much, for the present, as I have seen of the *vie intime* of London; as other vistas open out before me I will let you know. I feel, keenly, that it is an excellent thing for me to have come here. I expected it would prove so, but it *feels* so, even more than I expected. I am very glad I wasted no more time in Paris. I shall work here much more and much better, and make an easier subsistence. Besides it is a comfort feeling nearer, geographically, my field of operation at home. I feel very near New York. I have been revelling in a subscription to Mudies:—All this about myself, a subject which you will desire that I should not scant. I was deeply grieved to hear from William that he had been weak and disabled, thro' his dysentery, so much longer than I supposed. I fondly believed he was well again, and I trust he is now. Tell him I thank him much for his strictures on some of Newman's speeches in *The American* of which I quite admit the justice. It is all along of my not seeing proof—I should have let none of those things pass. The story, as it stands, is full of things I should have altered; but I think none of them are so inalterable but that I shall be easily able in preparing the volume, to remove effectually, by a few verbal corrections, that Newmanesque taint on which William dwells. I wish any of you would point out anything more you think subject to modification.—I have received since being here a letter from Aunt Kate (written before she had gone to Cambridge to see Bob's baby) in which she speaks of father's having been a trifle less well. But I hope this was but a fleeting shadow. Give him all my love and blessing and ask him if I can do anything for him in London.—The advent of Bob and his Babe must have been a very interesting and agreeable episode. I wish I could have shared in it; and that, failing that, Alice would write me about the Babe. Bob's verses are surprising, and very touching: fearfully so, in fact. They have, as you say, a touch of inspiration; and are a strange proof of the reality of the need for poetic utterance—for expressing that which transcends our habitual pitch. It is an affecting groping for form—and finding it. I am sorry for his domestic troubles, which seem strange over here, where there are so many hungry servants looking for work.

I wish I could do something for Mary. Is there any modest thing I can *send* her—not a trinket or a ribbon, which would be a mockery. Think of s'thing, and let me know. I have (as I said) just heard from Aunt Kate to whom, as I may not be able to answer her letter directly, (I mean instantly,) pray make a point of forwarding this. It will tell her about me *en attendant*. Tell my sister, with a kiss, that I am now daily awaiting the return of that missing letter of her's. Farewell sweet mother.

Your fondest
H.J. Jr.

P.S. I have it at heart to add that just before leaving Paris I was obliged to draw for the first time in a year, on my letter of credit. The expense of breaking up there and coming here compelled it. But don't imagine from this that I am going to begin and bleed you again. I regard the thing as a temporary loan—and I have amply sufficient money coming in to me in these next weeks to repay it in two or three remittances. I shall not draw again for another year—and had not done so, up to this time, from the first few weeks of my coming abroad. You needn't commiserate me for my *Tribune* cessation, as it was only two days since that I received payment for my last letters, written six months ago. If it had come sooner, I shouldn't have had to use my credit. I don't miss the *Tribune* at all; I can use my material to better advantage.—I am forgetting to wish you a Merry Christmas. I shall eat a solitary Christmas dinner tomorrow—if indeed one can be procured at an eating-house, which Sabbath-wise, here, I doubt. If not I shall fast! But I hope your own feast will be succulent and sociable and that you will spare a thought to the lone literary exile.

1. The young man was Theodore E. Child of Merton College, Oxford, later Paris correspondent to London newspapers and editor of an Anglo–French journal, the *Parisian*. Their warm friendship, rooted in their common love of France and French letters, endured until Child's death in 1892, "prematurely and lamentedly, during a gallant professional tour of exploration in Persia" (HJ in the preface to vol. XIV of the New York Edition).

To William James

Ms Harvard

3 Bolton St. Piccadilly.
Jan. 12*th* [1877]

Dear William.

I have lately received three letters from home—one from you, with Sheldon's first cheque; one from father, with second cheque; and one from Alice. I will answer yours first, as it came first, but you may share your joy with the others, to whom give also my thanks and blessing. Tell Alice that her lost letter was some time since returned from Baltimore, and that her precious words are not squandered. I have also received a couple of notes from you, and have paid your *Medical Record* bill, and subscribed for another year. I have deferred scandalously sending you gloves; but I now enclose a couple of pair (I hope they are not too ornamental) on the sole condition (since you countermanded the original order) that you accept them as presents. Mind you that. They are in different envelopes.—I am by this time an established Londoner, tho' I have no particular adventures to relate. I have passed these five weeks in profound tranquillity and seen no one. The one or two persons I saw on first coming I have not since beheld, and my only view of the "world" has been in dining once at the Smalley's—a very savoury interruption to the lugubrious fare of one's London ordinary. Or rather, I forget: a lady whom I met at the Smalley's, a great friend of theirs, very amiably bade me to a banquet of her own; and not being proud I went, and sat thro' a heavy London dinner, composed of fearful viands and people I didn't know. But I took in a very nice, ugly woman, Mrs. Hill, wife of the *Daily News,* and on the other side of me sat a great beauty, Lady Gordon, daughter of Sir William Herschel[1] —and on the other side of her, Sir Charles Dilke. I have also been bidden by Lady Pollock (thro' the Smalleys) to call upon her, she being an *admiress* of my literature (!)—tho' who she is I haven't an idea. So, doubtless, my London horizon is opening. I have no doubt it will, gradually, and that the day will come when all my endeavor will be to contract it. The weather has been uninterruptedly atrocious. It has rained here for three months in torrents; half England is under water, and there is great consternation and misery. It is a great depression and a great inconvenience, as walking just now is my principal pastime, and it has been almost impossible. In spite of this I like London better and better and am very glad I didn't delay another hour to come here. For the practical convenience of life (except *fires*), living as I live, it is immeasurably inferior to Paris—no *cafés*, no restaurants, no Boulevards, no kiosks, no theatres, (that one can go to), no evening visits etc. But it is more interesting—much; and the incommodities and drearinesses are of a sort that I shall feel less as time goes on, while other resources will grow, that would never grow on the Continent. *Ce n'est pas, pourtant, que je lâche cette bonne vieille France.* I am tired to death of her, but England, and all its uglinesses and hypocrisies, make one think not worse of her but better. I have just called in my landlady to pay my bill, and her deadly wooden-faced "respectability," with an avidity, beneath, every whit as grasping as the French, and not a grace to glaze it over, makes me feel as if, beside such a type as that, the most impudent Paris *cocotte* were a divinity. But this is foggy "spleen." London *is* agreeable to me, as well as interesting, and I am in excellent humor with it. My lodgings are excellent, the service perfection, and the situation *ditto*. Physically I am (as always) much better since being in England. In Paris, indoors, I had always two physical ennuis—cold feet and sore throat. Since being here I have not had a trace of them. I have also done a good deal of work—(sent a lot of stuff to the *Nation*, which you will probably recognise). I shall be able to work much more here than in Paris.—So much for myself. I am very sorry that your own work has exhausted you so much, and I trust that in vacation you will lay in a sufficient stock of strength for future contingencies. Tell father it was a great pleasure to see his hand-writing again, and I perceive in it no trace of shakiness—a great improvement on the note he wrote me some time since. But I was much distressed by your mention of mother's sanitary eccentricities. Kiss the lovely creature all over for me, and repeat the process as often as necessary until she is completely cured. Make her write to me and tell me all about it. Your letter enclosed one from Bob, written just after his return from Cambridge, which filled me with an extreme sense of the grimness of his lot, and made Bolton Street and my existence here, seem like a festering sore on the bosom of Justice. But I can't help it, any more than he can! Your suggestion to send him *Punch* was a blessed one, and was instantly acted upon. Tell me this. Does father, as he used, mail the *Graphic* to him from home? If not, I will post it to him weekly— the expense is nothing; and if he *does*, I will send him something else. (*Please see that this question is answered.*) Apropos of which I will send father (tell him) the *weekly* edition of the *Times* which they have just begun (Jan. 1st) to issue. I am sure the *Mail*, with its ponderous mass of local news, twice a week would sicken him. (I will begin tomorrow.) I am extremely sorry to hear of the way father is losing money, as well as of Aunt Kate's reverses. Is it a serious discomfort? Whatever it is I hope it will stop there, and go no further. Isn't it true that prices have, on the other hand, fallen very low? The way gold is going down (105.) is a great advantage to me, as to the drafts I receive.—I am sorry Godkin's course strikes you as so vicious—I had been wondering much what you thought of it. Seeing no American paper but the *Nation*, I had supposed not exactly that its tone was the correct thing, but that there was much reason in it. From here it all looks shocking bad, and I give up trying to discriminate. Over here things have reached the farcical stage. The Turks are making fools of assembled Europe, and Russia backing down. But everyone nevertheless, expects war in the spring. Your remarks on *Daniel Deronda* were most sagacious. The book is a great *exposé* of the female mind. Tell Lathrop, particularly, from me, of my interest in his troubles, good wishes etc. And T. S. Perry a father! He writes me the letters of a child! I will write as things unfold. Meantime I bless you all, particularly my poor suffering Mammy.

Yours ever
H.J. Jr.

1. Lady Hamilton-Gordon was the grand-daughter, not daughter, of the famed astronomer.

To Mrs. Henry James Sr.
Ms Harvard

3 Bolton St. Piccadilly.
Jan. 31*st* [1877]

Dearest mother—

I don't remember exactly how long it is since I last wrote home; long enough, I suppose to make you expect another letter. Meanwhile, two days since, came your letter of the 15th ult; and I hastily resume the pen. I say I resume it, but of late I have hardly laid it down; for in addition to my regular writing I have never had so many letters to write as during the last two months. I have numberless correspondents over here (in Paris, Rome etc.) and I no sooner slay one crop than another springs up. I have written since I came to London some three or four dozen letters. Remember this when I seem too silent.—Evidently, however, if I wish to give you an account of myself here I must write often, for my observations promise to accumulate at such a rate as to outstrip an ill-regulated memory. You will infer from this that I am beginning to "go out." Even so; I am getting quite into the current of London life, and the extreme quietude of my first weeks is being rapidly transmuted. I will try and remember what I have been doing, to entertain you withal. I have dined out a great deal—and yet up to this time I have delivered but *one* of my letters of introduction (in addition to the one given me by Gurney). Henry Adams, in the matter of letters, has come up to time very handsomely and placed me under great obligation to him. Never criticize his "manners" again. Mrs. Wister also has sent me half a dozen introductions—more, I am afraid, than I shall present. The first that I can recall in the series of banquets was at Andrew Lang's a friend of Benson—a young, Oxford and literary man, with a "picturesque" wife. He is a clever and pleasant fellow and writes much in the *Saturday Review, Daily News, Fortnightly* etc. Then I dined at Sir Williams Power's—with whom it will take too long to tell the history of my acquaintance. Suffice it that he is a very pleasant and polite Irishman, a son of Tyrone Power, the actor, a K.C.B., and a friend of the Emmets, Duncan Pell etc. (Miss "Posie" Emmet was staying with him.) There I took in Mrs. Cashel Hoey, a curious and interesting specimen of a wondrous type—the London female literary hack.[1] She is the authoress of that novel you used always to be reading, to the neglect of your household duties (*A House of Cards*) and, in quite another line, of many of the "social" articles in the *Spectator*. We got on like houses afire, and she revealed to me, between the courses, her most *intimate* history. She is a typical London product. Then I dined with Benson again, with some Oxford men. (Benson is an angel; but he seems sad and over-worked.) Then I travelled to Notting Hill, and feasted with the Ashburners, who had heard of my being in London and wrote to me to come. I was very glad to be able to do so; tho' 'twas a rather "pathetic" affair. They live in a remote, depressing quarter, and seem not without domestic dreariness. They were very friendly, and seemed to cling to me for society. I got an impression of their living in such deadly tranquillity that my coming was really a social event for them. Miss Annie was graceful and subdued—she looks older, and she speaks very affectionately of Alice admiringly of her letters. The little Walter (now big) is very beautiful and like Daniel Deronda, "seraph-faced." The other boy, George, is not, but he seems clever and interested in some "art-school" to which he goes. He showed me some of his drawings, which were not bad.—The next day, I think, I dined at Smalley's—a splendid banquet, all of famous men. (S., by the way, is a real benefactor to me. He has made me temporary member, for instance, of his Club, a small and modest one, the Savile: but it is convenient for several purposes, and as I pay the dues, the thing, I believe, can be indefinitely prolonged.) At this dinner were Browning, Motley, Froude, Kinglake, Mr. Pierrepont[2] and half a dozen other men whom I was glad to see. I found myself next to Kinglake, with whom I quite fell in love—a most delicious, sweet old man, as urbane and deferential as Emerson, and with an old-English-gentleman quality in addition. The next day I lunched at Sir Frederick Pollock's—Lady P., an amiable, mildly pretentious woman, being addicted to *littérateurs* and theatrical people. She admires Bret Harte, knows Howells, and has written about "American literature" in the *Contemporary Review*. Then I dined with Mrs. Edward Dicey, sister of Mme. Laugel and a very nice woman; and the young lady I was to take in having failed, sat next Anthony Trollope, and found him a very good, genial, ordinary fellow—much better than he seemed on the steamer when I crossed with him. (I forgot to say that after Smalley's dinner I had a long talk with Browning, who, personally, is no more like to *Paracelsus* than I to Hercules, but is a great gossip and a very "sympathetic" easy creature.) On Saturday of last week I went down to Weybridge (a charming place) to spend Sunday with the Cross's—friends of Benson (who also went) and of the Gurneys. They know a great many literary people, and their chief distinction seems in their being the most intimate personal friends of George Eliot. They live very modestly, but their house is the only one at which G.E. stays. Mrs. Cross is a most delightful, genial, witty old Scotch lady, and the two persons she seems to like best in the world are George Eliot and Mrs. Gurney. There was a quite charming little man staying there—Pigott, the Examiner of Plays; and I spent the day walking over the beautiful Surrey hills. Alice will be interested to hear that George Eliot is a great admirer of Miss Thackeray's literature.—Yesterday I dined with one of Adams's friends—Sir Robert Cunliffe. He and his wife are a very charming friendly young couple and seem inclined to treat me with profuse hospitality. Lady Cunliffe is one of the prettiest, frankest of the *Anglaises* that I have met. It was a big dinner—Sir Erskine May, clerk of the House of Commons, George Trevelyan (Macaulay's nephew) and wife, F. T. Palgrave, etc. etc. I sat between Mrs. Woolner, wife of the sculptor (to whom Henry Adams has also given me a letter), and Mrs. Ford, widow of the author of the old books about Spain—an entertaining specimen of the rather battered London female diner-out. (What strikes me here is that everyone is someone or something—represents something—has, in some degree or other, an historical identity.) Tomorrow I go out to Hammersmith, to dine with Moncure D. Conway, who wrote me an elaborate note, (I have never seen him,) begging me to do the same.[3] I don't expect to make him my bosom friend, but I accepted his invitation for civility's sake. The day after, I go to dine with James Bryce (of the *Holy Roman Empire*) whom I have not seen, but who had, the other day, the "civility" to call upon me spontaneously. (I think he did this as a friend of Benson's.)—So you see, with all this, beloved mammy, I am very well *lancé* and your response, in your last letter, to my picture of my stupid Christmas is now much of an anachronism. (Even as I write comes close upon the postman's knock another invitation from Lady Pollock!) When I think that the Season has not yet begun, and that when it does the social wheels here move just fifty times as fast, I begin to tremble. But I shall do, not overdo; and shall get a great deal of profit and wisdom out of it all. I find it, as yet, intellectually and personally, awfully easy.—

Many thanks, dearest mammy, for your domestic news, which seem reasonably good. I had not heard of Joseph Ripley's death, and can well conceive of poor Helen's desolation. I suppose Cousin H. P. will be something of a *planche de salut* for her. I am very sorry father's working powers don't increase more rapidly; I'm afraid he greatly misses them. Give him my filial love. I have just got a note from Bob, enclosing several copies of verses. They have great and real beauty, in spite of their queerness and irregularity of form, and I shall be curious to see whether this form will grow more perfect. They are as soft as moonbeams in a room at night—so strangely pure in feeling.—Tell Alice not to bother about the "expense" of her gloves; 'tis absolutely nothing; only write to me in reimbursement.—Ask father or William to cut out my *Balzac* from the February *Galaxy,* respecting the inner margin, and kindly enclose it in a letter. The magazine is sent me;

but I want duplicates and can't buy it here. The account of Etretat etc. in the January *Galaxy* was most incredibly misprinted.[4] Apropos of such matters don't imagine that in the description of the Fleurières in the *American* I have betrayed the Childes by reproducing Varennes. *Nullement.* It is another and much finer place in that country—Château-Renard. I have lately written a good deal for the *Nation*, and shall, for the present, probably continue, and I suppose you recognise most of my things—but not all.—But I must close, sweet mother, this long letter. I will try and write oftener, more briefly. Give Sarah Sedgwick my love and tell her I hope much she will be able to come out. Love and blessings on everyone else from your fondest

H.J. Jr.

1. Frances Johnston Hoey was a cousin of Bernard Shaw.
2. Edward Pierrepont (1817–1892), U.S. Minister to England during 1876–77.
3. Moncure D. Conway (1832–1907), American clergyman, lived in England and wrote on American subjects.
4. "The Letters of Honoré de Balzac," *Galaxy*, XXIII (February 1877), 183–195, later included in *French Poets and Novelists* (1878); "From Normandy to the Pyrenées," *Galaxy*, XXIII (January 1877), 95–109, reprinted in *Portraits of Places* (1883).

To William Dean Howells

Ms Harvard

3 Bolton St.
Feb. 2d [1877]

Dear Howells.—

I sent you a few lines three days since with my last bundle of copy; but now comes your letter of Jan. 20th which prompts me to send a few more.—I quite understand that you should not be able to begin another serial by H.J. Jr. until after the lapse of a year at least. Your readers and your contributors would alike remonstrate. I shall be glad, however, if you would begin to print a *six-months' tale* sooner than a longer one, to do something of those dimensions. But I should not make use of the subject I had in mind when I last alluded to this matter—that is essentially not compressible into so small a compass. It is the portrait of the character and recital of the adventures of a woman—a great swell, psychologically; a *grande nature*—accompanied with many "developments."[1] I would rather wait and do it when I can have full elbow room. But I will excogitate something for the shorter story, and shall endeavor to make it something of an "objective," dramatic and picturesque sort. Only let me know well in advance when you should commence publication. In January '78?—I agree with you in thinking that a year seems a long time for a novel to drag thro' a magazine—especially a short novel that only fills one volume when republished. But I think that the real trouble is not that any novel that the *Atlantic* would publish in a year is too long, but that it is chopped up in too fine pieces. Properly such a thing as *The American* should have been put thro' in five or six months, in numbers of thirty or thirty-five pages. To wait a month for a twenty minutes' nibble at it, would, it seems to me, if I were a reader, put me into a fatally bad humor with it. I have just been making this reflection apropos of your little "Comedy"[2]—which is extremely pretty and entertaining. But one wants to go through with it. Your young-lady talk is marvellous—it's as if the devil himself were sitting in your inkstand. *He* only could have made you know that one girl would say that another's walking from the station was *ghastly!!*

Yours ever

H.J. Jr.

1. HJ sketches in an early form his plan for *The Portrait of a Lady*.
2. Howells' *Out of the Question*, published in the *Atlantic*, February-April 1877.

To Henry James Sr.

Ms Harvard

Athenaeum Club
Pall Mall
Feb. 13*th* [1877]

My dearest Dad—

I received this a.m. your letter about sending you the weekly *Times* etc.—besides having received a long and excellent letter from William of Jan. 28th. Many thanks for both, especially for yours, as a proof of recovered vigor. I have been meaning any day for a week to do what you ask about the *Times*, and have delayed it only because a journey over into the City is a serious enterprise, taking time. But I shall do it immediately. I shall likewise be very happy to send the *Graphic* to Bob—but where shall I send it? This morning came to me a note from Carry (to thank me for some gloves I had sent her on Christmas), telling me that she "supposed I know all about Bob's Mary's having come back to Milwaukee") and speaking as if they intended to remain. You don't mention this, and I am anxious to know whether poor Bob has found himself forced to suspend farming. I hope not and should be glad to hear. Meanwhile, subscribing to a journal for a long time I don't know where to have it sent. But I will try Whitewater.—I am writing this in the beautiful great library of the Athenaeum Club.[1] On the other side of the room sits Herbert Spencer, asleep in a chair (he always is, whenever I come here) and a little way off is the portly Archbishop of York with his nose in a little book. It is 9:30 p.m. and I have been dining here. An old gentleman put himself at the table next me and soon began to talk about the "autumn tints" in America—knowing, heaven knows how, that I came thence. Presently he informed me that he was the son of Sir Richard Westmacott, the sculptor; and that the old gentleman on the other side of him was a nephew of Lord Nelson etc. etc. I give you this for local color (it is a great blessing, by the way to be able to dine here, where the dinner is good and cheap. I was seeing arrive the day when London restaurants, whose badness is literally fabulous, would become impossible, and the feeding question a problem so grave as to drive me from the land. I am not sure that some day it won't). I have been spending of late rather quiet days and have not seen anyone in particular. But I go to breakfast tomorrow with Lord Houghton, who invited me of his own movement. H. Adams and Mrs. Wister had each sent me a letter for him; but I have not presented them, 1st, because I heard his house had lately been burnt down; 2d, because I had an idea he was much battered, bored and beset. But if the mountain comes to Mahomet, it is all right. He wrote to me (as "Dear Mr. James," which, indeed, is what all the English do, before they have ever seen you) and asked me to breakfast, having heard of my existence I don't know how. On Thursday I breakfast with Andrew Lang, at his club, to meet J. A. Symonds, and tomorrow I dine with the spasmodic but excellent little Dicey (who was in America) and whom, with his ugly but equally excellent wife, I met the other day at James Bryce's. I lunched a few days since at Lady Pollock's. with a lot of people, whom Lady P. left to scramble after her to the dining-room as they could, she, an aged woman, having marched out with a little infantile Lord Ronald Gower—not so handsome as his name. Lunched also with the Cunliffes, very kindly, but mildly-interesting people, and sat next Samuel Laurence, the artist who did your bad portrait in the diningroom—a very kind, soft little man: who when I told him he had done my father's portrait, said that was what every American told him. I went today to see Thomas Woolner, the sculptor, to whom H. Adams had given me a letter—a good plain, conceited fellow and respectable artist, living, with an intensely pre-Raphaelite wife, in a charming old house, full of valuable art-treasures: a delightful place. Adam's other letter was to F. T. Palgrave, on whom I left it a week ago, but who has taken no notice of it. But perhaps he will, yet. *Don't breathe a word of this.* Tell William I prized his letter highly, and make Alice get from the Athenaeum, Mackenzie Wallace's *Russia,* a new book which every [one] here is talking about.[2] It is most interesting. Farewell, dearest dad. Write me again when you can and believe me your loving son—

H. James Jr.

1. The historian John Motley obtained for HJ guest privileges at the Athenaeum.

2. HJ wrote an unsigned review of this book for the *Nation*, XXIV (15 March 1877), 165–167.

To William James

Ms Harvard

3 Bolton St. Piccadilly
Feb. 28*th* [1877]

Dear William.

Since last writing home I have received two letters from you: the first on general topics and very welcome; the second a request to get you a *Maudsley*,[1] which I immediately did. I hope it has safely reached you. Meanwhile, the wheel of London life, for me, has been steadily revolving, turning up no great prizes, but no disappointing blanks either. I go on seeing a good many people, and yet I seem to myself to be leading a very tranquil life. I suppose it is because my relations with the people I see are very superficial and momentary, and that I encounter no one of whom I hanker to see more. All the Englishmen I meet are of the "useful-information" prosaic sort, and I don't think that in an equal lot of people I ever received such an impression of a want of imagination. Sometimes I feel as if this process of "making acquaintances" in a strange country were very dreary work: it is so empirical and experimental, and you have to try one by one so many uninteresting people to hit upon even the *possibly* interesting ones. I hope it won't be often repeated, and that I shall be able to settle down in England long enough to keep, and profit by, any sense of domestication that I may acquire.—I have dined out a few times lately; but not so often as a while ago. I think I mentioned that Lord Houghton had asked me to breakfast—where I met half a dozen men—all terrible "useful-information," and whose names and faces I have forgotten. But he has invited me again, for a few days hence, and sent me, very kindly, for the season, a card for the *Cosmopolitan*—a sort of talking-club, extremely select, which meets on Wednesdays and Sunday nights. I was taken there a while ago by Frederick Locker, Boott's friend (B. gave me a note to him) (a very nice fellow,) and, amid a little knot of Parliamentary swells conversed chiefly with Anthony Trollope—"all gobble and glare," as he was described by someone who heard him make a speech.—I lunched the other day with Andrew Lang to meet J. Addington Symonds—a mild, cultured man, with the Oxford perfume, who invited me to visit him at Clifton, where he lives. Also, Albert Dicey (he who is America with Bryce[2] and who is a very good fellow in spite of his physique) asked me to lunch with Henry Sidgwick. About Sidgwick there is something exceptionally pleasant (in spite of a painful stammer). He has read *Roderick Hudson* (!) and asked me to stop with him at Cambridge. Further, as to lunches, I lunched yesterday with poor Leslie Stephen, whom, however, rendered more inarticulate than ever by his wife's death,[3] I find an impossible companion, in spite of the moral and intellectual confidence that he inspires. I had but a glimpse of Miss Thackeray, who has likewise been greatly knocked up by her sister's death, and is ill and little visible.[4] She inspired me with a kindly feeling. All this in spite of the fact that, theoretically, I don't lunch out at all; as it spoils a morning's work. I dined 'tother day with one Robarts, at his club; he having made up to me I know not why. Tho' civil, he belongs to the type of Englishman one least endures—the big Englishman who looks like a superior footman, with a turn up nose and an indented chin. At his dinner were several unmemorable men—very legal: he is a practising barrister. I also dined some days since with Mrs. Rogerson—I think I have told you who she is; a clever, liberal woman who invites me to dinner every four or five days. This was a sort of theatrical banquet with the whole Bateman family, who are patronized here socially. They sat however below the salt and I at the summit with Lady Hamilton Gordon who is on the whole, though almost upwards of fifty, the handsomest woman I have ever seen. She has the head of an antique cameo. I dined yesterday with Boughton, the painter (an American—Londonized), a good plain man; and with two other painters who happened to be remarkably pleasant fellows.—When I add that I lately feasted also with Mrs. Pakenham, an American married to' a British general, to whom Mrs. Wister sent me a letter, (a very nice woman with a very nice husband) I shall have exhausted the list of my adventures. I must have told you that I have for the present the frequentation of the Athenaeum Club (thro' Motley) and that I find it a little heaven here below. It transfigures the face of material existence for me: and alas! I already find it indispensable. I also have a temporary membership of another club—the small and modest Savile. It is very respectably composed—supposed, I believe, to be particularly so; but after the Athenaeum it seems dreadfully caddish, and I shall resort to it only when the latter fails me. When that melancholy day comes I shall feel at first as if London had become impossible: the having it makes such a difference. The Athenaeum is a place it takes sixteen years for a Briton to become a member of!—if things go very smoothly.— I am more and more content to have come to England, and only desire to be left soaking here for an indefinite period. I positively *suck* the atmosphere of its intimations and edifications.—This is a very personal letter, as I suppose you desire; and I trust you will answer without waiting for them to be asked. What is your "Herbert Spencer elective"?—to which you have alluded, but without explaining its sudden genesis. Whatever it is I am glad you like it. I often take an afternoon nap beside Herbert Spencer at the Athenaeum, and feel as if I were robbing *you* of the privilege. A good speech of Matthew Arnold's, which seems to be classical here: "Oh, yes, my wife is a delightful woman; she has all my sweetness, and none of my airs." I hope the family circle prospers. Tell Alice to get from the Athenaeum Lord George Campbell's *Log letters from the Challenger:* a delightful book. Tell her also I saw the Ashburners the other evening and they struck me as more lively. I received yesterday a long call from F. T. Palgrave, who is not *sympathique,* but apparently well intentioned. He said G. Eliot's picture of English country-house life in *Daniel Deronda* might have been written by a housemaid! *Don't repeat this, for particular reasons.* In fact F. T. P. stuck in pins, right and left. Write all you can, bless you all.

H. James Jr.

1. Henry Maudsley, *The Physiology of Mind* (1876).
2. An allusion to Bryce's book on the American Commonwealth.
3. Stephen's first wife, Thackeray's younger daughter, Harriet Marion.
4. Anne Isabella Thackeray, later Lady Ritchie.

To Alice James

Ms Harvard

Athenaeum Club
Pall Mall S.W.
(3 Bolton St. Picc.)
March 2 [1877]

Dearest sister:

I enclose you a letter from Ivan Tourguéneff which I received this a.m. in the belief that it will entertain you and the domestic circle.[1] Tho' slight it is pleasant. *Please show it to no one outside of the family,* and return it, in the envelope, by the first person who writes.—This is not meant to be a letter, *chère sœur.* It is very late at night and I am in the delightful great drawingroom of the Athenaeum Club where I have been reading the magazines all the evening, since dinner, in a great deep armchair with such a comfortable place to repose my book and such a charming machine to sustain my legs! I don't want to excite your animosity—but I might, were I to depict the scene that one may usually view here— in this same drawing room, at 5 o'clock in the afternoon:—all the great chairs and lounges and sofas filled with men having afternoon tea—lolling back with their laps filled with magazines, journals, and fresh Mudie books, while amiable flunkies in knee- breeches present them the divinest salvers of tea and buttered toast! I don't write, because I sent William a long letter three days since. But write me, then!

Ever your
H. J. Jr.

1. The letter, dated from Paris 28 February 1877 and written in French, speaks of the failure of his new novel, *Virgin Soil;* expresses regret at HJ's absence from the French capital; and contains an allusion to Zola's *L'Assommoir* as "not an immoral book—but devilishly dirty." Turgenev adds: "If I were a cartoonist for *Punch* I'd amuse myself by representing Queen Victoria reading *L'Assommoir*."

To William Dean Howells

Ms Harvard

3 Bolton St. W.
March 30th [1877]

Dear Howells—

I am supposed to be busily scribbling for lucre this morning; but I must write you three lines of acknowledgment of your welcome long letter. Its most interesting portion was naturally your stricture on the close of my tale, which I accept with saintly meekness. These are matters which one feels about as one may, or as one can. I quite understand that as an editor you should go in for "cheerful endings"; but I am sorry that as a private reader you are not struck with the inevitability of the American dénouement. I fancied that most folks would feel that Mme de Cintré *couldn't*, when the finish came, marry Mr. Newman; and what the few persons who have spoken to me of the tale have expressed to me (e.g. Mrs. Kemble t'other day) was the fear that I should really put the marriage through. *Voyons;* it could have been impossible: they would have been an impossible couple, with an impossible problem before them. For instance—to speak very materially— where would they have lived? It was all very well for Newman to talk of giving her the whole world to choose from: but Asia and Africa being counted out, what would Europe and America have offered? Mme de Cintré couldn't have lived in New York;

104

depend upon it; and Newman, after his marriage (or rather *she,* after it) couldn't have dwelt in France. There would have been nothing left but a farm out West. No, the interest of the subject was, for me, (without my being at all a pessimist) its exemplification of one of those insuperable difficulties which present themselves in people's lives and from which the only issue is by forfeiture—by losing something. It was cruelly hard for poor N. to lose, certainly: but *que diable allait-il faire dans cette galère?* We are each the product of circumstances and there are tall stone walls which fatally divide us. I have written my story from Newman's side of the wall, and I understand so well how Mme de Cintré couldn't really scramble over from *her* side! If I had represented her as doing so I should have made a prettier ending, certainly; but I should have felt as if I were throwing a rather vulgar sop to readers who don't really know the world and who don't measure the merit of a novel by its correspondence to the same. Such readers assuredly have a right to their entertainment, but I don't believe it is in me to give them, in a satisfactory way, what they require. —I don't think that "tragedies" have the presumption against them as much as you appear to; and I see no logical reason why they shouldn't be as *long* as comedies. In the drama they are usually allowed to be longer—*non è vero?*—But whether the *Atlantic* ought to print unlimited tragedy is another question—which you are doubtless quite right in regarding as you do. Of course you couldn't have, for the present, another evaporated marriage from me! I suspect it is the tragedies in life that arrest my attention more than the other things and say more to my imagination; but, on the other hand, if I fix my eyes on a sun-spot I think I am able to see the prismatic colors in it. You shall have the brightest possible sun-spot for the four-number tale of 1878.[1] It shall fairly put your readers eyes out. The idea of doing what you propose much pleases me; and I agree to squeeze my buxom muse, as you happily call her, into a hundred of your pages. I will lace her so tight that she shall have the neatest little figure in the world. It shall be a very joyous little romance. I am afraid I can't tell you at this moment what it will be; for my dusky fancy contains nothing joyous enough: but I will invoke the jocund muse and come up to time. I shall probably develop an idea that I have, about a genial, charming youth of a Bohemianish pattern, who comes back from foreign parts into the midst of a mouldering and ascetic old Puritan family of his kindred (some imaginary locality in New England 1830), and by his gayety and sweet audacity smooths out their rugosities, heals their dyspepsia and dissipates their troubles. *All* the women fall in love with him (and he with them—his amatory powers are boundless;) but even for a happy ending he can't marry them all. But he marries the prettiest, and from a romantic quality of Christian charity, produces a picturesque imbroglio (for the sake of the picturesque I shall play havoc with the New England background of 1830!) under cover of which the other maidens pair off with the swains who have hitherto been starved out: after which the beneficent cousin departs for Bohemia (*with his bride, oh yes!*) in a vaporous rosy cloud, to scatter new benefactions over man—and especially, woman-kind!—(Pray don't mention this stuff to any one. It would be meant, roughly speaking, as the picture of the conversion of a dusky, dreary domestic circle to epicureanism. But I may be able to make nothing of it. The merit would be in the amount of *color* I should be able to infuse into it.) But I shall give you it, or its equivalent, by November next:—It was quite by accident I didn't mention the name of your admiress. Nay there are two of them! The one I spoke of, I think, is Lady Clarke—a handsome charming woman, of a certain age, the wife of a retired and invalid diplomatist who lives chiefly on her estate in Scotland. She takes in the *Atlantic* and seems to affect you much. The other is Mrs. Coltman, a modest, blushing and pleasing woman, who also has the *Atlantic*, and who can best be identified by saying that she is the sister of the widow of A. H. Clough, the poet—Lowell's friend. She is to take me some day soon down to Eton to show me an inside-view of the school, where her rosy little British boys are. Both of these ladies descanted to me on the *Atlantic*, and your productions and said nary a word to me of my own masterpieces: whereby I consider my present action magnanimous! *Àpropos:* the young girl in your comedy is extremely charming; quite adorable, in fact; and extremely real. You make them wonderfully well.—What more shall I say?—Yes, I find London much to my taste—entertaining, interesting, inspiring, even. But I am not, as you seem to imply, in the least in the thick of it. If I were to tell you whom I see; it would make a tolerably various list: but the people only pass before me panoramically, and I have no relations with them. I dined yesterday in company with Browning, at Smalley's—where were also Huxley and his wife and the editor and editress of the *Daily News:* among the cleverest people I have met here.[2] Smalley has a charming house and wife, and is a very creditable American representative; more so than the minister who, I am told, has never returned a dinner since he has been here. Browning is a great chatterer but no *Sordello* at all.—We are lost in admiration of Mr. Hayes; may his shadow never grow less. Blessings on your home.

Yours always truly
H. James Jr.

1. HJ outlines his plan for *The Europeans,* published in the *Atlantic,* July–October 1878.
2. Mr. and Mrs. F. H. Hill.

To Thomas Sergeant Perry
Mf Duke

Athenaeum Club
Pall Mall
April 18th 77.

Dear Tom—

I have to thank you for two letters, both of which were very welcome and one of which arrived two days since. I am very glad that my Lindau Musset was so opportune; I thought I could safely assume that you would like to see it. Both of your letters contain various little facts of interest which, but for you, I should apparently have languished in ignorance of—I am thankful for instance for your telling me that the editor of the *North American Review* (who is the brute?) admits articles of only fifteen pages, as the information comes just in time to save me from sending him a paper on George Sand which I have just finished, *Apropos* of which the current *Quarterly Review* (April) contains a clever article of G. S. by Andrew Lang, who in addition to all his other scribblements works daily on a prose translation of Homer in old-fashioned "picturesque" English, edits Aristotle's *Politics,* and labors at his favorite theme, primitive civilization (McLenon, Lubbock etc.) His great gift is an extraordinary facility. I send you herewith the cheap (and nasty) reprint of *Terres Vierges* which John Turgenieff lately sent me—having kept it only to review it. The nice edition is not yet out. The book will disappoint you, as it did me; it has fine things, but I think it the weakest of his long stories (quite), and it has been such a failure in Russia, I hear, that it has not been reprinted from the Review in which it appeared. Poor T. is much cut down. He wrote me the other day: "*La fortune n'aime pas les vieillards*"[1] and the miserable prospect of war (which is all that is thought or talked of here) won't cheer him up. I should not find myself able conscientiously to recommend any American publisher to undertake *Terres Vierges.* It would have no success.[2]

I am sorry that in the "new deal" you speak of you don't get some engagement. I trust it may yet come. It is interesting to hear that Howells may come to Berne; and between ourselves I am glad in so far as it may interrupt his "comedies." I thought the last (in spite of pretty touches) a feeble piece of work for a man of his years—and sex! Yes, William Black is like him—only less so; inferior in talent, but in better luck as being a Londoner etc. Yes, also, I have read and relished Wallace's Russia (I reviewed it in the *Nation.*) So Sedgwick is to leave the *Nation?* What a sense it gives of our literary poverty to think that one can't fancy who will replace him? The last passion here in "American literature" is *Helen's Babies*[3] which sells by the 10,000 and is chiefly bought by the *haute noblesse.* Farewell, with blessings on your dame and daughter.

Yours ever
H. J.

1. HJ gives only a part of Turgenev's sentence in the letter of 28 February —"*la fortune n'aime pas les vieillards.*" The Russian added " *même en littérature.*" He also expressed the hope that perhaps later the book might encounter a more favorable opinion, "*Je me donne la petite consolation de la croire.*"

2. HJ had obtained authorization from Turgenev for Perry to translate his novel into English.

3. A novel by John Habberton.

To Henry Adams

Ms Mass. Historical

(3 Bolton St. W.)
May 5*th* 77

My dear Adams.

Of course this letter has been mentally begun several dozen times before this; and equally of course, London being London and the huge high-pressure machine you know, it has never found a moment when it could emerge from my yearning intellect. I wanted to write to you, but I consoled myself for delay with thinking that the longer I waited the more I should have to tell you. I have waited so long now that I am quite embarrassed with confidences, and I have let so many of my impressions grow old that some of them have forgotten that in their innocent youth they were very lively. I have really become something of an old Londoner; I am, for instance, so stupidly, prosaically, insensibly, at home, in this blessed asylum of an Athenaeum Club that I feel as if I were losing half its charm—a charm to be properly enjoyed by a Western barbarian only in a flutter of luxurious appreciation. But the flutter will come back when I am turned forth in the cold world again!—I suppose you have heard from any member of my family whom you may have lately encountered that I am having a "beautiful time" and drinking deep of British hospitality. Such a view of the case is in the main correct; but in writing to my relatives I ransack my memory for every adventure that has befallen me and turn my pockets inside out; so that they receive, and possibly propagate, an exaggerated impression of my social career. I didn't come here on a lark but to lead my usual quiet workaday life, and

I have limited myself to such entertainments as was consistent with this modest programme. But I have little by little seen a good many people, gathered a good many impressions and largely enjoyed things. Brutally speaking, I like London exceedingly. I find it very much the place for me, and when I first came here (for I liked it from the first) I seriously regretted that I had wasted time in not fixing myself here before. That, however, I have ceased to regret; for it is a great advantage to be able to compare London with something that is not London—an advantage to one's self I mean: not always an advantage to London!

Your introductions rendered me excellent service and brought about some of the pleasantest episodes of my winter. I am an old friend of the Cunliffes; I have seen, for London, a good deal of them. A capital couple they are, and their friendliness and attentiveness have been more than fraternal. Cunliffe himself is out of town, in some (by me imperfectly realised) militia duty in the country: but I spent an afternoon with him just before he departed. We went out to Richmond by train one lovely day, and took a long and charming walk in the Park: one of those agreeable things one can do easily and compactly here. The last I saw of Lady C. (whom I find a most sweet, frank, comfortable creature) was at the private view of the Royal Academy, where I walked about with her and pretended to think some of the dreary daûbs worth pointing out to her. You can't, after all, say to an English-woman, even if she be as gentle and liberal as Lady Cunliffe, that you think her nation fatally unendowed for the arts, and her Royal Academy the biggest vulgarity of the age. The exhibition this year seems like a collection of colored lithographs from music sheets.— Lord Houghton has been my guide, philosopher and friend—he has breakfasted me, dined me, conversazioned me, absolutely caressed me. He has been really most kind and paternal, and I have seen, under his wing, a great variety of interesting and remarkable people. He has invited me to an evening party tonight (but you see I prefer to sit here and scribble to you; it's half past 11); and to a 6th or 8th breakfast next week. So you will perceive he has done very handsomely and I will defend him with my latest breath!

Palgrave I have not seen so often; but I have seen (not to say heard!) a good deal of him when we have come together. I have been two or three times to see him of an evening and have sat late talking with him *de manibus rebus.* At first, to speak frankly, I didn't like him; but each time we have met I have thought better of him. He pitches into people too promiscuously; but this, I think, is but a conversational habit begotten of the exuberance of his faculty for talking, and in the long run I suspect he will turn out as kind as he is clever. He *is* a most mighty talker, and a very good one. Woolner and his picturesque and amiable wife I have seen three or four times—the last one on the occasion of his showing me two watercolors (a Cotman and a Bonington) which he was on the point of sending out to you. He wanted to know what I thought of the selection. I approved it highly and thought the Cotman [illegible] superb. There was another C. which I a little preferred (an old Normandy house:) but only for extrinsic reasons—such as your already having a marine Cotman. Woolner's choice is quite the stronger picture. I find W. a very honest, vigorous fellow and, for an Englishman, quite a handsome sculptor.—I said above that I have seen a good many people—which is true with the emendation that I have had very little contact with individuals in the mass. I have formed no "relations" of any consequence, and made no intimacies; what I have done has been simply to get a rough sense of London, to feel that it is a place where almost anything or any one may turn up, and to like it accordingly. I like it so well that I shall certainly, if nothing interferes, make it my local anchorage for the rest of the time that I remain in Europe; which will more probably be long than short. Heaven knows one is an outsider here: but the outsider that one must be in Europe one is here in the least degree. So at least, I feel; and at any rate I have got thus far with London, that I am not afraid of it —not at all. At the same time I don't think I could stomach any long residence here that should not be interspersed with periods (in summer and autumn) of the continent.—There are twenty pages of egotism for you; but I believe that both you and your wife will take it kindly. I have left myself no space for inquiries as to your own present situation; but I am re-assured by my impression that this is always intrinsically comfortable. I suppose you are on the point of exchanging Boston for Beverly—bless them both. I only wish you a less ferocious May than this, here, which is paying us off for what seemed a very innocent winter. Give my friendliest remembrances to your wife and believe

always very truly yours
H. James Jr.

To Henry James Sr. and Alice James
Ms Harvard

Embley,
Romsey. Hants.
May 20*th* [1877]

Dearest father and sister.

I address you both together for economy's sake, and I pray you to divide my letter impartially between you. I have favors from both of you to acknowledge: from sister the charming gift of an American blotter brought me by Sara Sedgwick: from father the letter of May 2d received three or four days (or more) ago. I was very grateful for the letter, as it was a long time since I had seen the paternal hand. The blotter gave me an exquisite joy, and sister could not have chosen a more sympathetic gift. It adorns my table and transfigures my room. *Apropos* of Sara Sedgwick I will give you news of her without more delay. I went down to Tilgate to see her on Tuesday last, and by Mrs. Nix's invitation dined and spent the night. Sara looked to me old and shrunken, but she seemed very cheerful and happy: though I should think the very dull life she must be booked for at Tilgate would be a rather severe test of her cheerfulness. Her cousin, Mrs. Nix, is an extremely pretty, charming and attractive woman—a most lovely being, in fact, to whom I quite lost my heart, and whom I am greatly indebted to Miss Ashburner (*tell her this*) for having introduced me to. She is married however, to a man grossly and painfully her inferior—a snob of the snobbish, I should say. The place is very beautiful (at least I thought so until I had seen *this* abode of bliss); but the life is I should think of a quietness beside which Kirkland Street is Parisian and Quincy Street a boulevard.—I must take up the thread of my London life where I left it last, I suppose: only I forget exactly where I left it, and I find I tend more and more to forget where I have been and whom I have seen. *Apropos* of this Sara S. tells me that you labor under the impression that I "go out immensely" in London, have a career etc. Disabuse yourself of this: I lead a very quiet life. One must dine somewhere and I sometimes dine in company; that is all. I have been to several dinners the last fortnight, two or three of which I can't for my life recall, though I have been trying for the last ten minutes in order to enumerate them all. I can mention however that I dined one day at Lady Rose's, a big sumptuous banquet where I sat on one side, next to Lady Cunliffe. (Lady Rose is one of the easiest, agreeablest women I have seen in London.) Then I dined at the banquet of the Literary fund, invited nominally by Lord Derby, the chairman, in reality by good Frederick Locker. I sat next to young Julian Sturgis, and opposite his papa (Russell S.) but the thing was dull and the speech-making bad to an incredible degree— dreary, didactic and witless. As many Americans would certainly have done better. Then I feasted at Mme Van de Weyer—a feast and nothing more, some unrememorable fine folk. Then a pleasant dinner at Hamilton Aïdé's, whom Alice will remember as the author of novels which she used to read in the days of the "Fanny Perry intimacy." He is an aesthetic bachelor of a certain age and a certain fortune, moving apparently in the best society and living in sumptuous apartments. The dinner was in particular to George Du Maurier of *Punch* a delightful little fellow, with a tall handsome wife like his picture-women. I sat on one side next Mrs. Procter, widow of Barry Cornwall, (mother of Adelaide P.) a most shrewd, witty and juvenile old lady—a regular London diner-out. *H.J.* "Tennyson's conversation seems very prosaic." *Mrs. P.* "Oh dear yes. You expect him never to go beyond the best way of roasting a buttock of beef." She has known everyone.

113

On t'other side was a very handsome and agreeable Mrs. Tennant, an old friend and flame of Gustave Flaubert. She was brought up in France. I dined a week ago at Lady Goldsmid's—a very nice, kindly elderly childless Jewess, cultivated, friend of George Eliot etc. who is of colossal fortune and gives banquets to match in a sort of country house in the Regents' Park. *H.J. to a lady after dinner.* "It's a very fine house." *The lady.* "Ow—it's like a goodish country house." I sat at Lady G's next to Mlle de Peyronnet, a very nice English-French youthful spinster, whose mother with whom I afterwards talked (Mme de P.) is, though an English-woman, the Horace de Lagardie who used to write *causeries* in the *Journal des Débats,* and of whom there is a tattered volume somewhere in Quincy Street. I met the mother and daughter (there is another daughter, Lady Arthur Russell, whose husband I have been introduced to and talked with at the *Cosmopolitan*) again at an evening crush at Lord Houghton's, of which the Princess Louise (a charming face) was the heroine; and where also, much *entourée,* was the Miss Balch whom Alice will remember at Newport, red-faced and driving in a little pony-trap, and who now figures in England as a beauty, a fortune and a fast person. She *is,* strange to say, divinely fair, not at all red-faced, smothered in pearls and intimate with the Marchioness of Salisbury (with whom, that is, I saw her hob-nobbing and who looks as if she had just cooked the dinner). Such is life—or rather Balch; who is living with another American spinster of the *décolleté* order, a Miss Van Rensselaer to whom Anthony Trollope (at Lord Houghton's) introduced me on the strength of having overheard her say that she heard I was present, and that I was the person she desired most to see!! *Notez bien* that the rooms swarmed with famous grandees. Miss V. R. by her American "chattiness" exhilarated me more than any *anglaise* I have talked with these six months, and though she was vulgar, made me think worse of these latter, who certainly are dull, and in conversation quite uninspired. (Anecdote of Mrs. Kemble's. *Frenchman sitting next to young Anglaise at dinner, who has said nothing for three quarters of an hour. "Eh, Mademoiselle, risquez donc quelquechose!"*) *Apropos* of Lord Houghton: I breakfasted with him again lately—a very numerous breakfast— of the *Philobiblions*: mostly ancient gentlemen, and pretty dull. I went some time or other to another dinner at Mrs. Rogerson's, promiscuous and easy like most of her dinners, and with men preponderating: Mackenzie Wallace (*Russia*) Augustus Hare (*Walks in Rome* etc.) old Alfred Wigan, the actor, Lady Gordon etc. I have dined furthermore at the Morton Lothrop's (of Boston) who has been staying in London, and in rather solemn and dullish fashion, at Mrs. Coltman's who is a sister of Mrs. A. H. Clough, with whom (strange as it may appear) I am staying since yesterday p.m., and until tomorrow a.m. at this beautiful place. Tho' you don't suspect it, this is Whitsunday, and all the world leaves London. Mrs. Clough sent me a very kind note (through her other sister, Mrs. Godfrey Lushington) asking me to come down here and stay with her aged parents, Mr. and Mrs. Smith. I had determined for the present to "stay" nowhere in England; but the temptation to get out of London for thirty six hours was great—to say nothing of seeing this lovely Hampshire country. The rest of the household have gone properly to church, and I sit in the library in a great deep window, looking out, while I scribble all this base gossip, into green gardens, and the oaks and beeches and cedars of a beautiful park. The place is a very vast and very fine one, tho' as Mr. Smith (a charming rosy old gentleman of eighty-two) tells me, not at all a "crack" one. In America however it would be "goodish," having a drive of rhododendrons four miles long! These kind and friendly people have come into it only two or three years since, I believe, through the death of Mrs. Smith's brother, Mr. Nightingale, uncle of Florence N. Mrs. Smith is also a rosy octogenarian and the old couple are even now creeping about together on the lawn, like Philemon and Baucis. Mrs. Clough is a stout and genial widow, of, I should suppose, mildly—very mildly—"liberal" tendencies, but not of commanding intellect or irresistible brilliancy. The whole household however *respire d'honnêteté* and kindness; Mrs. Coltman's rosy children, with their German governess, are sporting down one of the avenues, before me. There are of course several other people staying in the house, and I have a plan, after the lunch, to take a long walk, over to the New Forest, with a very nice young fellow who is one of the number. The place and the country are of course absurdly, fantastically fair. But I must break off, as I must go out on the lawn and say a word to Mr. and Mrs. Smith, who don't come to breakfast and whom I haven't saluted for the day. I will finish this evening.

3 Bolton St. May 22d I had no time to resume my letter at Embly, and I hastily close it here, having returned last night. I have just received Alice's note enclosing Grace Norton's, and the thought of poor Jane's approaching end saddens me too much to write more. It is a great shock to me, as Sara Sedgwick had spoken as if she were quite on the way to recovery. What a strange fate for that genial, generous woman, so willing to live and with so many reasons to live! If all this were less true she might be living longer! I have just written to Grace.—I stopped over, another day at Embly, and drove yesterday through the New Forest: an enchanting country. On my way home I stopped at Winchester and saw the Cathedral. I have just received (*tell her, mother, when you write*) a long and delightful letter from Aunt Kate. Farewell. I fancy you all feel a personal grief as to poor Jane Norton—I send a few poor photos.

Ever your loving
H. James Jr.

To William James

Ms Harvard

3 Bolton St. W.
June 28th [1877]

Dear Brother—

It is a good while ago now since I received your letter of May 27th; since when also I got a note from father, in which he spoke of sending me a post office order from Osgood, and the German translation of my novel. Both of these have come; for which many thanks. Did you ever see such vile impudence as the translator's performance on the *dénouement* of the tale? and the "cheek" of the man in sending it to me with his "compliments"![1] If those are your Germans I give them up.—I *do* congratulate you on arriving at your holiday, and I hope it will yield you the most priceless satisfaction, of every kind. By the time this reaches you, you will probably be lying alongside of one of those small cedars, with your head on a neatly-massed stone, wrapped in the enchantments of Paradise. For you, as for all the others, I trust these may prove infinite.—It is so long since I have written to you that you will expect me to have many wonders to relate: but in fact I have very few. The season has brought me—thank the Lord!—no increase of diversions; it would be absurd to pretend or attempt to work if it had done so. In fact I have been little in the world as the world goes here! Just after I last wrote, I went for twenty-four hours down to Oxford to "Commemoration"—James Bryce, who as Regius Professor of Civil Law, presents, in a gorgeous crimson robe, the honorary D.C.L.'s having invited me, very kindly, to stay at his college (Oriel). I occupied there some pleasant rooms and found the thing very jolly. I have written of it, however, somewhere and won't say much here.[2] In the A.M. I breakfasted with little Charles Wyman of America (Mrs. Whitman's brother) who is studying "History" at Oriel. Then I went to commemoration—then I lunched at All Souls with Montagu Bernard—a big feast and a charming affair: then I went to a beautiful garden fete at Worcester College: then I dined with the little Oriel Dons, in the common-room. After which I took the late train, with Bryce, back to London. I have dined out hardly at all. Two or three unmemorable dinners at the frequently-inviting Mrs. Rogerson's:[3] a pleasant one with good people, at Mrs. Edward Dicey's: a most amusing one at Greenwich with Woolner: the annual Greenwich dinner of a sort of Bohemianish-literary-artist-club; composed, however, not of first class men, but of persons somewhat of the Hepworth-Dixon calibre; he looking like a third rate Bulwer, making the principal speech. The dinner was wondrous for fish and champagne and the occasion most entertaining. A lot of hard-working London professional men frankly taking a holiday are not such a bad lot—if for nothing else than the handsome share of the individual (even if he himself is not remarkable) in the magnificent temperament of the race, which comes out so strongly, and on the whole so estimably, at such an affair.—I got another day in the country by going down to lunch with my old friend Coulson near Richmond. It was a lovely day and a lovely region and we walked and lounged for a while delightfully in Richmond and Sudbrook Parks. I have also been to two garden-parties at the Duchess of Argyll's—she having invited me at the friendly prompting of George Howard. They are very pretty and full of fine folks, some few of whom I knew, and could talk to. But my intercourse with the family did not get further than shaking hands with the poor dropsical (or paralytic) Duchess and the Marquis of Lorne. I didn't even have a chance of putting on my face before the Prince of Wales, as yesterday (the last party) most of the people managed to do.—I dined one day this week at Mrs. Dugdale's—a niece of Lord Macaulay (daughter of Lady Trevelyan) and a nice friendly little woman. The next day I feasted with Mme du Quaire whom I used to see in Paris at Mme de Blocqueville's—a big, fashionable blonde, English widow of a Frenchman of some position, I believe, who lives half in London, half in Paris, and gives dinners and is liked, in both places. I took in a queer very clever old woman, Mrs. Alfred Wigan, an ex-actress, who, with her husband, appears to be much in circulation in London society. Indeed all her talk was—"Yes, as the Queen said to me the other day at Osborne"; and "the dear Princess Beatrice is so deliciously *naive*." I dine today at Charles Rose's (Lady R's son) who seems a very nice fellow, lives like a lord, and invited me a month ago.—The only other "outing" I have had, but 'twas rather an *inning*—was taking Julia Ward Howe and daughter over St. Bartholomew's Hospital. This sounds like a queer errand for me; as indeed it was. But a very good young fellow, the Warden of the Hospital had asked me to come and see it; and as Mrs. Howe had demanded of me to show her some of London, I've killed two birds with one stone, and got credit with both parties. But the mission would have been for you; the hospital is most ancient and interesting—with nothing in it—but the

118

patients later than the twelfth century, and one of the most beautiful old Norman chapels you can see.—I must break as I have got to go and see your—excuse me but I must say, accursed friend Miss Hilliard, who had turned up here and writes me a note every three days, appointing an interview. I do what I can; but she will certainly tell you that I neglect her horribly. Do you admire her, particularly? She is, I suppose, a very honorable specimen of her type; but the type—the literary spinster, sailing into-your intimacy-American-hotel piazza type—doesn't bear somehow the mellow light of the old world. Miss H. announced her arrival here to me by writing to ask me to take her to the Grosvenor Gallery and Rembrandt etchings and then go out and dine with her—at Hammersmith miles away!—at the Conways! And this a maid whom I had never seen!—I have in the interval of my two sentences driven over to the remote region of Paddington and back, at an expense of three shillings, to see Miss H. whom I did not find. But she will nevertheless deem that I have neglected her.—Excuse the freedom of my speech, which I have not stinted, as I have no reason to suppose that you are "soft" upon her.[4] (Of course I went immediately to see her, after the Grosvenor Gallery proposition, which I was utterly unable to accept. I spent a large part of a Sunday afternoon with her.) Tell mother I also instantly called upon Mrs. Van Buren, who sent me a note, just as she was leaving town. I saw only her two little daughters—two amiable little sprigs of Fishkill. I have just heard from Baron Ostensacken that he is here, and hope to see him tomorrow, and get news of you. Lawrence Walsh and his Uncle called upon me yesterday, and seemed in good spirits: but as they are living at an inn in the City, and seem much disposed, and very competent, to take care of themselves, I don't suppose I shall see much of them; especially as I believe they spend but five or six days. Sara Sedgwick has just gone back to the country, suddenly, after a short stay in town during which I saw less of her than I should have liked. She was exhausted with London, and gave up a visit to the A. Dicey's, during which I was expecting to approach her more, as she was to be much nearer. But I did two or three things for her, and went to see her when I could. She seemed in good spirits and very lovely and pleasant to be with.—I went (two days since) to see the Ashburners the last thing before they sailed and sent you all my blessings by them. Unfortunately I had nothing else to send—save to Alice, a small tribute, which I hope will reach her safely, and which she is not to sneer at because it doesn't bear the mark of the *fabricant* with whom she is familiar. It is by the most correct artist here—the cream of the cream—who leaves her old friend far behind. I informed myself carefully, at the highest sources: wrote to the Princess of Wales.—I got yesterday a note from Lord Houghton who had had a fall from his horse in the Park and was slightly crippled asking me to come in (he lives near) and sit with him. I of course responded. He is a queer, but most kind and human old fellow and is getting better.—Also I had another call from Lady Selina Bidwell, whom I think I have mentioned. This time she had not the pretext of Joukowsky's picture, which I have sent away; but being in town (from Brighton) for the day and near my lodging, she comes up *en bonne camaradé* for a little chat. And talk after that of the coldness and stiffness of the English aristocracy. And Lady S. is the best of women—not at all adventurous or "fast." I had also yesterday a visit from Frederick Wedmore, an amiable weakling of the aesthetic school who writes in the *Academy*. (He is noted for the close of one of his articles: he was speaking of Dutch painting. "Then—Cuyp." That was all the sentence.) I enclose a notice of *The American* from the *Daily News*. I esteem it a considerable compliment that Frank Hill, the editor, a fiercely busy man, should have found time to read it, and write me a very good, appreciative little note about it; which I should enclose if I hadn't lost it. (He didn't write the notice.) The *American* will be reviewed (I learned) in the *Saturday Review*; probably indifferently well, as 'tis by Walter Pollock, a very amiable mediocrity. *Apropos* of this matter, I forgot to thank father for enclosing poor T. S. Perry's note of distress to you about the treatment of *his* article in the *Nation*. I am very sorry for his distress, and wrote to him. The notice was respectable; but it was helpless and unperceptive in poor Garrison (as regards *me*) to cut out his comments.—Behold all the base gossip I can invent. When

I next write to you I probably shall have taken flight to some rural retreat. I shall certainly not stop in London to the end of July, as I until lately purposed, or supposed I purposed. It is too hot and noisy and I find it impossible (especially living where I do—in Mayfair) to fix my attention upon work, and I must without delay get to work at my novel for next year, the beginnings of which must be ready by the autumn. I have besides no people I care for to stay here for, and no invitations ahead. I don't know where I shall go; but I shall go somewhere. I am afraid of the dullness of the English watering place—afraid of lonely chop, for breakfast, for lunch and for dinner, in a lodging on some genteel, cockneyfied Crescent or Terrace. But I shall try it, as soon as possible; and if I break down I shall go abroad, where I hope, in any event, to go in September. (Of course I expect to be back here for the winter.) (Address always *here*, for I shall keep a lien on my rooms.) I wish you all every joy, and (especially father) complete invigoration. Little Jim Putnam came again to see 'tother day, and I have asked him to dine with me somewhere in the country, day and place yet to be fixed.—Mrs. Kemble has left town for Switzerland; and I miss her as we had become very good friends. Write me all about Newport and about everything—about your *philosophical* prospects. Tell Aunt Kate with infinite love that I will answer her two letters directly I get out of this dusty, noisy, headachy Babylon, where, in spite of having decked my two balconies with flowers and awnings, the turbid atmosphere palls upon me.

Ever dear brother, your fond

H. J. Jr.

1. *The American* was translated as *Der Amerikaner oder Marquis und Yankee* (Stuttgart, 1877). The translator, Heichten-Abenheim, supplied a happy ending and took other liberties with the text.

2. "Three Excursions," *Galaxy*, XXIV (September 1877), 346–356, revised and reprinted as "Two Excursions," *Portraits of Places* (1883).

3. Mrs. James Rogerson, daughter of HJ's London friend Mrs. Duncan Stewart, "a clever liberal woman, who invites me to dinner every four or five days."

4. Miss Hilliard may have contributed some elements to the character of Henrietta Stackpole in *The Portrait of a Lady*. Scrawled across the back of this letter in W. J.'s hand are the words, "Do you notice the demoniac way in which he speaks of the sweet Miss Hilliard."

To William James

Ms Harvard

3 Bolton St.
July 10*th* [1877]

Dear William—

Yesterday came your letter of June 24th (having taken a most extraordinary time for its journey—15 days—) containing your excellent photograph, Alice's note about her hat (which I will comply with) and last but not least, the startling news of Lowell's application for me to be his Secretary in Spain. This is altogether news to me, Lowell not having written to me a word on the subject. I know not what to think of it, and in the complete absence of data, almost wish either that I knew much more, or knew not the fact, as yet, at all. If the appointment comes to me I suppose I shall decide to accept it, tho' the rose will not seem to me to be altogether without thorns. It will cost me something to give up London, which I have thoroughly taken up with, and to forfeit for three or four years the opportunity of work. I suppose a secretary of legation cannot with dignity and propriety contribute light articles to periodical literature; and yet I have an idea also that without writing occasionally, the salary is not sufficient to maintain me in great ease. On this and on other points I am quite in the air and in the dark. I am sufficiently excited by the prospect to feel a sensible disappointment if it comes to nothing, and am quite ignorant of how far Lowell's choice of me carries with it a presumption of my getting the place. At moments it seems too good to be true: for a salaried post enabling me to do a small amount of first class work at leisure and remit this constant mercenary scribbling, has long been my delightful dream. I am also, as you may suppose, inflamed at the idea of seeing and knowing Spain. To Lowell himself I am of course most devoutly grateful. But I seriously dread the climate—especially the confinement at Madrid during the summer heats. There are likewise other things. But I won't, for good or for ill, count my chickens before they are hatched; I will only wait patiently for the event and above all for further information. If the event hangs fire, (as the suspense to me is, as regards my personal plans and arrangements, materially awkward) I wish you would write me such information as you can gather, as regards probability, salary etc. I don't like to write to Lowell until he has written to me about the matter.—[1]

You see I am still in London, tho' a week ago I hoped to have got off by today or tomorrow. But London is not a place where, after seven months residence, one can pull up stakes abruptly; and as the weather has lately (until today) been extremely cool, I have lingered on. What has kept me last has been an invitation from Charles Gaskell (H. Adams's friend) or from his wife, Lady Catherine G., to go down for three days to Wenlock Abbey, their place, or one of their places, in Shropshire. I was on the point of declining it as I was deadly desirous to get away from London, when, by an odd chance, came a letter from H. Adams saying— "If Gaskell asks you to Wenlock don't for the world fail to go"; and adding other remarks, of a most attractive kind: the upshot of which has been that I have accepted the invitation, and go on the 12th, to stay to the 16th. It is, according to Murray's *Shropshire,* a very exquisite place: a medieval Abbey, half ruined, half preserved and restored.—For the rest, I have in these latter days neither seen nor done much in London: though somehow, in the simple paying of farewell calls, etc., the days have melted away without remunerative occupation. I am aching to get into some quiet rural spot and at work: for the last fortnight here, I have been utterly unable to fix my attention. Until this Spanish news came I had meant directly after my return from Wenlock, to take boat, by night, straight from Newhaven to Dieppe, and settle down there (or at some place near it on the Norman coast) for the next six weeks. But if I am really to go before long to Madrid, I would rather remain in England until I start. I hope by the time I return from Wenlock I shall hear something definite; for I don't even know whether to begin work upon a novel I have projected for next year. If I go to Madrid I shall postpone it; and if I don't must begin without more than an already extreme delay. I have scarcely dined out. Once at Mrs. Rogerson's, to meet Eugene Schuyler (with whom, and Mackenzie Wallace I two days later breakfasted). Once at Smalley's, in company with Huxley, Senator Conkling of New York (a most extraordinary specimen!) the Edward Diceys, Mr. Eliot (the "household" man, of Boston) etc: a most singular medley: Conkling "orating" softly and longwindedly the whole dinner-time, with a kind of baleful fascination. On Sunday (two days since) I dined *en famille* at the Huxleys. I wish you knew H., himself. I lunched once at Lord Houghton's at one of his great medleys—Miss Rhoda Broughton ("Cometh up as a Flower"), William Black, a little red-faced cad of a Scotchman who says "aboot," "doobt" etc.: Capt. Burnaby ("Ride to Khiva") poor little Frederick Wedmore and others. Today I had dear Benson· (whom I haven't seen in months) to breakfast: I lunched at the Andrew Lang's, and I dine at Mme Van de Weyer's for which last I must now swiftly dress.—11:30 p.m. I have just come in from dinner at Mme Van de Weyer's, a big luscious and ponderous banquet, where I sat between the fat Mme V. de W. and the fatter Miss *ditto;* but was rewarded by the presence and by some talk with, the adorable Mrs. Lyulph Stanley. I can think of no other gayeties or gossip. I went the other night to a musical party at Mme du Quaire's, where I saw the once famous Mrs. Ronalds of America, who has lately turned up here again, and who though somewhat "gone off," as they say here, is still as pretty as an angel. I also lunched at the Greek *chargé d'affaires,* a very nice fellow, whom I knew at the Athenaeum (which I still frequent and prize) and who entertained Mrs. Howe and daughter, and the Baker family. I also lunched at Mrs. Pakenham's and ate strawberries (three) as big as my fist.—I did what I could further about Miss Hilliard, who has left London: called again upon her and saw her, and went to a party at the Boughton's in order to meet her, where, having found her I quitted Mrs. Mark Pattison for her and adhered to her for the rest of the evening. She is a good girl: her faults are that she is herself too adhesive, too interrogative and too epistolary. I have received (I think) seven notes and letters from her, for two or three that I have written her.—

Your account of Class-Day sounded very pretty; but prettier still was the announcement of your speedy departure for Newport; which I hope will be fraught with rarest charm. Many thanks for your criticisms on my articles (George Sand etc.) which are much to the point and very useful. Farewell; love to all—

from your fond brother

H. James Jr.

1. James Russell Lowell had been appointed by President Hayes to be American minister to Spain. Nothing came of his request for HJ, the State Department taking the sensible view that one inexperienced diplomat in a legation sufficed.

To Henry Adams

Ms Mass. Historical

Wenlock Abbey.

Shropshire.

July 15*th* [1877]

My dear Adams—

Just before I left London came to me your letter giving news of the arrival of your case of drawings, which I was glad to hear were uninjured and to your taste. The expense of carriage was *not* paid in advance, and you have doubtless by this time been made responsible for it. All I paid was a trumpery sum to the consul, which I have forgotten, but which I will try and recollect when we meet. Very oddly at the same instant that I received your letter, with its hearty injunction to go to Wenlock should the occasion offer itself, came a gracious note from Lady Catherine Gaskell inviting me to the same enchanting spot. I was on the point of going abroad, but the coincidence of these solicitations seemed a thing not to be made light of; so I deferred my departure for two or three days and came down here on the 12th ult. This is my last day, and I can't let it pass without thanking you for your share in bringing about so agreeable an episode. I had seen next to nothing of Gaskell and his wife in town. With him I had had but ten minutes talk, and Lady C. I had but admiringly looked upon. (I had been unable to accept their invitation to dinner.) It was therefore all the more meritorious of them to invite me hither, where they have come only for a week, to interrupt London and be alone. By this time I feel as if I knew them almost well—as well, without the "almost," I certainly like them. Gaskell I find an excellent fellow, an entertaining companion and the pearl of hosts. We have talked together as people talk in an English country-house when, during the three days of a visit, two, alas, turned out too brutally pluvial. This is a rather big thorn on the Wenlock rose, which, however, on my first day, bloomed irreproachably. A rose without a thorn, moreover, is Lady Catherine G., of whom you asked for a description. I can't give you a trustworthy one, for I really think I am in love with her. She is a singularly charming creature—a perfect English beauty of the finest type. She is, as I suppose you know, very young, girlish, childish: she strikes me as having taken a long step straight from the governess-world into a particularly luxurious form of matrimony. She is very tall, rather awkward and not well made, wonderfully fresh and fair, expensively and picturesquely ill-dressed, charmingly mannered, and, I should say, intensely in love with her husband. She would not in the least strike you at first as a beauty (save for complexion); but presently you would agree with me that her face is a remarkable example of the classic English sweetness and tenderness—the thing that Shakespeare, Gainsborough etc. may have meant to indicate. And this not at all stupidly—on the contrary, with a great deal of vivacity, spontaneity and cleverness. She says very good things, smiles adorably and appeals to her husband with beautiful inveteracy and naturalness. There is something very charming in seeing a woman in her "position" so perfectly fresh and girlish. She will doubtless, some day, become more of a British matron or of a fine lady; but I suspect she will never lose (not after twenty London seasons) a certain bloom of shyness and softness.—But I am drawing not only a full-length, but a colossal, portrait.—As for the place, you will know without my telling you what I think of that. This is a Sunday morning, with a great raw rain-storm howling outside; but though this unpleasantness has lasted forty-eight hours it has really not put me out of humour with Wenlock. The morning after my arrival, luckily, Gaskell and I started off and

126

made an heroic day of it—a day I shall always remember most tenderly. We went to Ludlow, to Stokesay and to Shrewsbury and we saw them all in perfection. You spoke of Stokesay, and I found it of course a gem. We lay there on the grass in the delicious little green, beside the wall, with every feature of the old place still solid and vivid around us, and I don't think that, as a sensation, I ever dropped back, for an hour, more effectually into the past. Ludlow, too, is quite incomparable and Shrewsbury most capital. The whole thing made a delightful day. Gaskell had proposed another for the morrow, but I am sorry to say that the heavens *dis*posed, otherwise. There is, however, a very handsome entertainment in simply loafing and lounging about such an interesting old house as this. I imagine, from what G. tells me, that it is better now than when you saw it—has more of its ancient detail uncovered and disentangled. Gaskell also tells me to say that, in the very act of writing to you, he is deterred by the fact that I have got the start of him; so he keeps over his letter till he has the occasion to himself. He furthermore calls my attention to the screen you sent him on his marriage and which occupies a distinguished position in the drawing room, and bids me say that he and his wife consider it their handsomest appurtenance. It is indeed very handsome and "reflects great credit" as the newspapers say, on American workmanship. I pretend, patriotically, to Gaskell, that in America *nous n'en voyons pas d'autres*; but, in fact, I seem to myself to recognise in it the exceptional inspiration of your wife. —But I must remember that my letter, though written on a rainy day, may not in your reading of it under Beverly skies, have that assistance to your excusing its length.—I go back to London tomorrow, simply to pick up my luggage and depart for the continent, where I expect to spend four or five months in some quiet corner, favourable to work: at the end of which, D.V., I shall resume the thread of my British existence. I feel as if this thread had spun itself quite sufficiently thick to be, for the future, the main cable, as it were, that binds me to Europe. I appreciate your warning as to what that same future may lead to, and I know that, when the day comes, as I suppose it must, for snapping the cable, I shall need a very heroic tug. But I go on the plan that the safest remedy for the homesickness of after-years will have been to get all, and not less than all, one can now. I had heard from my brother William, of your ceasing your Cambridge work, and of the sort of labor and reputation that you are, as you say, going in for. May the former be as agreeable as the latter will doubtless be abundant! Even from Wenlock, London-and-(prospective)-Italy, I find a pulsation of my soul to envy you your Washington winter: but when it is over I shall find another to welcome you here. I hope your summer is a comfortable and happy one, and even believe it, knowing as I do in how rare a degree Beverly combines the charm of nature and of society!—But Lady Catherine comes in from the "chapel"—you remember the chapel—to inform me with her own easy lips that lunch is being served. Commend me humbly to your wife, the memory of whose merits even the presence of those of Lady Catherine does not obscure, and believe me

very truly yours
H. James Jr.

To Mrs. Henry James Sr.

Ms Harvard

3 Bolton St. Piccadilly
August 6th [1877]

Dearest mammy—

This morning came to me your letter of the 23d July: to my great satisfaction, as it seemed a long time since I had heard from home. Ten days before this had come a note from Alice telling me of the arrival of her hat; and a good while earlier a letter from William (enclosing his photo: which is excellent): but this I think I have acknowledged. I am extremely glad the hat was a hit—and a fit: the more so as I all but trimmed it with my own hands.—My last letter home was to Aunt Kate; and spoke of my departure from London as imminent. You see it has not taken place: I am really spending the summer in this murky metropolis. When the hour came on which I had planned to go, I found myself too unwilling to leave England and quite gave up the idea for the present. England is quite the most profitable and interesting place just now, to my sense, that one can be in: it is a very interesting time to be here. I felt as if, really, I couldn't give up the English newspapers of a morning. So as London is now as "quiet" as the grave and very seasonably cool, here I am still.—You say nothing about the great commotions at home, but I imagine that since you wrote you have had plenty of time to watch them and deplore them.[1] I hope you haven't had any particular cause. But do they make you feel very uncomfortable? There was such a full daily account of them in the *Times* that one knew all about the matter here. I won't talk of it though, as it seems to have subsided; and here, too, one feels nearer to the horrible butcheries which during all these summer days are going on on the Danube, and which are so elaborately reported in the English papers.[2] What with these, and the American riots, and the iniquities of the reactionary party in France,[3] and the helpless drifting of poor old England between the Scylla and Charybdis of siding with Turkey and giving rope to Russia—civilization seems in a very pretty condition. My "castle in Spain" is completely laid low: but to my on the whole very moderate regret. I should from the "civil service reform" point of view, have been from my entire inexperience, a very unfit person for the post; and should probably, as regards business, have been very uncomfortable in it. Lowell passed thro' London lately, and I dined with him, in company with William Story, who has just gone to America to look after his affairs. Seeing Lowell renewed a little my regret at not going to Madrid; I should have liked to be *en route* with him for Spain, with the prospect of an even moderate salary. But my regrets were not acute, and I suspect that a year of Madrid would have contented me. And this (as it would have quite broken me up here) would not have been worth while. Lowell was extremely pleasant and gentle—I don't think he is in love with his prospect: but he struck me more than ever as being but little of a man of the world: for a diplomatist, very little. I don't believe he will understand half of what he sees at Madrid; but he is evidently determined to make as good and discreet a minister as he can.—This is almost all the "society" I have had this long time—save a very pleasant episode of a couple of days at a country-house, a week since. I spent them at the Dugdale's in Warwick-shire, and they were very charming. It is a glorious old place—an immense park: oaks six hundred years old, browsing deer etc; the house—quite a "great" one—was full of easy, friendly people; and the combination of the spacious, lounging, talking-all-day life, the beautiful place, the dinner-party each night, the walk to church across such ideal meadow paths with such a lovely young Miss Bouverie (the product of similar *agréments* in Devonshire)—all this was excellent of its kind. Staying there was Sir Garnet Wolse-ley, the victor of the Ashantees, a couple of years since, and pro-prietor of a very charming wife with whom I became quite "thick." If I had chosen earlier in the season to "go in" for this kind of thing I suppose I might have a good deal more of it: but it suits me much better for the present not to. I have promised to go two days hence to see Sara Sedgwick again; and after that I think I shall try to get away from London, as I am feeling much the desire to exchange its atmosphere for something lighter and purer. I shall go somewhere to the seaside; it hardly matters where.—I am extremely glad that your Newport arrangements work smoothly and that you have enough society. I hope that you are staying on there, and that father's prosperity does not wane. Has he got Alice's phaeton? You never say anything more about the little dog. I hope he isn't dead, or stolen. And Aunt Kate and William, (if they will excuse my mentioning them after the dog): I trust the former got my last letter, and that the latter will write to me from the Adirondacks or wherever he is. You had better forward him this letter. I am glad to hear that poor Wilky is getting out of his deep water, and wish I could do something to improve the "tem-perament" of Bob.—I am sorry poor Annie Ashburner strikes you as dull: but there is nothing to vivify her mind or stimulate her wit in the very small corner of "British middle-class" life in which her lot here is cast. I hear from Scribner and Co. that they punctually sent to father the money they owed me (£60.00) and I trust I made it clear that he was to be so good as to keep it. As it turns out they might have sent it straight to me, since I have remained in England: but I directed otherwise when I thought I was on the point of going abroad. I have just drawn a part of the money and will also draw the rest.—This is "Bank Holiday"—Sir John Lubbock's *festa:* the universal midsummer spree. It is a great blessing; but the diffusive hordes of the hot British populace do not beautify the empty dull streets. Yesterday was a very "close" Sunday; and in the afternoon, to take the air, I went down the river to Gravesend; but there was no air, and it was a dreary affair. Aunt Kate will be glad to hear that I abstained from the classic Gravesend treat—"tea and shrimps"; offered me by *such* tea-maidens! I am thinking of going to Isle of Wight—to Ventnor. But you shall hear. Farewell, dearest mammy, with love superabundant from your sympathetic son

H. James Jr.——

Tell Alice that I had carried her old hat to Brown's when her note came; but that the trimming is to be simple and inexpensive and that she will not regret having it. I will tell Sara Sedgwick to call for it when I go to see her.

1. The national railroad strike in the U. S. which led to federal regulation of wages.
2. The Battle of Plevna in the Russo-Turkish war had just been fought.
3. Indirect censorship of Republican journals and other political moves were occurring in France in anticipation of a new election.

To Macmillan & Co.

Ms BM

3 Bolton St. Piccadilly.
August 7th [1877]

Messrs Macmillan & Co.
Dear Sirs:

It was mentioned to me some time since by my friend and countryman Mr. J. W. Smalley that you had inquired my address of him with some apparent intention of making a proposal to me with regard to the simultaneous issue here of a novel of mine lately published in Boston by Messrs. Osgood & Co. viz: *The American.* As, in fact, I did not hear from you, I supposed that you had subsequently decided otherwise: but the circumstance I mention gives me a certain ground for myself making you a proposal. I am disposed to collect into a volume a series of papers published during the last four or five years in American periodicals (the *North American Review,* the *Galaxy,* the *Nation* etc.) upon French writers. I should like to publish the book in England; I have taken, and propose to take, no steps with regard to its appearing in America. It would consist of some 13 or 14 articles, of various lengths, and would make a volume, I should say, of about 325 (largely-printed) pages. It would treat of writers of the day, and I should call it "French Poets and Novelists." The table of contents would be about this:

Balzac's Novels
Balzac's Letters
George Sand
Gustave Flaubert
Alf. de Musset
Théophile Gautier
Ivan Tourguéneff
Ch. Baudelaire
Théâtre Français etc.

Should you feel disposed to undertake the publication of such a volume as I speak of? I shall be glad to learn about what your inclination may be.

> I remain, dear Sirs,
> respectfully yours
> Henry James Jr.

To Grace Norton

Ms Harvard

> 3 Bolton St. Piccadilly
> August 9*th* [1877]

It was very strange, dear Grace, my coming in last night and finding your most welcome letter. Strange because I had just returned from the country, whither I had gone in the morning to pay a pre-arranged visit to Sara Sedgwick; because Sara had read me part of a letter she had lately received from Charles (which gave me a good deal of detailed information about you); and because, lastly I had (partly in consequence of Charles's letter) come in with a perfect intention of doing, before I went to bed, what at any time for three weeks I had been on the point of doing— writing to you.—I didn't write to you on the spot; I simply read your letter, which, for the hour, made me feel too sad to write. It is very sad, dear Grace, but I can hardly even wish that it had been less so. It is terribly sad, and it brings tears of the deepest affection and sympathy to my eyes. But to feel something of your pain with you, and to tell you I feel it, is all that I can do! I cannot thank you tenderly enough for telling me truly how it presses upon you; for you will understand what I mean when I say that I almost *wish* to feel—far away and out of contact with your life as I am here—the reality of Jane's having gone. I wish to share your consciousness of it, and not to idly dream that time is doing a whit more to lighten that consciousness than it really does. Even before I read your letter I had often said to myself that there was something cruel in your finding yourself again in that summer stillness of Ashfield, where every object in nature must be a quickener of pain. And now what you say gives me a stronger sense of your accumulation of memories and of how the present must be completely at the mercy of the past. But there is one thing which is not at the mercy, I believe, of anything else: that personal philosophy, of whatever nature it may be, which is our refuge in the last resort. It is made up out of the mystery of our hearts and our experience, and the most intelligent of us have it, I believe, when it is most needed. That you have it—that you are not demoralized and weakened, but that you may be trusted to *bear* sorrow as well as feel it, is a necessary conviction for any one who has known you.—I sit writing in a dusky London street, on this midsummer day; but as I write my spirit takes a long effectual flight and I can seem for a moment to be near you in that clear, crude, still, New England air— among those hills and woods and streams that are not of this old, over-conscious world. I wish we might take a walk together;

and if we did I should not be afraid to talk about Jane. At this distance my sense of her death is chiefly in the feeling—of which a man at such a time must often become conscious with regards to a woman whom he has loved without being in that closeness of intimacy which produces *professions* of affection—that now my affection may be as frank and tender as the tenderest, may become part of the tenderness of our belief in the purity and goodness that make a reason for living, an object of invocation which nothing in this life of accidents and obstacles can contest our right to invoke. It is no small thing to have known Jane for one, who, like myself, has taken the line of trying to study and represent human character; and in so far as this knowledge is a thing to be thankful for, let it be said of you, with whatever mitigating force the words may have, that you knew her best! Your writing to me was a great kindness in the midst of or at the end of (as I hope it is in some degree) the terrible number of letters that you have probably, sooner or later, undertaken to answer.

——I should be very glad to tell you all that is at all phraseable about my life; but just now (in the middle of a London August) there is very little to tell. I spent three or four hours yesterday at Mrs. Nix's very beautiful place and found Sara Sedgwick apparently very reasonably well and happy. Her cousin—do you know her?—is a very—a particularly charming and attractive person: but her cousin's husband is not, and I should think that a certain British dullness would be often Sara's portion. The creature most odious to me in the world is the English narrow middle-class Tory! But it must be a pleasure, and a profit, to Sara, to live in a place of so much natural loveliness.—I am lingering on in London long after the "Season" has quite passed out of my consciousness, partly for convenience and partly because it seems—at this empty, uninterrupted time—a good occasion to digest and look over and set in order, all those impressions that the winter and spring have left me. These impressions are very numerous; I could tell you a good many of them, but in writing of them I hardly know where to begin. I feel now more [at home] in London than anywhere else in the world—so much so that I am afraid my sense of peculiarities, my appreciation of people and things, as *London* people and things, is losing its edge. I have taken a great fancy to the place; I won't say to the people and things; and yet these must have a part in it. It makes a very interesting residence at any rate; not the ideal and absolutely interesting—but the relative and comparative one. I have, however, formed no intimacies—not even any close acquaintances. I incline to believe that I have passed the age when one forms friendships; or that every one else has!—I have seen and talked a little with a considerable number of people, but I have become familiar with almost none. To tell the truth I find myself a good deal more of a cosmopolitan (thanks to that combination of the continent and the U.S.A. which has formed my lot) than the average Briton of culture; and to be—to have become by force of circumstances—a cosmopolitan, is of necessity to be a good deal alone. I don't think that *London*, by itself, does a very great deal for people—for its residents; and those of them who are not out of the general social herd are potentially deadly provincial. I have become in all these years as little provincial as possible—I don't say it from fatuity and I may say it to you; and yet to be so is, I think, necessary for forming, here, many close relations. So my interest in London is chiefly that of an observer in a place where there is most in the world to observe. I see no essential reason however why I should not some day see much more of certain Britons, and think that I very possibly may. But I doubt if I should ever marry—or want to marry—an English wife! This is an extremely interesting time here; and indeed that is one reason why I have not been able to bring myself to go abroad, as I have been planning all this month to do. I can't give up the morning papers! I am not one of the outsiders who thinks that the "greatness" of England is now exploded; but there mingles with my interest in her prospects and doings in all this horrible Eastern Question a sensible mortification and sadness. She has not resolutely played a part—even a wrong one. She has been weak and helpless and (above all) unskillful; she has drifted and stumbled and not walked like a great nation. One has a feeling that the affairs of Europe are really going to be settled without her. At any rate the cynical, brutal, barbarous pro-Turkish

Henry James, age forty-two or forty-three

attitude of an immense mass of people here (I am no fanatic for Russia, but I think the Emperor of R. might have been treated like a gentleman!) has thrown into vivid relief the most discreditable side of the English character. I don't think it is the largest side, by any means; but when one comes into contact with it one is ready to give up the race!—I saw the Lowells and can testify to their apparent good-humor and prosperity. It was a great pleasure to talk with Lowell; but he is morbidly Anglophobic; though when an Englishman asked me if he was not I denied it. I envied him his residence in a land of color and warmth, of social freedom and personal picturesqueness; so many absent things here, where the dusky misery and the famous "hypocrisy" which foreign writers descant so much upon, seem sometimes to usurp the whole field of vision.—But I shall in all probability go abroad myself by Sept. 1st: go straight to our blessed Italy. I hope to be awhile at Siena, where you may be sure that I shall think of you and of how I shall think of you. Thank you for waiting to see my things as they are printed at home. I confess that the fashion and the company in which they usually come back to me here makes me want rather to hide them away than to show them. To care for them I must wait till I put them into volumes. Certainly I will tell Alice to send you things, and with indefinite pleasure. What you say about your having found relief in reading my book touches me more than I can tell you. I send you (it's the shortest way) a little English sketch.[1] It has small weight, but may please you. Give my affectionate love to your dear mother and to Charles, and tell Charles that I have a standing and most positive intention of writing to him. He must not doubt of this; but desire it.

Yours always, dear Grace, in all tender affection,

H. James Jr.

1. Miss Norton probably had been reading *The American.* The "English Sketch" would have been "An English Easter" in *Lippincott's Magazine.*

To James R. Osgood

Ms Cornell

3 Bolton St. Piccadilly.
Sept 8*th* [1877]

My dear Mr. Osgood.

I have kept the copy for *Watch and Ward* very long; but the truth is I have been unable to bring myself to the point of really sending it to proofs. I have been half hearted about it, and have kept putting this off from week to week. I have at last decided, however, not to retreat from the answer I originally gave you, and I send back the sheets by this post. I have *riddled* them with alterations and made a great mess for the printer. I must absolutely see proofs. This will possibly delay publication (with my delay already) beyond the time you thought it well for the book to appear; but I would rather give up the whole thing in that case than forego the proofs. This is a rigid condition. I will attend to them immediately and make no more delay. The book could still come out by Christmas, which I suppose is what is to be desired. I enclose (I omitted to put it with the sheets) the three lines of preface.[1]

Yours very truly,
H. James

1. *Watch and Ward* had appeared in serial form in the *Atlantic Monthly* during August-December 1871. Osgood now issued it (in the first and only edition during HJ's lifetime) in book form, elaborately revised.

To Henry James Sr.

Ms Harvard

Sept. 19*th* [1877]
39 Avenue d'Antin

Dear Father.

This morning was my weekly crisis—the day on which I look for letters from home. But none arrived—nothing but the dreary *Nation,* handed in to me alone, as it has been of late pretty often. But of course you have all plenty to do, and I don't complain.

Only write as often as you can. Last week came simply three lines from mother, enclosing the very short note you had received from William. I was very glad to get this, with its fine account of his long walks and climbing, for I haven't heard from him in many weeks. I am sorry to see by an allusion in his note that the state of his eyes has kept him from writing. I hope that he will soon be able after his return to give me *de ses nouvelles*. But now I shall have to wait another week before anything will come from you. (For mysterious reasons I never get any American letters save on Thursday or Wednesday.)—I wrote you just before leaving London, so that you will understand my having come hither. I came over on the 9th, and accomplished my usual performances on the odious channel. I have taken for a month a couple of shabby little rooms just off the Champs Elysées, (above the Palais de l'Industrie,) which have a charming view of tree-tops and autumnal verdure. Here, while I stay, I shall do some work, if I succeed in learning not to keep looking out of the window. Paris seems very agreeable, in its own Parisian way; but it makes me feel terrifically glad that I have given up trying to live here. London is worth five hundred of it. The weather, until today, which is bad, has been charming but too cool, and I feel the discomfort of this horrid European autumnal atmosphere which always begins by the 10th of September to make it detestably cold indoors, while you sit writing. It makes me long for the warmth of Italy; for here I am sitting in a Cardigan jacket, and yet I have had no summer. William's account of his self-precipitation into the bosom of nature excites my envy; I wish I could have had something of the sort, and next summer I shall certainly try to get it. But this is an interesting time to be in Paris, where party strife waxes more and more dangerously fierce and the future certainly looks dark. I missed Thiers's funeral by two days; they say it was a most impressive spectacle. But the impression one gets here of the irreconcilability of parties is something sickening; if it makes trouble a month hence (at the election for the new Chamber) one will really have to give up the French. After my residence in London and my acquired familiarity with the large, manly British individual, these latter seem to me like an awfully ugly and bilious little race. But France

is certainly in a hundred respects a more civilized country.—I have
seen three or four people: Ivan Tourguéneff, Mrs. Kemble, Mrs.
Lombard etc. Tourguéneff came in from the country to breakfast
with me yesterday; but the affair was very sad. He is in a very melancholy state of mind over the more and more ominous disasters
of the Russian army and shows it painfully. He expects a total
failure and collapse on the Russian side, and says that the badness
of their generals and the viciousness of their system (having ignorant grand-dukes as commanders-in-chief etc.) can produce no
other result. And even this result will produce no "up-rising" of
the Russian people. The Czar, he says, can, with impunity, do
absolutely what he chooses with them. Tourguéneff says that he
himself doesn't sleep and has dreadful visions all night long: altogether, he is very unhappy. He also takes a very dark view of the
future here; he expects a *coup d'état* a month hence. I go out to
see him at Les Frênes (his place) three days hence and shall breakfast *par la même occasion* with the Nicholas Tourguéneffs, who
live near.—I expected to find here Paul Joukowsky; but he has
not yet come back. He arrives however, immediately, and I shall
be glad to see him; but Russians, just now, are depressed and depressing company. I have done nothing else but go three or four
times to the Théâtre Français, which I enjoy, but not as I once
did. *Ce que c'est de nous!* I saw last night the good old H. W. Huntington who is the same amiable optimist as ever—even to admir-
ing Victor Hugo's speeches. I also dined with my young Jewish
friend T. E. Child, of London, who is now Paris correspondent
of the *Daily Telegraph*. This is a long letter in exchange for nothing.
I hope you are well and active and in the midst of lovely autumn
weather—crimson trees and cerulean skies. I shall probably have
some more money sent to you while I am absent from London,
if you don't mind: you will always know what it means. Please
tell Alice I paid for her hat before I left London (£2.10) and (as
I was rather short) drew on you for the equivalent sum. Farewell,
dearest Dad.

Love, all round from your fondest
H.J. Jr.

To Alice James
Ms Harvard

Rome Nov. *2d* 1877
45 Capo le Case

Dearest sister:

Your letter, which was forwarded to me the other day from London, contained the last news I have received from home, and I should have answered it before if the languor of Italy had not so potently taken possession of me. (I had written you before leaving Paris that I was coming here; so that you will not be surprised at my date.) I thank you, however, none the less for your charming note, from which I have had to extract all possible satisfaction, as it has not been followed as yet by a letter from anyone else.—I left Paris for Turin on the 16th and came quickly to Florence where I spent a week. When the moment came for coming away (from Paris) I was little disposed to execute my plan, for various reasons; and did so rather for conscience sake and the desire to get warm than because I longed for the spree. Once I entered Italy it seemed very charming; but the minor degree of delight in its more picturesqueness which the years have brought—so different from my former visits, makes me feel old and fat. The truth is I am preoccupied with a desire to get back to London (or at least Paris) and work more attentively than I can do in this traveller's life. I shall probably make but a short thing of this stay in Rome. Meanwhile the weather is glorious, and the present autumn, all over Europe continues to be the most remarkable on record, the nights being as fine as the days. Rome is as yet very void of the herd of strangers, and bating the hideous cockneyfications that are going on, ought to be very delightful. But it has changed, and I have changed. It *is* delightful, but it seems, comparatively, common-place and familiar; tho' this I suppose only proves, how thoroughly I had enjoyed and appropriated it in former years.—I have seen of course a great deal of the Bootts, whom I found in Florence and because I had been assuring them for the last two years that I would come and see them here, it was *au fond,* in a large measure, that I got into the train. I must add that they appear thoroughly to appreciate the civility. They seem very well, though poor Boott himself appears much older. He strikes me for the first time as an old man and looks much more aged than of yore—seems also more weary and motionless. Lizzie looks thin and older too, but is apparently well and has become an accomplished paintress. I detest the method she has imbibed from Couture, whom she exactly reproduces, with its charmless absence of delineation and detail, but she practises it, such as it is, with much vigor and even brilliancy, and constantly does better. She is as industrious and prolific as ever and, I believe, intends to send home soon a collection of things, by which you will see her improvement. She is happier I imagine than she has ever been in a sort of antique friendship with the excellent Miss Bartlett, who is as excellent as ever, and, by the way, spoke to me yesterday of the great pleasure she had had in seeing you in America, and of her admiration for your physical beauty and grace. Did I ever tell you by the way, that these things formed (I think I forgot it at the time) the principal conversation of James Lowell when he was in London last summer; resting upon a dinner at which he had met you somewhere, and at which he was also, as he said, singularly struck with the beauty of your costume. "She was so beautifully dressed"—he repeated it several times. I have been wondering ever since what you had on. It couldn't have been the Walker hat—at a dinner. Perhaps it was the black lace scarf.—I have obtained a lodging here in the bosom of a Roman family; that of the Cavaliere Avvocato Spinetti—a rather ragged and besmirched establishment. But I pay little and have lots of sun. I have seen no one but the Bootts and Miss Bartlett, save poor ill-wedded, soured, yet withal clever, Mrs. Tilton, and her repulsive husband.[1] The poor Terrys of former fame are down in the world, having lost two thirds of their property; and Story is in Boston, where perhaps you see him. I hope devoutly that everything is comfortable at home: that father is well and that William's eyes are better. *Send this to Aunt Kate.* Has Bob found anything more to do—has he permanently giving up farming? How does

Wilky write? Tell me of these things and others. Kiss my dearest parents and believe me of my sister the fond

H. J. Jr.

P.S. I have said nothing of what must have been your latest sensation—Sara Sedgwick's engagement.² Much as you will miss her I am sure it will have made you glad. What does Miss Grace say? I saw William Darwin at his sister's in London and thought him a good fellow—"prepossessing" (by the British standard.) But I had only a mere glimpse of him. I thought on that occasion that Sara seemed flushed and excited, but didn't suspect she was being wooed. It must all have been done very quickly. I have no doubt she will manage to be very happy in England, and will have married into a kind, humane set of people. I am glad, for I shall thus sometimes see *her*, and you must come out and do the same, both to her and to me. I hope that another year or so and prosperity in London will give me a little dwelling (of some sort) of my own, where I may offer you hospitality.

1. J. Rollin Tilton, American painter, called by HJ "a very queer genius"—"great on sunsets" but "the most blatant humbug in his talk." Tilton lived in Rome in the Palazzo Barberini until his death in 1888.
2. To Charles Darwin's son, William.

To Grace Norton

Ms Harvard

Paris, Dec. 15*th* [1877]

Dear Grace.—

I hoped after getting your letter of October 15th, to write you from Siena, But I never got there. I only got to Rome (where your letter came to me); and in Rome I spent the whole of the seven weeks that I was able to give to Italy. I have just come back, and am on my way to London whither I find I gravitate as toward the place in the world in which, on the whole, I feel most at home. I went directly to Rome some seven weeks since, and came directly back; but I spent a few days in Florence on my way down. Italy was still more her irresistible ineffable old self than ever, and getting away from Rome was really no joke. In spite of the "changes"—and they are very perceptible—the old enchantment of Rome, taking its own good time, steals over you and possesses you, till it becomes really almost a nuisance and an importunity. That is, it keeps you from working, from staying indoors, etc. To do those things in sufficient measure one must live in an ugly country; and that is why, instead of lingering in that golden climate, I am going back to poor, smutty, dusky, Philistine London. Florence had never seemed to me more lovely. Empty, melancholy, bankrupt (as I believe she is), she is turning into an old sleeping, soundless city, like Pisa. This sensible sadness, with the glorious weather, gave the place a great charm. The Bootts were there, staying in a villa at Bellosguardo, and I spent many hours in their garden, sitting in the autumn sunshine and staring stupidly, at that never-to-be-enough appreciated view of the little city and the mountains. Your letter, in Rome, dear Grace, was a great pleasure to me; but it was a pleasure in which there was a great deal of pain. You ask me not to attempt to "answer" those parts of it which are an expression of your grief; and I confess that even if you had not said this I should not know what to oppose to so keen a suffering. I feel, on the whole, as if I had very little mission to comfort or console anyone, and this feeling is not lightened in the presence of a sense of bereavement that I understand and share so deeply as yours. All one can say is that life brings with it the better as well as the worse, and that while we suffer and talk and call out in vain, we do still live and profit to some extent by the chances of life.—But I can say nothing to you, dear Grace, but that I think of you and understand everything and give you all my friendship. To full-grown human beings, it seems to me, there is nothing to be said but that.

I have had an autumn of things rather than of people and have not much to relate in regard to human nature. Here in Paris, for a few days, I find I know really too many people—especially as they are for the most part acquaintances retained for the sake of social decency rather than of strong sentiment. They consume all my time, so that I can't even go to the Théâtre Français! In Rome I found the relic and fragments of the ancient American group, which has been much broken up—or rather broken down. But neither in its meridian nor in its decline has it had any very irresistible charms. The chief quality acquired by Americans who have lived thirty years in Europe seems to me a fierce susceptibility on the subject of omitted calls.—

Public matters here, just now, are more interesting than private —and in France indeed are as interesting as can be. Parliamentary government is really being put to the test, and bearing it. The poor foolish old Marshal has at last succumbed to the liberal majority, and has apparently no stomach to renew his resistance.[1] Plevna is taken by the Russians and England is supposed to be dreadfully snubbed. But one is only snubbed if one feels it, and it remains to be seen how England will take the Russian success. But one has a feeling now—to me it is a very painful one—that England will take anything; that over-cautious and somewhat sordid counsels will always prevail. On the continent, certainly, her ancient "prestige" is gone; and I almost wish she would fight in a bad cause, if only to show that she still can, and that she is not one vast, money-getting Birmingham. I really think we are assisting at the political decadence of our mighty mother-land. When so mealy-mouthed an organ as the *Times* is correctly held to represent the sentiment of the majority, this *must* be. But I must say that even the "decline" of England seems to me a tremendous and even, almost, an inspiring spectacle, and if the British Empire is once more to shrink up into that plethoric little island, the process will be the greatest drama in history!—This will reach you about Christmas-time, and I imagine you reading it at a window that looks out upon the snow-laden pines and hemlocks of Shady Hill. That white winter light that is sent up into a room from the deep snow is something that one quite loses the memory of here; and yet, as I think of it now, it is associated in my mind with all kinds of pleasant and comfortable indoor scenes. I am afraid that, for you, the season will have no great animation; but you will, I suppose, see a good deal of infantine exhilaration about you. My blessings on all the infants, especially on dear little Margaret, to whom I sent a few days since a rather fat letter, which I hope she safely received.—I am told Godkin is gone; you must greatly miss him. But I am glad he has gone nearer the *Nation* again. I don't know whether it is that that it wants; but it seems to me nowadays greatly to want something. It needs more strings to its bow.—I wonder whether you ever hear from Lowell, and am pretty sure you do—I should like very much to know what you hear, and feel almost inclined to beg the "loan" of one of his letters as the only expedient known to me for getting a particle of news of him. He has as good as promised *not* to write to me and here there is no indirect way of hearing of him. But I shall try the experiment of writing to him, little success as it formerly has had!—I trust your mother is well—to whom, when you speak of reading aloud to her, I wonder what you read. I shall presently send you a book—a little book of essays that is coming out in England. Don't mind at present if you don't see such things of mine as appear in the American magazines. It is an odious way of seeing them, and now they are likely always to be reprinted in volumes. I am ashamed this time to send another message to Charles to the effect that I mean to write to him shortly. I have done it, I fear, too often. But give him my love and—I *will* write! Give my tenderly affectionate remembrances to your mother and let me tell you again that my thoughts are constantly keeping you company.

Ever dear Grace, very faithfully yours

H. James Jr.

Before I write again I shall probably be in England, have seen Sara Darwin and shall be able to give you my personal impression that she has done a good thing!

1. Marshal MacMahon had formed a short-lived royalist cabinet after the October elections.

To Alice James

Ms Harvard

3 Bolton St. Piccadilly
Dec. 29*th* [1877]

Dearest Sister.

I have before me your letter of Dec. 11th, which has come to console me at this dusky and ineffectually-festive moment. I gave you the "flatteries" of my letter from Rome as I received them, without any retouching whatever, and am glad if, being accurately reported, they should seem to you so highly-colored as to be fabulous. I wrote to father just after getting back to London, and since then I haven't laid in any great stock of allusions. This is a dismally rainy Sunday and I have just risen from my temperate lunch of a "chop" and a pint of ale—neatly served (as neatly as smutty English table-cloths allow) by the zealous, *h*-transposing Louisa. This will carry me to dinner (at 7:30) which I shall partake of at the St. James's Club, an establishment I have taken up with in default of the acutely missed Athenaeum. It is, however, a very pleasant place; chiefly a resort of foreigners (of the superior class) and the younger members of the Corps Diplomatique. It is the haunt of all the young attachés and secretaries of legation, and as one dines there better, and sees more men under sixty, than at the Athenaeum, it will in some degree make up to me for my loss. Also, as I pay a monthly subscription to it I have more of a certain sort of a feeling of liberty than at the A. Someday or other, I suppose, if I wait long enough, I shall be elected to the Reform; but there is no danger of it, I am afraid, this year. I have seen Christmas out and kept it by going (in pursuance of an invitation given last summer) to spend it with Mrs. James Leigh at Stratford-on-Avon. Her mother was there and the weather was brilliant; these circumstances, and the picturesque old house, with its big fires and its hangings of holly and mistletoe helped me through my thirty-six hours. Likewise a Christmas tree for the little girl and a tea-party for the children of the people about the place; large red-cheeked *infants* who kept bobbing curtsies and pulling their forelocks. But the Leighs themselves are not interesting. J.L. is an excellent liberal, hardworking, parson, but with the intellect and the manners, of a boy of seven; and his wife who (except for strength of will) is inferior both to her mother and sister, is a sort of perverted Helen Perkins, hating her position in England, detesting the English, alluding to it invidiously five times a minute, and rubbing it unmercifully into her good-natured husband. She has a certain charm of honesty and freshness, and her fault is in the absurd anomaly of her position. I cannot imagine a stranger marriage. Poor Mrs. Kemble looks on and wonders what her daughter can make of her future here.[1]—I have seen no one else since my return and have made no calls at all; save indeed that I went a couple of days since to the Ashburners', thinking that Theodora Sedgwick was there, to whom I should pay my respects. But she was not with them and I saw only the poor deaf Annie, the pampered Walter and the rest. Sara Darwin has invited me to come and see her either on the 5th or the 20th next. I can't leave town again now, and have chosen the 20th or 27th; but as soon as I have seen her I will let you know all my impressions.—I dined the other day with Frederick Macmillan, the junior partner of the firm, who has lived in New York, married an American wife and is a nice young fellow and very friendly. The appearance of my book, which they are publishing, has been delayed by my being abroad, but I am now reading the proofs again, and I hope it will come out soon. It will be pretty, but not one of their prettiest. They have asked me to give them my projected tale in the *Atlantic* for simultaneous publication in their magazine; but this can in all probability not be arranged. I value the offer, however, as a sign of extension, and it will serve for the next time.—(*Mention this, please, to no one.*)—I hope you have had a little Christmas of some kind, and that you have some more consonant weather than this too abundant rain, which gives me lumbago and kindred rheumatic ills—ills to which I am sorry to say I grow more liable as I advance in years. I have had in the last six months a good deal of neuralgia etc.; but I am learning how to take care of myself. I hope Wilky and Bob and their families are keeping their heads up, that father is prosperous, mother rosy and

William the better for his New Year "vac." (as they say here.) For sister, I assume that she is always brilliant and serene. Would it add to her serenity to knit brother a couple of pairs of *crimson silk socks* for evening wear. This is what British maidens do for their brothers, and I am sure that sister would be sorry to be excelled by such as these. The socks should be of a darkish shade and a coarse silk. They are then very handsome and very useful. *Verbum sap.* I sent two humble pairs of gloves just now and hope they come correctly.

Ever dearest sister your fondest
H. James Jr.

1. Mrs. Kemble recorded HJ's visit in *Further Records* (1891), pp. 233–234.

To William James

Ms Harvard

3 Bolton St.
Jan. 28 [1878]

Dear William.

Your letter, dictated to mother and accompanied with a note from herself, arrived some two days since; and more lately came another little letter from dear Mammy. It was a great satisfaction to hear from you at last; but I was sorry to find that you were still obliged to borrow other peoples' eyes. I hope that by this time you have got pretty well master of your own. It is a pleasure to hear however, that apart from your eyes you are robust and elastic and able to do your needful work without scamping. You go into no especial detail about anything: but your allusion to your possible visit to Baltimore and its results was highly interesting. May the visit, if you make it, be delightful and the results *solidissimi*.[1] I sub-scribed to the two periodicals instantly (with the missing *Mind*), and I enclose the two bills. Please, when you send the amount of these, do so by Post Office order. I have, also, just received the volume of Chauncey Wright's which I am very glad to possess and am much obliged for.[2] I have had no time to look at it.—In the way of news, the most recent is that I returned two hours since

149

from spending Sunday (yesterday) with Sara Sedgwick, at Basset. (I went on Saturday in time for dinner.) The visit was very pleasant, although it poured with rain from the moment of my arrival. Sara seems utterly unchanged by matrimony—neither exhilarated nor depressed: very sweet, soft, gentle and without initiative. She is in a densely English *milieu* and has a densely English husband. Both, however, are excellent in their way. Darwin is a gentle, kindly, reasonable, liberal, bald-headed, dull-eyed, British-featured, sandy-haired little *insulaire*, who will to a certainty never fail of goodness and carefulness towards his wife and who must have merit, and a great deal of it, to have appreciated merit so retiring, appealing and delicate as Sara's. He is fond of conversation and laughter, of books and etchings, and was particularly nice in his manner to Theodora.[3] The latter struck me as the brilliant feature of the affair. Whether or no it is from juxtaposition with the British Female, but at all events Theodora appeared a miracle of beauty, elegance, grace and intellectual sparkle. She strikes me as greatly improved—probably by the influence of Charles Norton. Sara, as I say, is wholly unmodified. But I have no doubt she will be reasonably happy, and she certainly did a wise thing (so far as one can tell) in marrying. Her house is a very pretty roomy villa, with charming grounds and views, completely in the country, though in the midst of a very agreeable residential suburb of Southampton. She is surrounded by plenty of solid British comfort, and judged by American habits would appear to be mistress of an opulent home. She had on Saturday a couple of genteel people (very pleasant ones) to dinner and apparently may have as much as she desires of the society of the "upper middle class": the more so as she keeps a very pretty brougham! Altogether, she struck me as very happy and comfortable, and I should have great confidence in Darwin and his prosaic virtues.—As regards other matters my London life flows evenly along, making, I think in various ways more and more of a Londoner of me. If I keep along here patiently for a certain time I rather think I shall become a (sufficiently) great man. I have got back to work with great zest after my autumnal loafings, and mean to do some this year which will make a mark. I am, as you suppose, weary of writing articles about places, and mere potboilers of all kinds; but shall probably, after the next six months, be able to forswear it altogether, and give myself up seriously to "creative" writing. Then, and not till then, my real career will begin. After that, *gare à vous!*—I find here today a note from Wilky inclosing two very pretty photos of his children, who seem, especially the boy, very handsome and solid and make me desire much to be near them. But poor W. gives a sorry account of his present business and says he means to leave it and look for a clerkship, in March. He seems to have a rude career; but I hope his wife eases him down. Please send me (the next who writes) Bob's Milwaukee address. I wish to send him the illustrated papers etc. for this year—as I did last. *So please make a point of this.*

Under the usual heading of my dinings-out there is very little to relate. I feasted some time ago (just as I was last writing, I think) with Augustus Hare (or rather an old aunt of his a genteel high Tory old lady). There I took out Lady Eastlake, widow of the painter; one of those dense, positive, accomplished specialising old London gentlewomen whom one so often meets. I dined also (as a contrast) with Henrietta Temple and consort. Her husband seems a very charming and attractive boy, and Henrietta was less undeveloped than I supposed. But they seem, in this huge metropolis, to be people of barely appreciable magnitude or maturity.—I also dined one day at Sir Garnet Wolseley's—amid the usual collection of rich accessories (it is a beautiful old house in Portman Square, filled with Queen Anne bric à brac to a degree that quite flattens one out) plain women, gentlemanly men etc. After dinner I was entertained of course (the men were all, I think, army men) with plenty of the densest war-talk. Sir Garnet is a very handsome, well-mannered and fascinating little man—with rosy dimples and an eye of steel: and excellent specimen of the *cultivated* British soldier. But my slight acquaintance is chiefly with his wife, who is pretty, and has the air, the manners, the toilets and the taste, of an American.—I went one night to a very pretty musical party at Hamilton Aïdé's, full of actors, actresses and artists, where Mrs. Ronalds (the American) who has appeared again in a miraculous way on the surface of London society, sang, very strikingly. Another night I went with Lady Gordon and Lady Wade (her sister) to see Henry Irving in *Charles I*; an occasion on which the combined wretchedness of the performance and satisfaction of the full-dressed audience—suggested to me *plus long* regarding the British mind than I can attempt to give a notion of here. From the continental point of view it made one think more basely of human nature. But of British artistry one cannot think too basely. I am going, in another hour, to dine with my friend of last winter Mrs. Rogerson, who has just returned from Scotland. Between her and the Smalleys, who were formerly near and dear to each other, there now reigns a mysterious "madness." I don't know the reason of it—and am simply sure in a general way that the fault (something bad has happened) cannot be with the Smalleys, who are generically irreproachable: but though it was they who introduced me to Mrs. R. I haven't dropped her; as to me she continues to be extremely *gentille*. I see little of the Smalleys, who are very *mondains* and dine out three times a day. They are a good example of the way people always (or almost always) make up for the extremes of their destiny. Reared in New England Abolitionism and asceticism they never had any "society" in the early part of their career, and in consequence they go in for it now, tooth and nail. It is curious to see the Londonisation of Mrs. S., a perfect and very pretty product of Watertown. But an end to this idle gossip, which I give you for local color's sake, and to gratify the intellectual femininity of mother and Alice. It is 7 o'clock and I must dress for dinner.—Nothing, of course, is talked of here but the War and the possible share of England in it. Three days since, this appeared great, but now that an armistice has been made, the excitement (for a moment it was intense) has diminished. The military and our aristocratic Turcophiles are certainly detestable (it was interesting to see them *en famille* at Sir G. Wolseley's) but one would detest them more if one did not want to keep one's skirts clear of the equally odious peace-at-any price, "Manchester"-minded party. An empire so artificial as that of Great Britain must be vigilant and jealous, not to begin to crack and crumble, and one has a feeling that from the day the vigilance and jealously hot "Manchester" get the upper hand, the ancient greatness of Britain has begun to decay. It may be that the ancient greatness of Britain has been an iniquity, an "hypocrisy" and an insolence: but to live here is (for me) to feel a kindness for the products of those energetic qualities of the race that are the compensation for its want of charm. At any rate I believe England will keep out of war for the reason that up to this stage of her relation to events in the East, her going to war would be simply for the sake of her "prestige," and that the nation as a whole, looking at the matter deliberately, have decided that mere prestige is not sufficient ground for a huge amount of bloodshed. This seems to me to indicate a high pitch of civilisation—a pitch which England alone, of all the European nations, has reached. It has been curious to see that all the French republican papers have lately been denouncing her fiercely for not pitching into Russia—the defense of prestige being a perfectly valid *casus belli* to the French mind.—It certainly remains to be seen whether in material respects England can afford to abdicate even such a privilege as that. I have a sort of feeling that if we are to see the déchéance of England it is inevitable, and will come to pass somewhat in this way. She will push further and further her non-fighting and keeping-out-of-scrapes-policy, until contemptuous Europe, growing audacious with impunity, shall put upon her some supreme and unendurable affront. Then—too late—she will rise ferociously and plunge clumsily and unpreparedly into war. She will be worsted and laid on her back—and when she is laid on her back will exhibit—in her colossal wealth and pluck—an unprecedented power of resistance. But she will never really recover as a European power, and will find that there is no chance in the armed-to-the-teeth Europe of our time for a country whose stubbornly aristocratic social arrangements make compulsory military service—the standing together in the ranks of peasants, "cads" and gentlemen—fatally impossible! Such is the vision I sometimes entertain, and which events, doubtless, will consummately bring to naught.[4]

Midnight. I have come in from dinner and will close this interminable scrawl before I go to bed. I dined, as I think I mentioned, with Mrs. Rogerson, with her usual little set of intimates: Sir Frederick and Lady Pollock, the Hills, Lady Gordon etc. But the dinner, I am sorry to say, was dullish, and I have nothing particular to relate of it. I am also tired, with a busy day and a walk down from Queen's Gate.—I hope everything is smooth at home and am very glad you are having so "glorious" (as mother says,) a winter. Here is it very much better than last and with nothing in the world to call cold. Thank mother for her letters; I hope father thrives in the fine weather. If you do go to Baltimore let me hear as much as possible about it. Goodnight!

Your faithful
H. J. Jr.

1. William James was being wooed by the Johns Hopkins to join their faculty.

2. Probably *Philosophical Discussions,* edited by C. E. Norton, which contained some posthumous essays by Wright.

3. Theodora Sedgwick.

4. This remarkable statement on the English character—prophetic of England's resistance to the Nazis—contains only one misjudgment: the class structure within the army did not work against compulsory service.

To Mrs. Henry James Sr.

Ms Harvard

3 Bolton St. Piccadilly
Feb. 17th [1878]

Dearest mother.

I am afraid it will seem to you a long time since I last wrote home—bating the few lines which I lately dispatched to Alice in answer to her letter of Jan. 27th. Since then has come your "strictly business letter" of Jan. 28th; and a note from William, asking me to dispose of his ms. Tell him (the note came yesterday) that I shall wait a day or two till I can carry the parcel (for safety's sake) *by hand* to the address he gives me. Meanwhile I hasten to reply to your strictly business letter. The incongruity that you point out, dearest mammy, resides simply in a defect of your own memory. You wish to know what I sent to meet the first draft I mentioned to Uncle Robertson—the one made between the last of July and the 1st Sept. I caused to be sent to father by *Scribner and Co.* a draft for *$300,* which they wrote me at the time had been duly sent, and *you, yourself, wrote me had been duly received.* I have not, unfortunately, kept your letter: but I remember it *most vividly.* It is singular that father and you should have forgotten it: but I imagine that if you meditate a little the thing will come back to you. Reinstating in its place this draft of $300 made and reimbursed last August, the report I made to Uncle R., which he quotes to you, and which you quote to me, tallies correctly with the account I rendered you. It is most strange you should have forgotten the *Scribner* draft. Don't you remember my writing to you after you had written to me mentioning its arrival, that I had caused it to be sent to father in prevision of my leaving London early, and that having in fact remained through the month of August I was sorry to have troubled him about it, as it would have had ample time to reach me here? Pray try and recall all this. I wish to heaven I had kept your letter. The draft was from Scribner in payment for two stories I had sent him: one the tale of the *Four Meetings* which you read: the second another tale which has not yet appeared. When you remember this, as I think you eventually will, you will see that we are quite square. I am sorry that I undertook to bother you in the autumn with this duty of receiving my moneys; I might have managed the affair less awkwardly. But I thank you very kindly for telling me that in case of my drawing again I need not mind leaving myself a certain time in your debt. I may have to do so once or twice during the coming months, but it will never be for long— never long enough for you to feel it. The reason for my doing so will be that the sudden extinction of the *Galaxy* by the *Atlantic* has been a material inconvenience to me.[1] The *Galaxy* had treated me for some time very well and last year, for instance, I drew $1200 from it. I expected to keep on doing, from month to month, the same; when suddenly, to my bewilderment, I learned that the *Atlantic* had swallowed up this convenient tributary. But this incommodity will be but temporary. I am taking, at last, a serious start with fictitious composition, and shall very presently begin to reap the fruits of it in a measure quite in excess of any advantage lost by stoppage of the chance to publish, in the *Galaxy*, small pot-

155

boilers of which I had grown very tired. So, if I am obliged to make two or three drafts in the course of the spring (and I am not *sure* that I shall be) have a little patience and believe that you will be very promptly reimbursed, not only in coin, but in reflected glory: of which latter article I propose to furnish myself with a very considerable amount. It is time I should rend the veil from the ferocious ambition which has always *couvé* beneath a tranquil exterior; which enabled me to support unrecorded physical misery in my younger years; and which is perfectly confident of accomplishing considerable things!—I sent father yesterday my book, just published by Macmillan, and which I hope will reach you safely.[2] Don't you think it very pretty?—Unfortunately it is a wretched moment, here, for a book to appear. The public is so preoccupied by the War, that nothing has any chance.—I am going to write a few lines to Alice; so I will close, dear Mammy. William wrote that father had been suffering for a day or two very severely, with a *gall-stone*. What does that mean—in the long list of human ills, the name is new to me? I hope it is to father, now, very old and of the past. Give him my love and believe me dearest mother your fondest

H.J. Jr.

Mrs. Norton—and Grace—are too sad to think of!

1. The *Galaxy* had ceased publication and sold its subscription list to the *Atlantic*.
2. *French Poets and Novelists.*

To Alice James

Ms Harvard

3 Bolton St. W.
Feb. 17*th* [1878]

Dearest sister.

I wrote you a short note a few days since, and said therein that you should very presently hear from me more plenteously. But I have just been writing a long letter to mother, and am afraid that today, also, I must restrict myself to a few lines. You tell me to keep plying you with social gossip, in so far as I have any, and I would fain to do so. But I have, today, no great stock of reminiscences. I have gone on dining out occasionally, but always pretty tamely: with Frederick Macmillan; with Mrs. Crompton, daughter of Mrs. Gaskell; with Mrs. Rogerson, again; with Leslie Stephen etc. At Stephen's I met the very charming woman (Mrs. Duckworth by name) who has, by a miracle, consented to become, matrimonially, the receptacle of his ineffable and impossible taciturnity and dreariness.[1] She is a most delightful, handsome specimen of a nice type of Englishwoman: but poor Leslie seems, since his engagement, in deeper intellectual mourning for his late wife than ever. It isn't even a *demi-deuil*. Present were poor Miss Thackeray and her juvenile husband (one Ritchie)[2]—the latter even out-silencing Stephen: and Miss T. herself the very foolishest talker (as well as most perfectly amiable, and plainest, woman) I have lately encountered. Compared with her conversation, *Miss Angel* is Baconian!—At Mrs. Crompton's I sat next to a rather nice, intelligent, short-haired Miss Cobden, daughter of the great C., who gave me an interesting account of her having prepared all the materials for her father's biography and put them into the hands of John Morley, to write the book. He has undertaken the task with enthusiasm, and Miss Cobden, who seems rather in love with him, is enchanted. Then I dined with the Albert Diceys, who are good, but decidedly too ugly, useful information-ish, grotesque-Oxfordish, poor-dinnerish etc., and too surrounded with emulous types of the same, not to make one feel that one can do better. I dined furthermore, one day, at a big house in Lancaster Gate, "to oblige Benson"—the dear good Benson whom you know, and who is more than ever angelical; only, poor boy, attacked with weak lungs and suddenly ordered off to the Riviera. He was staying with the Crossfields—old friends of his father's—Manchester people of colossal wealth, with the ugliest daughter in the world as heiress of it all. It was a curious example of a branch of the London world not "in society"—and with a "dance" afterwards. There were some dozen of the most fearfully dressed maidens I ever saw; and I took out Benson's sister, who is very nearly as nice as himself. But the pleasantest dinner I have lately assisted at was one given by John Cross, at the Devonshire Club, to a lot of men. I sat next to Frederick Harrison, who in spite of his aspect, complexion, hair-brushing etc, as of a provincial second rate dandy, is very good company. The contrast between Harrison's Comtism, communism etc, and his highly ornate and conventional appearance, is most singular.—I think that is all my junketing.—I went yesterday to see Sara Darwin who is in town for a few days, staying at Mrs. Litchfield's house, who has "lent" it, in that convenient English fashion, while she and her husband are away. Sara seems not in the least married—not enough so. She is as good and gentle as ever, but as listless and passive, and as, apparently, unconscious of a matrimonial "position" as when she used to wander along Kirkland Street. Theodora, as I said before, is superb! Another case of "superberness" is Henrietta Pell-Clark,[3] whom, and her lovely Leslie, I have seen several times. She is immensely "improved"—has opinions—and not bad ones—on English politics, society etc; says witty things about them. Her husband seems a most charming young fellow. I had them the other day to breakfast—having "got in," as they say here, plenty of eggs, fish, cutlets, cream, marmalade, muffins and other delicacies; and one night Leslie and I went to the House of Commons; a thing I should like to do often—it is very interesting—if it were not so difficult.—I have just been interrupted by a long visit from Sir Francis Doyle —whom you will know by name; he was lately Professor of Poetry at Oxford. It was "civil" and friendly of him (he is an old man) to come and see me: which he did, I suppose, because his nephew Charles Milnes-Gaskell put him up to it. (Gaskell is lodging just now—being in London without his wife—on the floor below me, in this house; and I have seen a good deal of him.) But I suppose he liked it, as he stayed an hour and a half. He is a very easy, genial old boy; but I can't retail his talk. Almost all my Sunday P.M. has fled—the precious time for dutiful calls.—We are trembling on the brink of War; but, I think, shall just graze it. Farewell, dear child.

Your loving H.

1. This was HJ's first meeting with the mother of Virginia Stephen Woolf.
2. Anne Thackeray had married Richmond Ritchie, a man younger than herself.
3. The former Henrietta Temple, Minny Temple's youngest sister.

To Henry James Sr.

Ms Harvard

3 Bolton St.
March 25*th* [1878]

Dearest Dad—

I have a letter from you of March 7th to acknowledge and to thank you for (enclosing me a letter which I re-enclose, as it may amuse you). I have been putting off writing until today because today brings.in the American post and I dreamed it might bring me some mentionable letter. But there was nothing—as so often occurs, but the solitary *Nation*, naked and unattended—and seeming to me, in these circumstances, most loathsome. I am getting to detest the sight of it. Such are the irritations of expatriation; they are, in fact, very numerous. But there are fortunately compensations; and I continue to find these in London, in very sufficient quantity. I have had of late no especial social joys, but I am constantly fonder of my London residence, and feel that I am getting cockneyfied for life. I have dined out a good deal for the last two or three weeks, and would fain enumerate these occasions for the benefit of Alice and mother. They have not been especially interesting; but I will try and remember what I can. As for instance that I dined one day with James Bryce—a dullish affair, redeemed mainly by the fact that he always talks well himself and that his pretty Scotch sister, who keeps his house, (she is but a lass in her teens) has the prettiest Scotch brogue. I took in a third rate female novelist, Miss Spedding, who writes under the name of Susan Morley. Does Alice know her works? If ever one meets a particularly pinched and prosaic British female, she is sure to be a Virgin novelist. Then, I think came a large dinner at Hamilton Aïde's, where I chiefly communed with the charming, handsome Mrs.

159

Henry Gordon, daughter of Mrs. Sartoris and niece of Mrs. Kemble. About this time, too, a dinner of formidable dreariness at the Coltmans' (whom I must have formerly mentioned)—a dinner like this:

illumined however, by my going in with a very pretty little Mrs. Milman (daughter-in-law of the late Dean of St. Paul's). I dined, then, quietly, with the amiable Andrew Langs; and also with Mrs. Crompton again, and took out her sister Miss Meta Gaskell (the Norton's friend); a most pleasing, amiable, sympathetic woman. Further, at Mrs. Pakenham's; and furthermore at the Edward Dicey's, where I went in with poor Miss Thackeray—further advanced toward confinement (though I believe it has not yet come off) than I have ever seen a lady at a dinner party. This is a thoroughly good, gentle creature; but exquisitely irrational. But I believe she is very happy with her infantile husband Richmond Ritchie. The next day I dined with the Spottiswoode's—deadly dull and not improved by my pairing with Mrs. F. T. Palgrave— the most unattractive form of the *Anglaise*. (And her brother, Charles Milnes-Gaskell, who is in town without his wife and who has rooms below me here, is such a nice, likeable fellow.) The Spottiswoodes, I should explain, are the great social representatives of science, in London. He is Secretary, or High Priest, at the Royal Institution and being rich people, they do the official dining and lionising. Their dinners are (from the gustatory point of view) memorable. After this I dined at the Russell Sturgis's, (who had asked me several times before): a huge, expansive, and expensive banquet. I took in the big Miss Van de Weyer, bursting in her corset, and sat between her and Miss Motley. After dinner came a London crowd, to hear Brandram recite from Shakespeare—poorishly. The Sturgis's is a materially brilliant, but not an interesting, *milieu*. I talked a bit with Lady Harcourt and went the next day (Sunday P.M.) to see her—she being in the same situation as Miss Thackeray. She is a good London woman. Two or three days since I dined with the Miss Lawrences'—two virtuous maiden gentlewomen of fortune, who live in a very pleasant old house in Whitehall and are fond of entertaining. (They are very pleasant, liberal, intelligent women.) I took in a young Russian Princess Troubetzkoy, who proved to be a grand-daughter of old Mme Taglioni, the ex-famous dancer. The Russian girl was clever and interesting, and talking French with her was a pleasant momentary lift out of British Philistinism. After dinner I was introduced to Taglioni, with whom I had a good deal of talk. (I had supposed she was in her grave.) She is an ugly little wizened old woman, but very entertaining and reminiscential. She has run through her various fortunes and in the evening of her days has settled in London, to give dancing lessons to the daughters of the aristocracy. She told me she was very well received *dans le monde.* "*J'ai ma position de femme mariée; et puis j'ai ma position de*—Taglioni." (She is married to, and separated from, a French nobleman.) I dined the other day with Mrs. Kemble and went with her afterwards to see Henry Irving in *Louis XI*—in which he is better than in anything else—which doesn't mean he is not pretty bad. Scatter all through this an occasional dinner with my friend Mrs. Rogerson (whose entertainments, though numerous, are always informal and easy—Whistler, the painter, has always been there of late) and you will have as complete a record as you need desire of my social existence. I suppose that to the family circle in the library it will seem an affectation in me to say that I find this same social existence rather stale and poor—composed of not especially interesting or superior elements. But, in fact, it is no blasphemy to confess to satiety after a certain amount of nestling in the lap of the "Upper Middle Class." One must give up looking for fresh and high impressions. And one must get used to finding (I must, at least) that I get tired of everything and blasé of everyone, and that I care not for much save the idea of doing some work. And yet, anomalously, I am, as I say, more and more attached to this great rotundity of London: doubtless because I find that such an attachment is an excellent condition for work. I have no more personal news. I am very well, thank God (as they say here); and I am getting toward the close of

161

my short serial for Howells, which I regret his delay in publishing.[1] But you will find it readable, I think, when it does begin.— The situation is very *tendue* and bellicose, though I know not what (if war occurs) England will fight either with, or for. She seems to be helplessly drifting; never did small statesmanship seem smaller beside great events.—Have you read Matthew Arnold's article on *Equality* in the *Fortnightly?* It is very charming. I cannot get over a feeling of pleasure that he writes just as he does; even his limitations have a practical excellence.—I am glad, dear daddy, that you are able to work; but are you never going to publish? I am glad too that you find pleasure in my *Essays;* but I am afraid they won't have much sale in America. How wretched of Alice to bring home a cold from New York; but I hope she brought something else. I am expecting a letter from her. I can believe that William "was a great *succès*," as the Americans in Paris say, in Baltimore, and I hope it will help him in Cambridge as well as at *B*. What is Bob doing—and Wilky, who wrote me that at this time he meant to leave his business? I am afraid that "*succès*" is not got there. Blessings on all and kissings on Mother.

Ever your

H. J. Jr.

1. *The Europeans.*

To Mrs. John Rollin Tilton

Ms Colby

3 Bolton St. W.

April 3*rd* [1878]

Dear Mrs. Tilton:

I thank you very kindly for your appreciative letter; over which, as I read it, I "grew faint," like Porphyro in Keats' poem,[1] as I regularly and systematically do over all emanations from Rome. You may be sick, you may be sad, dull, uncomfortable, justly indignant, (I devoutly hope you are none of these things;) but at all events you live in Rome, in April, in the prettiest *salottino* in Italy—and while this goes on you receive of the close-fisted Fate that governs our world more than you lose by her. I had rather be miserable in Rome than comfortable in London; which latter I am not at present, inasmuch as I am stupefied with a bad cold, and until just now I took for consolation to writing to you, had no diversion from the same but to stare wearily out of my window at the dirty drizzle of this misnamed springtime, against the great smutty blank wall of Lord Ashburton's house.[2] I have no stone-pines (only stovepipes) and statues to look at; no turquoise mornings and topaz afternoons—no palace frescoes or Roman drives. But you know I haven't, and it is not your fault. But it is not mine either, for I should certainly be in Rome at this hour if I had not fifty good reasons for being in London. If I had known how your winter was going to turn out I should have waited for those great events at almost any sacrifice. Still, even in Rome I could not have done more than *piangere* over the King's death[3] and the attendant impressions, and that I did here, every morning, at breakfast as I read the letters in the *Times*—I am very glad you have been putting Di Amicis into English[4] and I hope very much your labor will be rewarded by the public appreciation. I should say that much of him was decidedly worth translating. He is very touching and delicate and his *Constantinople,* which I looked through while in Rome, appeared to me really brilliant. How are all those good people, the Romans of the Decadence?[5] You see our friend Miss Bartlett rather more, I suppose, now that Mrs. Hawker has been removed. I have seen her (Mrs. H.) here and find her rejoicing in London. If she will give me the Palazzo Bonaparte I will gladly present her with 3 Bolton Street. I would even consent to share the Palazzo with Mr. H. There is nothing to tell you of here but war and weather. I have spoken of the latter topic and there is very little that is better to say about the former. London smells of gunpowder, and the tawdry old Jew who is at the head of this great old British Empire would like immensely to wind up his career with a fine long cannonade. But I hope very earnestly he will be disappointed, as the cause is a very shabby one. Remember that I always prize your letters and believe me, dear Mrs. Tilton, with kind regards to your husband,

very truly yours
H. James Jr.

Will you give my friendliest greeting to Mrs. Carson?

1. HJ was fond of this phrase from Keats's "Eve of St. Agnes."
2. On the north side of Piccadilly, at the west corner of Bolton Street, presenting an ugly brick wall to the window which HJ directly faced while he was writing.
3. Victor Emmanuel II died on 9 January 1878.
4. Mrs. Tilton translated and published Edmondo de Amicis' *Constantinople* (1878).
5. HJ uses the title of Couture's painting to refer to the American art group in Rome. He later described them, and the Tilton appartment, in *William Wetmore Story and His Friends* (1903).

To Lord Houghton

Ms Trinity

3 Bolton St.
Apr. 15<i>th</i> [1878]

Dear Lord Houghton.

I am most happy to do what you request—in the very small measure indeed of my ability. I enclose a note for Gustave Flaubert and one for Tourguéneff—though I think it very possible you know the latter. (I have left the note open, according to the rules of American civility—which has more rules than are commonly supposed.) If you *do* know Tourguéneff (or if you only make his acquaintance through my note) he will himself be the best possible introduction to the other men—the Frenchmen. It was through him that I made Flaubert's acquaintance, who was the only one of *ces messieurs* with whom I established personal relations. I am sure the others won't do me the honor to remember me, though I often used to meet them at Flaubert's. The latter is an excellent and interesting fellow, well worth knowing and worth all the others a hundred times over—both in genius and personal nature.

He is a great friend of Tourguéneff, and my respectful advice would be that you go first to see the latter and go with him to Flaubert's—he being an excellent introducer. He also knows Zola intimately, and Daudet (tho' rather less) and would be most happy to make you know them. I wish you a very happy journey to Paris and a speedy return.

Very faithfully yours
H. James Jr.

To Gustave Flaubert

Ms Louvenjoul

Londres
ce 15 avril [1878]

Cher monsieur Flaubert.

J'ose penser que vous n'aurez pas oublié le bon accueil que vous me faisez il y a deux ans, lorsque je venais chez vous le dimanche avec notre ami Tourguéneff. Le souvenir de ces causeries auxquelles j'assistais un peu en étranger mais bien en admirateur, me permet de croire que vous aurez la même bienveillance pour la personne très-distinguée qui vous remettra cette lettre—Lord Houghton—homme d'état et écrivain anglais, est amateur de tout ce qui se produit en France de neuf et de frappant. Il serait très-flatté que vous lui accordiez votre connaissance et s'estimerait heureux s'il rencontrait chez vous ce petit cercle de vos habitués du dimanche que j'avais souvent le plaisir d'y trouver: MM. Daudet, Zola, de Goncourt, etc. Lord Houghton s'intéresse vivement aux écrits d'Émile Zola et serait volontiers auprès de lui l'interprète du public très-nombreux et très-attentif qu'il possède en Angleterre. Je suis fort heureux, pour moi-même, de trouver une occasion aussi propice de me rappeler à votre bon souvenir et de vous remercier de nouveau de ces procédés amicaux par lesquels vous m'avez donné le droit de vous adresser un ami. Un homme de la valeur de Lord Houghton se trouve tout présenté rien qu'en le nommant, et j'ai voulu surtout le charger de vous exprimer mes amitiés et voeux très-sincères pour votre prospérité personnelle et votre travail. Voici le second hiver que je passe à Londres, mais je me promets d'année en année le plaisir de me retrouver à Paris au moment où vous y serez et de frapper bien discrètement à votre porte. Tout à vous, cher Monsieur Flaubert, d'admiration et de reconnaissance.

Henry James Jr.

To Henry James Sr.
Ms Harvard

[3 Bolton St.]
April 19th [1878]

Dearest Daddy—

Promptly arrived your note of April 2d, telling me that Houghton and Osgood had sent me a cheque etc. It was an error their sending it to you at all, as I thought I had made them understand that such things were always to come to me. I have written to rectify them, as also to rebuke them for their shabbiness—in terms which, I trust, will make them forswear it. They are, in truth, very shabby. Howells kept writing to me last year to remonstrate with me for publishing my little wares in the *Galaxy* and *Lippincott*; and when I send to the *Atlantic* the things they (that is the *Galaxy*, if it existed) might have had, Houghton pays me the half (or the two thirds) of what the other magazines did. But *j'y mettrai ordre.* I have written Houghton a letter *d'une bonne encre.* I have drawn on my letter of credit twice of late: but I shall soon repay you. Leslie Stephen has just accepted, with effusion, a short story of mine·for the *Cornhill.* It is in two parts and comes out probably in June and July. I will of course immediately send it you, and if I get them in time, I will sell the advance sheets, for simultaneous publication, in America—probably to *Harpers'.*[1] I don't know whether I have told you that Houghton and Osgood are on the point of republishing in a pretty little volume my tale of *Watch and Ward* which appeared some years since in the *Atlantic.*

Osgood wrote to me proposing it last summer, and at first I declined. But then I got hold of it and re-read it and it seemed to me a good way of turning an honest penny. So I have revised and very much rewritten it, and I think that—though very thin, and as "cold" as an icicle—it will appear pretty enough. If I get any fame my early things will be sure to be rummaged out; and as they are there it is best to take hold of them myself and put them in order. So I lately gave great pains to patching up *Watch and Ward*, and, as I have seen all the proof, suppose it will come out instantly.[2]—Thank you for the title page of your *Nature*, which I shall reverently peruse. I wish it every possible good fortune, but am afraid it isn't exactly a "selling" title.[3] Excuse so low a view of it.—When I last wrote I was rather seedy, and for awhile continued so. But I am better now, and that means very well. I am, normally, at present, very well *indeed*. Those visitations in my head are strange; but they are, fortunately, not frequent, and they have nothing whatever to do with "work."—This is Good Friday; I have had a hot-cross-bun for breakfast, and all the world is leaving town for Easter. I go tomorrow for two or three days to Florence Wilkinson, in Herefordshire. I have had of late but few sociabilities. I dined one day at Lady Harcourt's—a small dinner, pleasant enough: Lord and Lady Reay, Lady Ripon, Miss Motley, one Mansfield etc. Sir William Harcourt is a powerful, brutal, Britisher, humorous, not vicious, and of superior ability. Lady H. is an intense American (Boston physique) intensely Londonized. There is nothing like London for Londonizing one.—I also breakfasted on Sunday last with William Whistler[4] the painter, at his queer little house at Chelsea, on the river (near Carlyle's). His Sunday morning breakfasts are somewhat classical. He is a queer little Londonized Southerner, and paints abominably. But his breakfasts are easy and pleasant, and he has tomatoes and buckwheat cakes. I found there Sir Coutts and Lady Lindsay (the Grosvenor Gallery people)—who are very sociable (and Sir Coutts the handsomest man in England); Mrs. Duncan Stewart, Arthur Cecil the actor etc. Two days since I dined with Frederick Macmillan to meet Mr. Grove, the editor of their magazine, who had just been reading *The American* (these were the terms of Macmillan's invitation) "with great delight." There was also the estimable Craik (a partner in the firm), husband of Miss Mulock the novelist. Grove is a very jolly old fellow—one of those London men of letters who have done lots of unrecognized work. (He is sub-editor of Smith's Bible Dictionary and wrote much of it, etc.) He was very friendly, and I shall probably arrange with him before long for a serial in *Macmillan*—the obstruction being that the magazine is small, and, just now, overstocked. But it is only a question of time.—Relate these things to mother and Alice as my latest dissipations. Leslie and Henrietta Temple have just come back from Paris, Leslie more charming than ever (and indeed Henrietta ditto). They are just sailing and I have promised H. to go and bid her good-bye at Lady Rose's. So I must pause. I can think of nothing more that it is imperative to mention. Thanks for the notice of Howells's play, which, though very flattering, did not seem to attest a positive success. This indeed, as the thing read, was I should think, not in the conditions. I don't speak of the War-prospect; but they speak of nothing else here. Love and blessings on all, dear dad, from your faithful

H. J. Jr.

1. The story was "Daisy Miller," published in the June and July issues of the *Cornhill* XXXVII, 678–698, XXXVIII, 44–67. HJ did not move quickly enough to secure his American rights, and the story was promptly pirated.

2. James made more than eight hundred changes and refinements of punctuation in this early novel, which was published in Boston in May 1878. He never included it in the corpus of his work, speaking always of *Roderick Hudson* as his first novel.

3. This would have been the title page of the elder Henry James's last book, *Society the Redeemed Form of Man, and the Earnest of God's Omnipotence in Human Nature* (1879).

4. HJ makes a slip here, writing William instead of James.

To William James

Ms Harvard

3 Bolton St. W.

May 1*st* [1878]

Dear William—

Since I last wrote home two good letters have come to me—
yours of April 7th, and Mother's of the 15th ditto. I will answer
you first as I have written more lately to mother. It was very
agreeable to see your definite handwriting again, and I hope it is
a sign of real eye-betterment. Your letter was forwarded to me
more than a week since, while I was down in Herefordshire spending a couple of days with Florence Wilkinson. This had been a very
perfunctory performance; but it proved to be, for that short period, very comfortable. I am far from meaning, however, to go
back for a fortnight, as I got off only by falsely promising to do.
It is a picturesque ancient house, of the Tudor days (much mod-
ernized) with nothing to speak of in the way of grounds, but
standing in a very charming and what they call here "wild" country, close to the Welsh border. Mary Wilkinson and spouse were
also there, and she and her sister are both very nice, gentle, lady-
like women. Their respective husbands are also very good men.
St. John Matthews (Florence's) is a very handsome, distinguished
well-dressed personage, with very proper, polite manners and no
perceptive aroma of his native Birmingham. His cousin, Mary's
consort, is a hardworking London solicitor, much less *distingué*,
but very sharp and clever, and a Cambridge Wrangler. I walked
with him one morning up a very pretty little Welsh mountain,
and greatly enjoyed it. Mary W. is very sweet and innocent
(though chronically depressed by having no children) and, by way
of conversation, says to me, *àpropos* of nothing—"Is Mrs. James *very*
fond of London?" Is she? Ask mother. Mary is in fact lovely; but
the dullness, small provinciality, and "lower middle class" quality
of the conversation and the *milieu* are incompatible with close
relations. St. John Matthews is a "lower middle-class" Tory (of
the type of Sara Sedgwick's famous cousin) and one can't live or

pretend to attempt to live, with such people—especially when their only other outlook on the universe consists of fly-fishing. The Wilkinson family are, I opine, in adoration and subservience before St. J. M., whom they consider a Phoenix of gentility and pecunidity. (He seems, in fact, very pecunious.)—Coming back to London I dined at the Oxford and Cambridge Club with Alexander Carter, who had asked two or three other men—Sir David Wedderburn, who has been much in America, etc; and this is the only dinner party I have lately attended. It is still Eastertide, "every one" is out of town, and there are no invitations. I profited by the stillness to run down for a couple of days to the Isle of Wight and call upon our little friend Miss Peabody[1]—a design I had entertained more or less ever since she came to England. I had proceeded on the hypothesis that she was in solitude and desolation; but I found her *très-entourée,* having with her four other American women beside her mother, who is much better. But I enjoyed the wonderful prettiness of Ventnor and Boncherch, as well as seeing Miss P., with whom I walked on the downs and conversed, quite in the Boston manner. In spite of her five American women I think my visit was a benefaction to her and I am very glad to have made it. She was very nice, intelligent and charming; and it is a pleasure, immersed in Britishness as I am, to come in contact with the native *finesse* and animation of the American female mind; accompanied though it strikes me as being with a certain thinness of nature and with much circumstantial crudity. The Isle of Wight is charming; but I shall probably "do" my impressions of it and of the Wilkinsonian country. in an article; so I won't expatiate here.[2]—There were many interesting allusions in your letter which I should like to take up one by one. I should like to see the fair Hellenists of Baltimore; and I greatly regret that, living over here, my person cannot profit by my American reputation. It is a great loss to have one's person in one country and one's glory in another, especially when there are lovely young women in the case. Neither can one's glory, then, profit by one's person—as I flatter myself, even in your jealous teeth, that mine might in Baltimore!! Also about my going to Washington and its being my "duty," etc. I think there is much in that; but I can't whisk about the world quite so actively as you seem to recommend. It would be great folly for me, *à peine* established in London and getting a footing here, to break it all off for the sake of going to spend four or five months in Washington. I expect to spend many a year in London—I have submitted myself without reserve to that Londonizing process of which the effect is to convince you that, having lived here, you may, if need be, abjure civilization and bury yourself in the country, but may not, in pursuit of civilization, live in any smaller town. I am still completely an outsider here, and my only chance for becoming a little of an insider (in that limited sense in which an American can ever do so) is to remain here for the present. After that—a couple of years hence—I shall go home for a year, embrace you all, and see everything of the country I can, including Washington. Meanwhile, if one will take what comes, one is by no means cut off from getting American impressions here. I got ever so many the other day, from my visit to the six Boston ladies at Ventnor. I know what I am about, and I have always my eyes on my native land.—

I am very glad that Howells's play seemed so pretty, on the stage.[3] Much of the dialogue, as it read, was certainly charming; but I should have been afraid of the slimness and un-scenic quality of the plot. For myself (in answer to your adjuration) it has long been my most earnest and definite intention to commence at playwriting as soon as I can. This will be soon, and then I shall astound the world! My inspection of the French theatre will fructify. I have thoroughly mastered Dumas, Augier and Sardou (whom it is greatly lacking to Howells—by the way—to have studied); and I know all they know and a great deal more besides. Seriously speaking, I have a great many ideas on this subject, and I sometimes feel tempted to retire to some frugal village, for twelve months, where, my current expenses being inconsiderable, I might have leisure to work them off. Even if I could only find some manager or publisher sufficiently devoted to believe in this and make me an allowance for such a period, I would afterwards make a compact and sign it with my blood, to reimburse him in thousands. But I shall not have to come to this, or to depend upon it.—I received a few days since your article on H. Spencer, but I have not yet had time to read it. I shall very presently attack—I won't say understand, it. Mother speaks to me of your articles in Renouvier's magazine—and why have you not sent me these? I wish you would do so, punctually. I met Herbert Spencer the other Sunday at George Eliot's, whither I had at last bent my steps. G. H. Lewes introduced me to him as an American; and it seemed to me that at this fact, coupled with my name, his attention was aroused and he was on the point of asking me if I were related to you. But something instantly happened to separate me from him, and soon afterwards he went away. The Leweses were very urbane and friendly, and I think that I shall have the right *dorénavant* to consider myself a Sunday *habitué*. The great G.E. herself is both sweet and superior, and has a delightful expression in her large, long, pale equine face. I had my turn at sitting beside her and being conversed with in a low, but most harmonious tone; and bating a tendency to *aborder* only the highest themes I have no fault to find with her. Lewes told some of his usual stories chiefly French—the Frenchman who, coming out of a Berlin *salon,* said "C'est un peuple froid, sec et disgracieux," etc. There were various other people there; the Du Mauriers, Sir James Paget etc.—But enough of London.—I hope your Easter Vacation tuned you up and that you find comforting qualities in the advance of the spring. Mother said more than it made me happy to hear about Alice's having been of late a good deal enfeebled, but as she also mentioned a promising *régime* she had entered upon, I hope the news is better now. She also told me "all about" Miss Katharine Loring, whose strength of wind and limb, to say nothing of her nobler qualities, must make her a valuable addition to the Quincy circle.[4] Tell Alice I delight in the thought of her and she must send me her photo. I asked Miss Peabody about her, who said she greatly admired her, and had always timidly aspired to know her, but thought herself unworthy. I had shuffled your note, now so old, about the cravats and toothbrushes away under some papers, where as it remained unseen, I completely and characteristically forgot it. A thousand regrets. Just now, being rather low in pocket, I am only awaiting some money which must arrive from day to day, before *de me défaire* of the little sum needful for the purchase of your articles, which I will immediately send you.—

We expect to hear at any hour that war has broken out; and yet it may not. It will be a good deal of a scandal if it does—especially if the English find themselves fighting side by side with the bloody, filthy Turks and their own Indian sepoys. And to think that a clever Jew should have juggled old England into it! The papers are full of the Paris exhibition, which opens today; but it leaves me perfectly incurious.

Blessings on all from yours fraternally,

H. James Jr.

P.S. to letter to William. I enclose, though I suppose you have seen it, a notice of my book from the *Saturday Review.* The shabbiness of its tone is such as really—*n'est-ce pas?*—to make one think more meanly of human nature. It is evidently, by intrinsic indication, by Walter Pollock. I received the notice in the *Evening Post;* and hope you will send me any more that you see.—I am sorry Lizzie Boott's pictures are a *fiasco,* but understand the impression they must make. I am afraid both she and her father will feel it; and I hope it will at least have the effect of keeping her from returning to her detestable Couture.

1. Elizabeth Palmer Peabody (1804–1894), American reformer and feminist, a sister-in-law of Hawthorne; she probably served as model for Miss Birdseye in *The Bostonians.*

2. In "English Vignettes."

3. *A Counterfeit Presentment.*

4. This is the first allusion to Katharine Loring, who would later become AJ's closest friend and companion during her long illness.

To William James

Ms Harvard

The Reform Club
May 29*th* [1878]

Dear William.

You have my blessings indeed, and Miss Gibbens also; or rather Miss Gibbens particularly, as she will need it most. (I wish to pay her a compliment at your expense and to intimate that she gives more than she receives; yet I wish not to sacrifice you too much.) Your letter came to me yesterday, giving me great joy, but less surprise than you might think. In fact, I was not surprised at all, for I had been expecting to get some such news as this from you. And yet of Miss Gibbens and your attentions I had heard almost nothing—a slight mention a year ago, in a letter of mother's, which had never been repeated. The wish, perhaps, was father to the thought. I had long wished to see you married; I believe almost as much in matrimony for most other people as I believe in it little for myself—which is saying a good deal. What you say of Miss Gibbens (even after I have made you allowance for natural partiality) inflames my imagination and crowns my wishes. I have great faith in the wisdom of your choice and I am prepared to believe everything good and delightful of its object. I am sure she has neither flaw nor failing. Give her then my cordial—my already fraternal—benediction. I look forward to knowing her as to one of the consolations of the future. Very soon I will write to her—in a few days. Her photograph is indispensable to me—please remember this; and also that a sketch of her from another hand than your's—father's, mother's and Alice's—would be eminently satisfactory. This must be a very pleasant moment to you—and I envy you your actualities and futurities. May they all minister to your prosperity and nourish your genius! I don't believe you capable of making a marriage of which one must expect less than this. Farewell, dear brother, I will write before long again, and meanwhile I shall welcome all contributions to an image of Miss Gibbens.

Always yours
H. J. Jr.

To Henry James Sr.

Ms Harvard

The Reform Club
May 29*th* [1878]

Dear Father—

I have just been writing a line to William but I must write another to you, to go off by this post. I have told William what I feel about his engagement, and I imagine that it is what the rest of you, at home, feel, as well. Meanwhile I am waiting for a portrait of Miss Gibbens—a portrait photographic and epistolary;[1] without which I feel my present information to be very imperfect. Write me yourself about the young lady. You must have had her more or less in Quincy Street and have had opportunities to observe and estimate her. I am expecting from day to day to hear something from mother.—It was not about this, in particular, however, that I meant to write—but about a little matter I had in mind when William's letter came. I am going to inflict upon you another brief financial statement.—A short time since I was abruptly informed that I was on the point of coming up for ballot at the Reform Club—and, a few days after, that I had been elected—a regular member, for life. It came more suddenly than I expected, as I had received information at Christmas which led me to suppose that probably another year would elapse before I should be even balloted upon, and that even then my election was problematical. But they have treated me handsomely, and put me through after but a fifteen months' standing on the book of candidates. I owe it more especially, to the excellent Frank Hill, and Charles Robarts and also I think, a little to Sir Charles Dilke, who, poor man, appears to have found time (up to his neck in the House of Commons as he is) to read and be "struck" by my French essays. At all events, *j'y suis, j'y reste*—for ever and a day. It is a precious good thing for me—something of the kind had become indispensable—and makes me feel strangely and profoundly at home here. But there is no rose without its thorn; in a word I had to pay £42 entrance dues; and as I was elected

175

as a New Yorker, I wished both for my personal and national credit to pay the money instantly. I hadn't it in my pocket, and I determined to borrow it of you, on my letter of credit. I hesitated a little, because I have already drawn twice from this source, this winter, and but a fraction of the money has, as yet, been repaid. But I know what you would say, and how you would say it, were I to have a chance to ask you; so I settled the matter and took possession of this high advantage. (I have been lunching here today for the first time, and find the place all that I can desire and the lunch divinely cheap. I am writing this in the big tranquil library, looking out upon the green gardens of Carlton House Terrace, and furnished with a store of English literature sufficiently large and delightful to last me a lifetime.) I can easily and promptly repay you the money and shall in the course of a strictly limited time do so, together with the rest. But for this I did not expect again, for a long time, to resort to my letter of credit. At the present writing I have owing me £250, and if it would only pay itself down, I should disindebt myself instantly. By the autumn the sum will be doubled, at least; so you see I am not in want of funds. Still less am I in want of work. I have many irons on the fire, and am bursting with writableness. I can affirm therefore that whatever inconvenience my presumption may have caused you will be dissipated before it becomes acute. Enough; I don't venture to say more, for fear of disgusting you.—I have no great news, beyond this club business. I went down to Aldershot the other day to spend forty-eight hours at the Pakenhams'—they are situated there in a "hut"—and to assist at the review on the Queen's birthday. It was a charming episode; but I have written something about Aldershot, so I won't descant.[2] Two days since I dined at the Charles Roundells' with a lot of people—FitzJames Stephen, Alice's little worm of an historian (Green) and his wife, etc.[3] I sat next to Mrs. Green (who is, however, charming—just married) and on my other side had Stopford Brooke, who is a capital un-clerical creature; so that we greatly fraternized. I also dined with Leslie Stephen, on his return from his wedding tour. His new wife is a remarkably beautiful, lovely woman and has cheered him up amazingly: but I don't see what he has done to merit so grandly fair a creature.—I have taken Theodora Sedgwick to see pictures, and have learned from her that the Morses are here—upon whom I shall call, and try to be of service to Miss Fanny: though, what with work and London, and the multiplication, daily, of chance engagements and duties, it sometimes seems as if all time had flown forever, and bewildered madness would ensue. Bless you all, dear dad, *renseignez*-me about William's bride. I wrote lately, copiously. to Alice.

Yours ever
H. J. Jr.

1. HJ wrote "literary" but crossed it out.
2. "The British Soldier," *Lippincott's Magazine*, XXII (August 1878), 214–221.
3. John Richard Green (1837–1883), author of the *Short History of the English People* (1874). His wife, Alice Stopford Green (1847–1929), during her long widowhood became a writer and historian and remained a good friend of HJ's.

To William James

Ms Harvard

Reform Club,
Pall Mall. S.W.
15 July [1878]

Dear William:

I have just heard from mother that you had decided to be married on the 10th ult: and as I was divorced from you by an untimely fate on this unique occasion, let me at least repair the injury by giving you, in the most earnest words that my clumsy pen can shape, a tender bridal benediction. I am very glad indeed to hear that you have ceased to find occasion for delay, and that you were to repair to the happy Adirondacks under hymeneal influences. I should think you would look forward, in effect, to next winter's work more freely and fruitfully by getting your matrimonial start thus much earlier. May you keep along at a pace of steady felicity. The abruptness of your union has prevented me from a becoming punctuality in sending Alice a small material emblem of my good wishes; and now I shall wait till next autumn and the beginning of your winter life. I thank her meanwhile extremely for the little note—a charming note—that she sent me in answer to my own—and I feel most agreeably conscious of my intensification of kinship. I envy you your mountains and lakes—your deep, free nature. May it do you both— weary workers—all the good you deserve.

Ever your fond and faithful brother
H.J. Jr.

To William James
Ms Harvard

Reform Club,
Pall Mall. S.W.
July 23d [1878]

Dear Wm.

I just find your letter of July 8th, enclosing your wife's lovely photograph (which, having carefully, and as Ruskin says, "reverently," studied it, I re-enclose here, with a thousand thanks). You tell me that you were to be married two days later, but you are painfully silent as to details—say not a word as to the hour, or place, or manner of the ceremony—the officiating functionary, or any of those things which in such a case one likes to be told of. I should not forgive you for this if it were not that I count upon mother, after the event, writing to me in a manner to supply deficiencies. I wrote you briefly the other day, on first hearing that your marriage was coming off immediately—so that you know my sentiments about it. I can best repeat them by saying that I rejoice in it as if it were my own; or rather much more. I wish I could pay you a visit in your romantic shanty, among those mountains with which you must now be so familiar and which I have never seen. It will surely be the beginning of a beautiful era for you. You have only to go about your work, and health and happiness will take care of themselves.

—Yes, I know that it must be a sad summer in Cambridge, and my thoughts are constantly in Quincy Street. But I note what you say about the amelioration of poor Alice's symptoms.[1] She must have been having a tragic time; but I hope most earnestly it is melting away. I am much interested in the prospect of the Baltimore professorship, of which you speak, and surely hope that, since you desire it, you will quietly come into it. But I shall regret, on grounds of "general culture," etc. that you should detach yourself from Harvard College. It must, however, conduce to "general culture" to have Baltimore winters instead of Massachusetts ones. Bravo also for the Holt psychology and its coincidence with your labors.[2] May it go along triumphantly. I am very glad indeed that you were pleased with "Daisy Miller", who appears (*literally*) to have made a great hit here. "Every one is talking about it" etc., and it has been much noticed in the papers. Its success has encouraged me as regards the faculty of appreciation of the English public; for the thing is sufficiently subtle, yet people appear to have comprehended it. It has given me a capital start here, and in future I shall publish all my things in English magazines (at least all the *good* ones) and sell advance sheets in America; thereby doubling my profits. I am much obliged to you for your economical advice; such advice is never amiss, but I don't think I specifically need it. I think I am decently careful, and have no fear but that, after a little, I shall be able at once to live very comfortably, to "put by," and to make an allowance to each member of the family. This is my dream. I am very impatient to get at work writing for the stage—a project I have long had. I am morally certain I should succeed, and it would be an open gate to money-making. The "great novel" you ask about is only begun; I am doing other things just now. It is the history of an *Americana*—a female counterpart to Newman.[3] I have the option of publishing it in *Macmillan* or in the

Cornhill (with preference given to the former), and I hope to be able to get at work upon it this autumn; though I am not sure.— As regards *The Europeans* I am very sorry, and it is a great injustice to it, that it should have been advertised or talked of as a *novel*. It is only a sketch—very brief and with no space for much action; in fact it is a "study," like Daisy Miller. (I am just completing, by the way, a counterpart to *D.M.*, for the *Cornhill*.)[4] I have no personal news of any value. It is very hot indeed, at last— though not so terrible as I see by the papers it has been at home, as I am afraid Father and Mother and Alice and Aunt Kate must have felt to their cost. I shall be in London all summer, as I have plenty of occupation here. I have received several invitations to pay short visits, but have declined them all, save one for a week at Wenlock Abbey (Charles Gaskell's) on August 10th. I have just telegraphed a refusal to William Spottiswoode, the new President of the Royal Society who has a very charming place down in Kent. I shall, however, probably go to spend next Sunday with Sara Darwin. I rejoice in your rejoicings in my fat, and would gladly cut off fifty pounds or so and send them to you as a wedding-gift. I am extremely well, and though London heat is rather a vile compound, I, strange to say, like it. I was sure I had acknowledged the Post Office order for £15: a thousand pardons. I sent home the toothbrushes and cravats by Theodora Sedgwick; and took the liberty of joining to them the present of a pair of hair brushes, for travelling, in a leather case. I got only *six* cravats; and could not get them of the maker you designated. But I will send another six by a near opportunity. Read all this to Alice: it is a great pleasure to me to be writing to her too, as I always shall in writing to you. Here I sit with the uproar of Charing Cross in my ears, and envy you your strange woodland life. May it be excellent for you this summer. You had better forward this to Cambridge; it will eke out my correspondence there. Farewell; all my love to your wife. Seeing her photo. and getting an image of her beautiful face has made all the difference.

Yours
H.J. Jr.

1. The nervous prostrations to which AJ was subject had manifested themselves seriously during this summer.

2. This was the beginning of WJ's ten years of work on his *Principles of Psychology* (1889).

3. HJ's plan for *The Portrait of a Lady*.

4. "An International Episode," *Cornhill Magazine,* XXXVIII (December 1878), 687–713; XXXIX (January 1879), 61–90.

To John Foster Kirk

Ms Unknown

3 Bolton St. W.
July 29. [1878]

Dear Mr. Kirk:[1]—

I am afraid I can think of no suggestions for plates for my "English Vignettes"—and to tell the truth the somewhat impractical purpose of these few lines is to express my grief at my would-be-delicate and to-be-read-on-its own-account prose being served up in that manner. The thought is painful to me—and I call my protest unpractical because I suppose the enterprise is already under way. But I earnestly beseech you not to endeavor to equip anything I may in future send you in the same fashion. I think the text of illustrated articles is always supposed to be poor and perfunctory—written to the plates—and not read by those to whom I try to address myself. In this case, too, I regret the arrangement because it delays the appearance of the article, and I am as usual in want of the payment—Yes, I see in the English papers the record of the American thermometer, and melt, almost, in sympathy.

Very truly yours
H. James Jr.

1. Kirk was the editor of *Lippincott's Magazine,* in which "English Vignettes" appeared in April 1879 (XXIII, 407–418), illustrated, in spite of HJ's appeal.

To Mrs. William Dean Howells

Ms Harvard

Wenlock Abbey,
Shropshire.
Aug. 14*th* [1878]

Dear Mrs. Howells—

I must thank you very tenderly for your generous little despatch on the subject of "Daisy Miller." I am charmed to think that she struck a sympathetic chord in your imagination, and that having been, in fact, so harshly treated by fate and public opinion, she has had it made up to her in posthumous honors. She appears to have made something of a hit; for people appear to have found time to talk of her a little even in this busy and not particularly nimble-witted England. I thank you too for giving me a pretext to send you a reminder of the friendly memory I have of you and of the good wishes I always bear you. I have been hearing from your husband of your transmigration to Belmont and of the beauty of your house and situation there—a picture that fills me with envy even in the midst of English meadows. May your days be long in your new home, and all your occupations pleasant. One of these days—before it is a very old home—I shall come and knock at its door.

I am spending a few days in one of the most curious and romantic old houses in England—an old rambling medieval priory, intermingled with the ivied ruins of a once-splendid Abbey, dissolved by Henry VIII. The place is full of ghosts and monkish relics and is, in every way, delightfully picturesque; I wish that for an hour I might be a well-bred British young lady, so that I might make you a sketch of it. But the lunch-bell tolls, and I can't even stay to make word-pictures. Believe me, dear Mrs. Howells, with every benediction on your house and family,

Very faithfully and gratefully yours
H. James Jr.

To W. E. Henley

Ms Morgan

August 28*th* [1878]

My dear Mr. Henley—

I must thank you for your letter and congratulate you afresh. You evidently know your Turgénieff now and have nothing more to learn. I am extremely glad to hear you mean to write something about him and wish you all success. I don't think he is a one quarter appreciated, anywhere. My own attempt dates from a good while ago—1873—and if it were *à refaire* I should make a much better thing of it. I remembered, after my letter went, that "Faust" was included in the "Scènes,"[1] which I am very glad you have got hold of. I wish I had never read any of T., so that I might begin. You are right in saying that he is better than George Meredith. Rather! George Meredith strikes me as a capital example of the sort of writer that Turgénieff is most absolutely opposite to—the *un*realists—the *literary* story-tellers. T. doesn't care a straw for an epigram or a phrase—his inspiration is not a whit literary, but purely and simply, human, moral. G.M. cares, I should say, enormously for epigrams and phrases. He's a mannerist, a *coquette,* in a word: like that pitiful prostitute, Victor Cherbuliez. Turgénieff hasn't a gram of coquetry! Such at least are my perceptions.—I meant to have told you that I had found Mr. Stevenson's *Inland Voyage* a singularly charming affair; though he, too, perhaps is a little of a coquette. But the book has a great grace. Thank you for your good opinion of *Daisy Miller,* to whom I have written a *pendant* or counterpart.[2]

Very truly yours
H. James Jr.

1. Doubtless Turgenev's *Sketches of a Sportsman.*
2. "An International Episode."

To Alice James

Ms Harvard

Tillypronie, Aberdeen
Sept. 15*th* [1878]

Dearest Sister.

On this howling stormy Sunday, on a Scotch mountainside, I don't know what I can do better than give you a little old world news. I have had none of yours in some time; but I venture to interpret that as a good sign and to believe that peace and plenty hover over Quincy Street. I shall continue in this happy faith and in the belief that you are gently putting forth your strength again, until the contrary is distinctly proved. Behold me in Scotland and very well pleased to be here. I am staying with the Clarks, of whom you have heard me speak and than whom there could not be a more tenderly hospitable couple. Sir John caresses me like a brother, and her ladyship supervises me like a mother. It is a beautiful part of the country—the so-called Deeside—the mountains of Aberdeenshire—the region of Balmoral and Braemar. This supremely comfortable house—lying deep among the brown and purple moors—has the honor, I believe, of being the highest placed laird's house in Scotland. On such a day as this it is quite in the clouds; but I wish that, in the beautiful weather that we have been having, you might contemplate the glorious view of sweeping hills and gleaming lochs that lies forever before the windows. I have been here for four or five days and I feel that I have done a very good thing in coming to Scotland. Once you get the hang of it, and apprehend the type, it is a most beautiful and admirable little country—fit, for "distinction" and to make up a trio with Italy and Greece. There is a little very good company in the house, including my brilliant friend Lady Hamilton Gordon, and every day has brought with it some pretty entertainment. I wish I could relate these episodes in detail but I shall probably do a little of it in mercenary print.[1] On the first day I went to some Highland sports, given by Lord Huntly, and to a sumptuous lunch, in a coquettish marquee, which formed an episode of the same. The next day I spent in roaming over the moors and hills, in company with a remarkably nice young fellow staying in the house, Sidney Holland, grandson of the late Sir Henry; (his father married a daughter of Sir Charles Trevelyan, sister of my friend Mrs. Dugdale). Nothing can be more breezy and glorious than a ramble on these purple hills and a lounge in the sun-warmed heather. The real way to enjoy them is of course supposed to be with an eye to the grouse and partridges; but this is, happily, little of a shooting house, though Holland keeps the table—one of the best in England (or rather in Scotland, which is saying more) supplied with game. The next day I took part in a cavalcade across the hills to see a ruined castle; and in the evening, if you please, stiff and sore as I was and am still, with my exploits in the saddle, which had been sufficiently honorable, I went to a ball fifteen miles distant. The ball was given by a certain old Mr. Cunliffe Brooks, a great proprietor hereabouts and possessor of a shooting-lodge with a ball-room; a fact which sufficiently illustrates the luxury of these Anglo-Scotch arrangements. At the ball was the famous beauty Mrs. Langtry, who was staying in the house and who is probably for the moment the most celebrated woman in England.[2] She is in sooth divinely handsome and it was "extremely odd" to see her dancing a Highland reel (which she had been practising for three days) with young Lord Huntly, who is a very handsome fellow and who in his kilt and tartan, leaping, hooting and romping, opposite to this London divinity, offered a vivid reminder of ancient Caledonian barbarism and of the roughness which lurks in all British amusements and only wants a pretext to explode. We came home from our ball (where I took out two young ladies who had gone with us for a polka apiece) at 4 a.m. and I found it difficult on that morning, at breakfast, to comply with that rigid punctuality which is the custom of the house. But for all that we went on a twelve-mile drive and picnic through a glorious country and under a yellow autumnal sun, to the beautiful old baronial castle of Craigievar—a perfect specimen of Franco-Scottish architecture. There we sat on the grass, under the trees and towers and imbibed one of those admirable cold lunches which English butlers, whatever their faults, know how to put up so neatly in English hampers. Today our fine weather has come to an end and we are closely involved in a ferocious wet tornado. But I am glad of the rest and the quiet and I have just bolted out of the library to escape the "morning service" read by the worthy Nevin, the American Episcopal chaplain in Rome, who is staying here, to which the dumb and decent servants are trooping in. I am fast becoming a good enough Englishman to respect, inveterately, my own habits, and do, wherever I may be, only exactly what I want. This is the secret of prosperity here—provided of course one has a certain number of sociable and conformable habits, and civil inclinations, as a starting point. After that, the more positive your idiosyncrasies the more positive the convenience. But it is drawing toward lunch and I can't carry my personality quite so far as to be late for that.—I have said enough, dear sister, to make you see that I continue to see the world with perhaps even enviable profit. But don't envy me too much; for the British country-house, has at moments, for a cosmopolitanized American, an insuperable flatness. On the other hand, to do it justice, there is no doubt of its being one of the ripest fruits of time—and here in Scotland, where you get the conveniences of Mayfair dove-tailed into the last romanticism of nature—of the highest results of civilization. Such as it is, at any rate, I shall probably have a little more of it. I shall be here a few days more and then go, *via* Aberdeen and Edinburgh, to spend a few days with my hospitable, though somewhat irregular friend, Mrs. Rogerson. I spent a day at Edinburgh on my way hither (it's a long journey from London) and was immensely taken with its grand air. I shall hardly get back to town and settle down to my winter's work, which probably this year will be copious, before the last of the month. But I shall have had a very pretty holiday and have got all kinds of valuable impressions. Scotland is decidedly a thing to see and which it would have been idiocy to have foregone. Did I tell you I was now London correspondent of the *Nation?*[3] I parted with the good Gurneys just before leaving town; they will tell you an immense deal about me. Farewell, dearest child and sister. I wish I could blow you a little of the salubrity of bonnie Scotland. The lunch bell is striking up and I hurry off with comprehensive blessings.

Ever your faithfullest
H.J. Jr.

1. In "English Vignettes."
2. Mrs. Langtry (1852–1929) was the famous beauty known as "The Jersey Lily."
3. In this capacity HJ wrote his usual literary and artistic articles, and also several on British politics.

To Henry James Sr.

Ms Harvard

[Lothbary, Oct. 24, 1878]

Dearest father—

I have this moment received your letter of Oct. 11th, telling me that your affairs are in a bad way and asking me attend to the payment of my debts to you. I am extremely sorry to hear of your monetary embarrassments and feel, you may be sure, how well deserved is your reminder to myself. You must indeed have wondered why some of my reimbursements were not coming along. I had lately not directed any of the money owing me at home to be sent to you because I had the prospect of needing all that was forthcoming for my daily wants here and for paying a heavy bill. I thought it better to let the money come to me, directly, so that I might refund you out of it in proportion as I found this possible. Unfortunately it has not been coming in such abundance as to make the refunding begin as promptly as I very earnestly desired. Otherwise I should much sooner have bethought myself of Cambridge. All this, however, is now getting much better, and I was already on the point of sending you a draft for part of my debt. I remember vaunting to you in one of my late letters of the large sum I had received from *Harper* and the *Cornhill* combined, for a new tale, presently to appear in them. I suppose you wondered, very naturally, why I didn't accompany my vaunt with a specimen of the lucre; but in truth the major portion of the same was presently dedicated to my tailor who sent me in a bill for the first time in two years, and whose account was both pressing and not small. After deliberating a little, I decided to satisfy him first, as I preferred to owe money to you rather than to him. I mention this as an excuse for what must have seemed but a sort of flaunting of those £90 in your face. Now, however, as I say, I am getting out of the woods, and I enclose herewith a draft for £32, which may pass as a first installment and which I hope will seem to you the beginning of a serious reimbursement. I am sorry, it is not larger—very sorry; but I will follow it up as soon as possible. I shall still owe you £80; but if you don't mind my sending it to you in a number of *small* installments I think I shall be able to cut it down pretty promptly. Be assured that I shall use the most zealous endeavour to do so. I am working with great ease, relish and success. (My want of money and my borrowing from you last spring came from, *au fond,* a rather indiscreetly going abroad the preceding winter. It didn't seem at all indiscreet at the time; for I had the money in my pocket. But I ought to have kept it for the future; I didn't look ahead, and my three months on the continent were not as financially remunerative—in the way of generating work —as I had counted on their being.) I hope extremely that if you are in a tight place it won't last, and that in the meantime it is not productive of anything like acute discomfort. If I had known that you were in want of money I should have sent you the £32 I send today, a fortnight ago. But I was keeping it simply with the desire to make it, by waiting a little, a somewhat larger lump.— I am delighted to hear that Alice is better and earnestly hope never to hear anything else. Give her a brother's tender embrace. You alarm me very much by saying (Oct. 11th) that "it is an age since you heard from me." I wrote you (to Alice and mother) two long letters from Scotland, in September—one from Tilly-pronie and one from Gillesbie. I hope very much the Tillypronie letter didn't miscarry. I likewise wrote you a few days since from

Lord Portsmouth's. Love to mother and blessings on all. Ever, dearest daddy,

your faithful
H.J. Jr.

Oct. 24th

Send me any notices of the *Europeans* that you may see. See how well it is advertised here.

To Elizabeth Boott

Ms Harvard

The Cottage,
Milford, Godalming, Surrey
Oct. 30th [1878]

Dear Lizzie—

I haven't your last letter here, and I must answer it from memory —which will be easy to do however, because I remember its pleasant purport very vividly. Also that of your father's, which came with it, and for which I beg you to thank him very tenderly. I must entreat you both again to consider this as a kind of double effusion, addressed to you equally, and to try and stretch it out into something bigger and better than it is. I have just now so much writing on hand that if I can hit two birds with one stone I feel a kind of economical glee.—You are a marvellous critic, dear Lizzie, and in your observations on the *Europeans* you showed the highest discrimination. 1/ yes, Mr. Wentworth *was* a reminiscence of Mr. Frank Loring, whose frosty personality I had always in my mind in dealing with this figure. 2d The off hand marrying in the end was *commandé*—likewise the length of the tale. I *do* incline to melancholy endings—but it had been a part of the bargain with Howells that *this* termination should be cheerful and that there should be distinct matrimony. So I did [hit] it off mechanically in the closing paragraphs. I was not at all weary of the tale at the end, but I had agreed to write it in *one hundred Atlantic* pages, and its abrupt ending came from outward pressure—not from internal failing. 3d You are quite right to hate Gertrude, whom I also personally dislike!—Your sympathetic mind, and your father's, will be gratified to learn that the book is succeeding here quite brilliantly and in a manner to be very propitious to whatever I may do hereafter.—I am paying a short visit to an amiable friend in Surrey—a lovely little place, an hour and a quarter from London. She is a clever widow, (don't tell the Realist!)—Mrs. Greville by name, whom you may have heard me mention. She is not young, and she is ugly; but she has a touch of genius—a charming house—and a delightful mother, who lives with her. Also a very nice married sister, who is here on a visit. I am the only man in this trio of *devoted* gentlewomen; so you see I do well to stop in England! Today my hostess drove me seven miles through a lovely country to lunch with Tennyson who is an intimate friend of hers (to the point of her *kissing* him somewhere—quite *en famille*—every quarter of an hour) and who has in this part of the country an adorable estate where he spends three or four months of the year, alternating with his house in the Isle of Wight. He read out "Locksley Hall" to me, in a kind of solemn, sonorous chant, and I thought the performance, and the occasion, sufficiently impressive. Tomorrow I go to lunch with George Eliot who also lives near;[1] so you see I am in good company.—I suppose this will find you in Rome, where I hope your installation will be comfortable and your winter brilliant. I won't harrow you up by saying that you will miss Miss Bartlett; nor will you heed that I should. But I earnestly hope you will find a little civilized society, or some single Christian comrade. I have been seeing Mrs. Mason lately in London, where she still is, in very good spirits about her daughter's marriage. Young Balfour has been much with them and seems a decent, reasonable youth. But Mrs. M. is to me now less interesting than she has ever been, since she has become a sort of appendage to a rather ordinary English family and a devotee of a commonplace son in law! She is charmed with the Balfour people, who belong altogether to the class of "swells," and is going back to Scotland to stay many more weeks with them. She hopes this winter to get to Rome, before they go home in the spring for the marriage. Then the young people are to come out here again, and live in Liverpool, where Balfour (who is a younger son) is in business. Mrs. M. expects to live "near" them; but I don't know how she will manage it. International marriages have certainly their uncomfortable side! I have news from home both bad and good. Bad in that my father has lost a great deal of money; good in that Alice, thank heaven, is just lately a great deal better. This good more than balances the evil. But I am afraid that her health will remain for a long time delicate and precarious, and that they have a pretty sad, sober winter before them.—Thank your father for all his good literary advice—it falls in quite with a programme of my own, which will, I suppose, be more or less executed. I sent him (to 44) Swinburne's last volume,[2] which I hope has reached him safely and which I beg him to receive as a small token of my sentiments. (It contains by the way, with a great deal of unpleasant rubbish, a large number of magnificent passages and stanzas.) I hope the verses your father mentioned will, as a whole, prove suitable for his musical purpose. I also sent him an *Atlantic* and a *Harper*.—I trust dear Lizzie that you will find in your Roman situation, this year, the elements of happiness. You have them always, in your virtues and talents—your sweetness and light. Remember that one of the first elements in my happiness is hearing from you. My blessings to your father, to whom I before long will write.

Ever yours
H.J. Jr.

1. HJ's reminiscences of these occasions were written many years later and published posthumously in *The Middle Years* (1917).
2. The second series of *Poems and Ballads*.

To William James

Ms Harvard

Devonshire Club
St. James's, S.W.
Nov. 14*th* [1878]

My dear William—

I have only just now—by an extraordinary accident—received your note, from Keene Valley, of Sept. 12th. (The Reform Club is closed for repairs and meanwhile the members come here, where the servants, not knowing them and getting confused, play all kinds of devilish tricks with the letters.) This incident is perhaps all the pleasanter for the long delay; but I fear I must have seemed brutal in not acknowledging your letter and not mentioning in writing to the others. I can't do more than simply acknowledge it now—I can't write you a worthy reply. With it were handed me three other (English) notes, equally delayed, to which I have had to write answers, apologies and explanations (one of them was from William *Spottiswoode* the President of the Royal Society asking me to go down—a month ago—and stay at his place in Kent!) and as I have been working all the morning, particularly long, I am too tired for a regular letter. But I must congratulate you on your interesting and delightful remarks upon an "inside view" of matrimony. They fill me with satisfaction, and I would declare, if it were not superfluous, that I hope you may never take it into your head to take another tone. You evidently won't! I am as well pleased as if I had made your match and protected your courtship. I am hardly less grateful by your statement of your psychological development and prospects. May they daily expand and brighten and may your book, for Henry Holt, sweep through many an edition. (You had better have it published also here. I will put this through for you, if you like, when the time comes with ardor.) With your letter was handed me the *Journal of Spec. Science* with your article on the brain in animals and man, which I shall read; this a.m. came a letter from mother telling me how well you were going through your Lowell lectures. Please tell mother I have received her letter (it's of October 30th) and that I will very soon write to her. Give them this, meanwhile, to read, in Quincy Street, as a stopgap. I am delighted with the manner in which mother speaks of Alice's continued improvment—what a blessing it must be! I will say nothing of father's loss of money, of which I have written, and will again write, to mother.—I was much depressed on reading your letter by your painful reflections on *The Europeans;* but now, an hour having elapsed, I am beginning to hold up my head a little; the more so as I think I myself estimate the book very justly and am aware of its extreme slightness. I think you take these things too rigidly and unimaginatively—too much as if an artistic experiment were a piece of conduct, to which one's life were somehow committed; but I think also that you're quite right in pronouncing the book "thin," and empty. I don't at all despair, yet, of doing something fat. Meanwhile I hope you will continue to give me, when you can, your free impression of my performances. It is a great thing to have some one write to one of one's things as if one were a third person, and you are the only individual who will do this. I don't think however you are always right, by any means. As for instance in your objection to the closing paragraph of *Daisy Miller,* which seems to me queer and narrow, and as regards which I don't seize your point of view. *J'en appelle* to the sentiment of any other storyteller whatsoever; I am sure none such would wish the paragraph away. You may say—"Ah, but other *readers* would." But that is the same; for the teller is but a more developed reader. I don't trust your judgment altogether (if you will permit me to say so) about *details;* but I think you are altogether right in returning always to the importance of subject. I hold to this, strongly; and if I don't as yet seem to proceed upon it more, it is because, being "very artistic," I have a constant impulse to try experiments of form, in which I wish to not run the risk of wasting or gratuitously using big situations. But to these I am coming now. It is something to have learned how to write, and when I look round me and see how few people (doing my sort of work) know how (to my sense,) I don't regret my step by step evolution. I don't advise you however to read the two last things I have written—one a thing in the December and January *Cornhill*,[1] which I will send home; and the other a piece I am just sending to Howells. They are each quite in the same manner as *The Europeans*.—I have written you a letter after all. I am tired and must stop. I went into the country the other day to stay with a friend a couple of days (Mrs. Greville) and went with her to lunch with Tennyson, who, after lunch, read us Locksley Hall. The next day we went to George Eliot's.

Blessings on Alice. Ever your

H.J. Jr.

1. "An International Episode."

To Charles Eliot Norton

Ms Harvard

3 Bolton St. W.

Nov. 17*th* [1878]

My dear Charles—

That I did not instantly answer your letter of Sept. 22d is no proof that it was not a very great and particular pleasure to me to receive it. It is only an indication that I have had of late a rather lively stress of scribbling—that I have been much occupied and preoccupied, and that I desire to enrich the agreeable operation of answering you, with a comfortable margin of leisure. The margin this morning—this dusky drizzling morning, the perfect presentment of a London Sunday in November—is, I am sorry to say, not very wide; as I have been writing notes—those innumerable London notes—for the last hour and a half; and I have an engagement presently impending. But it is at least wide enough for me to shake hands across the seas and to tell you what a satisfaction it was to get a little directly personal news of you. I value all my old personal ties and friendships more than I can say, not being a lyric poet. They stretch with the years and with sepa-

Charles Eliot Norton

ration; they don't break, and the chord emits a deep, responsive sound whenever it is struck, at no matter how long intervals.— My occasional letters to Grace will have told you that I am very well and on very decent terms with the world and with life; also, perhaps, that I don't despair of being on even better ones. They will have given you an impression of the *generals* of my existence here, and perhaps sometimes even of a few of the particulars. As you know so well yourself, however, the particulars of even a tranquil London life, crowd fast upon each other's heels and rather outrun one's powers of notation. From time to time there have been things that I should have liked greatly to tell you and to talk to you of—and if I could always at the moment have taken up my pen we should very soon have been in conversation. But one can hope to preserve or *resolve,* in any way, but very few of the incidents of life. Some day or other, however, we shall have some long talks—and then I shall have many pleasant things to tell you of the frequent inquiries that people whom you know here make about you and the constant assurance I have had of the cordial remembrance in which you are held. I won't tell you—now at least—that going to see the G.H. Lewes's the other day in the country (where—in Surrey—they have acquired a very lovely little domain) they interrogated me *à votre sujet* and begged me to speak to you of them; because I believe you don't admire the fashionable authoress and would not be elated by this incident. Shall I even mention to you that, the day before, I went to lunch with Tennyson (I was staying, near him, with an amiable and clever, but fantastic and ridiculous, Mrs. Greville) and that he took me up into his study and read aloud—not very well—"Locksley Hall," from beginning to end? I don't know whether you saw anything of this author who personally is less agreeable than his works—having a manner that is rather bad than good. But whenever I feel disposed to reflect that Tennyson is not personally Tennysonian, I summon up the image of Browning, and this has the effect of making me check my complaints.— It was, in fine, dear Charles, a very happy inspiration of mine, two years since, to come to London to live; so thoroughly have

I attached myself to its mighty variety and immensity, so interesting do I find the spectacle of English life, so well do I get on, on the whole, with people and things, so successfully, on the whole, do I seem to myself to assimilate the total affair. As I think I have said to Grace, I am not at all Anglicized, but I am thoroughly Londonized—a very different thing. I have made no *intimate* friends here at all, but I have made a good many that are not intimate, and though I find much that is irritating and displeasing in many points of English life there are a hundred elements that I like and have a real tenderness for, in the personal character of the people. It seems to me many times the strongest and richest race in the world—my dream is to arrive at the ability to be, in some degree, its moral portrait-painter! Extremely interesting to me too, are the present problems and perplexities of public affairs—a constant drama. There are signs that the Tories are losing their lease of power and I have no admiration for the intellectual and administrative tawdriness of their incongruous leaders; but I must say that for a long time past I have been struck with the absence in the Liberal party, as a party, of the good old-fashioned sentiment of patriotism. A great deal of nonsense is talked, certainly, in the name of the "greatness of England"— but there are too many Liberals who strike one as willing to sacrifice it to the simple acrimony of party feeling.—Most interesting to me were your remarks about your Italian studies—and the personal interest of the great Italian time. I have lately been reading Burkhardt's *Renaissance* and feeling all that very strongly. I have always regretted not being able to go into it more; but I don't despair of finding means to do so yet. Meanwhile such things as your paper, the other day, on the Florence Duomo are a great incentive.—Your Cambridge winter will have begun and I hope it is promising well. I envy you your teaching, your relations with the generous and inquisitive mind of youth—(*is* it generous and inquisitive?) and all your beautiful researches and acquisitions. May all contentment and honor crown your labours. I have been hearing lately from Lowell, who evidently is not as yet a Madrilene. He pines for the *agréments* of Cambridge. But he has very kindly asked me to come this winter and share his exile. I shall certainly, if possible; but I have at present little faith in the possibility.— Farewell, dear Charles. Believe in my most appreciative good wishes. Give this thing, with my love, to Grace to read, as an earnest of what she shall before long receive. I hope your mother is at ease and your children prosperous. I am coming home for a year in 1880. Then we can talk.

Always very faithfully yours
H. James Jr.

To Alice James

Ms Harvard

Fryston Hall, Ferrybridge.
New Year's eve [1878]

Dearest sister—

I am sitting by my bed-room fire in this hospitable house (Lord Houghton's) during the useful hour that precedes the dressing-bell for dinner; and I am determined not to waste the time in musing and moralizing, while I gaze into the grate, upon the vanities of the closing year; but to turn it to what account I may by at least beginning a homeward letter long overdue. I left town a week ago, to spend a few days (including Christmas) at C. Milnes Gaskell's and then come here; carrying with me a dozen unanswered letters with the fond hope of getting them all off my hands before I returned to Bolton Street.[1] But I am sorry to say that this hope has been vain, and here, on the eve of my return, I am only, for the first time, driving my pen in earnest. You will take this as a sign that I have been very pleasantly occupied—which is true, to a considerable extent. But what more particularly, I found to go against epistolizing at Thornes[2] was Gaskell's beautiful and interesting library; for whenever I was not talking or walking, or lunching or dining, I was turning over the charming collection of books, in that charming great room. Here it is very much the same; though poor Lord Houghton's immense library was thrown into hopeless confusion at the time of the partial burning of his house, two years ago, and is now scattered all over the place. I have two letters from mother, received before leaving town, written, within a week of each other, in the early part of December. Please thank her for both of them and for the maternal spirit they breathe. She speaks of Uncle Robertson being apparently in a rather sad condition; but I hope he is getting back his abilities. I brought with me from London no particular news— save that I had dined out two or three times. I give you as usual the memorandum. With Mme du Quaire; present M. and Mme de Bunsen, Sir Frederick and Lady Eliot (whom I took in) Kinglake etc.—(Lord H. has just come into my room to know why I haven't come to afternoon tea, and, plumping himself into my armchair, is apparently lapsing into sociable slumber. He is a very odd old fellow—extremely fidgety and eccentric; but full of sociable and friendly instincts, and with a strong streak of humanity and democratic feeling. He has begun to snore violently and I must finish my letter as I can.) The other dinners I just mentioned were another at Mrs. Sartoris's—one at J. Cotter Morison's —and one somewhere that I can't recall. Morison's was entertaining—a large dinner of men. I sat between George Meredith the novelist and the Count de Kergokay, one of the French secretaries of embassy. G. Meredith is a singular but decidedly brilliant fellow, full of talk, paradoxes, affectations etc.; but interesting and witty, and of whom, if he didn't live in the country, I should see more. He hates the English, whom he speaks of as "they." "Their conversation is dreary, their food is heavy, their women are dull."—I passed at Gaskell's three or four days of sufficient, but not of first class, interest. The most interesting person there was the ever-delightful Mrs. Procter, whose talk is most delectable—full of genuine *English* wit and wisdom, and reflecting her admirably healthy and vigorous character and her immense experience of society. She has also come over here, and considering she is eighty years old, she is, at breakfast, lunch and dinner, a marvel. There was also the excellent and amiable Hamilton Aïde, a capital country-house man, polished and supple by much living in the world;[3] Sir Francis Doyle and his daughter—the former humorous, anecdotical, kindly and untidy; the latter a very nice handsome girl, always "staying" somewhere, and as frank and easy as an American.—Here it is very quiet, and the party very small. Lord Houghton however is very kind—he took me yesterday over to York to see the Minster, and the day before to call on the old Duchess of Somerset, the ex-"Queen of Beauty" (sister of the Hon. Mrs. Norton and grand daughter of Sheridan) who is staying in this country with her married daughter, Lady Gwendolen Ramsden. The Duchess has ceased to be a beauty, and is a dropsical, garrulous old woman. Lady Gwendolen you would *prendre en grippe*—just as you would Lady Margaret Beamont, whom I went with Gaskell to call on while I was at Thornes. The snow here has been profound (though a violent thaw has set in) and Gaskell drove me over to Bretton (the Beamont's place) in a delightful sledge. Such a picture as I found there of a drawling, lisping fine lady (Lady Margaret is a grand-daughter of the great Mr. Canning), enclosed in her great wintry park and her immense dusky, pictured luxurious house—with her tea table at one elbow and a table-full of novels at the other! Besides Mrs Procter and her daughter there is no one here but the family, including Lord Houghton's sister, the dowager Lady Galway, a rather unattractive old woman, whose lightest observations exasperate her brother. There is also a pretty Miss Bland, with a rare complexion, who has come for the impending York ball. The Miss Milnes's prove on further acquaintance very much nicer girls than they had ever seemed to me in town—which is but another example of the fact that the English should be finally judged only in their country dwellings, where they appear quite to most advantage. The Miss Milnes's, in fact, are charming girls, and the Hon. Robert is a very intelligent and clever young fellow for whose coming of age, a week or two hence, an extensive fête is being prepared.—I broke off to dress for dinner, and I have just come up, at 11.45, to finish my letter before stretching myself in my old mahogany four-poster. Our little company made, at dinner and afterwards a great deal of pleasant talk, in the course of which Mrs Procter said many good things. She abounds so, however, in reminiscences and in *esprit* that one of her speeches chases another from one's mind. She has known literally everyone. She said at dinner that once, at some dinner party, she sat next to Sydney Smith; and at the end of dinner—*Mrs. P.* "Who is that at the end of the table?" *S.S.* "Macaulay." *Mrs. P.* "What? The Macaulay? I haven't heard him speak a word all dinner." *S.S.* "I gave him several opportunities, but *you* always took advantage of them." After dinner she talked about Edward Irving whom she had known intimately, and about his relations with Carlyle whom she had known since the time he used, in his earliest London days, to come and borrow books from her step-father, Basil Montagu (whom Lord Houghton calls "a dreadfully dull creature") and walk away carrying them tied up in a blue calico pocket handkerchief.—But I must check this frivolous gossip, dearest sister, in which I have indulged in the hope of affording you a little innocent amusement. I shall take this letter with me to town tomorrow, to post it there, and shall perhaps be able to add, in a P.S. that I have found a line from Cambridge in Bolton Street. The New Year is just coming in, and I earnestly beg it may bring you an improved state of health. It is just 12 o'clock—1879. My blessings on it for all of you. I hope you are having a reasonable winter—here it is a very different affair from the two last, and the Yorkshire climate has given me back the chill-blains of infancy. Love to dear parents, from your *devotissimo*

H. James Jr.

1. HJ wrote Quincy Street, then crossed it out and substituted Bolton.
2. Thorne House was the Gaskell home in Wakefield, Yorkshire.
3. Also described by HJ as "an aesthetic bachelor of a certain age."

3
A Reasonable Show of Fame

1879-1881

3

A Reasonable Show of Fame

From the moment of his success with the "international" theme, Henry James recognized that he had at last touched the public pulse; the magazines were eager to have tales from him about the "American girl" in all her newness, brashness, and independence. She was markedly different from her European sisters. And the letters of the great period of his dining out and country visits, during the years that followed the success of "Daisy Miller," show how systematically James adhered to his course. He needed money, and he had an opportunity to earn enough to maintain his status of modest bachelordom. In these letters we see him eager to start on *The Portrait of a Lady,* but yielding to the wisdom of writing a series of shorter novels to "realize" on his success. In fast succession he sells for substantial sums three works, two of them minor masterpieces—*The Europeans, Washington Square,* and *Confidence*—the latter perhaps his least important work but one that yielded a substantial return. These earnings enabled him to buy the freedom and leisure to write his large novel. In our time such a writer might appeal to a foundation for a grant in order to free himself. James was his own "foundation." The ultimate fruit of his three short novels was his big novel, the one that marked the end of his first, his "international," phase. Its successful completion made him decide to revisit America, to return as the established novelist and man of letters he now was; and to see his parents and siblings after six years of life abroad.

The letters of these years have an expansiveness, a charming worldliness, the assurance of one who has found his place and is taking life in a large comfortable stride. He dines out as always; his brother William marvels at how he "works" at this, perhaps not understanding that the zeal he himself could show in a laboratory was the same as the zeal his creative brother was showing in the writing of fiction. If there is a bit of swagger in some of James's letters, it is the engaging swagger of the artist who knows he cannot be a best-seller—but knows too that he is esteemed, that cultivated people read him, that he is regarded as a novelist of high civilization; and he is aware constantly of being an American among the English, although he feels completely at home. He is now a member of two of London's celebrated clubs. The clubs were necessary to the bachelor; they represented the extension of his small Bolton street rooms into comfortable, spacious, elegant salons where he could have his meals and meet his peers. And then there were the delights of country visits, the various British ways of life from the opulence of the Rosebery-Rothschild Mentmore to the more humble abodes of James's middle-class friends. In this period he begins to form certain London friendships that will endure during all his years, moving in the circles both of London's "society" and its high bohemia. He revisits Paris in the fall of 1879; he goes to Italy in 1880. He renews his touch with his own country through the stay abroad of Henry Adams and his wife, and he meets the energetic "Mrs. Jack"—Isabella Stewart Gardner—who will offer him the type of the ardent American "collector" swooping down on Europe for great "spoils." One minor shock comes to him during this period. He writes a small book on *Hawthorne,* and the American press sees in it a denunciation of democracy. The passages that offended, as we read them today, show that he was grossly misread. He had spoken of the absence in America of certain ways of life which England enjoyed as a consequence of its long history; in doing this he simply echoed Hawthorne, but the American reviewers—even his friends—received his observations with misunderstanding, or irritation, or often irresponsible malice. From this moment dates the myth that James had lived too long away from his homeland to understand it. James regarded the matter as a tempest in a teacup, but it may have played a part in his decision to return, although he later doubted whether such a return was necessary. What he did need, he told himself, was to see his family; and he came home to enjoy at the same time both his fame and his notoriety.

To Grace Norton

Ms Harvard

Reform Club,
Jan. *4th* [1879]

My dear Grace—

I am always in your debt—so that I have learned to say to myself that a little more or a little less doesn't matter. Your letter of Nov. 19th lies open before me—I have just been reading it over and coming to the conclusion that on this occasion my indebtedness is at its maximum. I don't know which to thank you for first—your own appreciative remarks or your extracts from poor Miss Middleton's letters. (I don't know why I call her *poor* in that familiar way—I suppose simply because one can't help thinking with compassion of the lot, in that arid and afflicted South, of so nice a woman as she appears to be.) How funny that she should see—and remember, across the years—a likeness between Daisy Miller and my Cousin Gertrude. I can quite see what she means—a confession I make at the risk of receiving a compliment from you on my relatives. My cousin is in fact Daisy Miller at forty-five. I have sent you by the way two more *Cornhills,* containing another little story[1] which I hope will have reached you safely, and even have stirred up some of your English reminiscences. My very dear Grace, you are not, in the little matter of deciphering an (I confess) indifferent handwriting what Lady Hamilton Gordon is in general. She was what Howells, with editorial penetration, discovered—she was (and I hope still is) *douée*—which means "gifted," which is a word I hate. I grant you, however, that, pen in hand, I am not at all *doué* myself, and that I looked askance for a moment or two at your very neat facsimile of my hieroglyphics. What shall I tell you by way of a New Year's greeting? I have just come back from a week in Yorkshire where I was persuaded to go in honor of the Christmas-tide, which I spent half in the house of a friend I may have mentioned to you (Charles Milnes-Gaskell, a very pleasant, but more especially a very fortunate Englishman), and half under the hospitable roof of the venerable—if the word may pass in such a connection—Lord Houghton. These two episodes were of sufficient, but not of first class, interest. Gaskell's party was small and familiar—Sir Francis Doyle (G.'s uncle) and his daughter—Mrs. Procter and her daughter,—Hamilton Aïdé, etc. At Lord Houghton's there was no one of interest save the said Mrs. Procter—Houghton's house which was lately half consumed by fire being as yet not entirely restored to hospitality. I don't know whether you remember meeting Mrs. Procter, (the widow of Barry Cornwall) or whether Charles ever knew her. She is a great friend of mine and a singularly delightful old woman. Though in her eighty-second year she is a marvel of youth—pays cold country house visits at midwinter (you know what that means) and is the best talker, in a certain way, I have met in England. Her wit and cleverness are extreme and she has always lived up to her neck in the "world" and known clever and eminent people. The consequence is that she is an extraordinary compendium of wisdom and experience—I have met few people who have seemed to me to have observed people and manners to better purpose. Of Lord Houghton you have comparatively recent impressions. He is a battered and world-wrinkled old mortal, with a restless and fidgety vanity, but with an immense fund of real kindness and humane feeling. He is not personally fascinating, though as a general thing he talks very well, but I like his social, democratic, sympathetic, inquisitive old temperament. Half the human race, certainly everyone that one has ever heard of, appears sooner or later to have staid at Fryston. (I saw this in looking over the "visitors books" of the house.) This represents an immense expenditure of hospitality and curiosity, trouble and general benevolence (especially as he is not very rich.) His daughters are very nice and rather clever girls, who appear, like most of the English of both sexes, to much greater advantage in their native element, the country than amid the odious social scramble of London. Both of these Yorkshire visits of mine lay in a dark . . .

My letter was interrupted yesterday by my having to go off suddenly to keep an engagement for which the hour had struck.— I don't know quite what I was going to say, except that that Yorkshire smoke-country is very ugly and depressing, both as regards the smirched and blackened landscape and the dense and dusky population, who form a not very attractive element in that great total of labor and poverty on whose enormous base all the luxury and leisure of English country-houses are built up.—Last evening I dined with my friend Hamilton Aïdé, of whom I spoke just now—an amiable—very amiable—literary bachelor, who has charming rooms, innumerable friends and hospitable habits. I took in the *ci-devant* Miss Thackeray, with whom I had already considerable acquaintance, and in whose extreme good nature and erratic spontaneity I find something loveable and even touching. She has the minimum of common sense, but quite the maximum of good-feeling. (I suppose you will contest the thesis that that maximum and that minimum can exist together.) Miss Thackeray is at any rate very happy and satisfied in her queer little marriage. Her husband is, superficially, an ill-mannered and taciturn youth; but he improves much on acquaintance. Did I ever tell you how handsome—how beautiful—a person Leslie Stephen's new wife is? Perhaps you knew her of old. She has, literally, a beautiful face and head—but this is, I think, to the outside world, her main interest.—I hope you are having a comfortable and unembarrassed winter. I am afraid the ancient savagery of the New England clime has come back to you—as I see nasty hints of it in the American newspaper telegrams. Here too it is a violent and vicious winter. You may be interested to know that I hear my little "International Episode" has given offence to various people of my acquaintance here. Don't you wonder at it? So long as one serves up Americans for their entertainment it is all right—but hands off the sacred natives! They are really I think, thinner-skinned

than we! Much love to your mother and Charles, to whom I wrote a month since. Blessings on the young ones, and to yourself, dear Grace, all the best wishes of
yours ever faithfully
H.J. Jr.

1. "An International Episode."

To Mrs. Henry James Sr.

Ms Harvard

3, Bolton Street
Jan. 18*th* [1879]

My dearest mother—

I have before me your letter of Dec. 30th, with its account of your Christmas festivities and other agreeable talk, and I endeavour on this "beastly" winter night, before my carboniferous hearth, to transport myself into the family circle. You are right in pitying us over here for our odious winter—a more disagreeable one can't be imagined. Violent cold, torrents of driving sleet, poisonous pitch-black fogs—no abomination is wanting to it; and London, with the slosh of a snow-fall that has turned to rain and has resolved itself into soot-colored mud, is not, as you may imagine, delectable. I have paid for all this by a violent cold, and the worst sore throat I have ever had, which kept me two days in bed, and several others by my fireside. But I am happy to say that I have pretty well got rid of it now, and I hope that I have, once for all, paid my tribute to the rigor of the season. In the midst of all this I have been leading a very quiet life, and I have not at the present time (I am happy to say) sociably speaking many irons on the fire. I have dined out but two or three times in a long period. I met Sara Darwin at dinner at her cousin's Miss William's; but owing to an unfortunate misunderstanding in regard to the time she was to be in town I didn't see her apart from this. I am however to go a fortnight hence and spend a Sunday at Basset—I have so many questions I desire to ask her about you which I couldn't indulge in amid the publicity of a British dinner-table. She struck me as looking and seeming quite as well as when I saw her before she went to America.—I went some time since to a singular but very pleasant sort of entertainment —a dinner given by the Thackeray-Ritchies, in the refreshment-room of the South Kensington Museum, in honor of a brother of Richmond Ritchie who was at home on a vacation from India. It was chiefly a family affair—Ritchie, Freshfields, Brookfields etc.; but there were four or five outsiders, of whom I was one. It was very amusing, and after dinner the company wandered through the Museum, which looks very beautiful when lighted. I found my special entertainment in being placed with a most adorable little Mrs. Ritchie (wife of Miss Thackeray's boy-husband's eldest brother)—who *was* a Miss Brookfield, and whose mother, a delightful Mrs. Brookfield, also present, and whom I had met before, was an intimate friend of Thackeray, and the supposititious model partly of *Amelia* and partly of *Laura*. The said little Mrs. Ritchie, whom I met again the other night at a party, is not of commanding intellect or of brilliant beauty; she is even a little dull, and doubtless very *bornée*, as a good English-woman must and should be; but she has an enchanting charm of countenance and an intensity of feminine sweetness which I have seen equalled only in the ladies of my own family. If her mother was like her in her youth, I don't wonder Thackeray put her in a book—or tried to.—I dined also at Frederick Locker's —deadly dull—Lord and Lady Thurlow, General Hamley etc. Thurlows speechless, Hamley disagreeable, H.J. Jr. horribly *en-rhumé*, Lockers trivial, room freezing etc. Then a rather amusing dinner followed by a Sunday evening *conversazione,* at the Hertz's —German jews, living in a very pleasant old house in Harley Street, who are insatiate lion-hunters, and most naïfs in their pursuit of notabilities. They go in for having a literary *salon* and also have, I believe, every Sunday, when they first give a very good dinner, a very well-frequented one. The evening I was there, there were a lot of people, and I talked with Frederick Harrison,

Lyulph Stanley, C.G. Leland. W. Pater (who is far from being as beautiful as his own prose) etc.—Such, dearest mother, is the history of my small outgoings.—Mrs. Kemble has returned to town for the winter—an event in which I always take pleasure, as she is certainly one of the women I know whom I like best. I confess I find people in general very vulgar-minded and superficial—and it is only by a pious fiction, to keep myself going, and keep on the social harness, that I succeed in postulating them as anything else or better. It is therefore a kind of rest and refreshment to see a woman who (extremely annoying as she sometimes is) gives one a positive sense of having a deep, rich, human nature and having cast off all vulgarities. The people of this world seem to me for the most part nothing but *surface* and sometimes— oh ye gods!—such desperately poor surface! Mrs. Kemble has no organized surface at all; she is like a straight deep cistern without a cover, or even, sometimes, a bucket, into which, as a mode of intercourse, one must tumble with a splash. You mustn't judge her by her indifferent book, which is no more a part of her than a pudding she might make.—Mrs. Mason is also here for a few days on her way abroad, having been paying a visit of three or four months to the family of her daughters' intended. She is intrinsically as attractive as ever; but I find her I confess less interesting since she has become a kind of appendage or satellite to a little Scotch squirearchy. She seems immensely fond of young Balfour, who strikes one as an ordinary youth; and it is hard to interest one's self in her daughter, who, though sweet and maidenly, is unfinished and uncultivated. In this respect she resembles Mrs. Mason herself, who is redolent of American civilization. In no other country could such beautiful material have remained so unwrought. But I don't know why I should discourse at such length on these (by you) unseen and unheeded ladies.—Please tell William and Alice that I received a short time since their kind note, written on the eve of their going to Newport, and complimenting me on the first part of the *International Episode*. You will have read the second part by this time, and I hope that you won't, like many of my friends here (as I partly know and partly suspect) take it ill of me as against my "British entertainers." It seems to me myself that I have been very delicate; but I shall keep off dangerous ground in future. It is an entirely new sensation for them (the people here) to be (at all delicately) *ironized* or satirized, from the American point of view, and they don't at all relish it. Their conception of the normal in such a relation is that the satire should be all on their side against the Americans; and I suspect that if one were to push this a little further one would find that they are extremely sensitive. But I like them too much and feel too kindly to them to go into the satire-business or even the light-ironical in any case in which it would wound them—even if in such a case I should see my way to it very clearly. Macmillan is just on the point of bringing out Daisy Miller, An International Episode, and Four Meetings in two little big-printed volumes, like those of the *Europeans*. There is every reason to expect for them a very good success, as Daisy Miller has been, as I have told you before, a really quite extraordinary hit. I will send you the new volumes.—I am so glad my dearest sister is getting on so bravely and beg her to take this letter quite unto herself, and with it many embraces and benedictions. I am waiting both patiently and impatiently for that letter which it was foretold that she would write me.—I hope William and Alice were happy and merry at Newport— as poor dear Aunt Mary Tweedy, to whom I wrote the other day, must in her aged solitude, have been glad to have them. I desire greatly also to hear the upshot of Gilman's visit with his money-bag, and William's liability to be tempted by him.[1] The college would be very shabby to permit itself to be outbid, and I should be very sorry to hear of his having to give up the superior civilization of Cambridge. I have just been reading his two articles—the Brute and Human Intellect and the one in *Mind*, which have given me a very elevated idea of his abilities. Tell him I perused them with great interest, sufficient comprehension, and extreme profit. Farewell, dearest Mother. I send my filial duty to father, who I hope is worrying comfortably through the winter (I am afraid that since you wrote you have had some severe weather)—and, looking and listening always for a letter, remain

> your very lovingest
> H. James Jr.

1. Daniel Coit Gilman, the president of the Johns Hopkins, was seeking WJ for his faculty.

To Alice James
Ms Harvard

> 3, Bolton Street,
> Piccadilly. W.
> Feb. 26*th* [1879]

Dearest sister.

I received yesterday a charming letter from father—but I know he won't grudge my answering him by means of a short epistle to you. I am much pressed for time—and I *must* be short—so I will try to be sweet. Tell father I thank him tenderly for the agreeable things he says about the "Internat. Episode." etc. I feel as if I had done very little work to be so much praised, I should say, however, that *all* my friends here have not been displeased with the I.E., by any means; some of them have been highly appreciative. Macmillan has just published it with Daisy Miller etc., in two very pretty vols., which I have ordered to be sent to you. It is a Sunday morning and I have just been interrupted by a visit from Nadal, the little 2d secretary of legation here, to tell me that he is going to Paris for a month, for the first time, and ask for "advice." He is a most amiable nature but the feeblest and vaguest mind, and socially speaking, a perfect failure here—though he is not aware of it and it doesn't seem at all to have embittered him. He is a wonderful specimen of American innocence.—I forget whether I mentioned in writing last that I spent a Sunday at Sara Darwin's, and that she appeared much better than your account of her in America represented her being there. Mrs. Ashburner has just invited me to her daughter's wedding, two mornings hence—and tho' just now, being very busy, I can ill afford to give up a morning, I shall go, for politeness' sake. I have dined out the last three days—and had not done so, for some time before. 1st at Mrs. Inwood Jones's, a little lame old lady, a niece of Lady Morgan and heiress of her relics and of what is left of her society. It was pleasant—Browning, the Stansfelds, Charles Dilke etc. 2d at Lord Reays', with the Grant Duffs, Sir John Lubbock, Rutson etc. 3d at Lady Arthur Russells'—rather dull and dreary.—I am glad to hear that you are getting on, dear child, but I am very sorry that you are still so delicate. Has Mrs. Gurney yet launched her invitation to dinner either to William and Alice, or to you? Don't fail to let me know as soon as she does. I have just received a very pleasant letter from her, which I shall answer, please tell her, none the less appreciatively for a little invitation delay. I hope your winter is passing smoothly away and that you are getting those occasional intimations of better things which I used to sniff up so eagerly in my Cambridge walks. I lately heard from Lizzie Boott that her father had had a slight touch of fever which had driven him for a few days to Civita Vecchia. But he was better; she appears to desire greatly to *sell* some of her pictures, and I am afraid she finds it very hard. She is trying to place some things in London—but in this fierce market I am afraid they won't stand much chance. She has had two (very good) things here a year, in vain; but I am doing what I can (infinitesimally little) to help her. Tell father that I am much gratified by what he tells me of the success of the International Episode at home. I am sorry to say that, though I have my head full of urgent ideas for other tales, I have allowed myself to be diverted for the present into some other work. I have been induced by lucrative offers to write a couple of articles for the *North American Review;* and am now busy with the little book upon Hawthorne. As soon as this is off my hands I shall send you some more *études de moeurs.*

Love superabundant, dearest child, from your devoted brother

H. James Jr.

I enclose a note just received from Lizzie Boott (Feb. 17th). I am afraid poor Boott is "breaking up."

To William James

Ms Harvard

3 Bolton Street,
Tuesday March 4*th* [1879]

Dear William.

I regret with a sense of personal misery the continuation of your trouble with your eyes. I was at hopes it was passing away; and I can well imagine the restrictions it lays upon you. It was all the more noble of you, therefore, to have written me your note of Feb. 15, which came to me two days since. I had not very lately heard from Quincy Street and had begun to hanker for a line. Thank you for your commendation of the "International Episode" which, here, has been, tho' successful, less so than "Daisy Miller." The book, with the three tales, has already been out a fortnight; so you see it was too late for me to act upon your advice to include "Longstaff's Marriage." This latter surprised me, by the way; inasmuch as I had an idea this little tale had seemed but a poor affair. But if it has any virtue I shall still have plenty of chance to reprint it, as a few months hence, I shall have material for another collection of short things. I shall before very long gratify your "pining" for a "big novel"—or a bigger one at least than these last little things. I have just lately answered in the affirmative an appeal of Scribner's for a serial tale about a third longer than *The Europeans*. I am immediately getting to work upon it, and having a good idea in my head, I shall put it forward rapidly. They apparently stand ready to publish as rapidly. I was just getting under way with my little book upon Hawthorne when Scribner's proposal came; and as there was no imperative hurry about the Hawthorne, I have put it off two or three months. I had gone down to Hastings just before this, to spend thirty-six hours and have some talk with Julian Hawthorne, who is spending the winter there. He gave me little satisfaction or information about his father; but I enjoyed my day by the sea, and also got on very well with him. He has something personally attractive and likeable, though he is by no means cultivated or in any way illuminated. He detests England and the English, and reminds me so a dozen times a day. I can make allowance for his feelings, but I can't for a man in that state of mind continuing to live here. It is very unfair all round.—This is the only incident that has lately befallen me. I continue to dabble a little, as usual, in "London life," but I don't land any very big fish from its waters.—I like London more and more as a big city and a regular basis of mundane existence; but sometimes I get woefully tired of its people and their talk. There seems something awfully stale and stupid about the whole business and I long to take a plunge in something different. I feel as if it were only necessary to insert the small end of the wedge to begin and be as inimical as J. Hawthorne. But these emotions are of course mainly subjective, and appertain to one's feelings about any human society, in any big agglomeration of people. As things go in this world I am inclined to think that London is as good as anything, and to agree with Dr. Johnson that he who is tired of it is simply tired of life. I dined last night at the New University Club with Ernest Myers and four or five ci-devant Oxford men who are supposed to be choice spirits—Andrew Lang—a leader-writer for the *Times* etc. I suppose this strikes you as an attractive occasion and in the stillness of Harvard Street excites your envy and speculation. But it failed to give me a sense of rare privilege—owing partly, I think, to the *ungemütlich* associations I have, humanly, with Oxford—dreary, ill-favored men, with local conversation and dirty hands. (All the men in London, however, have dirty hands.) The other night, at Charles Godfrey Leland's—a queer literary party, composed of the ex-King of Oude and various third rate magazinists, just like something in Dickens or Thackeray. I was roped into a certain "Rabelais Club," which Leland has it greatly at heart to found, to resist the encroachments of effeminacy and the joyless element in literature. Leland is a very good fellow but a big half-Germanized Philadelphia boy, and I am afraid his club will evaporate as his Rabelaisians seem to me all very feeble and beneath the level of the rôle.[1] He's trying to get Lord Houghton as president or figure-head—also Gustave Doré etc. I have been looking to see where I have dined lately, but though I see various names none of them recall any particularly memorable occasions. If you dine out a good deal in London, you forget your dinner the next morning—or rather, if you walk home, as I always do, you forget it by the time you have turned the corner of the street. Familiarity with such occasions breeds contempt, and my impressions evaporate with the fumes of the champagne. I met James Bryce out at dinner somewhere the other night, and he walked home with me and sat and talked an hour. He is a distinctly able fellow, but he gives me the impression of being on the whole a failure. He has had three conflicting dispositions—to literature (History) —to the law—and to politics—and he has not made a complete thing of any of them. He is now however trying to throw himself into politics—to stand for the Tower Hamlets. I am afraid he won't succeed—he belongs to the class of young doctrinaire Radicals (they are all growing old in it) who don't take the "popular heart" and seem booked to remain out of affairs. They are all tainted with priggishness—though Bryce less so than some of the others. The man who is shooting ahead much faster than anyone else is Charles Dilke. His ability is not at all rare, but he is very skilful and very ambitious, and though he is only thirty-five years old, he would almost certainly, if the Liberals should come into power tomorrow, be a cabinet minister. I heard the other evening an interesting parallel drawn between him and George Trevelyan, who has fallen off, since his start, as much as Dilke has gained—thanks to "priggishness." This is very instructive, and if one has been living here awhile these comparisons are interesting. I must say, however, that, so far as my observation goes, pure political ability, such as Dilke's, doesn't appear a very elevated form of genius.—Tell Alice (sister) that I went to Annie Ashburner's wedding, and meant to write to her about it, but this virtuous intention was crowded out. Tell her Annie A. looked extremely pretty (in yellow satin, with a yellow veil) and appeared to great advantage. The breakfast was very sumptuous and agreeable and the whole affair pleasant, save that at the end, her angry father, coming with me to the door, broke out into a torrent of protestations and imprecations. I am afraid she has had no easy time—but S. Ashburner is a selfish old Turk. Farewell, I must close my letter. I hope you are beginning to breathe the spring, as we are, after the vilest of possible winters. Tender greetings to Alice, and to you earnest hopes of amelioration.

Ever dear William your devoted brother
H. James Jr.

1. Leland (1824–1903), American journalist and humorist, did found the Rabelais, a dining club which HJ occasionally attended during his early London years.

To Mrs. F. H. Hill

Ms Private

3 Bolton Street,
March 21*st* [1879]

My dear Mrs. Hill—

I must thank you without delay for the little notice of *Daisy Miller* and the "Three Meetings," in this morning's Daily News, in which you say so many kind things so gracefully.[1] You possess in great perfection that amiable art. But, shall I confess it? (you will perhaps guess it,) my eagerness to thank you for your civilities to two of my tales, is slightly increased by my impatience to deprecate your strictures with regard to the third. I am distressed by the evident disfavour with which you view the "International Episode;" and meditating on the matter as humbly as I can, I really think you have been unjust to it. No, my dear Mrs. Hill, *bien non,* my two Englishmen are not represented as "Arries"; it was perhaps the fond weakness of a creator, but I even took to myself some credit for the portrait of Lord Lambeth, who was intended to be the image of a loveable, sympathetic, excellent-natured young personage, full of good feelings and of all possible delicacies of conduct. That he says "I say" rather too many times is very probable (I thought so, quite, myself, in reading over the thing as a book): but that strikes me as a rather venial

219

flaw. I differ from you in thinking that he would, in fact, have been likely to say it with considerable frequency. I used the words because I remembered that when I was fresh to England and first began to "go out," I was struck with the way in which they flourished among the younger generation, especially when the younger generation was of the idle and opulent and pleasure-loving type. Depend upon it, it is not only "Arry" who says "I say." There are gentlemen and gentlemen—those who are constantly particular about what they say, and those who go in greatly for amusement and who say anything, almost, that comes into their heads. It has always seemed to me that in this latter racketing, pleasure-loving "golden-youth" section of English society, the very atmosphere was impregnated with slang. A year ago I went for six months to the St. James's Club, where (to my small contentment personally) the golden youth of every description used largely to congregate, and during this period, being the rapacious and shameless observer that you know, I really made studies in London colloquialisms. I certainly heard more "I says" than I had ever done before; and I suppose that nineteen out of twenty of the young men in the place had been to a public school. However, this detail is not of much importance; what I meant to indicate is the (I think) incontestable fact that certain people in English society talk in a very offhand, informal, irregular manner, and use a great many roughnesses and crudities. It didn't seem to me that one was bound to handle their idiosyncrasies of speech so very tenderly as to weigh one idiom very long against another. In a word the Lord Lambeths of the English world are, I think, distinctly liable, in the turn of their phrases, just as they are in the gratification of their tastes—or of some of them—to strike quiet conservative people like your humble servant as vulgar. I meant to do no more than just rapidly indicate this liability— I meant it to be by no means the last impression that he would leave. It doesn't in the least seem to have been so, with most people, and if it didn't sound fatuous I should say that I had been congratulated by several people whom I suppose to be of an observing turn upon the verisimilitude of his conversation.—If it didn't seem fatuous, too, or unmannerly, to inflict upon you so very bulky a bundle of exposition as this letter has grown into, I should go on to say that I don't think you have been liberal to the poor little women-folk of my narrative. (That liberal, by the way, is but a conciliatory substitute for some more rigid epithet—say *fair,* or *just.*) I want at any rate to remonstrate with you for your apparent assumption that in the two English ladies, I meant to make a resumé of my view of English manners. My dear Mrs. Hill—the idea is fantastic! The two ladies are a picture of a special case, and they are certainly not an over-charged one. They were very determined their manners should not be nicer; it would have quite defeated the point they wished to make, which was that it didn't at all suit them that a little unknown American girl should marry their coveted kinsman. Such a consummation certainly does not suit English duchesses and countesses in general—it would be quite legitimate to draw from the story an induction as to my conviction on that point. The story was among other things an attempt at a sketch of this state of mind, and, given what I wished to represent, I thought the touches by which the attitude of the duchess and her daughter is set forth, were rather light and discreet than otherwise. A man in my position, and writing the sort of things I do, feels the need of protesting against this extension of his idea in which in many cases, many readers are certain to indulge. One may make figures and figures without intending generalizations—generalizations of which I have a horror. I make a couple of English ladies doing a disagreeable thing—*cela c'est vu:* excuse me!—and forthwith I find myself responsible for a representation of English manners! Nothing is my *last word* about anything—I am interminably super-subtle and analytic—and with the blessing of heaven, I shall live to make all sorts of representations of all sorts of things. It will take a much cleverer person than myself to discover my last impression—among all these things—of anything. And then, in such a matter, the bother of being an American! Trollope, Thackeray, Dickens, even with their big authoritative talents, were free to draw all sorts of unflattering English pictures, by the thousand.

But if I make a single one, I am forthwith in danger of being confronted with a criminal conclusion—and sinister rumours reach me as to what I think of English society. I think more things than I can undertake to tell in forty pages of the *Cornhill*. Perhaps some day I shall take more pages, and attempt to tell some of these things; in that case, I hope, there will be a little, of every sort, for every one! Meanwhile I shall draw plenty of pictures of disagreeable Americans, as I have done already, and the friendly Briton will see no harm in that!—it will seem to him a part of the natural fitness!—Since I am in for it—with this hideously egotistic document—I do just want to add that I am sorry you didn't find a little word of appreciation for the two other women's figures in the *I. E.*, which I really think a success. (You will smile at the artless crudity of my vanity!) The thing was the study —a very sincere, careful, intendedly minute one—of the state of mind of a couple of American women pressed upon by English circumstances—and I had a faith that the picture would seem life-like and comprehensible. In the case of the heroine I had a fancy it would even seem charming. In that of the elder sister, no, I hadn't such a faith: she is too garrulous, and, on the whole, too silly;—it is for a silly woman that she is offered. But I should have said it was obvious that her portrait is purely objective— she is not in the least intended to throw light upon the objects she critizes (English life and manners etc.); she is intended to throw light on the American mind alone, and its way of taking things. When I attempt to deal with English manners, I shall approach them through a very different portal than that of Mrs. Westgate's intelligence. I was at particular pains to mark the limitations of this organ—by some of the speeches I have put into her mouth—such as the grotesque story about the Duke who cuts the Butterworths. In a word she is, throughout, an ironical creation!—Forgive this inordinate and abominable scrawl—I certainly didn't mean to reward you for your friendly zeal in reading so many of my volumes by despatching you another in the innocent guise of a note. But your own frankness has made me expansive—and there goes with this only a grain of protest to a hundredweight of gratitude. Believe me, dear Mrs. Hill,

very faithfully yours
H. James Jr.

1. The review was of *Daisy Miller and Other Stories.* HJ makes an interesting slip in referring to his story of "Four Meetings" as "Three Meetings," the latter being the title of a tale by Turgenev.

To Alice James
Ms Harvard

3, Bolton Street,
Piccadilly. W.
March 26*th* [1879]

Dearest child,

I have not heard from home in a dismally long time, but that is, I suppose, no reason why I should longer maintain my own silence. It is a cold, grey, squally Sunday morning, with a frequent flurry of snow in the air—one of the last spiteful contortions, I hope, of this truly detestable winter. My thoughts spread their wings toward the grey and tumbling ocean, and beat their blustering way across it, till they subside in the domestic tranquillity of Quincy Street. I am afraid your tranquillity is even too domestic, or too intense—that you have not as many social interruptions as you might like. It is for this reason that I feel like forbearing to flaunt my own little activities in your face—it seems a heartless, mocking performance. I do nothing new or wonderful, however, but simply jog along the very well-beaten ground of the broad highway of London life. It has become very familiar and commonplace, and is strikingly deficient in the quality of excitement. I have been dining out a good deal of late with "the same old set"—here are a few of the names: Roundells, Lady Reay, Mrs. Gordon, Dean of Westminster, Maxwell-Lytes, Mme Blumenthal (who has the prettiest house in London), Lord Thurlow, Fred. Macmillan, W.E. Forster's etc. etc. There is not much to tell of any of these affairs—they were generally speaking dull. Now that the flush of novelty is worn away, I have become very sensible of this quality (the dullness) in the London banquet. The genius of conversation in the great upper-middle class is not a dazzling muse; it is a plain-faced, portly matron, well covered up in warm, woollen garments and fond of an after-dinner nap. But I suppose this is her aspect everywhere, in the great mass of society. At the W.E. Forsters' the other night I met the whole Matthew Arnold family, and sat next his oldest daughter, a charming little creature, as pretty as an American girl and chattering as freely. I dine tonight at the Sturgis's (where the dinner will be superlative, but the play of intellect restricted), and next week at George Trevelyan's and two or three other places.

Wednesday. Sweet child, my letter was interrupted the other morning, and I have kept it till this p.m. in the faint hope that there would be something from Cambridge to acknowledge. But the American post, for a long time past, has been terribly meagre, and I received nothing yesterday but the usual solitary *Nation.* What shall I tell you, dear child? It is most vile weather, and I am shut up with a cold. My *femme de chambre* has just come in to see if I will have some lunch, and I have ordered (write it not—telegraph it not—to Aunt Kate!—) a cup of tea and some thin bread and butter. This domestic, by the way, lately succeeded the venerable Louisa, who had grown grimy in my service, and who went away to marry a deformed cobbler, dwelling in a little mews, out of Curzon Street. When she came I said—"You had better tell me your name, please." *She.* "Well sir, it might be Maria." "It *might* be?" "Well, sir, they calls me Maria." "Isn't it your name?" "My name is Annie, sir, but Missus (Miss Balls) says that's too familiar." So I have compromised and call her Annie-Maria. It is part of the British code that you can call a servant any name you like, and many people have a fixed name for their butler, which all the successive occupants of the place are obliged to assume, so that the family needn't change its habits.[1] *Apropos* of which a lady told me the other day that on his return from the United States the Dean of Westminster told her that in America there were no perceptible servants at all. "Haven't you really any, *somewhere?*" she asked me. This was at dinner, and there were half a dozen footmen behind our chairs. "Yes," said I, "but at dinner, for instance, they get under the table!" Apropos of the Dean of Westminster, I mentioned that I dined with him the other day, and he was cordiality and friendliness personified. He is a dear little tender-hearted demonstrative old Briton, and he placed me close to him at table (which was all decorated with American autumn leaves—little maple leaves such as you pick up in the gutters in Cambridge) and talked without ceasing of the charms and glories of the United States. I went in with a certain decent, dull old Lady Effingham who sat between us, and was greatly bored by his allusions, which she couldn't understand a word of.—Dear child, I hardly know what else to tell you. Last night, in spite of having staid in all day nursing my cold (I am sorry to say that this year they have been very frequent), I went to see Mrs. Kemble who was, though ill herself (as she has been all winter,) extremely remunerative, as usual. She is, *comme nature,* a head and shoulders (or rather half a dozen) above everyone else in London, and her conversation is strong meat. Her book (it will probably amuse you to learn) has been a quite *immense* success here and has brought her considerable money:[2] but she cares no more for it—for the book and the success —than for the sole of her shoe. She hasn't read a single notice of it.—Dearest sister, I must close; I wish I could hear you were well. But I trust the others are, and that you presently will be. I have just got a very friendly letter (spontaneous) from Nelly Grymes. I think I mentioned in writing last to William that I was getting on very well with a (short) novel which is to begin in the August *Scribner* and run through six numbers.[3] You will probably lament its appearance in that periodical; but this won't matter in view of its immediate republication both at home and here. And after all in *Scribners,* one's things are read by the great American people—the circulation, I believe is enormous. Last, not least, I am to be very well paid—$1500 for a thing not much longer than *The Europeans.* I have made in all (sale of book etc.)

by *The Europeans* (as yet) only about $1650—so you see that I go on enlarging. *Please speak to no living creature of this Scribner matter till the thing is announced by the magazine.* Please tell father that Harpers were to have sent him $125 for me, a fortnight ago; I hope it safely came. It is of course for him to keep. Why doesn't he send me his book?

Farewell in earnest, dearest sister, with blessings on the house, from your fondest

H.J. Jr.

1. HJ incorporated this in his story "A Bundle of Letters," written in the autumn of 1879.
2. *Records of a Girlhood: An Autobiography* (1878) had gone into a second edition.
3. *Confidence.*

To W. D. Howells

Ms Harvard

3 Bolton St.
April 7*th* [1879]

Dear Howells—

The amazingly poor little notice of your novel in the last (at least *my* last) *Nation,* makes me feel that I must no longer delay to send you three words of greeting and tell you with what high relish and extreme appreciation I have read it.[1] (I wish you had sent it to me. You ought to have done so, considering all the things I have sent you. I have had to go and buy it—for eight terrible shillings. If you could only appreciate that compliment!! But do send it, as it is; I want a copy to lend.) It is the most brilliant thing you have done, and I don't see how your own manner can go farther. I sometimes wish in this manner for something a little larger—for a little more *ventilation,* as it were; but in this case the merit and the charm quite run away with the defect, and I have no desire but to praise, compliment and congratulate you! All the last part in especial is richly successful—and the very ultimate portion triumphant. Bravo and go on—you have only to do so. You are sure of your manner now; you have brought it to a capital point and you have only to apply it. But apply it largely and freely—attack the great field of American life on as many sides as you can. Plunge into it, don't be afraid, and you will do even better things than this.—Over here, I am greatly struck with the extreme *freshness* of your book; (don't take the term amiss)—I mean that newness and directness of personal impression, of feeling as to what you write about, which is the most precious thing in literature—and which is in such vivid contrast with the staleness of tone and flatness of note of most of the writing here. But in America, I must add,—*je ne vois que vous!* I see with great pleasure that your book is largely successful.—I have no great news. I have just got my "Pension Beaurepas,"[2] and am wincing over some of the misprints—especially the missing of my cherished little opposition between Beaurepas and Bonrepos. But *che vuole,* you'll say, with my hand?—The English spring is coming in after a winter of all the devils, and life assumes a sufficiently tolerable aspect. London continues to possess and please me; I have passed a bargain with it forever. The die is cast and the deed is done. The harm, I mean is done. You can live elsewhere *before* you have ever lived here—but not after. Not that it is any great "harm" to live in this multitudinous world-centre.—You will see, I hope unresentfully, that I am to begin before long (in August) a short novel in *Scribner.* They wrote me a couple of months ago a sudden and advantageous proposal, with which I closed. It's to be but a small affair—like the *Europeans.* I had however a notion of offering it to you before assenting to Holland, but as this would have cost a month's uncertainty I decided I couldn't afford it. You must ask me for something. I am expanding considerably (in a literary sense) over here. Farewell, dear Howells. With every blessing—

yours ever
H. James Jr.

1. *The Lady of the Aroostook.*
2. This tale was published by Howells in the April 1879 *Atlantic* (XLIII, 388-392).

To Mrs. Henry James Sr.

Ms Harvard

3, Bolton Street,
April 8*th* [1879]

Dearest mother—

I have had for some days your letter of March 18th, and I must thank you for it this morning, though I have nothing very brilliant to narrate. Since receiving it I have been unwell, and life has been rather a blank. But I am better now and have risen again to my usual level—such as it is—of happiness. I am sorry to say I was taken about nine days since with one of those diabolical attacks of pain in my head which I have occasionally had before, and which, while they last, are very hard to bear. I was pretty miserable with this for almost a week, but I suffered acutely only three days and was in bed but two. This however was quite enough. Not knowing what else to do I sent for Dr. Wilkinson, who, however, I am sorry to say, rendered me though he came three times, no assistance whatever—though he consented to accept a goodly fee. He was however very "nice," and kind. But when one is ill one longs for one's dearest mammy, and short of that, nothing will avail. However, as I say, I am pretty much myself again, and have renewed the tenor of my way. I am ashamed to say that this attack had all the appearance of coming on, as it had done before, in consequence of a prolonged spell of deep potations of tea, into which I had little by little, for the past few months, suffered myself to be beguiled. English life is one large conspiracy to make one drink tea, and for a month previous to my illness I had grown quite reckless, though I daily feared a catastrophe. It served me right.—Of course I haven't seen or done much for a good many days. Easter is coming on, people are "going out of town for a while," with the astounding facility, and amplitude of resource that they exhibit in this operation— so for some time to come London will be delightfully quiet. I am going nowhere—but to stay here and work and be thankful. London is delicious in its momentary intermissions. Your letter contains a number of questions—I will try and answer them cat-

egorically.—*No* I am not working a great deal, dearest mammy—
but a very little deal. That thing in Lippincott was sent to him
a year ago, and he has kept it all this time to trick it out with his
vile engravings.[1]—I am horrified at my little book-notice in the
North American Review being printed as a signed article. It was
sent to the *Nation,* which when it arrived, had noticed the book,
and so passed it on to Thorndike Rice, who made in a mercenary
manner this mortifying use of it. It is very poor and was destined
to the obscurity of anonymity.[2] He has, however, a couple of
longer and better things of mine.—The "Pension Beaurepas" is
full of distressing misprints. *Bonrepas* should be "Bonrep*os*" etc.
"Allegory" should be *colloquy!*—"Lurking round" should be *looking round,* etc.—No, the thing in *Scribner* is *not,* by any means
the big "wine-and-water" novel.[3] I should never bring that out
in that painful periodical, while *Macmillan,* the *Cornhill* and the
Atlantic are all waiting for something. This is a short (but in subject, I think, dramatic and interesting) tale, in five or six numbers. The "wine-and-water" thing must await my larger leisure.
This will come, in portion at least, I hope, from the proceeds
of the just named.—I never in my life, to my knowledge, beheld Mrs. Schlesinger—though I have ceased to be surprised at
the wanton impudence and grotesque inanity of human gossip.
—It occurs to me that the story has reference to Sir Henry J.,
who is the bosom friend and fellow-flirt of William Harcourt.
The latter is distinguished for the almost brutal frankness with
which he conducts *his* flirtations under his wife's nose. I called
on her (Lady H.) yesterday—and if she were not such a "cold
lady" herself, one would, in spite of her in some respects satisfied
ambitions, pity her. But someday she will probably be the wife
of the British premier. Harcourt is much in what is called here
"the running." I meant by Sam Ashburner's "imprecations" that
when I left the house after his daughter's wedding feast, he came
with me alone to the door, detained me there and cursed the
whole thing in good set terms. It was a very painful explosion
of resentment and wrath—the more violent that he had had to
suppress it all the morning. He made no public demonstration;
but I suspect he unbosomed himself to others of the guests in-

dividually.—I have received father's book from Trübner—but really to read it I must lay it aside till the summer. I have however dipped into it and found a great fascination. I won't say that I shall understand it, but I'm pretty sure I shall enjoy it. It is a great success of appearance. Farewell dearest mother. I hope you are having a touch of spring. Love to Alice and father.

Your fondest
H. James Jr.

P.S. I enclose Bob Temple's last. Was there ever a more exquisite turn of fate than his being in a *pastoral* capacity?—having a cure of unspotted lambs!—I have just been writing to Howells to compliment him on his novel, which I have been reading with great enjoyment. Once granted the limitations of his manner, and more particularly of his tone, it seems to me wonderfully good—and the last part quite brilliant and triumphant. The whole thing greatly deserves its success—and I have been very happy to congratulate him heartily. I have no doubt I enjoy it still more here than I should at home.

1. "English Vignettes" had finally appeared.
2. A review of a memoir of the Rev. Francis Hodgson, which contained letters from Byron; titled "A Friend of Lord Byron," it appeared in the April issue (CXXVII, 388–392).
3. HJ had told his parents that his new novel would be to his former work "as wine is unto water." The novel would be *The Portrait of a Lady.*

To Mrs. Henry James Sr.

Ms Harvard

3, Bolton Street,
May 14th [1879]

Dearest mother—

It is Sunday morning—the end of it; and I am rather weary with the writing of several notes and letters. But I must still manage to dash you off a line of thanks for your letter of April 14th, which was accompanied with a note from father. You give me an account of William having gone to Milwaukee to see Bob, in consequence of the alarming report you had received about him.

I am delighted to hear he was reassured on the subject of poor B.'s balance of intellect and rejoice in the latter's having got rid of his unhappy newspaper. I hope he won't (whatever he does) embark in an *irritating* profession. He has tried so many things that I should fear there is nothing left for him to try. What a comfortless career of change, of restless variation! You must have been happy that William was free to go and see him, and I am very glad to hear it served William for a holiday better than might have been feared. I hope that his own domestic event has by this time happily come off and that the consequences are all satisfactory. You have never specified at all the time it was to take place; but I trust that you will let me know the moment it has done so.— I haven't much to tell you—I am working along and don't care for much else just now. I have sent half my novel to Scribner and am rapidly finishing the other half. It will be *very good indeed*— much better than *The Europeans,* which I never thought good.[1] As soon as this is finished I have plenty of other work and profit awaiting me—and this, as I say, is what I am chiefly thinking of. I long to get out of England for six months; but I shan't do it just yet. Three or four months hence, however, I hope to. I have few people or events to exhibit to you. I dine out from time to time—but thinking over these incidents I find absolutely nothing or no one worth talking of. To tell the truth I am very tired of the "common run" of the London world and of the British upper middle class. I can meet them and get on with them; but I can't expatiate upon them. I feel like going away and then coming back after six months and beginning afresh with a new lot— only to become weary of them after six months—or rather six weeks. Such is the penalty of having a nature so tiresomely framed as that of the "artistic" H.J. Jr. Mrs. Kemble remains the person here I take most comfort in—of her I don't tire, *si bien* that I am going down to stay with Mrs. Sartoris for three days next week, Mrs. K. being there. These two ladies don't love each other and I may possibly have some fresh sensations as a peace-maker. I will let you know. Thank father very much for his little word of warning as to my mind having been embittered by the "injustice" of English criticism of the "International Episode." Such warnings are always timely; but I honestly believe that it would be impossible to be less at the mercy of common criticism, than I. I know too perfectly well what I intend, desire and attempt, and am capable of following it in absolute absence of perturbation. Never was a genius—if genius there is—more healthy, objective, and (I honestly believe) less susceptible of superficial irritations and reactionary impulses. I know what I want—it stares one in the face, as big and round and bright as the full moon; I *can't* be diverted or deflected by the sense of judgments that are most of the time no judgments at all.—Don't think from what I said above that I am tired of London or care for it less. I like it and value it more than ever: but to live here happily I ought to be able to be *out* of it—wholly out of it—for three months annually. This I shall try in future always to accomplish—I have just declined another invitation from Lady Rose, whom I never see, now, to go and stay with her in the country. It is the third time she has asked me and that I have refused and she thinks me, I suppose, a great brute. But I can't help it—I have never been able to go—just now less than ever. Don't tell this to Aunt Mary Tweedy. I hope your spring has at last come (which is far more than ours has) and that Alice is getting some good of it. A tender blessing on her, and on all, dearest mammy, from your fondest

H.J. Jr.

1. Posterity has not confirmed this judgment. *The Europeans* continues to be read as a minor masterpiece; *Confidence* is all but forgotten.

To Alice James

Ms Harvard

Reform Club,
Pall Mall. S.W.
May 19 [1879]

Dearest sister:

I haven't written home in a good while but neither have I heard thence. It is a source of great affliction to me that I never hear from you; but far be it from me to urge you to exert yourself beyond your powers or to say aught to lead you to put pen to paper at untoward moments. I have a hope of getting something from home tomorrow, which is one of the American post-days, but I won't wait for this anxious chance—I will commune with my sister ere I retire to rest. I have been dining here (at the Reform) tonight—for the first time in a good many days. I have been gracing the festive board of various acquaintances for a succession of evenings and I confess it is most sweet, after a series of such performances, to mumble one's bone, as Thackeray says, in solitude, without the need of swallowing inscrutable *entrées* and tugging at the relaxed bell-rope of one's brain for a feeble tinkle of conversation. I have also, since I last wrote, been for two or three days in the country—i.e. paying a little visit to Mrs. Sartoris,[1] who had left town a short time before. Warsash is a small but very pretty place on the edge of Southampton water—some six or eight miles from Sarah Darwin's abode, and though thanks to this incredibly vile and wintry spring, the land was almost as naked as in January, I enjoyed the pure breath of the sea and the sight of the primroses, after so many uninterrupted months of the dusky London aether. There was no one there but Mrs. Kemble and the family—i.e. Mrs. Sartoris and her taciturn husband (the perfect ideal of the ill-mannered Englishman who improves —somewhat—on acquaintance) and the blowsy young Algernon and his wife. But Mrs. Sartoris is the most agreeable woman (literally) in England, and one of the most remarkable it is possible to see. She is extremely nice to me, "appreciates" my productions etc. and we get on preposterously well. One might have worse fortune than to sit and talk with Mrs. Kemble and her together, for the talk of each is first rate, and each is such a distinguished "personality." Mrs. S. has not the magnificent integrity of my sublime Fanny—but she plays round her sister's rugged *méfiance* like a musical thunder-storm. Meanwhile poor little Nelly Grant[2] sits speechless on the sofa, understanding neither head nor tail of such high discourse and exciting one's compassion for her incongruous lot in life. She is as sweet and amiable (and almost as pretty) as she is uncultivated—which is saying an immense deal. Mrs. Sartoris who appears (*sick* with fastidious-

233

ness as she is) to do her perfect justice, thinks very highly indeed of her natural aptitudes of every kind, and cannot sufficiently deplore the barbarous conduct of her mother leaving such excellent soil so perfectly untilled. (She speaks of course only privately of this—*please repeat it to no one.*) Of the dinners of which I have lately partaken I would fain give you some account but those things fall into a sort of shimmering muddle in one's memory and one is rarely tempted to try and keep them very distinct. One was rather interesting—or ought to have been (in point of fact it was rather dull)—a small feast given conjointly at the Devonshire Club by George Brodrick and Sidney Buxton. There were Tyndall and Charles Dilke and Grant Duff, and Sir John Lubbock and Chesney, the Editor of the *Times,* and Adam the whip of the Liberal party, and the hosts, and H.J. Jr. A few days later H.J. Jr. entertained a small and select circle at this club—John Cross, Edward Pigott, Andrew Lang and Mowbray Morris. The thing was pleasant and the dinner very good. It is an agreeable feature of this establishment that one can give a very genteel banquet for a very moderate cost, and I hope to reciprocate in the course of the next month or two a little more of the hospitality I have received—which sometimes burdens my conscience. I am trying to think over my other dinners, but for the life of me I can't remember half of 'em. There was one at the Bishop of Gloucester's, (I sat between the Bishopess and one of her daughters—a curious location, and not a lively one; the Bishopess being a regular Mrs. Proudie[3] and the daughter very deaf, I was sustained only by watching the fine sincere gallant-looking old face of Sir Henry Rawlinson (the orientalist) who sat opposite to me). Then there was one at the Stansfeld's at which I took in to dinner Mrs. Jacob Bright, the essence of Birmingham and the flower—a rather faded one—of the middle class. Then there was one at Lady Holland's where I took in a large, plain, buxom Miss Lowther, a young woman of high fashion and had on the other side of me Lady Carnarvon, who though "nice" and pretty, has not the genius of conversation. But I found compensation after dinner in a longish talk with a divine Lady Ridley, who to an enchanting beauty added the friendliest frankest grace and an acquaintance with my works.[4] Also in going to a sort of crush at Mrs. Tennant's, where I sat in the drawing-room alone for half an hour with the delicious Dolly, while all the rest were at supper. Miss Dolly Tennant is one of the finest creatures I have met here—as free and natural as an American girl, as handsome as the youthful Juno, and with the dimpled English temperament *en plus*.—I also dined at the American Minister's one day and sat between two very charming American girls—a crude, but most fascinating beauty from Philadelphia and a remarkably nice Miss Rutherford of New York.—I can think of nothing else, dear sister, just now, and this will doubtless satisfy you for the moment. I received yesterday a visit from T. B. Aldrich who had just returned from Spain and who seems plump, youthful and opulent. Whence comes the opulence?—and what was the purpose of this sudden dash at Spain, of which, to tell the truth, he appeared to have nothing very appreciative or discriminating to relate? I hope that the gentleness of spring will have brought some balm to your weary constitution. I am afraid it is very weary indeed—but I trust Nature,—i.e. mild airs and blooming shades, will hold out helping hands to you. I am awaiting news of William and his family and trusting it will be happy news. I embrace my parents tenderly.

Ever dearest sister your devotissimo

H. James Jr.

20th I am sorry to say that this morning has brought no letter! but I blame no one.

1. Mrs. Kemble's sister.
2. Daughter of Ulysses S. Grant, married to a Sartoris.
3. An allusion to a character in Trollope's *Barchester Towers*.
4. This series of dinners seems to be echoed in *The Wings of the Dove*, written twenty-two years later.

To Mrs. Henry James Sr.

Ms Harvard

3, Bolton Street,
[May 31, 1879]

Dearest Mammy—

I haven't time to write you today at any length—I only wish to enclose you without more delay the last fragment of my debt— which I do in a draft for £12. I am sorry to have been so long about it—but there are often inconvenient delays in my receiving moneys which have for some time been due to me.—I wrote father a short note the other day, and acknowledged a long letter which a few days before I had received from you (of May 13th, giving me an account of William's plan of building a house on the paternal estate). The house-building scheme is a very grace- ful one, and does great credit to Alice's intellectual audacity. I suppose they will baptise it, on the gate-posts, as they always do here, "Alice's Whim,"—or "Sister's Suggestion." Or a very good name would be "The Alices"—just as you see here "The Ferns," "The Hollies," "The Laurels" etc. The Spring is creeping on a little here, but it has been a truly loathsome one; and I have still great fires, night and day. I dine out a good deal, but I am happy to say that I keep pretty free of evening "smashes," as they don't at all agree with habits of matutinal labor. Besides which I get mortally tired of the "social element"—of the people, and the crowd, and the talk and the senseless professions, if I don't keep it within straight bounds. The amount of it some people can stomach here, and the way they can keep going, in harness, is a thing of wonder. Next week is Whitsun-Week and supposed to be "empty"—the civilized world going out of town. But nevertheless I dine out every day but one. That blessed *one*, when I don't! I gave Alice a list of my recent feasts—and the only ones I can think of to add to it since are three rather pleasant dinners— at the Playfairs', at Lady Reay's, and at Lord Belper's. At the last named I sat next Mrs. Millais, wife of the painter and *divorcée* of Ruskin—a very big, handsome, coarse, vulgar, jolly, easy, friendly Scotchwoman, and as unRuskinish a being as one could conceive. After dinner I had some talk with the young Duchess of St. Albans, she having solicited it (they all do!) on account of admiration for my works! The only big thing I have been to in the evening was a "rather good" party at Lady Harcourt's, where there were many pretty women.—Farewell dearest mammy. I enclose a little document of yours to show you we are, financially speaking, square. I owed you still, when you wrote, $185. Shortly after that I paid you $125 in a cheque from Harpers; which left $60 still to make up. These are represented in the £12 I send today. In the future I expect to give you money, not to take it from you!—I am expecting news of Alice's confinement to answer a letter she lately wrote me. Love to all, and tell William I shall write him a regular letter as soon as I have news of his paper from the editors.

Ever dearest mother, yours
H. J. Jr.

To Grace Norton

Ms Harvard

3, Bolton Street
Sunday a.m. June 8*th* [1879]

My dear Grace—

I have lying before me a letter of yours of which I will on no account mention the date, as I think there may be some slight chance of your having forgotten it. The paper is yellow and the ink faded with time; but as the sentiment which prompted it has I am sure by no means undergone a similar disfigurement I may allude with a certain boldness to its antiquity and trust you to believe that if *this* contemporary document is my first response to it, there are all sorts of excellent London reasons for the fact. And what can be better than a London reason? Nothing, surely, unless it be a London folly. In truth the follies here, half the time *are* the reasons; by the follies I mean the interruptions,

Grace Norton

the accidents, the innumerable engagements, the delusive and distracting social entanglements which interpose between one's bewildered vision and one's oldest friends all sorts of vaguely-grinning phantoms of acquaintances who demand for the time to be treated as realities, and yet who are so hollow and transparent that through their very substance one sees the images of the said old friends sitting afar off, neglected, patient, a little reproachful and divinely forgiving! But this morning, dear Grace, I am happy to say that I see you through no interposing British medium—it seems to me that I behold you in the highest relief and the most vivid distinctness, across an interval of the clear bright air that belongs to your customary summer habitation. I have settled in my mind that you have gone to Ashfield—or that if you have not you ought to have! I don't know why I say that—it's a strange world in which I pretend to talk to you even in jest about what you ought to have done!—I will go so far as to say that your letter came to me in the midst of the dark and dreadful winter from which even yet we can hardly be said to have emerged. It has been the most ingeniously detestable one I have ever known, and yet in spite of its horrors it has passed very quickly and left me with some pleasant impressions. It is difficult to talk to you about my impressions—it takes a great deal of space to generalise; and (when one is talking of London,) it takes even more to specify! I am afraid also, in truth, that I am living here too long to be an observer—I am losing my sense of peculiarities and differences—I am sinking into dull British acceptance and conformity. The other day I was talking to a very clever foreigner—a German (if you can admit the "clever")—who had lived a long time in England and of whom I had asked some opinion. "Oh, I know nothing of the English," he said, "I have lived here too long—twenty years. The first year I really knew a great deal. But I have lost it!" That is getting to be my state of mind, and I am sometimes really appalled at the matter of course way of looking at the indigenous life and manners into which I am gradually dropping! I am losing my standard—my charming little standard that I used to think so high; my standard of wit, of grace, of good manners, of vivacity, of urbanity, of intelligence, of what makes an easy and natural style of intercourse! And this in consequence, of my having dined out during the past winter 107 times![1] When I come home you will think me a sad barbarian—I may not even, just at first, appreciate your fine points!—You must take that speech about my standard with a grain of salt—but excuse me; I am treating you—a proof of the accusation I have brought against myself—as if you were also a dull-eyed Briton. The truth is I am so fond of London that I can afford to abuse it—and London is on the whole such a fine thing that it can afford to be abused! It has all sorts of superior qualities, but it has also, and English life, generally, and the English character have, a certain number of great plump flourishing uglinesses and drearinesses which offer themselves irresistibly as *pin-cushions* to criticism and irony. The British mind is so totally un-ironical in relation to itself that this is a perpetual temptation. You will know the things I mean—you will remember them—let that suffice. *Non ragioniam di lor!*—I don't suppose you will envy me for having dined out 107 times—you will simply wonder what can have induced me to perpetrate such a folly, and how I have survived to tell the tale! I admit that it is enough for the present, and for the rest of the summer I shall take in sail. When the warm weather comes I find London evenings very detestable, and I marvel at the powers of endurance of my fellow "factors", as it is now the fashion to call human beings. (Actors—poor blundering un-applauded Comedians would be a better name.) Would you like a little gossip? I am afraid I have nothing very lively in hand; but I take what comes uppermost. I am to dine tonight at Sir Frederick Pollock's, to meet one or two of the (more genteel) members of the Comédie Française, who are here just now, playing with immense success and supplying the London world with that invaluable boon, a topic. I mean the whole Comédie is here *en masse* for six weeks. I have been to see them two or three times and I find their artistic perfection gives one an immense lift out of British air. I took with me one night Mrs. Kemble, who is a great friend of mine and to my sense one of the most delightful and interesting of women. I have a sort of notion you don't like her; but you would if you knew her better. She is to my mind the first woman in London, and is moreover one of the consolations of my life. Another night I had with me a person whom it would divert you to know—a certain Mrs. Greville (a cousin, by marriage, of the Greville papers): the queerest creature living, but a mixture of the ridiculous and the amiable in which the amiable preponderates. She is crazy, stage-struck, scatter-brained, what the French call an *extravagante;* but I can't praise her better than by saying that though she is on the whole the greatest fool I have ever known, I like her very much and get on with her most easily.[2] But why should I analyse poor Mrs. Greville to you? She is worth mentioning however as one of a family who form a positive *bouquet* of fools. Her mother, Mrs. Thélusson, who is one of the nicest women I have seen, is a simply delicious and exquisite goose, and her sister Lady Probyn is touchingly devoid of common sense. "They are all geese, but Mrs. G. is a *mad* goose!" That remark was made to me the other day by a dear friend of Mrs. G's and may serve you as a specimen—as a reminder—of the amenities of London conversation.—What shall I say more? (Don't bruit the above, by the way, abroad at Ashfield!) I dined last night in a sort of American circle—at the house of C. Godfrey Leland, who has lived here many years and is (if you don't know it) a distinguished American author. I grieve to say that the occasion was not absolutely enlivening though after dinner there was one of those grotesque literary parties so common here, in which people are pointed out to you as having written the "most delightful" papers on the Icelandic dialects etc. The day before this I dined at the house of Mrs. Sutherland Orr, who is a very nice woman who writes in the *Nineteenth Century* against the "emancipation" of women (sensible creature) and has the further merit of being the sister of Frederic Leighton the painter (and new president of the Royal Academy) who is, in turn, the pleasantest (for simple pleasantness) man in London. The day before that I dined with three or four young men at a club, notably with young Arnold, a very intelligent clever fellow, a nephew of the sympathetic Matthew. I find young England often very pleasant—very ingenuous and intelligent. The day before that I dined with Mme du Quaire, where there were rather "smartish" people; and *ainsi de suite!*—I have seen a little this winter of your friend the John Clarks, but not as much as I should have liked. You know I am by way, as they say here, of liking them—"old black cat" and all. They have been a good deal bored this winter by having undertaken the guardianship of a couple of young girls (the Miss Van de Weyers) who have lately lost their mother, and have undertaken furthermore with these young ladies one of those common households which seem with the English a peculiar impossibility. It has ended in affliction and the poor Clarks have taken refuge again at Tillypronie, where if I remain in England I shall go once more and see them. But I shall not remain in England (you will perhaps be glad to hear that); I shall go abroad if possible, to breathe a little foreign (I hope a little Italian) air. But of course I shall return to London next year—I am a hopeless and helpless cockney, as I have told you before. Is that gossip enough, dear Grace? It is at least egotism enough. But I will add another egotistic item. I am just finishing a short novel which will presently appear in six numbers of Scribner.[3] This is to say please don't read it in that puerile periodical (where its appearance is due to—what you will be glad to hear—large pecuniary inducements); but wait till it comes out as book. It is worth being read in that shape.—I have asked you no questions—yet I have finished my letter. Let my blessing, my tender good wishes and affectionate assurances of every kind stand instead of them. Divide these with Charles, with your mother, with the children, and believe me, dear Grace,

always very faithfully yours,
H. James Jr.

1. HJ first wrote "some 107" times but then crossed out the word "some."
2. Mrs. Richard Greville. See letters of 30 October, 14 and 17 November 1878 for his previous encounters with Mrs. Greville.
3. *Confidence* appeared in *Scribner's*, vols. XVIII and XIX (August–December 1879).

To William Dean Howells

Ms Harvard

3 Bolton Street,
June 17th [1879]

Dear Howells,

Many thanks for the flattering note of the fair Washingtonian. These responsive throbs and thrills are very gratifying—as you of course have known for a long time. I had been meaning to write a word of answer to your letter of the other day, which was extremely pleasant, in all ways.—I am delighted to hear of the flourishing condition of my fame in the United States and feel as if it were a great shame that I shouldn't be there to reap a little the harvest of my glory. My fame indeed seems to do very well everywhere—the proportions it has acquired here are a constant surprise to me; it is only my fortune that leaves to be desired.—I hope very much to send you some time in the autumn a *short* story (size of the *Pension B.*). I don't see my way just now to promising anything larger, and for such a purpose I have a very good subject—a real subject—not a mere pretext like the P.B.—*en tête.* I am pledged to write a long novel as soon as possible, and am obliged to delay it only because I can't literally afford it. Working slowly and painfully as I do I need for such a purpose a longish stretch of time during which I am free to do nothing else, and such liberal periods don't present themselves—I have always to keep the pot a-boiling. The aforesaid fame, expanding through two hemispheres, is represented by a pecuniary equivalent almost grotesquely small. Your account of the vogue of *Daisy Miller* and the *International Episode,* for instance, embittered my spirit when I reflected that it had awakened no echo (to speak of) in my pocket. I have made $200 by the whole American career of D.M. and nothing at all by the Episode (beyond what was paid—a very moderate sum—for the use of it in *Harper's* Magazine). The truth is I am a very bad bargainer and I was born to be victimized by the pitiless race of publishers. Excuse this sordid plaint, and don't indeed take it too hard, for after all I shall have made this year much more than I have ever made before, and shall little by little do better still.—Don't regret having declined the *Episode*. I never offered it to you. You mistake in thinking it to be the same as a certain novel about a Europeanizing heroine touching which I wrote you. That is quite another affair and is a very long story. It is the same as the novel I just now spoke of which I am waiting to write, and which, begun sometime since, has remained an aching fragment.[1]—Why don't you take measures to issue your own things here as well as at home? It would be, I should think, well worth your while. The other day at a brilliant dinner party a lady sitting next me began eagerly—"You who are an American, *do* you know anything about Mr. Howells?—You know him personally? Oh, tell me *everything* about him. His books have enchanted me! Etc." I painted you in the tenderest tints, and I imagine there are many—or would be—if you would give them a chance—who would have the same bright yearning as my neighbor, who was not young or pretty, but who was a clever old woman of the world. What has struck me here is the almost absurd facility of success. Here are fifteen years that I have been addressing the American public, and at the end of a few months I appear to have gone as far with this one as I ever got at home.—I am very happy to hear of your turning projects for work—the blessing of nature and the smile of circumstance rest upon them all. I remember very well your childrens' "deserted city," with its bushy vistas of grassy cross-roads. I used very often to play there— alone! Won't you dine with me on the 20th to meet Turgénieff? I wish you might indeed. He is in England for a few days, and I have asked John Fiske to meet him, who will tell you of him. A happy summer and a bushel of compliments to your house.

Ever yours
H. James Jr.

1. *The Portrait of a Lady;* see *Notebooks*, p. 29.

To Elizabeth Boott

Ms Harvard

3, Bolton St.,
June 28*th* [1879]

My dear Lizzie—

I am in receipt of more missives of one sort and another, from
your father and yourself, than I can pretend to enumerate. I can
only say that I am very grateful for them all, and that if I haven't
appeared to notice them it is because London for the last month
has simply not left me breathing time. But I have welcomed
them none the less, and rejoiced, as I always rejoice, in every
symptom of your well-being and activity. This a.m. came the
postcard from Munich, and the other day the two photos from
Mrs. Cleveland. I was charmed by these, and I gleefully and gratefully selected the standing one, in the turban, which by the way
is admirably becoming. The other I have sent, from you, to Alice.
Flattered, dearest Lizzie? They are charming, but they are the
charming truth, and indeed though (especially the standing one)
they are better than such things usually are, they do but half justice
to your graceful and sympathetic personality. I am delighted that
you have fallen on your feet so speedily in Munich. I congratulate
you on everything, and I congratulate Duveneck on *you*.[1] I am
rather sorry that you are not going to a more famous instructor—
an acknowledged Master—or to a man who goes in rather more
for "high finish" (a term in which of course you will see a proof
of my degraded British philistinism); but I have no doubt that
Duveneck will be able to show you a good many things and
that under his genial influence your powers will increase and
multiply. Perhaps I may venture now to say that I am very glad
at any rate that you have put a corner between you and the late
Couture.[2] Round this corner may your fortune lurk! *Ma basta.*—
Your big panels went some time ago (or at least he some time
ago promised me to take them) to the little man in Fitzroy Square.
It cost me a pang to consign them to such an obscure corner—I
did so simply because it was a refuge—a shelter—for them. Jackson

& Graham would none of them and this at least is a place of safe-keeping. It is a place of nothing else, and a strange "opening" for your relations to recommend (a little third rate picture framer in a very unfrequented part of London)—but as I could propose nothing else myself I was fain to comply with your direction. The other two things I sent to the auction, but they have not yet been sold. It is a rascally little Jewish place, where they will sell them for. *very* little, and transmit you still less—but enough literally, I fear, to pay for the frames. I blush, dear Lizzie, to write you such confessions of helplessness to do something for you, and I am confounded by your pretending to thank me for what I have done. As yet I have done literally nothing. The £6.00 have never come. I am glad to hear the Thursby note and parcel were properly delivered, as, against your father's express injunctions, I was obliged to consign them to the hands of Brossy, who positively declined to give me Miss T.'s address. I knew in advance they would, as no London shop will *ever* do this.—Of news I haven't much. The London Season is drawing to a close and I welcome the fact with rapture. I have dined out almost every night for two months—*je n'en peux plus*. The Henry Adamses are here—very pleasant, friendly, conversational, critical, ironical. They are to be here all summer and to go in the autumn to Spain; then to return here for the winter. Clover chatters rather less, and has more repose, but she is very nice, and I sat up with them till one o'clock this morning abusing the Britons. The dear Britons are invaluable for that.—I think I told you my brother William had a man-child born to him, and the mother is very well. I met only the other night at dinner the most charming creature I have ever seen in my life (except *you*)—little Miss Bici Trollope.[3] I thought her adorable—*ma, adorable;* and I pine that she is not a Boston maid, so that I might go and see her. She has more of a certain subtle charm than any English girl I have ever met; and part of this doubtless was that she spoke so tenderly of you and your dear father. How could such a flower have blossomed on that coarse-grained Trollope stem?—But of this too *basta.* Thank your father for his letter of June 7th. I shall write to him when the Season has definitively closed. Every good wish for your Munich life. I go in half an hour out to dine and spend the night at Lady Waldegrave's, at Strawberry Hill (Horace Walpole's old house). *Addio*.

Yours devotedly
H. James Jr.

1. Miss Boott had begun studying painting with Frank Duveneck, an American artist who had established a large reputation.
2. She had worked for a long time in Paris with Thomas Couture.
3. Daughter of Thomas Adolphus Trollope.

To Mrs. Henry James Sr.

Ms Harvard

Reform Club,
July 6th [1879]

Dearest mother—

I this morning received a letter from you, which I have not at hand, so that I cannot acknowledge it according to the date. It was the one in which you acknowledge the receipt of a certain cheque for £12 which I lately sent you. A few days since came also a note from William, which I have not at hand either, but which was dated West Cedar Street. My last letter home was a tolerably copious address to William, so that I will give you the benefit of this such as it is. It is some time since I have written; but I have had many other things to do, and your benevolence will excuse me, as it has often done before. I gather from your letter that (except William's baby) there is nothing very new among you; but I hope your summer is turning out more agreeable than ours. Incessant rain and the darkest dismallest cold, are here the order of the day—a more melancholy and depressing apology for a summer can't be imagined. Constantly, as I sit in my room I have to light my fire,—and at moments almost my candles. Meanwhile one's London occupations accumulate, and at times, I confess one grows very weary of them. I don't think I shall again attempt to go through a London spring with unfinished work on my hands. The work suffers and one loses one's temper with the interruptions and interruptors. Fortunately these things are subsiding and a period of empty days is at hand. You say you hope I don't mean to spend July and August in London; but I do, distinctly—making up for lost time. And I don't object at all to the prospect. If the summer continues to be (as it promises) of this rugged complexion London will be, I think the most comfortable place. This will be the third summer I have spent here—so that I have had a chance to get attached to it. I have nothing very especial to relate, in spite of the fact that the days have been prolific in engagements. I have dined out, as usual, but I can't pretend to think where. A certain dinner at Lord Airlie's is impressed on my mind, owing to my having on that occasion marched up first into the drawing-room of another house by mistake (Lord Stair's): a rather awkward thing, with a room full of "smart" guests and a hall-full of flunkies witnessing one's discomfiture. The pleasantest dinner I can remember was the little meal to which Turgénieff came at my bidding, and which turned out very successful. There were five other men: Fiske, J. A. Cotter Morison, Ralston, J. Cross and Mowbray Morris.[1] James Bryce and young Arnold-Forster came in the evening, not having been able to come to dine, and it was all extremely pleasant, dear Ivan Sergéitch being at his best and most charming, which is not saying little. His simplicity and sweetness are as great as his wit and intelligence, and his conversational powers are flavored (excuse the culinary expression) by the most captivating *bonhomie*. The only other episode I can think of worth narrating was a visit I paid a week ago today to Lady Waldegrave's—the news of whose sudden death came out yesterday. She very kindly asked me (through Charles Dilke) to come and dine last Satuarday at Strawberry Hill and stop till Monday A.M. Dilke drove me down but I was able only to stay till just before lunch on Sunday, being engaged to dine in town. It was an interesting glimpse of a woman who has been a great social figure here, and if I had known she was to drop out of existence so suddenly (by disease of the heart) I should have found it even more noteworthy. She didn't strike me as the witty or clever person that I supposed she was, but as a very kind, honest and genial one. She kept a huge hotel, and the house— Strawberry Hill is an enchanting place—was filled with a multitude of "smart" people—the Crown Prince of Sweden, Duchess of Manchester, Lord Hartington (whose curiously public intimacy with the Duchess carries them everywhere together)—and twenty more members of the British peerage. The most entertaining to me was a famous old woman—a certain Maria Marchioness of Ailesbury (she is always called "Maria Marchioness" or simply "Lady A.") who has been a figure in the London world since time immemorial and who looked exactly the same forty years ago as she does today. On the Sunday morning, coming into breakfast I found her there alone, doing sums on the table-cloth, and I sat down beside her and we had a long colloquy before anyone else appeared. Lady Waldegrave is supposed to have left a social void that no one can fill—her house—(or her *houses;* she had three or four) was the great "saloon" of the liberal party.— I went this afternoon with the Henry Adamses to Lady Lindsay's Sunday reception at the Grosvenor Gallery—to which I had asked Lady L. to send them a card. They seemed to enjoy it greatly (I introduced Mrs. A. to Mrs. Duncan Stewart and Mrs. Procter)[2]— and they appear indeed to be launched very happily in London life. They are extremely friendly, pleasant and colloquial, and it is agreeable to have in London a couple of good Américan *confidents.* Tell William that John Fiske came to see me the other A.M. with one *White* of Harvard, who seemed a very capable youth—Fiske, who tells me that his lectures have been brilliantly successful, appearing also very happy and comfortable. Tell William also that George Palmer[3] has been to see me, and that he struck me very pleasantly, both as regards the intellect and the affections. All the Americans I meet indeed strike me as clever— light, bright, quick, keen etc.—I sent you yesterday a *Spectator* with an (I think with all respect *inane*) review of *Roderick Hudson* in it. The article (like all the articles on H. J. Jr.) was by Hutton, whose writing on this topic, ungrateful as it may seem to say so, depressed me by its essential *unintelligence* and the extreme narrowness which lurks under its liberal pretensions.[4] I also sent a *Blackwood,* with a very nicely-written little piece on the said H. J. Jr. I must bid you good-night, dear mammy, with every blessing on yourself and companions. If Aunt Kate is still in Quincy Street give her my tenderest love. (If she is not you might send her the letter.) I repeat that I hope your summer will not roast you, and that the two Alices, the nurseling, the two gentlemen and your indispensable self will pass it, somewhere or somehow, in comfort. Macmillan is just to bring out another volume of collected tales for me (*old* ones,) which I will enumerate in another letter.[5]

Farewell, dearest mammy, from your devoted

H.J. Jr.

1. John Fiske, the American historian, was visiting in London at the time; Cotter Morison was the well-known Positivist; W.R.S. Ralston was Turgenev's translator; John Cross would in a few months become the husband of George Eliot, and Mowbray Morris was editor of *Macmillan's Magazine.*
2. Mrs. Duncan Stewart and Mrs. Anne Benson Procter were two elderly London ladies cultivated by HJ, who enjoyed their conversation and evocation of London society of the past. For an account of these friendships see Edel, *The Conquest of London* (1963), the chapter entitled "Three Old Women."
3. George Herbert Palmer, professor of philosophy at Harvard.
4. R. H. Hutton, London editor, had written an unsigned review of *The Europeans* in the *Spectator;* he called *Roderick* "skilful and subtle" but "dreary in its total effect on the mind." He added "Mr. Henry James delights in dismal stories."
5. *The Madonna of the Future and other Tales,* published that autumn.

To Frederick Macmillan

Ms BM

3 Bolton Street,
July 14*th* [1879]

Dear Macmillan—

I meant to say to you today, but lost the opportunity, that if there is any money to my credit in consequence of the various publications of the last months I should take it kindly that you should give me some palpable symbol of it before you leave town. You intimated to me the other day that the proceeds of these publications were the reverse of copious—but I don't know whether you meant that they were nil. I prefer not to believe it at any rate without a definite assurance; and the fact of their being small would not prevent me from accepting them.

Another thing I meant to say is that if the copy for the "Madonna of the Future" should prove scanty for *two* volumes, I have one or two tales which I could easily add.

Yours ever, in haste—
H. James Jr.

To William Dean Howells

Ms Harvard

Reform Club,
[July 14 or 15 1879]

My dear Howells,

Your letter of June 29th, asking me for a novel for next year came to me three days since, and I have been thinking over your proposal. I am under certain pledges to the *Cornhill* and *Macmillan;* but having sifted them out and boiled them down, I have come to the conclusion that I may properly undertake to furnish you a glowing romance about the time you propose. That is if my conditions suit you. These bear on two or three points. For instance I have the desire that the next *long* story I write be *really* a long one—i.e. as long as *The American* at least—though very preferably told in a smaller number of long instalments. As you speak of having *four* novels in one year I am afraid this *won't* suit you. I think that what I should like would be six or seven numbers of twenty-five pages apiece. I should also like to begin about the middle of the year—June or July—hardly before, and not later.—I shall also feel inspired, probably, to ask more for my tale than I have done for any of its precedessors. If I publish in *Macmillan* or *The Cornhill* I can double my profits by appearing also in *Harper,* and I shall have, to a certain extent,

251

to remember this in arranging to appear in one periodical exclusively. But I shall not, in this respect, be at all unreasonable. You had better let me know how these things suit you before you announce me: especially the matter of length. I don't feel as if it would be worth my while to pledge myself so long in advance to furnish a *short* novel—a thing like *The Europeans* or like *Confidence,* now appearing in *Scribner.* I must try and seek a larger success than I have yet obtained in doing something on a larger scale than I have yet done. I am greatly in need of it— of the larger success.

Yours ever
H. James Jr.

To William Dean Howells

Ms Harvard

The Reform Club
[August 23d, 1879]

Dear Howells,—

If I had only kept over my letter of three or four days since, twenty-four hours, I should have written it, to better purpose, with yours of the 8th before me. I learn by this, to my satisfaction, that you are willing, with regard to my projected serial, to entertain the idea of simultaneity, and I hasten to be explicit, as you say, in respect to my terms in this case. Considering that the instalments are to be long ones, and the thing is to appear nearly a year hence, by which time I hope to have achieved a surcease of reputation, I don't see how I can ask less than $250 a number—the same price that was paid for *The Europeans,* and that Scribner pays me for the *Confidence,* which is in short instalments. I hope this will suit Osgood, and that you will find yourselves able to consent to the simultaneity of appearance with Macmillan of which I treated in my letter three days ago. I dwelt so on this in that letter, that it doesn't seem to me worthwhile to say at present anything about terms for exclusive publication, as in case the simultaneous business doesn't suit you I fear I should have to postpone writing a novel for the *Atlantic* alone. But I trust it will suit. I don't pretend to fix the *number* of instalments, more than to say *probably* not less than six and more than eight. Also it *may* be that I shall have to ask you to begin in *June:* but this I shall know later. I don't know that there is anything else to settle or to touch upon. I think I told you that my title would (probably) be "The Portrait of a Lady." But on this meanwhile please observe complete silence. And do let me hear from you at your first commodity.—I am so very glad that Leslie Stephen wrote to you immediately and I hope your matter may be settled. I should have liked to see the "wonderful ladies" at your hotel: but verily there are such everywhere!

Yours

H.J. Jr.

To Mrs. Henry James Sr.

Ms Harvard

42 Rue de Luxembourg

Sept. 14*th* [1879]

Dearest Mother,

I must write you a line, though there is absolutely nothing to tell you, to let you know that I am alive and well. I notified you of my temporary removal to this place, where I shall probably remain for most of the autumn. Paris seems extremely agreeable, thanks chiefly to lovely weather, and its contrast with the melancholy summer I had been passing in England. But the interest of the place has pretty well died out for me, and I thank my stars I have cast my roots elsewhere. One can be very contented and comfortable here, however, for two or three months, and I doubt not that you envy my situation. I have got a very tidy little lodging, on a big court, looking toward a garden, and I am working away with an interest and success of which you will in due time behold (and I trust appreciate) the results—which will eventually cover you, as my fortunate progenitrix, with honour. I have seen no one here, to speak of, but the Henry Adamses, who are here for three weeks on their way to Spain, and with whom I fraternize freely. I have become very fond of them—they are very excellent people. I have heard nothing from home since I have been here, and I shall be thankful for news when it comes. Beg father to write me a few lines—he hasn't done so in a long time. I sent you, dearest mammy, a few days since, my long promised portrait—two photos which I hope you think tolerable. They seem to me so, save that, though stout, I am *not*, in truth, by any means so corpulent as I look in the full-face view.—I enclose some French types for Alice: the *Zola* is an admirable likeness. I hope, dearest mammy, that your autumn is taking a happy turn, and that everything is well at home: especially Alice, and particularly father, and supremely William and his house-keeping venture, and essentially, dearest mother, your precious self. Have you a fine autumn and are the trees red and blue? Is Aunt Kate at home? I sent her my photograph and I sent her all imaginable love, and, always, her share of my letters. Farewell sweet mother; while I am here I probably shan't have much to write you. I am already homesick for London.

Ever your doting
H. J. Jr.

To Thomas Sergeant Perry

Ms Colby

Paris. 42 Rue de Luxembourg.
Sept. 14*th* 1879

Dear Tom,

Thank you very kindly for your pleasant little letter of Aug. 24th; which overtook me in this giddy capital, just after I had left Bolton Street for the autumn—happy to escape from malign influence of the dreary British summer. I have come hither to spend two or three months and *me retremper* a little in the sources of Gallic gayety. I needn't undertake a topographical description of Paris and its monuments, as you have probably not forgotten the Place de la Concorde, Arc de Triomphe, or the little kiosques on the Boulevards. It is the same old Paris, seeming transcendently civilized, after the grimy Babylon by the Thames, but one million times less interesting. This is well enough to come to for a gentle spree, but I am ravished that I no longer dream of living here and have struck my roots deep in Piccadilly. I lead a very quiet life—have seen no one (save the Hy. Adamses)—and not even, for *ventilatory* reasons, been to the theatres.

I John Morley, is a charming fellow[1]—still a young man (*de mon âge*)—and rather shy, but as they say in Boston, "VERY sympathetic".

II I hope very much Macmillan may take up your vol. of essays— if you had let me know, I should have been very glad to say good words for you to him, as I am tolerably "in" with them. But if he does publish it, don't nurse yourself in the fond illusion that he will give you a palpable sum of money in consequence. That is not the strong point of the good Macmillans. The book, at any rate, would have more readers in England than with us, for it is a patriotic fallacy that we read more than they. *We don't!*

III Don't read, in Heaven's name (or let any one else read) my Scribner novel, till it's republished.[2]

III Yes, I have just about finished a little book for Morley on *Hawthorne;* a difficult task, from the want of material and (as I think) slenderness of the subject. G. P. Lathrop[3] will *hate* it, and me for writing it; though I couldn't have done so without the aid (for dates and facts) of his own singularly foolish pretentious little volume. The amount of a certain sort of emasculate twaddle produced in the United States is not encouraging.

IV I have seen R. L. Stevenson but once—met him at lunch (and Edmund Gosse) with Lang. He is a pleasant fellow, but a shirt-collarless Bohemian and a great deal (in an inoffensive way) of a *poseur*. But his little "Inland Voyage" was, I thought, charming. I haven't read the other.

V You will probably have seen Frederick Myers[4]—a very pleasant, gushing, aesthetic Briton, but not powerful, to whom I gave a letter to John, whom I devoutly hope he didn't bore.

VI I know nothing of the *Academy,* which I never see, having wholly abandoned the perusal of the weekly press. I know far more of the English papers at home than I do in London—and here I never see the *Revue des Deux Mondes.*

VII I never saw Saintsbury, who seems so much and so strangely to interest you. I believe he is a schoolmaster.

VIII Yes the Tourguénieff dinner was charming—I wish you might have graced it. I shall see him, here, soon, by going into the country after him.

Ever yours,
H. J. Jr.

1. John Morley, statesman, historian, biographer; in his early years he was editor of the *English Men of Letters* series for Macmillan.
2. *Confidence.*
3. Hawthorne's son-in-law had written a study of the novelist (1876).
4. A founder of the Society for Psychical Research.

To Frederick Macmillan

Ms BM

Paris, 42 Rue Cambon.
28th September [1879]

Dear Mr. Macmillan,

In answering your note in regard to the proposed serial for next year in the Magazine, just before I left London, about a month ago, I promised you that I would let you know *definitely* about the matter as soon as I should have heard from the *Atlantic Monthly,* in which my plan was to publish the novel simultaneously with *Macmillan.* I have only just heard; but apparently the project can be carried out. There is a point which differs from your proposal, but I imagine that you will be able to accede to it: viz: that the novel begin in *July* rather than in *June.* This would be more convenient both to the *Atlantic* and to me. I should also mention that the monthly parts are to be pretty long—twenty-four or twenty-five pages; there will be, I suppose, about *eight* of them. I don't think there will be less than eight, and there may be *nine*. I wrote to you that your terms—£250—were agreeable to me, and if these details are not inconvenient to you, I suppose we may consider the matter settled. My novel is *probably* to be called "The Portrait of a Lady": but upon this I observe the Silence of death!——I received yesterday my account of the Sales of my books, from your people. The results are not brilliant—on the contrary—and I grieve that the books should not do better. It seems to me an anomaly that they don't, as they have been on the whole largely and favourably noticed, and apparently a good deal talked about. I hope better things for the serial—and also, if possible, for the "Madonna," which I suppose is about appearing, though I haven't yet received her. I am happy to say that I at last, some days since, consigned my *Hawthorne* to Morley.

Very truly yours
H. James Jr.

To Henry James Sr.

Ms Harvard

Paris 42 Rue Cambon.
11th Oct. [1879]

Dearest daddy,

I have delayed for so long writing home that I am almost ashamed to begin a letter today. I suppose I ought to begin with some attempt at an explanation of my long silence; but I am afraid I have none that you will think adequate. I have been much occupied, in one way or another, and Paris has not seemed to suggest anything that I should be in a great hurry to tell you. It is very cheerful and comfortable, and makes a salubrious break in my London life; but it offers me no interesting or important revelations. I was waiting, for a very long time for news from home, which came, a few days since, in a good letter from mother (without a date, but telling of Alice and Miss L.[1] having just gone to Cotuit; an episode which I hope was crowned with felicity). Mother says in this letter that she was waiting for my photos; which I trust safely arrived a day or two after. I have settled down to as steady going a life here as in London—*plus* the advantage of five weeks of *enchantingly* beautiful weather which I have enjoyed with extraordinary acuteness, thanks to the months of British gloom that had preceded it. The sunshine still lasts, and this will apparently have been a superb autumn. There have been various people here, off and on, who have given me at least enough society. The Henry Adamses, who are very good company, I frequently—almost daily—see; and we usually dine together at a restaurant. Henry is very sensible, though a trifle dry, and Clover has a touch of genius (I mean as compared with the usual British Female). Sara Darwin has been here with her husband, *en route* to Geneva, to pay a visit to Mrs. Crafts, who was also here, and who, with the vague-minded Mrs. Haggerty (the latter especially) sent many apparently very genuinely affectionate messages to mother and you. Sara D. was pale and feeble, but very gentle; and she and her husband are to be here again, for a longer time, on their return from Geneva. I tried the other day, and shall try again, to do what I can for them. Then there have been various English people, whom I have had to be more or less preoccupied with—Lady Wolseley the last in order; and for many days I have been as a nursing mother to the Andrew Langs, who have never been in Paris before and are as helpless and innocent as the Babes can be in the Woods. It is a "great pull" to catch the English abroad—they lose all their advantages, and are strangely insular and ignorant. I often think that we Americans are more "European" than they. I have to see that the Langs get their breakfast properly—put the right stamps on their letters etc. When they first arrived, they put on English stamps!—I went out the other day with Hamilton Aïdé, (to Bougival) to see the divine Turgénieff, and found him as delectable as ever, though a little gouty. I have been a good deal to the theatres, and looked at all the bookshops, where not a ray of interest shines. French literature seems at present utterly stricken with aridity. I sent Alice the other day, unread, a novel (*Jacques Vingtras* by Jules Vallès, the Communist) because Turgénieff has *highly* recommended it; but on coming to look into it afterwards I found it so disagreeable that if I had done so before, I shouldn't have sent it. I will send her, as soon as it appears, Daudet's forthcoming book *Les Rois en Exil,* which is said to be very good. And apropos of *sendings,* tell mother to let me know Alice (William's) size of glove, as before I leave Paris I wish to send her, as well as to our own Alice a few *gants de suède.* (Is A.J.'s no. 6½?)—I suppose you are beginning to face toward your winter, and I hope it will treat you kindly! I hope also that your autumn is as genial as ours—which if it is, it must be finer still. I expect to hear as well that Alice came back in good form from her south shore spree, and continues in a graceful (yet not too graceful) state of health. Mother told me for the first time of poor Aunt Kate's serious illness, as well as L. Walsh's death. (The latter seems a mysterious providence!) I shall write to Aunt Kate by this post, but as I shall write briefly I wish you would send her this letter. I hope she is completely restored. To hear of her being ill affects me almost in the same way as it would to perceive some derangement in the solar system. What do you hear from Wilky and Bob; the latter especially? Send me another of his letters.—I trust you are well, dear Daddy, and that your life is comfortable. Also that the blessed mother continues to thrive and bless. I hear from every one here that business, railways etc. are all flourishing now in the United States, but mother has never alluded to the improvement—so I am afraid it has not helped you appreciably. It may interest you to know that I am (for my next novel at least,) leaving the unremunerative *Macmillans.* I received for the first time a fortnight since their statement of accounts, for the *six* publications they have made for me; and it was so largely to their advantage and so little to mine, that I immediately wrote to Chatto & Windus, to ask *them* on what terms they would publish *Confidence* for me next Christmas. They instantly replied in so favourable a sense (offering me a substantial sum *down* for the copyright for three years) that I have closed with them; and I trust it will operate as a salubrious irritant to Macmillan, who wants my books very much, but doesn't want to pay for them! I did the same six weeks ago to Scribner & Co., who immediately offered me for the volume—*Confidence*—much better terms than Osgood (a sum down *and* a royalty, larger than O's); meanwhile I received from Osgood such a plaintive letter, more in sorrow than in anger, that I have given him the book—a weak proceeding, natural to the son of my father. I hope by the way that NONE of you are reading *Confidence* serially; if you will wait for the volume it will seem very much better. I don't think there is anything else of importance to tell you— save that I "greet" you all. I received a note from Cousin Mary Post, the other day, in London, asking me to come and see her. She thought I was there, and sent some affectionate message to you—being on her way to Torquay for the winter.

Love to all—from your
H.J. Jr.

I enclose two photos. for A. *No;* I can only get in one, but will send the other the next time.

1. Katharine Loring. See letter of 1 May 1878.

To Grace Norton
Ms Harvard

3, Bolton Street,
Dec. 21*st* 1879.

My dear Grace,

I can't help it—but it *is* like me; at least so all the world says— and some dear friends have gone so far as to intimate that it is a flattering and favourable image. What is the matter with it? It seems to me to represent a cheerful, amiable, inoffensive countenance—a face you would TRUST—*non è vero?* Perhaps you will say you couldn't trust it; but that perhaps will partially prove that you are of a sceptical, scoffing strain. No, I think I am really like that. I have another coming in, a few days hence, and I will send you—but I won't flatter myself with materially greater success.—Your letter came to me in Paris, where I had been spending three months; but now, within ten days, London again contains me. I had a plan of going to Italy before coming back; but the intense and unprecedented cold which is raging there (the trains between Rome and Naples blocked by the snow etc.) has led me to postpone my visit to the vernal months, when I shall be able to stay longer. I have spent three "Seasons" running, in this place, and my attitude toward a prospective fourth is that of evasion rather than enjoyment. Strange as it may seem, this dark, crepuscular midwinter, with its greasy fogs and eternal candle-light, is the part of the year I most enjoy here. London is so ugly and contains so many dismal things that the day-long dusk performs a kindly office, in draping and hiding them.—Nevertheless, with all its visible and invisible charms and disfigurements I am glad to find myself here again; it is the place in the world (not excluding Cambridge) in which I feel myself most at home. I have however seen no one in particular, and done nothing memorable since my return, and I have no London gossip to offer you. The country is in a very dismal state—everyone poor—the embarrassments of the government increasing, the anxiety about Afghanistan and India growing, without any increase of the means to deal with them. Old England is in a strange position—she has broken with her old traditions and she has formed, successfully, no new ones; she has her immense artificial Empire on her back, but the spirit that created this Empire has virtually died out, and she staggers under responsibilities which she formerly thought glorious. The only thing that she succeeds in doing is in making herself hated everywhere. As I don't hate her, I find this very sad; don't you? (I don't mean don't you hate her; but don't you find it sad?) Do you see what an anger she has stirred up in Italy?—by the preachings and lecturings of Mr. William Morris and his associates, who very naturally, don't want St. Mark's "done up," as they say here.[1] The Italian papers are furious at English "meddling." The papers here certainly do meddle too much, in the way of advising and moralizing about continental affairs, and they always do it with a want of tact. It seemed to me there was a great want of tact in getting up meetings to protest against the repairs of St. Mark's; the people concerned, good as their cause was, must have known little of Italy not to foresee how it would be taken there. St. Mark's won't be saved; the last time I was in Italy I received an impression of the love of newness and the vulgarity of the modern taste which does not permit me to suppose it. The Italians can so easily answer—"Beautify your own country a little, and leave ours alone!"—a stupid answer, but a natural one—Yes, I have heard all about Lowell's sad situation,[2] and expect to hear more a fortnight hence from Henry Adams and his wife, who have been with him for some weeks, and are soon to come to London for the rest of the winter. I have written to him several times, and if it had been at all possible I should have gone from Paris to Madrid to see him. He doesn't answer my letters—but I don't expect it.—I hope you have a comfortable Christmas in prospect—and yet what am I saying? How can any *anniversary* have comfort for you? But it will bring satisfaction, I hope, to your nephews and nieces who must always be vividly present enough to keep within limits the time you have to think of the absent. I hope Charles continues to grow, I won't say in grace, but in health and activity, as he grows in years. Give him my love and tell him I hope to find myself in that dear old library of his before another year is out. Yes, seriously, I am going home for several months. I have sent you a little biography of *Hawthorne* which I wrote, lately, sadly against my will. I wanted to let him alone. I wish you a happy New Year—I think I may do that. I think of you very often; and I never think ill!! Always, dear Grace,

very faithfully yours
H. James Jr.

1. William Morris' Society for the Protection of Ancient Buildings, founded two years earlier, had extended its campaign to the international scene.
2. Lowell was experiencing difficulties settling in as American ambassador at Madrid.

To Henry James Sr.

Ms Harvard

3, Bolton Street,
Jan. 11*th* 1880

Dear Father,

I must thank you for your letter acknowledging the receipt, and describing the perusal, of my little *Hawthorne,* which arrived last evening; together with a very sweet one from the mother of us all, of the same date (Dec. 29th). I am delighted you like the book so much—having been in hopes (which I had scarcely ventured to express) that it would please you. Mother thinks me very "bold," to have braved the probable wrath of the Boston critics; but I am not conscious of any great audacity. I should think the tone of the book gentle and good-natured enough to disarm reprobation, and to G. P. Lathrop I pay scarce anything but compliments. I am surprised, by the way, at your finding the printing of the *Hawthorne* so bad. It went through the press while I was abroad, and I saw less proof, in consequence, than I ought; but on looking it over I find nothing much to complain of save in *two* places the rather grave blot of a blank space left for a preposition, and two or three slight misprints.—*Apropos* of these matters, the Macmillans have offered me $1000 to do *Dickens* for the same series—they having long wanted the right man for the purpose. I greatly hesitate, however, and shall probably refuse: not on intrinsic grounds (for I should greatly like to do it;) but owing to want of time.[1] I wish during several months to come to have my hands free to work upon my forthcoming long novel, and Dickens would be a much more elaborate piece of work than *Hawthorne.* The thing is not settled however; *and it is meanwhile* AN INTENSE SECRET.—Julian Hawthorne takes my book about his father very kindly, and as he has now come to live in London (at Hampstead) I had him three days since to dine with me. He is much interested in your writing and in Swedenborg, and would greatly like you to send him your last book. He has not as yet, however, a fixed address; as soon as I hear it I will let you know it.

He is the author of the review of *Confidence*, in the last number of the *Spectator* which you will see. I think him of course quite wrong as to the *dénouement;* his own notions about it seem to me characteristically wrong-headed and crude.—I know there are quite too many "I" 's in my Sainte-Beuve[2]—they shocked me very much when I saw it in print, and they would never have stayed had I seen it in proof. I have no social news. The winter continues gentle (since the intense cold before Christmas), and I am living very quietly just now, and not going out at all, to speak of. I intend to cultivate a quiet winter, being, after three years of it, very tired of a promiscuous London life. I desire rest and leisure. Blessings on mother and Alice, and the others.

Ever yours
H. J. Jr.

P.S. I am very desirous to hear something more about Houghton and Osgood's disaster, etc.[3] Is the *Atlantic* at all shaken? I hope my *Confidence*, which they were just finishing to print isn't burned up—nor your own plates, etc. Have you seen Howells?—I received three or four days since a letter from Francis Boott from which I copy the following. (Jan. 3d) "I got a letter from your father lately, written with all his usual vigour. He says nothing of letters I wrote some time since to your mother and Alice, nor did they give me any credit for them by message. Do remember to say this when you write, and tell your sister *I am glad she is well enough to write to F. Morse.*"—He had spoken to me several times of these letters and of no notice being taken of them; and though I suppose your letter was meant as an answer on their behalf, this couldn't satisfy him. Alice will see he is still her old "Franky." I wish Lizzie *would* wed Duveneck!!

1. HJ ultimately did refuse.
2. HJ's review of *Correspondance de C.A. Sainte-Beuve* in the *North American Review*, CXXX (January 1880), 51–68.
3. There had been a printing-house fire.

To Isabella Stewart Gardner

Ms Gardner

3 Bolton Street
Jan. 29th [1880]

My dear Mrs. Gardner,[1]

If you "like being remembered," it is a satisfaction you must be in constant enjoyment of—so indelible is the image which you imprint on the consciousness of your fellow-men. For me the pleasures of memory are also equally keen; but they are naturally rather active than passive. I remember those most agreeable days last summer in London and Paris—those talks and walks and drives and dinners—with a tenderness which the past, directly it recedes a little, always awakes in my sympathetic soul, but which in this case is altogether of exceptional softness. All those were delightful hours—not only pleasures, but treasures, of memory. I went a few nights since to another "smash" at Lady Lindsay's—just like the one you were at—; and as I moved about I seemed to feel your ghostly presence on my arm, and the sensation gave the affair an interest much finer than the comparatively vulgar one which I trust I appeared to my neighbors to be taking. I have a happy faith that we shall Europeanize together again, in the future. But doubtless we shall, before that, Americanize; as I hold fast to my design of going home. I remained in Paris till Christmas, —and never went to Italy, as I intended. But I shall try it this spring. London is more London than ever; there is a black broth, by way of atmosphere, and a kind of livid gloom, by way of sunshine, outside; I am incarcerated with a cold, and taking something, with a big spoon, out of a sticky bottle; and yet I am for the moment very cheerful and comfortable. I think of the *plaisirs* and the ginger-bread at St. Cloud!—The Adamses are here, and have taken a charming house.—I am delighted you liked the little Hawthorne (do you remember the day it was finished?)—and happy in the general appreciation you tell me of. You are dear kind people.

Look out for my next big novel; it will immortalize me. After that, some day, I will immortalize you. Meanwhile, with very friendly regards to your husband, and love to those two jolly boys, I remain my dear Mrs. Gardner,

very faithfully yours,

H. James Jr.

1. Isabella Stewart Gardner (1840–1924), the Boston hostess and art collector, became at this time a good friend of HJ. He always fell in with her idea of "queenship" by posing as her loyal courtier and writing letters filled with his particular kind of ironic flattery. Commonly called "Mrs. Jack," after her husband, John L. Gardner, whom she married in 1860, she later built the Gardner Museum in Boston in the form of a Venetian palace. Here the one hundred letters Henry James wrote to her are preserved (by her orders) in the desk to which she consigned much of her correspondence. HJ characterized her as being "better at Grand Hotels than grand manners" and spoke of "the age of Mrs. Jack" to describe antiquarians seeking to shore up European artifacts in America.

To William Dean Howells

Ms Harvard

3, Bolton Street,

Jan. 31st [1880]

My dear Howells,

Your letter of Jan. 19th and its inclosure (your review of my *Hawthorne*) came to me last night, and I must thank you without delay for each of them.

I am very happy to hear the effects of the fire[1] were so minimized by the moment at which it took place; and evidently, both in your letter and in your article, you had been writing in a smokeless air. Your review of my book[2] is very handsome and friendly and commands my liveliest gratitude. Of course your graceful strictures seem to yourself more valid than they do to me. The little book was a tolerably deliberate and meditated performance, and I should be prepared to do battle for most of the convictions expressed. It is quite true I use the word provincial too many times—I hated myself for't, even while I did it (just as I overdo the epithet "dusky"). But I don't at all agree with you in thinking that "if it is not provincial for an Englishman to be English, a

Frenchman French, etc., so it is not provincial for an American to be American." So it is not provincial for a Russian, an Australian, a Portuguese, a Dane, a Laplander, to savour of their respective countries: that would be where this argument would land you. I think it is extremely provincial for a Russian to be very Russian, a Portuguese very Portuguese; for the simple reason that certain national types are essentially and intrinsically provincial. I sympathize even less with your protest against the idea that it takes an old civilization to set a novelist in motion—a proposition that seems to me so true as to be a truism. It is on manners, customs, usages, habits, forms, upon all these things matured and established, that a novelist lives—they are the very stuff his work is made of; and in saying that in the absence of those "dreary and worn-out paraphernalia" which I enumerate as being wanting in American society, "we have simply the whole of human life left," you beg (to my sense) the question. I should say we had just so much less of it as these same "paraphernalia" represent, and I think they represent an enormous quantity of it. I shall feel refuted only when we have produced (setting the present high company—yourself and me—for obvious reasons apart) a gentleman who strikes me as a novelist—as belonging to the company of Balzac and Thackeray. Of course, in the absence of this godsend, it is but a harmless amusement that we should reason about it, and maintain that if right were right he should already be here. I will freely admit that such a genius will get on *only* by agreeing with your view of the case—to do something great he must feel as you feel about it. But then I doubt whether such a genius—a man of the faculty of Balzac and Thackeray—*could* agree with you! When he does I will lie flat on my stomach and do him homage—in the very centre of the contributors' club,[3] or on the threshold of the Magazine, or in any public place you may appoint!—But I didn't mean to wrangle with you—I meant only to thank you and to express my sense of how happily you turn those things.—I am greatly amused at your picture of the contributing blood-hounds whom you are holding in check. I wish immensely that you would let them fly at me—though there is no reason, certainly, that the decent public should be bespattered, periodically, with my gore. However my tender (or rather my very tough) flesh is prescient already of the Higginsonian fangs. Happy man, to be going, like that, to see your plays acted. It is a sensation I am dying (though as yet not trying) to cultivate. What a tremendous quantity of work you must get through in these years! I am impatient for the next *Atlantic*. What is your *Cornhill* novel about? I am to precede it with a poorish story in three numbers—a tale purely American, the writing of which made me feel acutely the want of the "paraphernalia."[4] I *must* add, however (to return for a moment to this), that I applaud and esteem you highly for not feeling it; i.e. the want. You are certainly right— magnificently and heroically right—to do so, and on the day you make your readers—I mean the readers who know and appreciate the paraphernalia—do the same, you will be the American Balzac. That's a great mission—go in for it! Wherever you go, receive, and distribute among your wife and children, the blessing of

yours ever,
H. James Jr.

1. The Houghton and Osgood fire.
2. HJ's study of Hawthorne.
3. A section of the *Atlantic Monthly* devoted to reviews, commentaries, and short articles by various contributors.
4. "Washington Square", with illustrations by George Du Maurier, was to appear in England in the *Cornhill* (June–November 1880) and in the United States in *Harper's* (July–December 1880).

To Mrs. Henry James Sr.

Ms Harvard

3, Bolton Street,
Feb. 2d [1880]

Dearest mammy,

I have just received your sweet letter of Jan. 17th, enclosing the 2d photos. of Father, Alice, William and the Babe. The portrait of father in this one is delightful, better even than the first; but I should not suppose the likeness of Alice so satisfactory. Though very pretty, it looks a little staring and strained—whereas the first is purely lovely. She must be a most fair creature. The Baby, in all of them, is very considerable, and has a likeness to some different person in each pose.—This is not meant, sweet mammy, to be a long letter; indeed its chief purpose is one of sordid eagerness. You have alarmed me by mentioning that *Loring* told father that he was going to republish my *Bundle of Letters* as a little cheap pamphlet[1]—and you appear to mention it in a tone of some exultation, from which I infer that father innocently assented to the idea. In fact, Loring's proceeding is an impudent one—and if he has not carried out his plan by the time this reaches you, I wish very much that father would kindly give him warning from me. *He has no legal right to republish in any sort of book-form, however small or cheap, any article* contributed to any periodical, anywhere in the world, by an AMERICAN CITIZEN, without the formal leave of that citizen. I have written to the Harper's, offering to *sell* them for a substantial sum the copyright of the *B. of L.'s*—and that Loring should *steal* it beforehand doesn't suit me at all.—Excuse my appearance of vulgar greed; I am getting to perceive that I *can* make money, very considerably, if I only set about it right, and the idea has an undeniable fascination. It suddenly occurs to me that it is useless for poor father to trouble himself about the matter, inasmuch as if the Harpers accept my proposal (I sent it only last week) *they* will effectually come down on Loring and trample him out. I hope they will obliterate him. Therefore let Father not trouble himself further than to let me know what Loring does. That is all I wanted to say.—I have no particular London news—being rather seedy with one of the villainous colds that I am sorry to say visit more frequently my advancing years. I have been more or less shut up for a week, but am almost well. I have dined out a good deal (even with my cold, as to back out of a London invitation to dinner which one has accepted three weeks before, is a proceeding justified only by mortal illness). I am afraid you are sick of my barren enumerations, but as I haven't given you any in a good while here are a few of my dinners: Lady Arthur Russell, Lady Wolseley, Lyulph Stanley, George

Trevelyan, Comyns Carr, Russell Sturgis, Lady Ashburton, the Lord Justice's, Sir Curtis Lampson's, Mrs. Romilly's etc.—The Henry Adamses are here, and have taken a remarkably pretty house in the Bird Cage Walk (St. James's Park); such a house as I hope to have here some day, when I shall entertain my family. We have passed through a week of phenomenal fog—most blinding and disastrous, in which one couldn't see one's hand before the face. I am very sorry Alice can't write to me, but am glad she takes it easily—I will write to her all the same. I am very pleased about A. Rodgers.

Ever yours
H. James Jr.

1. HJ had contributed his tale "A Bundle of Letters" to an Anglo-French journal called the *Parisian* published in Paris (issue of 18 December 1879) by his friend Theodore Child. In doing so he lost the American copyright, and Frank Loring issued an unauthorized pamphlet in Boston, 24 January 1880, at 25 cents a copy.

To Henry James Sr.

Ms Harvard

3 Bolton St.
Feb. 15th 1880

Dearest Daddy,

I am grateful for your note of the 2d ult; enclosing Godkin's letter about my *Hawthorne*. The latter gave me extreme pleasure, and, proceeding from the undemonstrative G., was certainly very flattering. It is the most striking "tribute" I have ever received. Thank him very warmly for it when you see him next, and tell him it made me feel very "good." I am much obliged to you also for your attempted inquiries at Houghton and Osgood's, which have ceased to be necessary, as I received some time since a very reassuring note from Osgood himself. Further thanks for the two copies of Loring's edition of my *Bundle of Letters,* which are very pretty and concerning which I wrote you a rather irate note last week. I am still irate, the more so that you tell me that the thing is selling like Wildfire; but further reflection has satisfied me that I have probably no redress. I had, in my ignorance, an idea that copyright could be taken out at ANY TIME, and that the Harpers could yet do so. I now apprehend that they can't—so that I have lost five-hundred or six-hundred dollars that I might have made, simply by my foolish neglect of the precaution of writing from Paris to have my story copyrighted in advance. The thing had become public property, through my failing to do so, and Loring *had* therefore a legal right to reproduce it. But he had no moral right, and his doing so without asking my assent or offering me any profit remains a scandalous and impudent proceeding. I have not yet heard from the Harpers; but I am afraid they will write to me that it is too late for them to do any-thing—though in the case of *Daisy Miller,* which had already been pirated by Littell, and might therefore have been supposed to have fallen *dans le domaine publique,* this was not the ground they took. The thing will be a lesson for me, and I shall never in future publish ten lines in an European journal without copy-righting it in advance in the United States as I can easily do. Then I hope Loring *will* try to steal 'em, that I may have the satisfaction of coming down on him with the arm of the law. Meanwhile, will you kindly send me two or three more of his pamphlets. Since he has issued the thing, I may as well have 'em to give away, and they are very chastely "gotten up." I had the other day a long and interesting talk with Smalley, who (being a man of extreme acuteness and large information on all practical matters) gave me a great deal of excellent and helpful advice. He tells me that I "work" my reputation and my advantageous position (with regard to having command of both the English and Ameri-can markets) with absurdly little science and skill. (Not that I didn't already know it!) He recommends me not to deal directly with American publishers at all,—and never to *offer* them anything: but to put my things into the hands of a lawyer, as my permanent agent, whose business it will be to make the best possible bargain for me, in each individual case, with competing publishers desiring to bring out in the United States the productions that I am bring-ing out here. He has a healthy hatred of all publishers (and a great knowledge of them and their ways) and thinks that, once one is successful, one ought to deal with them altogether through one's solicitor. If I had dealt with the Macmillans through "my solicitor" they would not, for instance, have befooled me to the point of allowing them to appropriate all the profits of the sale of the little *Hawthorne* in America. I don't get a penny from its success there, and the example is an excellent one. On the other hand, if I dealt with 'em through my solicitor, I suppose that I shouldn't dine with Fred Macmillan (not that it matters) and that he wouldn't present me, as he did a few days since, under the influence of a groping remorse, with a beautiful set of Hawthorne's complete works, which he had imported in large-paper sheets from Osgood, and had charmingly bound for me by his most select binder here. Still, I would much rather have my "rights," and no presents. But a truce to this sordid minuteness in which you will not recognize your would-be gentlemanly child. I am much gratified by your incitements to assent to the *Dickens* project.[1] But I fear I shall shock you by saying I have altogether declined it for the present. It is altogether impossible I should think of it for a year to come. After that I should probably take to it kindly, and I can, in the meantime, read him over (a tremendous job!) at my leisure. But in case I do the thing, my interest (to become sordid again) would altogether be to do it quite independently of Macmillan—to write the monograph on my own hook and give it to the publisher who would offer most for it. Macmillan shall have it only by bidding highest! I enclose you a note from Paternoster Row, which will show you that I needn't fear to be left with anything on my hands; a note the more flattering as the L's[2] rarely publish novels—only Lord Beaconsfield's!—The story that I mentioned as soon to come out in the *Cornhill,* will not appear till June, and will then run through four numbers, and be about as long as (or a little longer than) the *Europeans.* Of course I shall carefully protect it in the United States, and am thinking, indeed, of making it over to a "solicitor" there.—You will not be disappointed I trust at learning that I am seriously intending to absent myself soon from London for a series of weeks. I am thinking of fleeing away and going down to Florence, for March, April and May—for the sake of quiet, isolation, and exemption from those London engagements and temptations which make it impossible (especially as the deeper entanglements of the season come on) to give quiet hours and fresh, unjaded attention to one's work. I dread another season (after the three successive ones I have had,) and I want to get vigorously forward with my long novel, which begins next August. This I see no prospect of doing here, and I shall therefore probably get off in the first days of March, as soon as I have finished a piece of *anonymous* work which I have promised to *Scribner*[3] and which you shall see in time (*Mention it not!*) I said just now I hoped you wouldn't be disappointed, because I shall cease to supply you with London tattle. You must however have got quite sick of the names of my Dinner-parties. I am dining out every day regularly, just now—have dined about forty times since I returned from Paris. Fancy the weariness of it—and don't wonder at my flight. I dine tonight at the Eustace Smith's—yesterday 'twas the Montagu Cookson's—tomorrow, Frederick Lehmann's. Much love to mother and Alice, and pardon the rank egotism of my letter.

Ever, yours
H. James Jr.

1. See 11 January 1880.
2. The publishers, Longmans, Green and Company.
3. An essay on the London theaters.

To Theodore E. Child

Ms Barrett

[London]
Feb. 17<i>th</i> [1880]</div>

Dear Child,

Here is the notice of *Nana;*[1] much longer, as usual, than I meant it to be, and also more heavy and solemn. *Mais ça se laissera lire.* Print it as soon as you can; I only make three conditions (you will say three is a big "only").

1° Please send me *two* proofs. You shall have them back on the instant.

2 PLEASE IF POSSIBLE PRINT IT LEADED. This I beseech you.

3 Please send me half a dozen copies of the paper.

—I ask for two proofs because I should like to send one to some particular American paper, of high repute, *in advance,* to play a trick, and take a mild revenge, on all the others who would steal it from the *Parisian* on the arrival of the latter. I should of course make said paper credit you with it. I earnestly hope you can have the article set up and proofs sent me so expeditiously as to be no inconvenience to you. How unutterably filthy is the book![2]

Yours ever, in haste for the mail

H. James Jr.

1. HJ's review of Zola's *Nana,* which he never reprinted, was published in Child's *Parisian,* No. 48 (26 February 1880), p. 9.
2. In spite of this remark, HJ had much to say in praise of the novel.

To Thomas Sergeant Perry

Ms Colby

[London]
Feb. 22*d* [1880]

Dear Tom,

A word of thanks for your note of condolence of Feb. 13th. The hubbub produced by my poor little *Hawthorne* is most ridiculous; my father has sent me a great many notices, each one more abusive and more abject than the others. The vulgarity, ignorance, rabid vanity and general idiocy of them all is truly incredible. But I hold it a great piece of good fortune to have stirred up such a clatter. The whole episode projects a lurid light upon the state of American "culture," and furnishes me with a hundred wonderful examples, where, before, I had only more or less vague impressions. Whatever might have been my own evidence for calling American taste "provincial," my successors at least will have no excuse for not doing it. Poor little Lathrop ought to be [*tear*] and put to bed, and forbidden the use of pen and ink. I am very happy to hear you have been doing something on the hapless volume, and I shall look out for it.—Yes, there is no denying that *this* is a higher civilization, in literary respects. As I expect to be in London for the rest of my natural life, you must indeed come and pay me a visit—it will only be a question of time—I will introduce you to every one you ever heard of (and as a general thing they will greatly disappoint you; it is the people you have *not* heard of that you will like). Last night I dined at a pleasantish (though not at all first rate) dinner of men, given by E. D. J. Wilson, one of the principal men on the *Times,* and a person of perceptible talent. There were Wemyss (pronounced Weems) Reid a remarkably nice fellow, editor of the principal paper in the North, the *Leeds Mercury,* and author of that interesting little Monograph on Charlotte Brontë published a year or two ago. He told me some very curious unpublished facts about the Brontë family; and offered some day to lend me some 750 letters of Charlotte, addressed to her friend E. N.[1] and containing the whole history of her life. A terrific offer!! (You must come over with your good lady, to help me read 'em.) Then there were Justin McCarthy (who is better than his novels, and a great journalist —he has also lately got into the House of Commons); and John Russell Young, a compatriot, of the New York Herald, and one or two others.—I think of going abroad in a week, for two or three months (probably to Florence) to escape from the importunities of the London season. Andrew Lang, who is rather knocked up with overwork, offers me his company, which I shall probably enjoy for part of the way. He is a very excellent, amiable fellow, of an infantine simplicity, like eight Britons out of ten, even the distinguished ones. We are expecting Lowell here, with mingled feelings (at least I am). I shall be delighted to have his company, but I tremble at what he will make of the arduous wreck of his position. It will bore him to death, and he will shirk it.[2] Love to your wife and daughters.

Tout a toi—

H. James Jr.

1. Ellen Nussey. The story of this correspondence has been published in our time and the importance of the letters is accurately assessed by James.

2. Henry James was wrong. Lowell adjusted himself to his new role, and thrived as minister to Madrid and later to London.

To Henry James Sr.

Ms Harvard

Florence,
March 30*th* [1880]

Dearest daddy,

It is a terrible time since I wrote to you, and it seems all the longer that I have been for a longer time than usual without Quincy Street news. My letters have been forwarded from London to Rome, whither I had expected to go almost directly on leaving England: but I shall telegraph for them today, and I hope that among them will be some happy tidings of my valued family. I left England just two weeks ago, and have been lost ever since in the relief and satisfaction of having eliminated myself from the whirl and hurry of London, and found time for meditation and contemplation. I spent five days (it will strike you as grotesque) at Folkestone, looking at the sea before embarking on it. Thanks to this fact, when I at last did so, I had a quiet and comfortable crossing; I enjoyed the "bath of cool solitude" at Folkestone, where the weather was lovely, more than I can say. I was three or four days in Paris, where the weather was more charming still (this is everywhere, in Europe, a remarkably beautiful spring), and then I started, via Turin and Bologna, for this place, where I arrived day before yesterday evening. I have been here but a day, therefore, and am now writing to you early in the morning at an open window overlooking the yellow Arno. Of course the first thing I did was to go and see the Bootts, who are still in the apartment, in town, that they have occupied all winter (they ascend to their villa tomorrow). They gave me a warm welcome and I spent a part of the day with them; we went together to San Donato, to the sale of Prince Demidoff's treasures, which is making such interminable talk here, and which I found extremely tiresome. The Bootts are the same old Bootts as ever—gentle and affectionate and appreciative, but exhaling a kind of impression of sadness. They show the marks of time a little; Frank is less irrepressible (which is an improvement) and Lizzie is if possible even more mouselike. She has lately been rather seriously ill, but seems now quite restored, and has thrown herself completely into the ministrations of Duveneck. She seems to spend her life in learning, or rather in studying without learning, and in commencing afresh, to paint in someone's manner. I have not seen any of her new things yet, but, I believe, am to go to the studio today, and make the acquaintance of Duveneck. When I have done so, I shall be able to tell you more. *Apropos* of such things, I received, the morning I left London, your and mother's short combined letter, enclosing the two notes from Mrs. Hunt, and her three photographs. I send you herewith my answer to Mrs. H. and leave it open, so that you may read it, and then please forward it. I needn't therefore expatiate on it. I have as yet no definite plan for disposing of my absence from England—save to turn it to as good account as possible. I don't know how favourable, as the spring goes on, and the weather grows more "relaxing," Italy will prove to literary composition. For the moment, it seems delicious, and all the ancient charm of the place takes possession of me again. Florence seems "quite too lovely." For the moment too, however, (for another two or three weeks) I am taking a holiday pure and simple—before settling down to the daily evolution of my "big" novel.[1] (I think I told you that I finished a little one, for the *Cornhill,* before leaving London. I also wrote an article which you will find some day in *Scribner's,* without my name, and which I beg you to keep a religious silence about. The said Scribners had asked me two years ago, to write a disquisition on the London theatres, to be richly illustrated; but though they were very pressing, I declined, owing to the dreariness of the subject. Since Gilder[2] has been abroad, however, he has ardently returned to the charge, offering me so rich a "guerdon or remuneration," as Shakespeare says, that I at last wrote the article, on condition that it should be profoundly anonymous. Gilder is delighted with it, but it will probably not appear for some time, as they are making the most elaborate—and apparently expensive—arrangements to illustrate it: sending out one of their draughtsmen from New York to draw Ellen Terry, etc. I mention all this in parenthesis for your entertainment, with the frantic prayer *that not a word of it be repeated* save to William and his wife.)³ I shall probably, at the end of a week, go down to Naples to spend five days and pay a long-promised visit to the peculiar Joukowsky;⁴ after which, and three or four days in Rome, I shall come back here.—I feel as if I were writing to you much in the dark, from having been without news of you for so long. I trust however that in spite of the darkness, I don't seem to stumble rudely against you, and express no sentiments that are not in harmony with your situation. I hope your springtime is as genial as this. I shall probably write you another line—that is, add a line to this, if I keep it over till tomorrow—after the receipt of my letters from Rome.—The last time I wrote you I think I said that poor Lowell, in London, seemed on the point of veritably losing his wife. I had this on my conscience for several days afterwards; for he got better news a little later. I see however that since I left London, he has been called back to Madrid by a repetition of the bad news, and by this time she may have really expired. Clover Adams promised to write to me; but her letter is probably in Rome. I can imagine no more dismal complication of embarrassments than those poor Lowell has been struggling with for the last many months. It seemed to me, in London, that they had made an old man of him—but it would be almost more correct to say that they had made a child.—I have left myself no space for messages; and I take a fresh leaf to enclose as a symbol of my pure affection. Love and blessing to every one—especially to each. Embrace the dear mammy, and imprint a kiss upon the brow of sister, to whom the next letter shall be religiously (or profanely) addressed.

Ever dear father, yours
H. James Jr.

1. *The Portrait of a Lady.*
2. Richard Watson Gilder, editor of *Scribner's*.
3. "The London Theatres" appeared in *Scribner's*, XXI (January 1881), 354–369.
4. HJ had not seen Joukowsky since their Paris friendship of 1875. Joukowsky was now a member of Richard Wagner's entourage.

To Charles Eliot Norton

Ms Harvard

Florence, Hôtel de l'Arno.
March 31*st* [1880]

My dear Charles,

I am sitting at an open window, this perfect spring morning, looking out on the yellow-green Arno with the little overhanging cabins of the Ponte Vecchio directly beneath me; and it is because I had a fore-knowledge, some time ago, that I should before long find myself in this happy situation, that I delayed answering your very welcome letter of so many weeks ago. I knew you would rather have an answer from Florence than an answer from London. And if I could only make this a real answer from Florence! If I could justify my delay by infusing into my letter some of the delightful elements that surround me! I have been here but two days, but the charm of Florence has already taken complete possession of me and assured me that my recollections were not illusions.—I left London a fortnight ago, spent a week in Paris, and then came almost directly here. I am going to Rome and Naples for a fortnight and then coming back here to remain (unless I go to Venice instead!) for some weeks. I find Italy the same delicious old Italy as ever—trying more and more to dis-Italianize herself, but, thank heaven, not succeeding half so well as she would like. The spring is particularly radiant, now that it has begun (for thanks to an extraordinary severe winter it has been rather behind the mark), and I have never seen the views about this place and the glimpses up and down the river, more delicately and divinely beautiful. I shall make you "feel badly," as we used to say, if I insist too much on this—for I should be sorry to give you too vivid a sense that Shady Hill is not the hill you used to live upon outside the Porta San Gallo. Of Florentine news I have not as yet much to give you—though I went to a dinner-party last night. They are putting a front upon the Duomo, but I don't know in what manner they are doing it, for the place is covered over with a huge screen of boards, under cover of which they can play what tricks they please. I spent a good part of yesterday in the Uffizi and the Pitti, where the pictures that were most my old friends gave me a greeting that was almost an intimation that they had been waiting for me to come again.—In another line, I was interested (very much) in going to see a compatriotic artist, Frank Duveneck, who was many years at Munich and has lately established himself here with a number of pupils. He is a "child of nature and a child of freedom," as Martin Chuzzlewit says; but he also struck me as much the most highly-developed phenomenon in the way of a painter that the U.S.A. has given birth to. His work is remarkably strong and brilliant, with a completeness about it that I should not have suspected from some unfinished things that were exhibited a long time since in Boston. I don't understand why he has not made more reputation —unless it be that he has apparently an almost *slovenly* modesty and want of pretention. I am told however that he was the pride and joy of the Munich School, which has been much depressed by his departure. I shall urge upon him the importance of his making himself known in Paris and London.—I must thank you tenderly for the good things you said about my poor little *opusculi*—especially the poor little *Hawthorne,* which appears to have had the fate of creating a very big tempest in a very small tea-pot. If it were not so childish and so farcical, it would be melancholy and mortifying; but the verdant innocence of it all saves it, to a certain extent, and it seems to me like the clucking of a brood of prairie-hens. My critics, either literally or essentially, seem to me all to have been of the hen-sex.—I must speak to you of Lowell, whom I saw every day, in London, during the week that he spent there previous to my departure. What has befallen him since, I have not yet been able to learn—knowing only that he was called back to Madrid just afterwards. Because this time she was really dying? —I don't know; I am quite in the dark; but if this has been the case you will already have learned it. I can imagine nothing more dismal and dreadful than his situation has been for all these months; and I must say that he showed the marks of it. He seemed old and worn—and yet he seemed wonderfully relieved at getting away from the prolonged misery of his situation in Madrid, giving himself up to it with an almost childlike simplicity: though indeed he could talk of absolutely nothing but his wife.—I trust that, whatever has happened, he will still come back to London, where I shall do my utmost to be comfortable and helpful to him—I have put off answering not only *your* letter, but all the other letters till I should have got to Italy, and have thus prepared for myself a day of reckoning which makes it important I should diffuse rather than concentrate myself. Therefore, dear Charles, for diffusion's sake I must say farewell. Mention the fact just stated, with all my love, to Grace, and tell her that *her* turn imminently impends. Would she prefer a letter from Rome or from Naples—from Siena *or* from Capri? *Commanda, signorina?* Say to her that I have an immense deal to thank her for, and beg her to wait but for a moment. I hope that you are well and that she and all of you are well. I bless you all and try and fold up with this a breath or two of Italian air. I shall see you before many months. Ever, dear Charles,

faithfully yours
Henry James Jr.

To Grace Norton
Ms Harvard

Sorrento,
April 9*th* 1880

My dear Grace,

I have several letters and other missives to thank you for; but though I have them lying here before me (they have kept me company throughout my journey from England), I will not further specify or enumerate them, lest I may remind you too vividly of benefits which, in your generosity, you doubtless forget as easily as you confer them. I wrote to Charles the other day from Florence, sending you a message and giving you your choice of the locality from which I should address you. You will admit that this was very handsome treatment—such as ought to make up a little for unbecoming delays. I am however, as you see, not waiting for your answer, but taking for granted that you would say "Sorrento, please," as easily as anything else. From Sorrento then I write to you, and send you many affectionate salutations. I wish I could send you something else,—a patch of the blue sea that stretches away to Naples and Capri—a few square feet of the pale purple that covers the gentle-looking flanks of Vesuvius—or even a bunch of the deep-coloured oranges that are hung, like Chinese lamps, in all the gardens and orchards, amid the tangle that their own foliage makes with the silvery dusk of the olives. I see these things —most of them—as I sit writing to you. I have a big window which stands open and directly overhangs the Sea. It is early in the morning, and I have just interrupted this epistle to partake of the matutinal tea. The bay of Naples lies before me like a vast pale-blue floor, streaked in all sorts of fantastic ways with currents both of lighter and darker colour. The opposite coast—Posilippo, Baiae etc.—is wonderfully distinct in the clear still light, and I can almost see the shapes of the villas, and the boats pulled up along the strand. Vesuvius sits there on my right, looking wonderfully serene as he smokes his morning pipe, and just beneath my window a boatfull of fishermen in red caps sends up a murmur of lazy sounds which mingles with the clash of little waves at the base of the cliff on which the hotel is planted. Let me not, however, be too geographical.—I left Florence just after writing to Charles, for an absence of some ten days. I spent but two or three —most lovely ones—in Rome, and then came down to these regions to pass three or four more with a friend[1] who is living at Posilippo at about an hour's drive from Naples. I made my little visit, and got part of my entertainment from observing the manners and customs of a little group of Russians with whom the said friend—a Russian himself—is surrounded. They are about as opposed to those of Cambridge as anything could well be—but to describe them would carry me too far. My friend lives in great intimacy with Richard Wagner, the composer and his wife, who are spending the year at Naples; but I did not avail myself of the opportunity offered me to go and see the musician of the future, as I speak no intelligible German and he speaks nothing else. The charms of Madame Wagner were depicted to me in the most vivid colours (she is the daughter of Liszt, the musician and the lady—Madame d'Agoult, who called herself Daniel Stern, and was formerly the wife of Von Bülow, from whom she is divorced, a curious collection of attributes!). But I kept out of the house, and went instead to look at the mutilated Psyche at the Naples Museum, which (by the way) (the Museum I mean) is as rich and interesting as you probably remember it. Two or three of the bronzes, and a couple of the small Greek bas-reliefs, are among the loveliest things of antique sculpture—to say nothing of the before-mentioned Psyche (she, I mean, who has lost the crown of her head and has her lovely face bent down; you will easily recall her). I drove yesterday afternoon from Castellamare to this place, along the famous and beautiful road which winds among the orchards of orange and olive and overhangs the sea. You probably remember it well, but I saw it for the first time. I spend but today here, how-ever, and then return to Rome and Florence. Rome has much of the old charm, but it had not all of it. The air of the modern water-ing-place has invaded it to a very sensible degree, and the gov-ernment are doing everything that the most diabolical ingenuity can suggest to destroy the dear old purely Roman quality. The enormous crowds, the new streets, the horse-cars (you might think yourself in Brattle Street!) the ruination of the Coliseum, the hideous iron bridge over the Tiber, the wholesale desecration of the Pincio, etc., are all so many death-blows to the picturesque. Nevertheless, of a lovely spring day, the place is still capable of exciting an agreeable emotion, and I could easily make shift to spend the next two months there. Florence seems to me on the whole less spoiled than Rome—but I think I discoursed of Flor-ence the other day in writing to Charles. I shall probably divide the rest of my stay in Italy between that place and Venice—a programme which will probably seem to you highly delectable. To me too it seems pleasant enough; but I confess that I am perpetually *sous le coup* as they say in French of a sense of having lost the freshness of my impressions, the keenness of my enjoyment. I don't mean through any particular catastrophe, but simply by the common curse of advancing life. So true it is that we are young but once! When I compare my feelings the first time I came to Italy with my state of mind today, it seems to me the difference between hot coffee and cold. *Then* every glance was a sensation, and every sensation a delight; *now,* the finest sensation I have had is this of writing to you. This after all, however, is not so bad—it proves at least that my heart still beats.—I am very glad to be away from England during all this electoral turmoil. Much of it is interesting; but you can't have only so much as interests you—you must have so much more as well. The Liberals are coming in with a vengeance; but I shall not rejoice unless they make a better figure in office than they have made in opposition, where, to my mind, their attitude has been singularly arid and dreary. They probably, however, will rise with the occasion. Dear Grace, as I have only one day here, I will leave you for a long walk or a drive.

I bless you, and all those that are with you, and remain your *devotissimo,*

Henry James Jr.

1. Paul Joukowsky.

To William Dean Howells

Ms Harvard

Florence,
April 18th [1880]

Carino amico,

The most *caressing* epithets of a caressing language are not out of place in regard to the particular motive of my writing to you. My imagination seeks eagerly for anything that will ease me off a little and rob my letter of its sting. This sting resides, brutally speaking, in my earnest wish that you may find it not fatally inconvenient to begin my promised serial in *October* instead of *August!* A postponement of two whole months!—the thing will probably have to you an impudent sound. But I throw myself on your mercy and urge upon your attention that the story shall be a 100 percent better by each day that you have to wait. My motives for this petition are twofold. In the first place I withdrew a month ago from London and its uproar, its distractions and interruptions, in order to concentrate myself upon my work. But if London is uproarious, Italy is insidious, perfidious, fertile in pretexts for one's haunting its lovely sights and scenes rather than one's writing-table; so that, in respect to my novel it has been a month lost rather than gained. In the second place I think I wrote you before that I lately finished a serial tale for the *Cornhill*. This has proved by the editor's measurement longer than by my own, so that instead of running through *four* numbers, it will extend to *six*. As it begins in *June* they will make it terminate in *November;* and it will be agreeable to *Macmillan* that the novel for them and you, shall not begin till the thing in the *Cornhill* is virtually leaving the scene. Behold, dear Howells, my reasons; I trust they will seem to you worthy of a compatriot and a Christian, and that the delay won't cause you any material discomfort. It will leave me a chance to get forward a good deal further than I should otherwise do, before beginning to publish. I shall assume that I have touched you by the appeal, and shall proceed in consequence; but a line in answer (to 3 Bolton Street Piccadilly) will nevertheless be very welcome.—Come back to Italy as soon as you can; but don't come with a masterpiece suspended in the air by the tenderest portions of its texture; or else forbid yourself the pleasure of paying your proper respects to this land of loveliness.—I have just come back from a ten day's run to Rome and Naples, and shall be in this place for the longer or shorter time that I remain absent from England. Florence is delightful, as usual, but I am lacerated with the effort of turning myself away from Rome, where I feared I shouldn't do much work, but which is to Florence, as sunlight unto moonlight.—I hope that, putting aside the untoward incident embodied in this letter, everything is well with you. I read your current novel[1] with pleasure, but I don't think the subject fruitful, and I suspect that much of the public will agree with me. I make bold to say this because, as the thing will be finished by this time, it won't matter that my rude words discourage you. Also, I am in a fine position to talk about the public's agreeing with me!—But if you do, sometimes, I don't care about the others! Greet me your wife and children, and believe me your *devotissimo*—

H. James Jr.

1. *The Undiscovered Country.*

To Alice James
Ms Harvard

Florence,
April 25*th* [1880]

Dearest sister.

I think I announced in my last letter home that the next time I should write, you should be the object of my favours, and as this declaration has probably thrown you into a fever of expectation and impatience, I will prolong no further a silence of which I am already much ashamed. I am well aware that an abominable interval has elapsed since I last gave you news of me; but I on my side also have been waiting for a token from Quincy Street,—a token which however arrived three days since in the shape of a letter from mother, with date of March 28th (it had been delayed some days in London, where my letters during a temporary uncertainty as to address had at my request been retained). Thank our dearest mammy effusively—it is the letter in which she speaks of William's beginning to build his house, of the death of Wilky's father-in-law, etc., enclosing the letter from Bob describing Mr. Cary's funeral. I hope these events are having comfortable consequences; i.e. that William has chosen a happy model for his dwelling, and is seeing it rise to the skies with magic swiftness; and that Wilky's wife and children will be eased off, financially, by the demise of their relative. I got a characteristically quaint letter from Wilky about a month ago (telling me that something I had sent him had "identified me to his memory," and speaking in the highest terms of the conjugal and domestic virtues of his wife). In Bob's letter, enclosed by mother, he (Bob) sent me a graceful message (à propos of Hawthorne,) but I can't make out whether or no he had received quite a long letter I wrote him before leaving London. If so I trust he will answer it—and will mother kindly mention it to him?—I wrote home last from Florence, and in Florence behold me still. In the interval, however, I took a short run down to Rome and Naples, spending in the latter place (or rather at Posilippo) three days with Joukowsky, who is the same impracticable and indeed ridiculous mixture of Nihilism and bric à brac as before, and who is living in great intimacy with Richard Wagner, the composer, who is spending some months at Naples, and whom Joukowsky thinks the greatest and wisest of men. He endeavoured to *m'attirer chez lui* (that is J. did;) but I kept away because Wagner speaks no French and I no German, as you are probably aware. Jouk.'s present plan— it will probably last about six months—is to go and live at Bayreuth "*afin de prendre part au grand œuvre*": that is to paint decorations for Wagner's operas. But as he believes that the Nihilists will presently overturn every human institution and make *place nette,* in order to begin afresh, he may not put this project into execution. He is always under somebody's influence: first (since I have known him) under Turgénieff's, then under the Princess Ourousoff's, whom he now detests, and who despises him, then under H.J. Jr. (!!) then under that of a certain disagreeable Onéguin (the original of Turgenieff's Neshdanoff, in *Virgin Soil*), now under that of Wagner, and apparently in the near future under that of Mme W., who is the daughter of the Abbé Liszt and Daniel Stern (Mme d'Agoult) and the divorced wife of Von Bülow, the pianist.—Naples, as regards her nature, seemed to me enchanting; but the vileness of her humanity took the edge from my enjoyment of the outlines of Vesuvius and Capri, and the classic blue of the Bay—all of which things I would give fifty times over for an hour of Rome, where I spent, very happily, five or six days. The pleasantest of these I went out and passed with Somerset Beaumont (a man you may have heard me speak of in England) who is living at an enchanting old Villa at Frascati, one of the loveliest places on earth. This day, which was in itself most charming, derived an extra merit from the contrast of Beaumont's admirable, honest, reasonable, wholesome English nature with the fantastic immoralities and aesthetics of the circle I had left at Naples,[1] and which contained three or four other members I have not mentioned. At Rome I dined one day at the Story's, who were very friendly and *adulatory,* and another at Eugene Schuyler's, in company with the Waddingtons and their brother-in-law M. de Bunsen.—Florence just now is very lovely, and fairly favourable for work. I see more or less of the gentle and pure-minded Bootts; but less than I should do if they did not live up upon their hill top (to which they sometimes since removed again); the labour of scaling which under an Italian sun offers terrors to an individual prone to liquefaction. The simplicity of Bootts' mental constitution only increases with age, but as it does so becomes easier to accept. Lizzie is also ever more acceptable than ever. I see no one else of importance here, though it is a place where one is liable to tea-parties; I have to call, for instance, on Constance Fenimore Woolson, who has been pursuing me through Europe with a letter of introduction from (of all people in the world!) Henrietta Pell-Clark. Constance is amiable, but deaf, and asks me questions about my works to which she can't hear the answers.[2] I shall probably remain absent from England till June 1st, my state of mind being divided between relief and regret at being away from London now. It is an excellent thing for me to be away, but my homesickness is keen, and I blush to confess that I have arrived at that prosaic maturity when the picturesqueness of Italy seems at times to but half console me for the lack of my club and my London habits. Love to father and mother and aunt. (I hope the latter sometimes sees my letters.) I greet you dearest sister on both cheeks.

Your fondest
H. James Jr.

1. HJ seems to have been greatly shocked to find his old Parisian friend in a veritable nest of homosexuals.
2. Miss Woolson's privately printed diaries and journals, edited by Clare Benedict, show that HJ called often and took her to galleries and museums in Florence. These meetings are recounted (in light disguise) in her tale "A Florentine Experiment." See Edel, *The Conquest of London* (1963), the chapter entitled "Fenimore."

To J. W. Cross

Ms Private

Florence,
May 14*th* 1880.

My dear Cross.

I have just heard of your marriage, and I must give myself the satisfaction of sending you a word of very friendly sympathy on the occasion—which I beg you to communicate, in the most deferential form, to your illustrious wife.[1] Receive my heartiest congratulations and good wishes, and try and fancy that they have hovering about them the perfume and promise of a Florentine Maytime. I have congratulated friends before on their approaching, or accomplished, nuptials; but I have never had the privilege of doing so in a case in which I felt (as today) all the cordiality of mankind mingling with my individual voice. Don't let the mighty murmur drown my feeble note, by the way; but remember that I am what the newspapers call a "distinct factor" in any sense of the good-will of your fellow-mortals that you may now enjoy. Don't on the other hand dream of answering this hasty note—you have probably so many letters to write. I am on the point of returning to England and I shall see you then. I wish I could fold into this sheet a glimpse of the yellow Arno, the blue-grey hills, the old brown city which your wife knows so well and which she has helped to make me know.—But I will only attempt to insert, again, a friendly handshake from

your very faithfully
Henry James Jr.

1. Cross had married George Eliot.

To Henry James Sr.
Ms Harvard

3, Bolton Street,
June 20*th* [1880]

Dearest Daddy—

I wrote to mother about ten days since, and just afterward received a short letter from her—the one in which she enclosed Miss Phelps's article on my *Hawthorne* (which seemed to me, by the way, very repulsive in its hysterical imbecility—an appalling revelation of morbidness). I am very grateful to her, as usual, for her least word—very grateful, I mean, to mother. Since then also, William has arrived, as he will already have written to you, and I have him domiciled here in the apartment beneath my own. It is very delightful to see him again, and we have had much interesting talk, which as well as most other things, he seems to enjoy. I have been, however, rather disappointed in his physical condition, or was so, at least, at first. He looks very well, but he arrived in a very sleepless state, which (naturally enough) appeared to make him feel very miserable. This however is passing away, his sleep is returning, and with it his disposition to exert himself. I have no doubt he will do very well for the future and will draw much renovation from his holiday. I find him very little changed, looking no older, and with the same tendency to descant on his sensations—but with all his vivacity and brilliancy of mind undimmed. How he finds me he will have told you, and I hope will have given you a favourable picture. I have of course questioned him minutely about the family group and all cognate matters, and his answers only quicken my desire to behold it again. It is very possible therefore that I shall sail for home earlier in the autumn than I at first intended—the more so that to do this will be in many ways a convenience to me, to say nothing of the better passage. I shall not settle this, however, for another month, and then will let you know. It is *not* probable, all the same, that William and I will return together. He will remain here, I suppose, about three weeks more; but what he will do on the continent he has not settled—probably spend his time in Switzerland. He has not yet seen any one of particular interest, as he has not hitherto felt able to exert himself in this way; but yesterday I had some men to meet him at dinner at the club, which he much enjoyed. They were not however, persons of particular distinction and he will not attempt to go in much for the "social side," which if he desires to recruit, is wise.—I hope your summer is going on comfortably and that all things are well with you— with Alice, in particular. The other Alice and her baby you must miss, to judge by the attractive account William gives me of both. Tell Alice James that I thank her very prettily for the calligraphic pen, and will bring her something almost as neat (as a gift) when I come home. Farewell, dear Dad, embrace mother and sister and believe me

> your faithful son
> H. James Jr.

To Mrs. Henry James Sr.

Ms Harvard

> 3, Bolton Street,
> July 4*th* [1880]

Dearest Mammy.

Your letter of June 20th came to me yesterday, and I must answer it without delay. It found William still with me, though later in the day he left town, to go and pay a short visit to Sara Darwin and take a look at the Isle of Wight. I am afraid my first letter, after his arrival gave you a more gloomy impression of him than I have been justified in taking since. After he had been here a few days he began to recover his sleep and with it his strength and his spirit; and most of the time he appears to have been able to do with impunity and with enjoyment the principle things he has desired. He has seen his friends the philosophers (Hodgson, Robertson, Bain, Sully, Hughlings Jackson etc.) and of Hodgson in particular has seen a great deal. (He likes the last mentioned extremely and describes him as most sympathetic.) All this has been interesting and even exhilarating to him, and I am very glad he has managed it, for he has managed little else in the way of seeing people and has been able to avail himself almost not at all of the social opportunities I have wished to offer him—(in the way of dining out etc.). This however is highly natural, for as he justly says, it is poor work going through all the formal preliminaries of acquaintance with people whom you never expect to reap further profit of friendship from. He has preferred to use his time for other things—knocking about London, keeping out of doors etc.; all of which has done him good. He has been most genial and sympathetic to me, and I have greatly enjoyed his talk and his company—having learned more from him about home affairs in a half hour's conversation, than in a year of letter-writing. I must say, however, that even at best there remains more of nervousness and disability about him than I had supposed, and I can't get rid of the feeling that he takes himself, and his nerves, and his physical condition, too hard and too consciously. As he takes himself however, so one must take him; but I wish he had a little more of this quiet British stoutness. I am delighted with what you tell me about the advantages of his wife and babe; he has let me read some of the former's letters to him since he has been here, and they breathe a sweetness and devotion which must indeed be full of help and comfort to him.—I hope our own Alice has made a good thing, with Miss Loring's help, of the journey to the White Mountains. You will tell me of the event when you next write, and I shall be delighted if it proves a happy one. Give my tender love to the Sister and tell her to profit by some hour of coinciding vigour and virtue to write me a few lines. I see you are having it hot again; but I hope you are keeping cool, all the same. Your sketch of Anna Rodgers's marriage-doings was interesting and shows the family in rather a vulgar light; but people must be left to take their satisfactions where they seem to them to lie; and the incidents you mention will have at least had the advantage of furnishing Aunt Kate and Cousin Helen with subjects for conversation for an unlimited period. I am very sorry you are to be deprived of Aunt Kate's society for the whole summer; but I trust her ministrations to Cousin Helen will prolong the latter's life.—Touching myself personally I am able to give you no great news. I have carried on my London habits in a great measure independently of William—went for instance the other evening to a party at Devonshire House to which he was indisposed to accompany me. I am much more interested in my current work than anything else—and am a good deal bothered with the number of transitory Americans who come to see me, with appeals (tacit or explicit) for "attention" which I have neither time nor means to show them. (Tell Alice, however, that William Loring has never turned up.) Don't think I am trifling with your affections too much in the matter of coming home in the autumn if I say that in spite of my having written you last that I was thinking of starting sooner, it may be that I shall judge it best again to delay it. Nothing is settled yet, positively, but as soon as it is I will let you know. Several excellent reasons have turned up within the last week to make me think of waiting a while longer, and you may be sure that if I decide to do so, I will set them forth to you in a manner not only to take the edge from your disappointment, but to minister to your joy. If by waiting a while I become able to return with more leisure, fame and money in my hands, and the prospect and desire of remaining at home longer, it will be better for me to do so; and this is very possible. When I *do* come, I wish to come solidly; and in this respect a few months will make a great difference. I am eager to go now, but next year I shall be still more so. All this, however, will become clearer to me in two or three weeks; and then I shall make it clear to you.

Blessings on father and sister, and on yourself, dearest mother, from yours ever fondly

H.J. Jr.

To Mrs. Henry James Sr.

Ms Harvard

3, Bolton Street,
July 20*th* [1880]

Dearest Mammy—

I must write you but a short note, for I am sorry to say your poor old infant is rather seedy. I am just recovering from one of those wretched sieges of pain in my head which I have had so often and which are so very unprofitable. I have had longer ones than this (was but two days in bed) but rarely more acute; though on the other hand I have the satisfaction this time of having seen a definite cause—in the fact that I got a violent chill from sleeping too much exposed to the air during a night in which the temperature suddenly changed from hot to cold.[1] This brought on a savage rheumatic, or neuralgic, headache; but I had this time a less metaphysical physician than poor old Wilkinson, who assuaged my pain with considerable promptitude. Now I am feeling much better, and I will try and not do it again. But they are strange and loathsome fits.—I have two letters, one from father of July 1st (which I sent on to William) and your own of July 9th which came last night. Both of them were full of tender affection and gratified me very much, and I shall send yours also on to William. He left me a week ago, feeling and seeming everyway very much better than when he arrived. The last thing he did was to go down to Lady Rose's and spend a few hours, which he enjoyed apparently so much that I was sorry he couldn't have more of it. They have taken a most picturesque old house in Surrey; Lady R. was delightful, and the party a very pleasant one, containing the Henry Adamses, some other people, and her charming and attractive daughter Mrs. Clark.—Frank Boott and Lizzie have just come in, having arrived here last night, to see some cousins whom they have lately discovered, some of whom live in the country and others in London. They seem very well and friendly, but they don't like London (which they don't know at all) and don't pretend to like it. Frank lags very much in the cousin-business which has chiefly been conducted by Lizzie, apparently with very agreeable results. They are to spend two or three weeks in the country, and I shall apparently not see much of them.—My last letter dearest mammy, will have prepared you and father for what I now speak of as a decision—namely my putting off my journey to America till sometime next year. I am afraid you will be rudely disappointed, but I hope your disappointment will not survive the knowledge of my good reasons for the change. These, briefly expressed, are that I am not yet ready to go. I took my passage, a month ago, in the *Gallia* for August 21st, and I have not yet given it up; but I shall shortly do so.—I have an insurmountable objection to going home with my long novel which begins two or three months hence, but half completed, and having settled down to steady work again as soon as I get home; and on the other hand it would be a feverish and impracticable scramble to finish it before the time I first intended to go—in October. I am to get a good deal of money for it (i.e. from the *Atlantic* and *Macmillan* together, if it runs a year, as it probably will, 6000 dollars, £1200); and therefore I wish to carry it on quietly and comfortably —the more so as I have just been correcting the opening proofs and that they seem to me very good. In the second place there is a considerable probability that I shall at last come to the point and undertake to write the Life of Dickens; and if I do this, I must do it here, and not go home with the task on my hands, unexecuted. I must do it on the spot, as much as possible in London.[2]—There dearest parents, are part of my reasons for putting off my return; and when you see that they redound to my profit, glory and general felicity, and therefore, by intimate implication, to yours and my sister's, you will, I think easily accept them, and reconcile yourself to a little more waiting. My delay has nothing to do with my not wanting to go home: on the contrary, I wish to go keenly, and see a thousand uses and satisfactions in it; but I wish to do it in the best conditions and to return in a word with a little accumulation of opulence and honour. (Send this letter if you think best, to Aunt Kate but please mention to *no one else that financial statement I made you about the novel, nor the other information about the Dickens*.) On this then I take your blessing and your embrace, and assume that for the present you will philosophically cease to expect me.—I am delighted that Alice has taken a successful breathing-spell in your formidable summer and hope her experiment has been happy to the end—if the end has come as I trust not. I trust she built a monument somewhere of forest leaves (or rather of New Hampshire granite) to the divine Miss Loring, who appears to unite the wisdom of the serpent with the gentleness of the dove. *Apropos,* I found on my table the other day Mr. William Loring's card and Alice's note of introduction. He had just left them at my door, but had neglected to put on the card the faintest inkling of an address; in consequence of which I have been unable to follow him up in any way. In all this measureless London I can't of course ascertain where he lodges, and he I suppose, having forgotten that he didn't leave an address, thinks me of small civility. I have been hoping he would bethink himself and come back; but he has not yet done so. Will his sister, in writing to him, please mention these facts, and my regret at having been so helpless in the matter?—The London season has virtually terminated, to my ineffable joy. It has to me been full of weariness, interruptions, barren engagements, expensiveness and general bewilderment—all injurious to quiet work. I shall never spend another at a time when I have any work to do. If I pass May, June, July here again, it will be because I can afford to be idle. Lots of people with introductions, friends from abroad, passing Americans etc., have been poured out upon me; and the measure has been too full—containing as it has done also, all my usual London engagements and preoccupations.[3] The outsiders never understand that you are already a man busy to the verge of desperation when they arrive, and they are the successive grains in the load that breaks the camel's back. The latest arrival is little

Bob Emmet, who made his way, two days since, to my bedside, and whom to get rid of, I have had to ask to dinner. He seems, however, an amiable, genial youth. This letter is of course addressed equally to father and you, but you must thank him none the less, particularly for the glowing speeches—the *ardentia verba* —of his of the 1st July, which enclosed the two extracts for Mrs. Orr.[4] These I have read with much interest. I have not yet sent them to Mrs. Orr, because I have been intending from one day to another to go and see her; and I shall now presently do so. I want to tell her personally of the pleasure her interest in his book gave father. What he said about William's Alice and the Boy made me regret acutely that another interval is to intervene before I see them; but their charms will only be a little riper. I hope the two are in good way at Petersham. The few hours William and I spent together at Losely Park (the Roses') made me feel that William's charming conversational powers would make him such a boon in the British country-house that he might easily spend his whole summer, gratis, in going triumphantly from one to another, where such birds are rare, and I wished he might stop awhile longer and try it; but what he is doing is of course much more truly hygienic. I hope your heat is over and that you are not the worse for it. Also that Alice will try another outing. Tell her that I am particularly sorry on *her* account that she is not to behold me so soon; for I know that she languishes for me and that her disturbed health is doubtless in some degree caused by this languishment. I too languish, but when I do come I will come in a style that will make up for delays. Thank Mary greatly for her message, and tell her I shall certainly go to Milwaukee. I hope Aunt Kate, who, I suppose, is a kind of "bed-chamber-woman," as they say here, to Cousin Helen, is in some cool and sympathetic spot. Farewell, dearest mammy and daddy. I have written you a longer letter than I intended, and that I have done so without evil results proves me to me that I am all right again. Waft your blessing across the seas to your faithfullest

H. James Jr.

P.S. I have got but a postcard from William, from Cologne. He will already have written to you that he crossed to Holland, passed through Amsterdam, Antwerp, etc. I expect daily to hear that he has reached Switzerland whither I have several letters to forward to him.

1. This self-diagnosis may be questioned. It is to be noted that HJ had similar headaches earlier, in the wake of visits from his brother William or after periods of extreme frustration or anxiety.

2. Though he had apparently decided not to write the life of Dickens, he seems here to use the Macmillan proposal as one way of explaining his further delay in visiting his family.

3. WJ saw his brother in a different light. "The way he worked at paying visits and going to dinners and parties was surprising to me, especially as he was all the time cursing them for so frustrating his work." He added, speaking from his philosopher point of view, "he is better suited by superficial contact with things at a great many points than by a deeper one at a few points." (WJ to parents 13 July 1880).

4. Mrs. Sutherland Orr had published an article on Howells' work in the *Contemporary Review* "more discriminating than I usually find such things." HJ described her to Howells as "a pleasant, clever, accomplished woman, in bad health, with no eyesight, and of rather a philosophical turn."

To William Dean Howells

Ms Harvard

3, Bolton Street,
July 20*th* [1880]

Dear Howells.

I send you today forty eight printed pages of my novel[1]—which should have gone to you five days since, but that just as I received the sheets from the printer I was taken with a sharp attack of illness which kept me in bed for three days, unable to use a pen. This is the first moment I have got my wits about me again. (I had a terrible siege of neuralgic pain in my head, to which, I am sorry to say, I am woefully liable.)

What you have herewith are the sheets of Macmillan containing the first part (number) of the story and the greater portion of the second number. You shall have in two or three days the rest of the second and the whole of the third. After that the sequel will flow freely. You will see that the first part is *very* long (twenty six and a quarter pages of *Macmillan*) (which will make, I should say, just about the same of the *Atlantic*). The following numbers will, as a general thing, probably be shorter by two or three pages. I wrote you that *October* was the month fixed for beginning here; but I am afraid I did not make as clear to you as I ought (as I was indeed myself rather inattentive to the fact at the time) that for the *Atlantic* this must mean the *November* number. It is only by your publishing a fortnight after Macmillan, rather than a fortnight before, that I can secure the English copyright: an indispensable boon. This is what Harper is doing with my little *Washington Square,* which beginning in the *Cornhill* in *June,* began in Harper in July. Don't worry about the *Portrait of a Lady* being stolen in the few days interval of time that may elapse between the October *Macmillan* arriving in New York, and the *Atlantic* coming out; for Houghton & Mifflin will please immediately have the thing copyrighted for me, and each number of Macmillan will contain (as the current *Cornhills* do) a footnote duly setting forth that I have taken out the American copyright and will have my pound of flesh from whomsoever infringes it. In *November* then I look for you to begin. I feel as if I had done nothing but delay and disappoint you with regard to this production; but you see what it is to have given me a boundless faith in your *bonté*. Prove it once more.

I am much obliged to you for the pretty volume of the *Undiscovered,*[2] which I immediately read with greater comfort and consequence than in the magazine. My first impression of it remains, however (and you have probably found it the general impression) —that it is the most *entertaining* of your books. The subject is interesting and the character of Boynton very finely conceived; but the spiritism, which at the beginning one looks to see more illustrated, vanishes from the scene, and the Shakerism which comes in, seems arbitrary and unaccounted for. You strike me, once you have brought in Shakerism, as not having made quite enough of it—not made it grotesque or pictorial, or whatever-it-may-be, enough; as having described it too un-ironically and as if you were a Shaker yourself. (Perhaps you are—unbeknown to your correspondents and contributors!!—and that this is the secret of the book!) Furthermore, I think Egeria is the least individual and personal of your heroines; and I resent her suburban matrimony with Mr. Ford (whom I don't care for, either) at the end. On the other hand the subject is a larger and heavier one than you have yet tried, and you have carried it off with great ease and the flexibility which shows how well you have learned your art. Excuse this diatribe, which is really cool as accompanying an appeal, on my own part, to your consideration. I have as usual no personal news. The only important things that can happen to me are to die and to marry, and as yet I do neither. I shall in any case do the former first; then in the next world, I shall marry Helen of Troy. My brother has been spending a month with me and has left for Switzerland. I shall be writing you again in a few days.

Yours ever faithfully
H. James Jr.

1. *The Portrait of a Lady.*
2. Howells' *Undiscovered Country.*

To Grace Norton

Ms Harvard

Grove Farm,
Leatherhead.
July 26*th* 1880

My dear Grace.

It seems to me better that I should write you a short note than none at all; so here is a hearty handshake, compressing many greetings and questions. I wrote to you some three months since from Sorrento; and hope the letter safely reached you, in spite of the vagaries of the Neapolitan post. After that I spent a series of weeks in Florence, in the midst of the sweet springtime, and then came back to this sterner, though still agreeable, clime, where I have for the last six weeks been struggling with the high tide, and the breaking waves, of the London Season. That is now virtually over, thank the powers of mercy; and I am taking breath for a couple of days under the genial roof of the Russell Sturgis's. You knew them, I think, while you were in England; but I don't know that you were ever at their lovely place, deep in the bosom of charming Surrey. Anything greener, rosier, breezier, more fragrant and more *cushiony* on the part of nature, cannot well be conceived—a place to reconcile one completely to a passive as distinguished from an active life. Socially speaking the characteristics of the spot are a religious confidence in the coming repast and an absence of fatiguing intellectual flights. Russell Sturgis is a dear, delightful old fellow and Mrs. S. the kindest, easiest and handsomest of hostesses. If she is very expensive to keep that is nothing to the pausing visitor, who simply enjoys what I just now enjoyed—an exhibition in the dining-room by a great goldsmith who had come up from London with his wares and had tumbled out on the table a heap of temptations in the shape of diamond necklaces for £6000, etc.—Italy, to go back a moment, was more Italy than ever and I am more helplessly infatuated with it. I came away with immense regret and hope to spend a part of next winter there. You will rightly infer from this that I am postponing that visit to my native land which I must have mentioned to you as likely to occur this coming autumn. I have found, quite lately, a great many good reasons for putting it off a while; and if you are so kind (as you will be) as to share my own regret at this necessity, you will perhaps extract comfort (as I do) from the reflection that when I do go home it will be with a hungry eagerness and a determination to remain a long time. The event will certainly come off some time next year. When you write me, don't reproach me overmuch with my delay, for I already feel much shame at having trifled with the affection of several gentle spirits who had found means to take pleasure in the prospect of seeing me soon.—I have had my brother William in town with me for a month—enjoying London quietly and very eclectically; but he is now rambling through Switzerland and enjoying a freedom that Britain cannot give. I was conscious this year of being overdosed with London and shall not soon again, I think, spend the months of June and July there. The machine is altogether too big, and too brutal in its operations, and the quality of social existence fatally sacrificed to quantity. The quantity is particularly excessive if one happens to have valued work to do; and in this case one neither does one's work properly nor enjoys the things that prevent one from doing it. One of my latest sensations was going one day to Lady Airlie's to hear Browning read his own poems—with the comfort of finding that, at least, if you don't understand them, he himself apparently understands them even less. He read them as if he hated them and would like to bite them to pieces.—I see Lowell only by glimpses; he is so terribly mundane and moves in such exalted spheres. He is apparently going straight through the mill; but now that his wife is better he appears to take to it kindly—which is very well, as there seems to be nothing else for him to do. I read in the *Times* that you are roasting alive in the U.S.A.; but I trust that you catch the passing breeze at Ashfield, and I hope that Charles and the children (among whom I include yourself) are preserved from blight by it. Give my blessings to Charles; if I go to Italy next winter I shall take his book with me, and indulge thereby then three or four passions at once—friendship, the love of knowledge, and the love of *Italia mia.*—The lunch-bell sounds, and I must hurry off to justify that confidence that I just now spoke of in the qualities of the victuals. You are probably at this moment sitting somewhere under the trees and looking at opposite hills. I am doing the same—that is I shall be, this afternoon; but the hills in my case will be the great lawny slopes of Norbury Park. Nevertheless I wish I were with you in your more untutored landscape. Is George Curtis always near you, and do you often see him? This question is inane, for of course if he is at Ashfield, you meet everyday; and I meant it only as a pretext for asking you to give him my very friendly remembrance. Farewell, dear Grace, for today. Don't forget me, but if you remember me, let it be leniently; and believe me

ever faithfully yours
H. James Jr.

To Eliza Lynn Linton

Ms Unknown[1]

[August 1880]

My dear Mrs. Linton.

I will answer you as concisely as possible—and with great pleasure —premising that I feel very guilty at having excited such ire in celestial minds, and painfully responsible at the present moment.

Poor little Daisy Miller was, as I understand her, above all things *innocent*. It was not to make a scandal, or because she took pleasure in a scandal, that she 'went on' with Giovanelli. She never took the measure really of the scandal she produced, and had no means of doing so: she was too ignorant, too irreflective, too little versed in the proportions of things. She intended infinitely less with G. than she appeared to intend—and he himself was quite at sea as to how far she was going. She was a flirt, a perfectly superficial and unmalicious one, and she was very fond, as she announced at the outset, of 'gentlemen's society.' In Giovanelli she got a gentleman—who, to her uncultivated perception, was a very brilliant one—all to herself, and she enjoyed his society in the largest possible measure. When she found that this measure was thought too large by other people—especially by Winterbourne—she was wounded; she became conscious that she was accused of something of which her very comprehension was vague. This consciousness she endeavoured to throw off; she tried not to think of what people meant, and easily succeeded in doing so; but to my perception she never really tried to take her revenge upon public opinion—to outrage it and irritate it. In this sense I fear I must declare that she was not *defiant*, in the sense you mean. If I recollect rightly, the word 'defiant' is used in the tale—but it is not intended in that large sense; it is descriptive of the state of her poor little heart, which felt that a fuss was being made about her and didn't wish to hear anything more about it. She only wished to be left alone—being herself quite unaggressive. The keynote of her *character* is her innocence—that of her *conduct* is, of course, that she has a little sentiment about Winterbourne, that she believes to be quite unreciprocated—conscious as she was only of his protesting attitude. But, even here, I did not mean to suggest that she was playing off Giovanelli against Winterbourne —for she was too innocent even for that. She didn't try to provoke and stimulate W. by flirting overtly with G.—she never believed that Winterbourne was provokable. She would have liked him to think well of her—but had an idea from the first that he cared only for higher game, so she smothered this feeling to the best of her ability (though at the end a glimpse of it is given), and tried to help herself to do so by a good deal of lively movement with Giovanelli. The whole idea of the story is the little tragedy of a light, thin, natural, unsuspecting creature being sacrificed as it were to a social rumpus that went on quite over her head and to which she stood in no measurable relation. To deepen the effect, I have made it go over her mother's head as well. She never had a thought of scandalising anybody—the most she ever had was a regret for Winterbourne.

This is the only witchcraft I have used—and I must leave you to extract what satisfaction you can from it. Again I must say that I feel 'real badly,' as D. M. would have said, at having supplied the occasion for a breach of cordiality. May the breach be healed herewith! . . . Believe in the very good will of yours faithfully,

H. James

1. The text given here is reprinted from the biography of Mrs. Linton by George Somes Layard, *Mrs. Lynn Linton: Her Life, Letters, and Opinions* (1901). A Victorian bluestocking, Elizabeth Lynn Linton (1822–1898) wrote fiction, pioneered on "the woman question," and practiced spiritualism. She had written HJ to ask him whether Daisy Miller was "obstinate and defying, or superficial and careless," and told him that an argument over the story had lost her "the most valuable intellectual friend I ever had."

To Mrs. Henry James Sr.

Ms Harvard

Lord Warden Hotel
Dover.
Sept. 11*th* [1880]

Beloved mammy.

A line of response to your tender letter of Aug. 23d: the one in which you enclose the head-ache prescription from Alice, etc. Perturb yourself not, sweet mother, on the subject of my head-aches, of my exhausting life, of my burning the candle at both ends, of my being nipped in the prime of my powers—or of any other nefarious tendency or catastrophe. You will have seen William by this time, and he will have chased such dusky delusions from your mind. I never was better, more at leisure, more workable, or less likely to trifle in any manner with my vitality, physical or intellectual. I wish you could see me in the flesh—I think a glance would set your mind at rest. *En attendant,* cradle it in the conversation of William—who if he doesn't draw a rosy picture of me, will be false to a sacred trust. He must have been, by this time, at home for nearly a week, and I am very impatient for some word either from himself or from you or father, on the subject of his voyage and his arrival. May such a word speedily reach me. As for me, you see where I am. I have been at this place about a week, and as I find here perfect quiet and fresh sea-air (both equally favourable to work) I shall probably remain some days more—I wish to keep out of London for the rest of this month. In October I shall *perhaps* go for a week or two to Scotland; but I have no other plans. I last communicated with home by means of a letter to Aunt Kate, despatched from my friend Mrs. Carter's house, near Kenilworth, and which she probably will have passed on to you.—After that I spent a couple of days at Sir Trevor Lawrence's, in Surrey, and then came straight hither. Dover is not (save in a very moderate degree) a watering-place, and is therefore more agreeable to a truly refined mind than the other places along this coast which are. The British middle-class

305

mob which inundates them at this period depresses the soul—to say nothing of squeezing the body. I fled howling from Folkestone, to which I went before coming here—lost in wonder as to whether it was a harder fate to have no dinner at all, or to find a place at the *table d'hôte*. It is a beautiful season—there has been no rain since the 1st July (it did nothing but rain before) and hotter weather, this last fortnight, than I have yet seen in England. A fine English summer is certainly a very lovely thing—there is a mild mellowness about it which is infinitely comfortable. But it comes only once in five years, and then is only six weeks long.—I hope you are now at the end of your own perspirations, and that none of you are really the worse for them. I am very glad father has written to Mrs. Orr; it will give her real pleasure. She is a genuinely serious woman. I hope to see the letter. Much love to her and to the sister, whom I thank tenderly for the remedy. It is sweet to take the same doses as one's sister.

Ever, dearest Mammy, yr.

H. James Jr.

To Grace Norton

Ms Harvard

Reform Club,
Sept. 20*th* 1880

My dear Grace.

I am not without confidence that you will understand me when I say that I am glad you are sorry that I am not yet coming home! Your very pleasant letter of Aug. 27th contains expressions of pain from which I absolutely extract pleasure. It was not for this, however, that I determined not to come—for the pleasure of your welcome would have been even greater than that of your regret—as it will be still, in fact, some time next year.—I saw your nephew, and got him to come and dine with me, which was all he could do, as he was leaving for the Continent the next day. I was most happy to see him, as I should have been to help him in any way in my power; and he seemed to me a very pleasant and intelligent youth—making himself very agreeable. I admit however (since you mention it,) that he appeared to me rather old and *posé* for his years. But I take an interest in seeing all the young Americans I can; living as I do away from home, I wish to guard against the reproach—and indeed the real disadvantage—of not knowing what manner of generations are growing up there.—I infer from what you say that you will be getting back to Shady Hill about the present time, and I hope you will find a pleasant autumn awaiting you there. I have recollections of Cambridge Octobers (and even Novembers) which are really very tender, and agreeable. May you lay in a few such memories this year. I am back in London again after a certain amount of wandering and small visit-paying. Just now however I have been spending a fortnight at Dover—an odd place to choose for a seaside retreat, but by no means bad on experiment. I am in London for the present, "for good," or only for short absences—that Saturday-to-Monday "staying" which strikes one sometimes as one of the pleasantest features of English life and sometimes as one of the most detestable. About the New Year I hope to go for six months to Italy—but this is as yet indefinite.

I have seen no new figures or friends of late, and have been cultivating work and unsociability. I go in an hour to bid farewell to my friends the Henry Adamses, who after a year of London life are returning to their beloved Washington. One sees so many "cultivated Americans" who prefer living abroad that it is a great refreshment to encounter two specimens of this class who find the charms of their native land so much greater than those of Europe. In England they appear to have suffered more than enjoyed, and their experience is not unedifying, for they have seen and known a good deal of English life. But they are rather too critical and invidious. I shall miss them much, though—we have had such inveterate discussions and comparing of notes. They have been much liked here. Mrs. Adams, in comparison with the usual British female, is a perfect Voltaire in petticoats.—Thank you so much for telling me of the kind things George Curtis feels, thinks and says (above all) about me and my doings. It is a real pleasure to me to think that I may have given him pleasure. I understand quite what you mean about the absence of local colour in *Washington Square,* a slender tale, of rather too narrow an interest. I don't honestly, take much stock in it—the larger story coming out presently in *Macmillan* and the *Atlantic* will be a much more valuable affair.—I am very glad Howells was able to come to Ashfield: it must have been very pleasant to all concerned. His slowly and honestly-won success is something I can heartily congratulate him upon—though his last novel did not seem to me his best. He goes in for local colour but he doesn't always select the prettiest "shades."—Farewell, dear Grace, and God bless you. What I write you is always partly for Charles—and even for those of the children who will listen to it. Margaret does, perhaps.

Ever yours very faithfully

H. James Jr.

To Alice James
Ms Harvard

3, Bolton Street,

Oct. 13*th* [1880]

Dearest child.

The red socks are very lovely and most beautifully worked. They will add alike to my comfort and credit, and I will sport them, in very low shoes, at the next country house I go to stay at. I thank you tenderly, and rejoice that you have had ability for the sustained industry to which they testify. The hat also has just reappeared, and if you will only have patience I will undertake to make up handsomely for past disappointments. These last days have brought me nothing else from home save a short letter from William written from Cambridge on Sept. 30th. Please thank him for it and tell him I will very soon answer it. He speaks again of his apartment in Louisburg Square, but doesn't give me the address, which I should like to have, for writing to him directly. Please let it be sent me, together with Wilky's and Bob's, which I asked for in my last. I hope that William's quarters will prove comfortable and that his winter will bring him prosperity. I suppose you will see him and his wife and babe less than before—but the change of circumstances will make it more of an "excitement" to do so.—I have nothing to relate—the less so as I wrote to you a few days since at some length. I am sorry to say I am rather under the weather with the first sore-throat (on my part that is) of the winter: which was aggravated by my spending an hour yesterday in a very cold church, to see my friend Mrs. Carter married: a rather dreary occasion, with a weeping bride, a sepulchral clergyman, who buried rather than married her, and a total destitution of relatives or accomplices of her own, so that she had to be given away by her late husband's brother! I enclose you an effusion just received from Mlle Blaze de Bury—as a specimen of the style of a French *jeune personne.*

Ever yours
H. J. Jr.

P.S.—William tells me you have been lately in very good health —which makes me very happy. Persevere in this graceful behaviour.—I dined last night (not to the advantage of my cold) with William Hoppin,[1] who also had Lowell. The latter enjoys his life here and is a good deal made of—is invited to make addresses, figure at public dinners etc—Destroy Mlle Blaze's letter.

1. William Hoppin was Lowell's first secretary at the American legation in London. His unpublished journal of his residence in the British capital furnishes many glimpses of HJ's London life. See Edel, *The Conquest of London* (1963), the chapters entitled "The Two Secretaries" and "A Position in Society."

To Mrs. Henry James Sr.

Ms Harvard

3, Bolton Street,
Oct. 31st 1880

Dearest mother.

I have a letter of yours, of almost a fortnight since (of the date
of Oct. 5th) to acknowledge; but I have waited, partly because I
had been writing, before, with some frequency, and partly because
this is the quiet part of the year in one's London life, and little
has happened to me that is worth narrating. Your letter tells me
of Alice's conservatory (a delightful idea), of the further postponement of William's house, the news of my engagement to the
young lady in Bangor, etc. This last report I need scarcely tell
you, is a slight mistake.—I am not just now making any matrimonial arrangements, though I constantly hear that I have been
(somnambulistically, I am afraid) "very attentive" to numerous
spinsters and widows, and also that many of my well-wishers
think that I should be "so much happier" if I would only marry.
The last source I heard this opinion quoted from was my friend
Mrs. Brookfield, a delightful person who lost her husband many
years since. As she is however about sixty years of age and was
at one time, I believe, in peril of marrying Lord Houghton, I
suppose her remark was purely disinterested. I expect soon to hear
that I am engaged to Mrs. Procter, aet. eighty two. I have indeed
proposed to her several times, but she seems to think she can do
better. As poor old William Hoppin, the American Secretary of
Legation here, age sixty seven or so, was lately reported to be
about to espouse Mrs. Duncan Stewart who is eighty three or so,
you will see to what an advanced period people here are assumed
to keep up their interest in life.—You will also see, from these
wandering allusions, how little of interest I have to tell you. I am
very little just now in society, and have paid, this summer and
autumn, almost no country visits. Six months ago I was over-
whelmed with social entanglements and wishing for a period of
leisure ahead, took in sail in every direction as much as possible—

i.e. "neglected" people, didn't leave cards, edged away when I sent them, etc. My manoeuvre completely succeeded, as such manoeuvres almost must here, for you only circulate so long as you keep in view, and no one can flatter himself that he is of sufficient importance to be remembered if he doesn't wish to be. I have had a number of weeks of undisturbedness and shall be thankful for many more; but when (if ever) I wish to join the giddy throng again, I can easily do so by turning on the screw for a month or two. Though people here easily forget, they are easily reminded, and are always very glad to see you after an absence. One of the comforts of this society also is that you never have to give an account of yourself, to say where you have been or what you have been doing. No questions are asked, or if they are, the vaguest answers suffice. People never *appuyer,* and at bottom know very little about each other. Excuse this disquisition, which will not particularly interest you. The winter has fairly begun, though society has not—but it has begun in a fairly bright and wholesome way, and this Sunday morning, on the edge of November is as brilliant and pleasing as that which is probably shining into your windows in Cambridge.—Mrs. Kemble is back from the continent, and her return is to me always a valuable, social, moral and intellectual resource. She always talks as if she were going to die the next month, but fortunately her previsions are not realized, and every now and then she has explosions of vitality (I don't mean merely of temper) which ought completely to reassure her. I took her last night (or rather went with her, inasmuch as Hamilton Aïdé took her) to see *William and Susan* at the St. James' Theatre —a *fade* rehash of Douglas Jerrold's drama, and she wept with such ferocity during the last act that I was glad we were in the seclusion of a box. Her sobs resounded through the place!—Mrs. Duncan Stewart is in Paris, enjoying it much, in spite of not having been there for forty years. She wrote me some time since that if she didn't go there now, again, she was afraid she never might have the chance, and that her stay abroad would be a delightful memory to her for the rest of her life! She evidently means to live to one hundred and ten. These things make one feel (at thirty-seven!!) delightfully young and they ought to make you feel equally so, dearest mammy, even at your superior age! (I enclose an economical note of Mrs. Stewart's, for the amusement of Alice, who will destroy it.)—I have dined out lately but once or twice. The other day, with my poor friend Mrs. Rogerson, who has just taken a house about five feet square for the winter. A small London house is certainly the smallest thing in nature. Mrs. R. has many domestic troubles and every year that she has come to London I have seen her on a more modest footing and with a smaller establishment. This year she has a tiny dwelling between two shops, and her diningroom retinue is reduced to a maid and a little page—the last round of the ladder! But her hospitality remains always, in proportion, the same, and I am very sorry for her. Her husband is a fierce drunkard and muddles away the funds. Fortunately he doesn't show much, in London.—But a truce to this cockney gossip!—I hope these October days have been agreeable in Quincy Street. Is the greenhouse finished? It will be a graceful appendage to the premises and to Alice—or rather Alice will be a graceful feature in it. I have been delighted to hear that she is in more comfortable health this year, and trust this letter will not find her otherwise. I wrote to her the other day.—You say that William is reconsidering his plan of suppressing the parlour of his house—which I am glad to hear. He drew a diagram of the non-parlour for me, and speciously explained it—but I thought ill of it afterwards and meant to tell him so before he left. It would be as awkward for him *in the long run* not to have a regular parlour as it would be for him not to own a dress-coat or a high hat.—Your account of Howard James as a book agent was interesting, though it makes one smile to think of him as an apostle of culture.[1] But I should think his plausible personality would assist him greatly and I hope much he may succeed. I wonder if he could create a "popular demand" for the productions of his brother or his nephew?—I am very pleased that you have liked *Washington Square* and hope you will do so to the end. Macmillan is to bring it out shortly in two volumes, with a couple of smaller pieces (reprinted). It has been well-noticed here, but I have heard nothing of it from America, save an abusive review of the first number, in the *Tribune.* I sent you yesterday the *November* Macmillan—and if father sees any noteworthy notices of the beginning of a *Portrait of a Lady* he might send them to me. I can't say that American criticism (or indeed any other) of my things edify me much, but they usually amuse me. *Washington Square* in America, is to be published in a volume by Harper.—I heard from Aunt Kate a short time since. I suppose she has left you, but please thank her for her letter—she shall soon have one from me. I shall write next to father, who I hope is well. Has he got an answer from Mrs. Orr? I haven't seen her yet and think she is still abroad. Don't forget to give me the *three* addresses—William's, Wilky's, and Bob's.

H.J. Jr.

I sent Alice a little book—*Mrs. Grote*—the other day. Did it come?

1. Howard James (1828–1887) was the youngest son of William James of Albany, thus HJ's youngest uncle.

To Grace Norton

Ms Harvard

3, Bolton Street,
Nov. 7th [1880]

My dear Grace.

I feel as if your good note of the middle of September from Ashfield deserved a *serious* answer; but as I am afraid I can't give one serious enough, I will not make a point of pitching my response in that key. It continues to please me a good deal that it should have displeased you that I should not have come home "as intended." This result is largely forwarded by my glowing consciousness of the intention of repairing my omission next year: if it were not for this, indeed, I should really feel very sorry for (or rather, with) your sorrow. As it is, I simply let it gratify me *en attendant.*—Yes, it was half a dozen reasons—a vulgar promiscuous lot—and not one, exquisite and incomparable—that detained me. Would it have been, by the way, an "exquisite" reason that I

313

should have plighted my troth to a daughter of these islands? On the whole, doubtless, yes; though one must twist one's intellectual neck a little to see it in that way. It may interest you (as it has amused me) to learn that there is a generally felt (or expressed) desire in the circles in which I move, that I should take the graceful step to which you still more gracefully alluded. But in that matter, dear Grace, I shall always be awkward. No man can answer for the future; but I have impinged far enough on my own to speak of it with a certain familiarity, and in its atmosphere of morning twilight I don't discern the particular figure which you seem to have *entrevue*. Describe it a little to me, and I shall be surer; but meanwhile, to my ear, a great silence reigns ahead. Not a gloomy one, however; for I am resigned in advance. I am unlikely ever to marry. If I were to tell you the grounds of this conviction you would think me dismally theoretic. One's attitude toward marriage is a part—the most characteristic part, doubtless—of one's general attitude toward life. Now I don't want to calumniate my attitude toward life; but I am bound to say that if I were to marry I should be guilty in my own eyes of an inconsistency—I should pretend to think just a little better of life than I really do. You will say that if one marries (properly) one's opinion of life greatly improves—and one ought to give it that chance. To give it that chance is not, I think, an obligation of justice—the *risk* takes it out of that category; but it is a very becoming act of generosity. That indeed is certain; but I am not moved to that way, because I think my opinion of life on the whole good enough. I am attached to it, I am used to it—it doesn't in any way paralyse or incapacitate me (on the contrary), and it doesn't involve any particular injustice to any one, least of all to myself. Then there are other impressions. An amiable bachelor here and there doesn't strike me as at all amiss, and I think he too may forward the cause of civilization. All this is part of the reason why I am not going to marry *next month*. It may not however, carry me beyond that!— After all, I *have* been serious—even in implying just above that I am "amiable"!—I am still serious, dear Grace, when I say that I thank you truly for your appreciation of the little fiction I have been sending you in the *Cornhill*. It had a very definite artistic intention; but most readers miss that (at all times) and I am happy that you should have found it. I am also touched by what you say about my "English accent"—though not touched in so good a place. I know up to a certain point what you mean by my having lost my sense of the truth of things at home—but I don't believe I know as much as you mean it. I *am* more attuned to English life now—that catastrophe has come to pass! But as regards the little story, I have been surprised that other readers (American) besides yourself, should have found it so false in the matter of "local colour" as they have appeared to do. Its weakness in this respect is, I should have said, negative; local colour is not made a point of—is left out. I don't think it has been violated as much as has two or three times been intimated to me.—I have begun a long novel in Macmillan (better than *Washington Square*) which you will see in the *Atlantic,* and which I don't send to you in the English pages because it is rather on my honour that I should not (out of respect to the *Atlantic*) introduce *Macmillan* into the United States—I haven't a grain of personal news. London is waking up again, a little, for the winter, but there is little doing as yet, and I don't dine out yet awhile—for which I am glad. I have had a quiet but profitable summer, and read a good deal. If you desire a book both solid and brilliant, try George Trevelyan's *Fox*.[1] Apropos of such books, please tell Charles I am to write to him in a day or two to thank him for his own beautiful volume which I have waited to do, only to read it.[2] I am just terminating this pleasure, and he shall hear from me. I hope to spend one of these coming Sundays at Basset where I shall see the youthful Lily and "pump" her about you all. Lowell is in Scotland, staying at the Duke of Argyll's, lecturing in Edinburgh etc. He is much better, steadily.

Yours ever

H. James Jr.

1. *The Early History of Charles James Fox* (1880).
2. C. E. Norton, *Historical Studies of Church Building in the Middle Ages: Venice, Siena, Florence* (1880).

To William James

Ms Harvard

Reform Club,
Nov. 27*th* [1880]

Dear William.

I sent you last p.m. the two volumes of Rosmini,[1] done up separately and registered; and I hope they will arrive safely. Don't talk of refunding.—A few days before, I had received a very welcome letter from you, in Alice's hand; and should have addressed this answer to her if I had not begun merely with the intention of notifying you about the book. As it is, I can now hardly do more. This is a Saturday afternoon, and I go very presently down to spend Sunday at Lord Rosebery's—so I have only a moment. (If the party at Mentmore proves interesting I will write of it to Quincy Street, whence I received, the same day as yours a dear letter from mother.) It gives me great pleasure to hear that your work this year leaves you leisure for reading and study, which must be a great satisfaction. It is the position I desire more and more to arrive at—which I am happy to say I tend to do. Thank you for what you say about my two novels. The young man in *Washington Square* is not a portrait—he is sketched from the outside merely and not *fouillé*. The only good thing in the story is the girl. The other book increases, I think, in merit and interest as it goes on, and being told in a more spacious, expansive way than its predecessors, is inevitably more human, more sociable. It was the constant effort at *condensation* (which you used always to drum into my head—*àpropos* of Mérimée etc—when I was young and you bullied me) that has deprived my former things of these qualities. I shall read what G. Allen and Fiske reply to you in the *Atlantic,* but shall be sure not to enter into what they say as I did into your article, which I greatly appreciated.[2]—I spent last Sunday at William Darwin's, very pleasantly, owing to beautiful cold, crisp weather and to Sara seeming very well and happy. I am very sorry your lodgings smell of soup, especially as I have lately wholly abjured it by the advice of Dr. Andrew Clark, whom I had to consult for matutinal nausea, which has vanished by the suppression of the pottage. Tell them in Quincy Street that I will speedily respond to Mother's letter. Say to Alice (sister) that I send her a new hat a week or two hence by Mrs. Mason, who has kindly offered (taking a great interest in the episode) to carry it. It came home this a.m. and is much superior to the other. Love to your own Alice and baby. I will send them some benefits the first chance I get.

Tout à toi.

H. James Jr.

1. Antonio Rosmini-Serbati (1797–1855), Italian philosopher. HJ may have sent Rosmini's basic work, *Sistema Filosofico.*

2. WJ's article in the October 1880 *Atlantic* was "Great Men and Their Environment," in which he challenged the determinism of a Spencerian disciple, Grant Allen.

To Mrs. Henry James Sr.

Ms Harvard

Mentmore,
Leighton Buzzard
Nov. 28*th* [1880]

Dearest mammy.

I received a good letter from you a few days ago, and as I have more leisure at this moment than I may have for some days to come, I will address you a few affectionate lines. (I have forgotten the date of your letter; but it was the one which enclosed that touching communication from poor Bob describing his health etc.) I wrote yesterday, briefly, to William, and he will, I suppose, give you the benefit, such as it is, of my note. This is a pleasant Sunday, and I have been spending it (from yesterday evening) in a very pleasant place. "Pleasant" is indeed rather an odd term to apply to this gorgeous residence, and the manner of life which prevails in it; but it is that as well as other things beside. Lady Rosebery (it is her enviable dwelling) asked me down here a week ago, and I stop till tomorrow a.m. There are several people here, but no one very important, save John Bright[1] and Lord Northbrook, the last Liberal Viceroy of India. Millais the painter has been here for a part of the day, and I took a walk with him this afternoon back from the stables, where we had been to see three winners of the Derby[2] trotted out in succession. This will give you an idea of the scale of Mentmore, where everything is magnificent. The house is a huge modern palace, filled with wonderful objects accumulated by the late Sir Meyer de Rothschild, Lady R.'s father. All of them are precious and many are exquisite, and their general Rothschildish splendour is only equalled by their profusion. Lady R. is large, fat, ugly, good-natured, sensible and kind; and Lord R. remarkably charming—"so *simpatico* and swell*," as the young lady in Florence said: that is, *simpatico* as well as swell.

I have spent a good part of the time in listening to the conversation of John Bright, whom, though I constantly see him at the Reform Club, I had never met before. He has the repute of being often "grumpy"; but on this occasion he has been in extremely good form and has discoursed uninterruptedly and pleasantly. He gives one an impression of sturdy, honest, vigorous, English middle-class liberalism, accompanied by a certain infusion of genius, which helps one to understand how his name has become the great rallying-point of that sentiment. He reminds me a good deal of a superior New Englander—with a fatter, damper nature, however, than theirs. There are no ladies save a little Mrs. Godley, the *effacée* wife of a wonderful universal-information and high-sense-of-duty private Secretary of Gladstone, with whom (Godley himself) I also walked this afternoon; and a graceful Lady Emma Baring, daughter of Lord Northbrook, whose prettiness, as is so often the misfortune of the British damsel, is impaired by protruding teeth. They are at afternoon tea downstairs in a vast, gorgeous hall, where an upper gallery looks down like the colonnade in Paul Veronese's pictures, and the chairs are all golden thrones, belonging to ancient Doges of Venice. I have retired from the glittering scene to meditate by my bedroom fire on the fleeting character of earthly possessions, and to commune with my mammy, until a supreme being in the shape of a dumb footman arrives, to ventilate my shirt and turn my stockings inside out (the beautiful red ones imparted by Alice—which he must admire so much, though he doesn't venture to show it), preparatory to my dressing for dinner. Tomorrow I return to London and to my personal occupation, always doubly valued after forty eight hours passed among *ces gens-ci,* whose chief effect upon me is to sharpen my desire to distinguish myself by personal achievement, of however limited a character. It is the only answer one can make to their atrocious good fortune. Lord Rosebery, however, with youth, cleverness, a delightful face, a happy character, a Rothschild wife of numberless millions to distinguish and to demoralize him, wears them with such tact and bonhomie, that you almost forgive him.[3] He is extremely nice with Bright, draws him out, defers to him etc., with a delicacy rare in an Englishman. But, after all, there is much to say—more than can be said in a letter—about one's relations with these people. You may be interested, by the way, to know that Lord R. said this morning at lunch that his ideal of the happy life was that of Cambridge, Mass., "living like Longfellow." You may imagine that at this the company looked awfully vague, and I thought of proposing to him to exchange Mentmore for 20 Quincy Street.—I have little other personal news than this, which I have given you in some detail, for entertainment's sake. I am very glad you sent me Bob's letter, which gives me a sense, most affecting, both of his trials and his advantages—I mean his good spirit, the esteem in which the railway people hold him, and his capacity for work. I hope the latter will soon return to him, but that, also, he may not again have to tax it so hard. I wish he had a little more of the Rothschild[4] element in his existence, and that I could do something to help him. Perhaps some day I may. —I spent last Sunday (from Saturday to Monday) at Sara Darwin's, whom I found apparently very well and bright—as lovable and natural as ever. I also beheld little Lily Norton and her grotesque resemblance to Charles. She seems to flourish, in a rather colourless way, under an amiable and talkative French governess. While

I think of it, *àpropos* of nothing, *please send me a good photograph of Garfield*—I want to see his face. I hope the house is quiet and happy. I wrote a short note to father the other day, and will soon send him a longer one. (My note enclosed some cheques, and I hope came safely.)—I trust Alice's oral regimen is still a resource. I am sending her presently another hat, which I will write her more about, when I know the exact day it leaves, so that she may get it from Mrs. Mason, who takes it. I embrace you dearest mother, and also your two companions.

Ever your fondest
H. James Jr.

1. John Bright (1811–1889), son of a miller, was a leading opponent of the Corn Laws. He served in various posts in Gladstone governments from 1868 onward.

2. Between 1875 and 1928 Lord Rosebery's horses "won every great race with the exception of the Ascot Gold Cup." See Robert James, *Rosebery* (1963).

3. Archibald Philip Primrose, fifth earl of Rosebery (1847–1929), was to be foreign secretary and, in 1894–95, Prime Minister.

4. HJ wrote "Mentmorish" but crossed it out and substituted "Rothschild."

To William Dean Howells

Ms Harvard

3, Bolton Street,
Dec. 5*th* [1880]

Dear Howells.

I didn't mean to put the screw on you to the extent of *two* volumes of native fiction,[1] and am much obliged to you for your generosity. I shall not attempt to read the books just now, but keep them for the larger leisure of a journey abroad, later in the winter. Dizzy's *Endymion*,[2] which is the actuality of the hour here, has almost fatally disgusted me with the literary form to which it pretends to belong. Can the novel be a thing of virtue, when such a contemptibly bad novel as that is capable of being written —and read? Perhaps, however, Aldrich and the *Grandissimes* will reconcile me to this branch of art. I asked you about the latter because I had observed one or two notices of him which seemed to indicate (in superlative terms) that the Great American Novel had at last arrived; but from the moment that public opinion had not forced him on your own perusal, I was willing to give the G.A.N. another chance.—Your strictures on my own story seem to me well-founded (don't say that I don't take criticism like an angel). The girl is over-analysed, and her journalistic friend *seems* (whether she is or not) overdrawn.[3] But in defense of the former fault I will say that I intended to make a young woman about whom there should be a great deal to tell and as to whom such telling should be interesting; and also that I think she is analysed once for all in the early part of the book and doesn't turn herself inside out quite so much afterwards. (So at least it seems to me— perhaps you will not agree with me.) Miss Stackpole is not I think really exaggerated—but 99 readers out of a 100 will think her so: which amounts to the same thing. She is the result of an impression made upon me by a variety of encounters and ac- quaintances made during the last few years; an impression which I had often said to myself could not be exaggerated. But one must have received the impression and the home-staying American doubt- less does not do so as strongly as the expatriated; it is over here that it offers itself in its utmost relief.—That you think well of Lord Warburton makes me regret more than I already do that he is after all but a secondary figure. I have made rather too much of his radicalism in the beginning—there is no particular use for it later.—I must have been strangely vague as to *all* the conditions of my story when I first corresponded with you about it, and I am glad to have wrung from you the confession that you expected it to be in six numbers, for this will teach me to be more explicit in future. I certainly supposed I had been so in this case—the great feature of my projected tale being that it was to be long—longer than its predecessors. Six months, for a regular novel, is a very small allowance—I mean for dealing with a long period of time and introducing a number of figures. You make your own stories fit into it, but it is only by contracting the duration of the action to a few weeks. Has not this been the case in all of them? Write one that covers a longer stretch of months or years, and I think you will see that it will immediately take more of the magazine. I believed that in this case you positively desired something voluminous and I believed equally that I had announced my voluminosity well in advance. I am afraid that it will be a characteristic of my future productions (in, I hope, a reasonable measure), but I will be careful to put the points on my i's.—I complain of you that you will never write to me save of the weather—as if you had just been introduced to me at an evening party! That is very well: especially as you describe it beautifully—but I would rather you told me what you are doing, writing, enjoying, suffering, hearing, seeing. About all these things you are very mysterious. Your description of the impudent Cambridge winter, however, is vivid —with the earth like a stone and the sky like a feather. Here the earth is like a Persian rug—a hearth-rug, well besprinkled with soot.—I hear every now and then that you are soon coming abroad; but I sincerely hope you won't have the perversity to take just the time when I am coming home, as I hope (this time seriously) to do next year. Your wife, I am sure, would not do this. Tell her I believe it, and remain

faithfully yours
H. James Jr.

1. Probably Thomas Baily Aldrich's *The Stillwater Tragedy* and G. W. Cable's *The Grandissimes: A Story of Creole Life,* both published during this year.
2. Disraeli's last novel.
3. The characters of Isabel Archer and Henrietta Stackpole in *The Portrait of a Lady.*

To Grace Norton

Ms Harvard

Kerris Vean, Falmouth.
Dec. 28*th* 1880

My dear Grace.

Christmas day is over, but your valuable letter (of the 14th) revives the festive feeling. I thank you tenderly for it and send you in return all greetings for the dawning year. Just hereabouts it is dawning in darkness and storm—both in the physical and the political world. I am in the middle of Cornwall—the rainiest county in England, and am just now listening to the music of an Atlantic gale and the "swash" of deluged window-panes. I am afraid I shall extract but little sympathy from you when I tell you that I am staying (since last evening) with our friends the John Clarks—the "old black cat" and her appreciative spouse. They live habitually in Scotland, but they have taken a house this winter on this Southern Shore, for the benefit of Lady C's health, and she is getting mild mugginess to her heart's content. The climate here is of the softest and the vegetation almost that of the Riviera; as I am fond of warm moisture I should also relish it—save on the days when it pours from sunrise to sunrise, which are six out of the seven. I have been spending Christmas with some military friends at Plymouth,[1] which is a big garrison town, just on the Cornish border; and on terminating my visit there, I came over here for three days, foreseeing the extreme in-doors tranquillity which I in effect find. But I also find much kindness, much talk, much food, much fire, much general amenity and appreciation. You will believe this last when I tell you that we were (Sir John and I) in the very act (at breakfast) of discoursing of you—in what glowing terms you may fancy—when your letter came in. Poor Sir John appears to retain the most ineffaceable, and really devoted, memory of Jane. Your essay on matrimony is charming and ought to be published somewhere—in the *Fortnightly* or the *Cornhill*. My single individuality is quite unworthy of it. Still, I shall not make it public; I shall make it private. That is I shall take it to my heart and assent to everything it contains. But I shall not marry, all the same. I am happy enough as it is, and am convinced that if I should go further, I should fare worse. I am too good a bachelor to spoil. That sounds conceited—but one may be conceited, in self-defense, about a position with which the rest of the world associates a certain idea of the ridiculous.—I am glad you are reading my long story—though that is not the way to read it. My theory is (it may be my conceit again) that it will bear reading again as a whole. It is much the best thing I have done—though not the best I shall do. You are both right and wrong about Minny Temple. I had her in mind and there is in the heroine a considerable infusion of my impression of her remarkable nature. But the thing is not a portrait. Poor Minny was essentially *incomplete* and I have attempted to make my young woman more rounded, more finished. In truth everyone, in life, is incomplete, and it is [in] the work of art that in reproducing them one feels the desire to fill them out, to justify them, as it were. I am delighted if I interest you; I think I shall to the end.—Thank my dear Margaret for her lovely Christmas card. I sent her three or four some ten days ago, but after I had despatched them remembered (I sent them from the shop) that I haven't written on one of them a word of greeting. Tell her I greet her now, most gratefully and affectionately. It is very touching to me to be so constantly remembered in the season of inconstancy—I mean the season of quick living, quick-growing youth.—I passed a beautiful Christmas day at Plymouth; a large part of it in walking through the the grounds of Mount Edgecumbe, which overhang Plymouth Sound and are almost hatefully beautiful. I am very sorry your stay at New York was cut short—but if you lost nothing better than Sarah Bernhardt, you may console yourself; as I regard her as the great humbug of the age. I hope the measles haven't sprouted again and I send my blessing both to those who have escaped and those who have suffered. I wrote lately to Charles, and I send him my love.

Ever yours
H. James Jr.

1. HJ was the guest of General Pakenham, commanding officer in the Government House at Devonport, at his official residence on the edge of Plymouth Sound. The General, a nephew by marriage of the Duke of Wellington, was married to "a former American belle" now "intensely Anglicized."

4
Homecomings

1881-1883

4

Homecomings

In the months preceding his return to America, Henry James worked and journeyed—worked with great steadiness and craft at the novel he felt would be the cornerstone of his fame. The writing of *The Portrait of a Lady* is told in the previous and ensuing letters: he would have returned earlier to his family, but felt he wanted to be completely free of this task; moreover, he told himself it would be an advantage for him to have the novel come out in book form while he was on the scene in his homeland. It was still running its course in the magazines—in England in *Macmillan's* and in America in the *Atlantic*. During its serialization it yielded him a large income—$500 a month. It gave him financial security and a feeling of great freedom. This animates his letters as he travels about the Continent, spending many weeks in Venice—one of the large experiences of his life—and taking the fullest "possession" (as he liked to say) of that unique water-city. In the hot season he went north, first to Lake Como and then to Switzerland where he did some climbing as in his youth. In the Engelberg he visited Mrs. Kemble; then he returned to London to meet his sister Alice, who had come abroad with her friend Katharine Loring. James paid a series of country visits that summer—the Russell Sturgises at Leatherhead, Lord Rosebery at Mentmore, his publisher Frederick Macmillan at Walton-on-Thames; and he inspected certain beautiful old houses in Somerset. As he journeyed, he wrote, and when *The Portrait of a Lady* neared its end, he went to Scotland, to Tillypronie, Cortachy, Dalmeny, Laidlawstiel. In October he embarked for Quebec and, after a swift journey, found himself again in Quincy Street. He had been away six years.

Once home, he wrote few letters, and the rest of the story of his homecoming may be read in his long diary-notes, in his *Notebooks* recorded during his stay in America. His decision to return proved wise. He was able to see his mother during the last weeks of her life; she died quite suddenly while he was in Washington, and her death colored his entire stay during the first part of 1882. In the diary-notes we have not only his feelings about America—the way in which it had shrunk to his Europeanized eyes—but his mourning and melancholy after his mother's death, and his affirmation that he had made a wise choice of domicile. Europe was his physical home, however much he might remain a spiritual American. He had long ago reconciled these two sides of his temperament. "I am thirty seven years old" he wrote on 25 November 1881 (he was actually thirty eight). "I have made my choice, and God knows that I have now no time to waste. My choice is the old world—my choice, my need, my life." This problem, he tells himself, "was settled long ago," and his letters to his London friends, to Fanny Kemble or Lord Rosebery and even to mere acquaintances, show how homesick he was for the way of life that had become his own in the British capital.

He returned to England in mid-1882 and made his "little tour" of France during that summer. He had settled in for the winter in Bolton Street when word came that his father was dying. The letters tell the story of this final break with his homeland—his winter journey, his life in Mount Vernon Street with his sister, his quarrel with William James (if one can use so violent a word for their verbal sparring) at this time. He was the second son, but the father had made him executor of his will. He took this task seriously. Then he went abroad again—not to return for two decades. It is fitting that this stage of his life, embodied in these letters, should end with an extraordinary letter to his Cambridge friend Grace Norton—the letter which embodies his philosophy of "living through," his message to all who despair and who would want to put an end to existence, his assertion of the life-giving principle that guided him through his own periods of anguish and loneliness. He writes:

I don't know why we live—the gift of life comes to us from I don't know what source or for what purpose: but I believe we can go on living for the reason that (always of course up to a certain point) life is the mostly valuable thing we know anything about and it is therefore pre-sumptively a great mistake to surrender it while there is any yet left in the cup.

He goes on to equate consciousness with life, as he always did, and proclaims the stoicism of his own nature. It is a noble letter— one of the noblest he ever wrote. But it was time to return abroad. "Home" no longer existed for him in Cambridge. He set out anew for the Old World. He had long ago "appropriated" it; he was now in full possession of it. His fame assured, *The Portrait of a Lady* recognized as a remarkable work—in time it would attain the stature of a "classic"—he planned to resume his life in Bolton Street almost as if he were starting a new career.

To Mrs. Henry James Sr.

Ms Harvard

The Durdans, Epsom.
Sunday Jan. 10*th* [1881]

Dearest mammy.

I have written home since I heard last, but I will not stand upon ceremony; especially as it is now some fortnight since my letter was despatched (to father, from Government House, Devonport). That letter, I suppose, was safely received, and when I return tomorrow to town I suppose I shall find some missive from home; at least I hope I shall. I finished successfully my little Christmas visit in Cornwall—spending some five days (after leaving the Pakenhams') at Falmouth with my good friends the John Clarks, who have taken a house (a very charming one) in that mild moist climate for the Winter. Sir John drove me (a matter of two days) to Penzance and the Land's End—and the weather was soft enough to make an open vehicle perfectly comfortable. Cornwall has a charming old-world, far-away-from-London quality, and the sea, about the strange, lonely, grassy, rocky Land's End, only asked a little more sun to be of an Italian blue. The Clarks were according to their wont, most kindly, talkative and harmlessly fussy, and the episode was agreeable, including a pleasant visit to two very pleasant Miss Sterlings daughters of John Sterling,[1] clever, individual maiden sisters of a certain age, who have a charming house and gardens on a bosky crag overhanging the sea, some three miles from Falmouth. I had a week in London on my return and then came, yesterday afternoon, down to this place, to remain till tomorrow Monday. By "this place" I mean one of the several residences of the fortunate Roseberys—a small, so-called bachelor house, of a sporting character, close to Epsom Downs, where the Derby is run—over which delightful grassy, breezy expanse I have just been walking for an hour—in company with Lord R. and George Augustus Sala![2] The latter gentleman, with G. W. Smalley, forms the rest of the company—the house being "quiet," owing to the condition of Lady R., who was confined (disappointingly, of a girl!) only a week ago. This is a delightful house, full of books, of entertaining old sporting pictures (to say nothing of several charming Gainsboroughs and Watteaus), and worth to my mind, a hundred times over all the grandeurs of Mentmore. Lady R. is not missed, her husband's company is better (he is extremely pleasant, intelligent and friendly); Smalley is, as usual, replete with good talk and inexhaustable information about all current London topics (of which—topics—one sometimes gets very tired), and Sala, whom I never knew before, is ripe, red-nosed, genial, easy, jolly and full of reminiscence; a Bohemian on his good behaviour.—I return to town, tomorrow, as I say; and as soon after that as I can I shall try and leave London for foreign parts, where I shall remain till the summer. I wish to escape from both the pleasures and the pains of this too-complicated land and find leisure to think, to work, to read. I shall keep this till I get back to Bolton Street to see whether there is not a line from you there. I am writing in the billiard room, a most delightful apartment, and Smalley and Sala are talking. I was obliged to stop on Sunday (the conversation just mentioned was so interesting) and I brought my letter away in my pocket. This morning (Tuesday, 11th) I find yours of the 27th, telling me of various matters, but especially of William's having given up the idea of building upon father's land. I am very glad of this—both because it certainly seems better that he shouldn't put all his eggs into one basket (I mean all his money into one edifice,) and second because in that position there would have been I should think, rather too much of Siamese-twin-ship. One wishes to be morally united to one's family; but after a certain age, one doesn't wish to be materially united—at least, too closely. If I were he, I would hire a neat house, at Cambridge at a sufficient distance from Quincy Street to make of the two dwellings two distinct and unamalgamated homes.—I finished my visit at the Durdans yesterday morning, and came up to town with Rosebery, who is a very delightful creature. He reminds me a good deal of Wilky—a successful and glorified Wilky: if W. had been to Eton and Oxford, had inherited an Earldom and a great fortune, and then had married a Rothschild, with a greater fortune still. Before breakfast, yesterday, having played awhile with the large, fat, dimpled daughter (I mean first born daughter) of the house (Lady Sibyl Primrose, aged a year and a half), I walked again over the Epsom course, which was in an entertaining condition, owing to the presence of large numbers of race-horses from the training-stables in which that neighborhood abounds, who were being exercised by grooms and diminutive jockeys: some of them being the property of Lord R. who is a great patron of the Turf.—He asked me to go with him in the afternoon to the House of Lords to hear Lord Lytton defend his late viceroyship in India (against the Duke of Argyll); but I was obliged to decline, having many other things to do that must be done before I get away from London. I hope to do this by the middle of next week. After that it will probably be the last of London (socially speaking) for me, for a good while to come; as I shall (if nothing prevents) remain away till after the Season is over; and then after spending a few weeks in Eng-land in the summer, embark in the early autumn (still if nothing prevents) for the United States. I have had a great deal of it, and laid up a great fund of impressions: but, socially, I am tired of it and want to leave it for a year. My ideal, after that, will be to come back here and make a permanent *pied-à-terre* of it—but spend in it only six months of the year.—I enclose you a note I have just received from Miss Cross, the eldest (and least *douée*) of the sisters—in answer to one I had written about George Eliot's death. This event is really very sad: she, poor woman, had begun a new (personal) life: a more healthy, objective one than she had ever known before. I doubt whether she would have written, but she would have lived—and after all, at sixty, and with a great desire to live, she was still young. Please burn Miss C.'s letter.—I read between your ingenious lines that Alice's hat is better to look at than to wear and hope she won't *gêner* herself to say so. I embrace both her and the Daddy. Also you, dear Mammy.

Ever your loving
H. James Jr.

1. John Sterling, best remembered as a central figure in a literary group called after him the "Sterling Club," which included Carlyle, Tennyson, Mill, Lord Houghton, and others. HJ's father had met Sterling during his journey abroad in 1843.
2. The journalist and traveler.

To Thomas Sergeant Perry

Ms Colby

Reform Club
Pall Mall S. W.
Jan 24*th* 1881

Dear Tommy.

Thanks for your good letter, which was the more welcome as it was long since I had heard from you. I thought you would be interested in Zola's article[1]—though he appears to interest you less than with all his views—his vanity, stupidity, fetidity etc., he does me.—I don't know what I have to tell you in particular. There are only two subjects of conversation here—Ireland and the weather; and you have these for yourself at home. The Irish muddle is desperate, and the weather is the coldest known for fifty years: the snow mountains-high in the streets, the thermometer proportionately low, the temperature ferocious. If I had nothing else

Thomas Sergeant Perry

to do I think I should run over to Ireland: which may seem strange to you on the part of one satiated in youth with the Celtic genius. The reason is that I should like to see a country in a state of revolution. I think I am more sorry on the whole for the English than the Irish. The latter have entirely departed from the turpitude of their ancestors and want only to do justice and consent to reforms; while it would be vain to pretend that the latter are not a totally impractical people. This government can neither satisfy them, shut them up, nor part with them; the problem seems insoluble.—If we are cold, you of course are colder. But you are also lighter, brighter, fresher; and you haven't stale black fogs commingled with your frost. But we are not on such terms that we need talk about the weather. I take much pleasure in what you tell me about the welcome that will be extended to me in the U.S.A. on my return. I take much pleasure too in the idea of that return, though I feel that I must be prepared for the worst. If the people who write in the newspapers form themselves into a committee to wait upon me, I fear there will be little left of my flaccid form. My good relatives occasionally forward me specimens of such vulgar idiocy that I long for the Day of Judgement.—What you tell me of Howells's isolation on his hill-top is quite what I supposed of his situation—which I regret much, for it seems to me that it would be of especial use to him to see more of men and women—especially the former. In this case he wouldn't make 'em so queer in his books. I am glad you repudiate that unwholesome young Brown, who came to me with a note of introduction and whom I thought a base little creature, and a specimen of a debilitated people. He represented himself as your most intimate friend —which rather depressed me; though I didn't believe it. I haven't read the two Russian books you speak of—but mean to read Gogol's one of these days. It is one of my few complaints of London that it is a bad place to read in—one has opportunities to do so many other things. But I have read the book of London—i.e. as Dr. Johnson would say, the book of Life, and I have got a good deal of information out of that. I should like to shut myself up in a good library for a year; and as soon as I can afford to stop writing long enough, shall do so. Thank you much for "chuckling" over my long story—which, when it is finished, will be the best thing I have done, in spite of an impudent lack of incident—or of what is commonly understood to be such. In spite of this, I believe the interest goes *crescendo* to the end. My aim is to hold it to the last page; and the story contains the best writing of which I have hitherto been capable. But I mean to surpass it, *de beaucoup*. I mean also to "quit" for awhile paying so much attention to the young unmarried American female—to stop, that is, making her the central figure: which is of necessity a limitation. I saw Lowell yesterday, who was, as always, very pleasant, and enjoys England, in spite of his antagonistic Yankeeism and the prolonged and depressing invalidism of his wife. I hope that yours has quite ceased to suffer in that way. Give her my love and to your gentle offspring.

Ever yours
H. James Jr.

1. On *Le Roman experimental*. Perry's article on "Zola's Essays" appeared in the *Atlantic Monthly*, XLVII (January 1881), 116–118.

To Alice James

Ms Harvard

3 Bolton St. W.
Jan. 30*th* 1881

My dear Alice—

It seems to me a long time since I have written home,—though I forget when my last letter departed. I suppose however this is a proof that it was a good while ago. Meantime I have got one from you (of Jan. 4th.) enclosing a portrait of Garfield, and accompanied by a brief postscript from Father. I am grateful for the photograph of the president-elect—the more so that I like his face, which though, I ˙think, peculiarly "self-made," is a good type of the self-made, and pleasant and manly in expression; much more potent than poor Hayes's. It now decorates my mantel-shelf side by side with an image of Helen Post in the costume of Rebekah at the Well, just sent me from Dresden. Your letter acknowledges the hat—though I note that it dilates more upon the beauty of the stuff than that of the fit. Nevertheless I hope you have been able to wear it, before or behind, beside, or below—or somehow or other. When I come back I expect you to be clad in it on our first meeting—and it must not look too fresh!—Your letter gives little other news—save that you didn't see Sarah Bernhardt (no great loss, I think), and that William Robeson has married a French adventuress. The latter strikes me as a flat performance and I trust that his connection with the family (in the matter of plantations etc.) doesn't bring the lady into our circle.—There have been only two subjects here—Ireland and the weather. The latter is now thawing hard (or rather, soft), but for ten days it was unprecedented in British annals, and for aught I know may begin again. The snow was mountains high, the cold ferocious, and London life impossible. It put a stop to everything—milk, butter, coals, cabs, water, gas, dinners; the only thing it stimulated was conversation. As I say, however, it is mild again; and now we are as stupid as usual. On one of the worst nights I managed to go in a hansom-tandem, to dine at Lord Airlie's—where I found that only a small circle of the nobility—the Dalhousies, Blandfords, Frederick Leveson-Gower etc. had been able to arrive. If it had lasted, I should have started a brougham by the week, as cheaper much, than tandem cabs. I have lately dined out very little, owing to my having given out three weeks ago that I was just starting abroad; in consequence of which I am supposed to have done so, and have been left quiet—to my great convenience The last two dinners I have eaten were at Lady Selina Hervey's (I think I told you she had taken a third husband—she being also his third wife); and at Mrs. Stanley Clarke's (Mary Rose). The latter is a singularly pleasant woman and very friendly: the dinner in question was apparently "for" H.J. Jr.—to enable him to meet Mrs. C's particular friend Mrs. Perugini (Kate Dickens), who, however didn't turn up. Putting aside the queer Rose-Sloane-Stanley-Prince of Wales-Stanley Clarke muddle, Mrs. S. C. leaves nothing to be desired. She is delightfully good-looking, and has, among other advantages, the finest "form" in London. It is true, as I have already written you, that I am going abroad, but not for another week. I shall, to begin with, spend three weeks in Paris, and from there will write you of my further intentions. Thank you for your little criticism on the "Portrait." Yes, it appears unnatural, certainly, that Isabel should fraternize with Henrietta, but it wouldn't if I explained it. I have been afraid to do this, because there are so many explanations in the story, which, I think, is rather overburdened with them. Perhaps you think I shouldn't be able to explain it—but I believe I could. The biggest laudation I have got of the tale here has been from Lowell, whom I send it to every month, and he comes down handsomely about it. A lady told me lately that Hutton (of the *Spectator*) told her that he (H.) "devoured" it; then, at a second sitting he *read* it! This I consider very high honour.—I paid John Cross a longish visit some little time since and sat in his poor wife's empty chair, in the beautiful little study they had just made perfect, while he told me, very frankly, many interesting things about her. She was surely an extraordinary woman—her intellectual force and activity have, I suspect, never been equalled in any woman. If, with these powers, she had only been able to see and know more of life, she would have done greater things. As for the head itself, it was evidently of the first order—capable of almost *any* responsibilities. She led a wonderfully *large* intellectual life—and Cross said that her memory and her absolute exemption from the sense of fatigue, were more amazing the more he knew her. He, poor fellow, is left very much lamenting; but my private impression is that if she had not died, she would have killed him. He couldn't keep up the intellectual pace—all Dante and Goethe, Cervantes and the Greek tragedians. As he said himself, it was a cart-horse yoked to a racer: several hours a day spent in reading aloud the most immortal works. Browning has a theory that she "went back on" Lewes after his death: i.e. made discoveries among his papers which caused her to wish to sink him in oblivion. But this, I think, is Browningish and fabulous.—Farewell, dear child. I enclose a P.S. to father.

Ever yours
H. James Jr.

To Mrs. Henry James Sr.

Ms Harvard

Reform Club,
Feb. 7*th* [1881]

Dearest mother.

I received from you three days since a letter of which I have forgotten the date, and which lies at home on my table. It was the one which enclosed a characteristic effusion (apropos of Christmas) from Wilky, and gave me the good news that Alice had for some time been in *belle-santé!* This latter information gives me the liveliest pleasure, as I beg you to let her know. It would be a graceful use of her exuberant health to write occasionally to her exiled brother, and I shall expect a weekly letter from her. The rest of your news was good—that is, it wasn't bad. I agree with you that it would be pleasant to see William living in a house of his own: there must be a certain want of majesty in his present *installation.* —You see I am still in London; I find it as difficult as usual to get away.—One cause has conspired with another to detain me for the last fortnight, but I shall definitely cross to Paris on Wednesday (day after tomorrow) Feb. 9th. I shall be there two or three weeks, and after that shall probably make a stay of equal length somewhere on the Riviera. If one lives in England one acquires a sun-hunger which must occasionally be satisfied. I have been doing nothing striking lately—keeping quiet more than anything else. I went the other evening to a ball (a sort of entertainment I rarely frequent) and took a Marchioness in to supper. The ball was at Lady Louisa Mills's, who is supposed to give the prettiest in London, and the Marchioness was her of Blandford, who will someday be Duchess of Marlborough; when the incident I mention will doubtless be her proudest boast! I dined at the Sturgis's (who caress me very much) a day or two since, in company with the Speaker and his wife and the Harcourts. The Speaker is a great hero here just now, in consequence of his *coup d'état* in the Commons[1] and it was rather interesting to see a man who had suddenly leaped into history. His act was a wise inspiration, for Parliamentary government was rapidly being proved a humbug. The political atmosphere is red-hot: there is only one word in Society—the abominable Irish. They are, I think, abominable; for their wrongs are certain to receive at the hands of Gladstone and Company the fullest consideration, and the most substantial redress. Yet they will consent to nothing that belongs in the least to the realm of practicable politics. There are surely bad races and good races, just as there are bad people and good people, and the Irish belong to the category of impossible. Dr. Wilkinson came to see me a couple of days since, and wants them governed by the sword—by a reign of terror. This is all rubbish, as I think the rest of his opinions are. He thinks Disraeli wise and beneficent, Gladstone abominable, Bismarck a saviour of society etc. In short the politics of middle-class Toryism and the *Daily Telegraph,* mixed up with a queer, musty Swedenborgianism: an unsavoury compound. The traces of the great storm have passed away—though it is blowing, raining and sleeting today in a way to make me rather wince at the prospect of my bad quarter of an hour on the Channel. I have seen no one lately of high interest. You will have already heard of poor old Carlyle's death, concerning whom the papers are most effusive. He had been dying of sheer old age for months, or rather years, and was praying for the *coup de grâce.*—(In another style) I have been more or less visited (discreetly though) by Lewis M. Carnes, who married Serena Mason, and who is of that illiterate and uncultivated New York man-of-business type (though a very decent fellow) which restricts conversation to the narrowest limits. He asked me the other day (having been three or four months in England) what a *Tory* meant, and I found he had no idea whether the present English government was liberal or conservative, and what were the respective politics of Gladstone and Disraeli. He smells strongly of Broadway and yet appears proportionately untutored: I don't mean in manners, but in "culture." I see Lowell every now and then, who is extremely pleasant to me, and of a simplicity as of childhood or of Brattle Street! His poor wife is still quite helpless. He goes about a good deal, but I think is not much of a success—his conversation (as a reputation for wit etc.

had preceded him) is found disappointing. I don't see how he *should* get on with London; he is so completely "out of it"—so alien to London traditions, feelings, dialects, etc. Add to this that he doesn't care a straw for it, and is perfectly indifferent to its opinion. His opinion isn't worth much. With me, as I say, Lowell is always charming and no one speaks so well of the "Portrait." Apropos of which matters I sent father the *Spectator* on *Washington Square,* though I suppose he takes the paper. The writer of the article is Hutton, who pays me a compliment by the elaboration of his talk. There is an element of truth (about my dryness, etc.) but the thing as a whole only makes me smile—his point of view seems to me so false, sentimental and second-rate. I don't think he has any sense 1° of form; 2° of reality; 3° of what a picture of human life positively is. I had a discussion on this, last evening, with Mrs. Kemble, whom I'd gone to see to bid her good-bye, in which she agreed strongly with Hutton, though she has definitely more understanding of things, and more observation than he. She takes much interest in my productions, but thinks they fail of justice to—I don't know exactly what! She is, however, a delightful woman to discuss with—she is so deeply in earnest, so perfectly honest, and so admirably intelligent; not to mention that she recites Shakespeare *àpropos* of everything, and last night treated me to some of the most beautiful speeches in *Measure for Measure.* But she has a great fund of old British philistinism in her, mixed up in the strangest way with a freedom of judgment which is as great as any I ever knew.—I must close, dear Mammy: when next I write you it will be from Paris. I wrote quite lately to Alice and to father. You say nothing of Aunt Kate, but I hope you sometimes send her my letters. I embrace you, not less than the others, and remain sweet mother

Your devotedest
H. James Jr.

1. The Irish Nationalist members had fought various measures by a system of "obstruction" which brought the House of Commons to a standstill. The Speaker of the House, with great energy, had brought a forty-hour sitting to an end on his own responsibility.

To Thomas Sergeant Perry

Ms Colby

Paris Feb. 16*th* 1881
(Hotel Continental)

Dear Tommy.

I received this a.m. your confidential communication touching Howells and the editorship of the *Atlantic*. I observe the secrecy you enjoin, congratulate Howells and commiserate Aldrich.[1] The former will greatly enjoy his freedom, I should think, and has well earned it. He has led for years a life of bondage which I never could have endured for a month. Now that he has more time and opportunity he will probably do still better work, and I hope will enlarge a little his studies and his field.—As for Aldrich, he seems to me good enough for the *Atlantic* and the *Atlantic* good enough for him.—I came abroad a week ago, and am going to pass three or four months *dans la douce Ausonie:* won't you come? I mean I am going to Venice, Rome, Florence, et cetera. I have been lingering a little in Paris, which as usual seems splendid and charming. I write this at a window looking over the Tuileries (gardens); the sun is as bright as April, and I have been standing on my balcony and watching a lot of Parisian athletes play *au ballon* beyond the gilded rails which you will remember. I have also just bought two books—Merimée's Letters to Panizzi and Zola's *Naturalisme au Théâtre,* which I lay down unopened, until I have answered your letter. You will probably think that at least as regards Zola this is no great sacrifice to friendship. I don't think you did him justice in the *International,* which the proprietors amiably send me every month.[2] Zola has his faults and his merits; and it doesn't seem to me important to talk of the faults. The merits are rare, valuable, extremely solid. However, I don't care much. You say that literature is going down in the U.S.A. I quite agree with you —the stuff that is sent me seems to me written by eunuchs and sempstresses. But I think it is the same every where—in France and in England. I suspect the age of letters is waning, for our time. It is the age of Panama Canals, of Sarah Bernhardt, of Western wheat-raising, of merely material expansion. Art, form, may return, but I doubt that I shall live to see them—I don't believe they are eternal, as the poets say. All the same, I shall try to make them live a little longer!—Yes, I know Matthew Arnold very well and like him much. I was pleased to hear that he told a friend of mine the other day that "Henry James is a de-ah!" I am sorry for your ice and snow, your hard sky and still harder earth. It makes me feel rather "mean" to be going down to Nice. However, the worst must be over. If there was anything worth sending you here, I would do so: but there isn't. Love to your wife and daughters.

Tout à vous—
H. James Jr.

1. Thomas Bailey Aldrich succeeded Howells as editor of the *Atlantic Monthly*.

2. Perry had published an article, "M. Zola as a Critic," in the *International Review*, X (February 1881), 144–153.

To Frances Anne Kemble

Ts Lubbock

Hôtel de Noailles,
Marseilles.
Feb. 24*th* [1881]

Dear Mrs. Kemble,

It is time I should ask you for some news, and give you some, first, as a bribe. I didn't wish to write to you while I was in Paris, because I don't think you care much for things that come from Paris—except caps and dresses. I have been spending twelve days there, and departed day before yesterday; and here I am pausing a little on my way to Italy and warming myself in the rays of this splendid Provençal sun. I stopped yesterday at Avignon, and "did" the place in an exemplary manner—that is I went over the old palace of the Popes and walked beside the Rhône, to admire the bare, dusty-looking landscape of rugged rock and smoke-coloured olive. Marseilles is rather amusing, like all seaports; and I took a

long drive this morning beside the sea to a restaurant in the fau-
bourgs where it is obligatory to eat a mess of *bouillabaisse,* a formidable dish, demanding a French digestion. It was served to me
on a charming terrace, overlooking the blue Mediterranean and
the Château d'If, where Monte Cristo began his adventures. Look
out of your window at Cavendish Square, and tell me what you
think of breakfasting out of doors. I don't like to torment you with
telling you that the air is as soft as it is bright, and that, having come
down to meet the spring, I have already met and embraced it—
and yet if the statement makes you think rather worse than usual
of the climate you live in, it will only make you think more kindly
even than usual of me. There is nothing very interesting to tell
you of Paris. I saw my various friends there, but thought the
"Frenchified American" rather a poor type. They eat and drink
very well and know a good deal about petticoats and *bibelots—
mais ils sont bien corrompus*—in a feeble sort of way, too. I went to a
French dinner-party and was struck with the conversational powers
—i.e. the vivacity, quickness, smartness, et cetera, of the people. They
don't care who is looking or who hears—which the English do,
so much, when they talk or move![1] I went several times to the
theatre—but saw only two things of importance, Alex. Dumas's
new piece, the *Princesse de Bagdad,* hollow, sentimental and nasty,
but brilliantly acted; and a much better thing, *Divorçons,* by Sardou,
at the Palais Royal. The latter is genuine comedy, without French
morality, from which Heaven deliver us, and if you had been on
the spot I think I should have almost attempted, in spite of the
impurity both of the atmosphere and of the piece, *de vous y attirer.*
I am going in a few days to Nice, but am waiting here till the
Carnival, which is now raging there, is over, as it makes, I am told,
an intolerable crowd and bustle. After that I shall probably betake
myself to Venice. A friend of mine, writing to me the other day
from Rome, said, "Hamilton Aïdé is here, as sweet and fresh as a
daisy!" So you see he is appreciated in foreign parts. Allow me to
wonder what has happened to you since I saw you last—nearly
three weeks ago—and to hope that nothing has, on the whole.
I am afraid you have been having a foggy life, but I trust that is

the worst. You will soon be out of your tunnel—the vernal month of March is at hand. I shall write to you after I get settled a little in Italy; and meanwhile, if you have the benevolence to address me, please let it be to 3 Bolton St., W. I am afraid you miss me, because I miss you: which makes me only the more yours very faithfully

Henry James Jr.

1. For a further account of this dinner see the following letter.

To Henry James Sr.

Ms Harvard

Hôtel de Noailles. Marseilles.
Feb. 24th, 1881

Dearest father.

I must write, decidedly, without waiting longer. I have been for some days without letters, and must be so for some days longer. till I stop long enough to have them forwarded; but meanwhile I have a conviction that something is waiting for me in Bolton Street.—something, I mean, from my natal house. I hardly remember when I last wrote home: a few days, I think, before I left London, which befel about a fortnight since. I crossed the channel comfortably enough, and spent some twelve days in Paris —which were several more than I wished. I care less and less for the Paris that one sees and has to do with during a short stranger's stay there: though I have no doubt there is another which, if one lived there, one could extract an intellectual subsistence from. The banality of the former has ended by overwhelming me; mainly perhaps owing to the low style of culture of my friends and compatriots who are all very good, but whose horizon is bounded on one side by the *Figaro* and on the other by the Théâtre Français. The famous "dullness" of London is an intellectual carnival beside that. Nevertheless I breakfasted and dined with them, hypocritically; but I don't think I should be able to go through the process again.—The pleasantest relations I have there are with the Childes, who are intelligent and in many ways superior, and whose windows open only upon *l'ancienne* France. They were very kind to me and, if you please, gave a dinner of six or eight people *in my honour!* (They are—especially Mrs. C.— very appreciative readers of H.J. Jr.) The dinner was of men, all French and very pleasant—though it would be long to tell you who they were—all men, save my old friend Madame Jameson, who however is almost a man, or at least a boy, in virtue of an extreme "larkiness" and hilarity. The most entertaining person was M. Guillaume Guizot, son of the old G., and professor of English literature etc. at the Sorbonne. It appears (again if you please) that he had desired much to meet me (excuse egotism), owing to a perusal of my little book on Hawthorne, for whom, in his quality of French Protestant and "Puritan," he has a great admiration. He was most effusive and fraternizing, repeated whole passages of my book to me, with a most extraordinary accent, etc. He had a phrase which I should have liked my critics to hear: he was speaking of the beauty of Hawthorne's genius in comparison with the provinciality of his training and circumstances. *"Il sortait de toute espèce de petits trous—de Boston, de—comment appelez-vous ça?—de Salem, etc!"* At the dinner above-mentioned, I was of course greatly struck with the lightness and brightness of the French conversational tone: but I must say there was nothing in the talk that seemed to me very valuable, and it lacked that quality of having the atmosphere of the British Empire round it which belongs to the more laboured speech of London. In Paris, I sus- pect, it is always the little Parisian horizon. *On ne sort pas de là.* I am out of it now, however, and rejoicing in the splendid sun of Provence. I have come down to meet the spring, and I have met it already in perfection: though I don't like to tell you so, for fear of making you quarrel with your own fine frost. I came in twelve hours (day-before-yesterday) from Paris to Avignon—where by the way I met poor Edward Jackson, of Boston, who had just lost his pocket-book containing his letter of credit, money, passport etc. (You had better not bruit this abroad, by the way, as he may find them again.) I spent a night and day at Avignon, where I found a southern sun, and last evening, in three hours,

came on here, where I am sitting with an open window in a fireless room (looking South). Marseilles is a high bright, handsome,
bustling seaport, with streets that succeed rather well in imitating
Paris. The feeling of the warm southern air is most delightful; I
breakfasted this morning on a terrace out of doors, overlooking
the blue Mediterranean and the Château d'If, where the adventures
of Monte Christo [sic] began. This was a restaurant half an hour
from the town, beside the sea, where it is obligatory to go and
eat bouillabaisse a sort of mess of fish, coloured with mustard.[1] I am
already tired, however, as I always am after a week or two in
France, of French eating—the messes, sauces, greases etc. combined
with the extreme predilection for the table, of the natives, male
and female, who all look red and fat while they sit there.—I forgot
just now to say (not at all àpropos of this) that I saw, in Paris, a
good deal of Tourguéneff, to whom, as he was laid up with the
gout, I paid three longish visits. We had made a plan to breakfast together, but I received, just before, the inevitable telegram.
He seemed and looked a good deal older than when I saw him
last; but he was as pleasant and human as ever. On the other hand,
I can't get over the sense that the people he lives with (the Viardot
circle) are a rather poor lot and that to live with them is not living
like a gentleman. The Tourguéneffs of the Rue de Lille were
as friendly, or rather as affectionate, and hospitable, as usual; I
don't think they have a great deal of light, but their sweetness
is something ineffable. The virtues of the Jacksons is nothing to
theirs; and this en plein Faubourg St. Germain!—I will send my
letter just as it is, without adding more; and when I get my packet
from London I will write again. I hope you are not refrigerated.
Love to all from yours ever, dear Daddy,

H. James Jr.

1. HJ's culinary knowledge may be faulted here: the lemon-yellow color
is not that of mustard but of saffron.

To Thomas Bailey Aldrich

Ms Harvard

San Remo, Italy.
March 8*th* 1881

Dear Aldrich.

Putting aside the peculiar malignity of your writing to me in such a beautiful hand, your note of Feb. 14th gives me great pleasure. I am very glad indeed that you are to take hold of the *Atlantic* and I hope it will give you comfort, as you will undoubtedly give it honour. My gladness is not mitigated by the fact that Howells relinquishes it, for I desire to feel with him on the subject, and I take for granted that after fifteen years' service he has an appetite for what they call in London when they go out of town every five days, a "little change." I trust you won't feel the need of change for a long time and I give you my blessing on your career. You will inherit the remainder of the ponderous serial which I am now shovelling into the magazine—it runs till the November (inclusive) number and it will at least have the merit that its large dimensions will, as regards quantity, simplify for you the editing of the rest of the number. *Apropos* of this, I send you by this post two more instalments of the same, in the proofsheets of Macmillan: those of June and July. The rest shall follow regularly. (They go to Houghton and Mifflin's, Park Street)—I have left London for three months, for a little change, and I write you these lines on the Italian Riviera, face to face with an orange grove, and a block (the shape of my window) of liquid cobalt. I am afraid that is not the sort of thing that a New England March offers you. The oranges are bad however (you can buy better in Washington Street) and the liquid cobalt is sometimes too liquid, for there has been overmuch rain. Is Mrs. Aldrich also to be editress? If so I engage to contribute for nothing. Give her my kind remembrances and believe me with all good wishes

ever truly yours
H. James Jr.

(3 Bolton St. Piccadilly W.)

To Mrs. Henry James Sr.

Ms Harvard

Genoa. March 16*th*. 1881

Dearest mother.

My last letter home was from Marseilles, three weeks ago, and by this time you will have received it. Meanwhile I have heard from you,—but not heard much. An old letter of father's, or rather a short note, accompanying some extracts from newspapers, has turned up after much delay, having I suppose been carried half round the world in the long-missing streamer Batavia. It is of the date of Jan. 18th and reached me about a fortnight ago (it also enclosed a short letter from Wilky, which I shall now answer). Your own subsequent letter is of Feb. 20th, and mentions Bob and Aunt Kate being at Cambridge etc.—which I was very happy to hear. You see I am still on my travels, which I will briefly relate. I went from Marseilles to Nice, which latter I found so little to my taste (besides being densely crowded) that I immediately came on to San Remo, where I enjoyed for ten days the society of Mrs. Lombard and Fanny—the former very feeble and very deaf, the latter "improved." San Remo was warm, quiet, lovely, and I stayed there till yesterday, when I came straight hither, along the rest of the Riviera. The railway, chiefly composed of tunnels, robs this journey of half its beauty; but the day was lovely, and I managed to enjoy it. Nothing can be sweeter and brighter than San Remo, though it has doubled in size and inevitable cocknification since I was there twelve years ago. The blue, blue sea, the orange-and-olive groves, the lovely walks and drives are most "attaching," and I should have stayed there longer if the hotels were not all on the *pension* plan and filled with English and German consumptives, who cause the meals to be served at impossible hours. I am stopping over in this place today, after which I proceed to Milan, where I expect to find letters—among which fortune may possibly vouchsafe me another word from home. From Milan I shall go straight to either Venice or Rome, I don't quite know which, and spend (in whichever I do decide upon) the greater part of the rest of my stay in Italy. I want to be quiet, and have time to do a little thinking and reading—privileges I have for a long time been too much deprived of.—Rome I should choose on its own merits, as one's life in Venice is rather too abnormal for my eminently natural habits; but Rome is infested with acquaintances, all ready to pour into one's existence the element I especially wish to avoid. I shall spend a week at Milan if it isn't too cold, which has the merit that I know none of its inhabitants. I have been solicited by the Bootts to join them in a trip to Sorrento, but have judiciously declined: whereby I shall probably not see them for another month or two. I suppose you know that they go home for a long visit in July. Perhaps you also know that (as I am told) Lizzie is much "talked of," in Florence, in the matter of Duveneck. I have no "inside view" of the case. Her marrying him would be, given the man, strange (I mean given his roughness, want of education, of a language, etc). But the closeness of her intimacy is hardly less so. I take it, however, that the said intimacy is simply the result of the total unconventionalism of the three persons concerned,—the third being Frank Boott. The latter thinks everything that Lizzie does all right, and is himself as simple as a milkmaid. Lizzie likes Duveneck, who is a very good fellow, and Duveneck likes her (no wonder, after all she has done for him); and none of them have any consciousness whatever of appearances. —But I didn't mean to write a disquisition on the subject.—It is very agreeable to me to be in Italy again (for instance sitting in this high-up room in a big, rambling rather dirty hotel, looking straight down on the picturesque port of Genoa, and having to shut out the blazing sun from my fireless apartment). I won't pretend that I care nearly so much for local colour as I used to; but there is something imperishable in the pleasure of finding one's self in Italy.—I was much interested to hear that poor Bob had managed to be a while among you—delighted that he was able to take some rest and recreation. I wish I could take him on a three months' tour over here. These things would be so fresh to him that he would enjoy them more than I, to whom they are stale. If he is still with you, give him my love and blessing. Tell Aunt Kate, in return for her message (that she doesn't write to me so as not to burden me to answer) that she needn't fear to overload me and that there are no letters more delightful and satisfactory to me than hers. Now that I am out here, I hope to have more time to write, too, than while I was in London. I hope Alice still goes on well—tell her that at Venice I shall think constantly of her. Tell father, who I hope is in health, that I shall write to him soon. I am much obliged to him for the Underwood letter about some article of G. P. Lathrop's: it is a most precious American document. I wish I could have more communication with William and his Alice—but there seem obstacles on both sides. He, however, at least, has my letters (to you) to read, if I haven't his. But on all this, and on other points, I reflect that I am waiting in a few days to take my passage in a Cunarder. I have of course read Grant Allen in the March *Atlantic* and think it seems prettily enough argued.[1] But I have no doubt William has a rejoinder, to which I wish all felicity. Bless you all, dearest Mammy.

Ever yours
H. James Jr.

1. See letter to WJ, 27 November 1880.

To Frances Anne Kemble

Ts Lubbock

Hôtel de la Ville, Milan.
March 24<i>th</i>, '81.

My dear Mrs Kemble,

Your good letter of nearly four weeks ago lies before me—where it has been lying for some days past—making me think of you so much that I ended by feeling as if I had answered it. On reflection I see that I haven't, however—that is, not in any way that you will appreciate. Shall you appreciate a letter from Milan on a day blustering and hateful as any you yourself can lately have been visited with? I have been spending the last eight days at this place, but I take myself off—for southern parts—to-morrow; so that by waiting a little I might have sent you a little more of the genuine breath of Italy. But I can do that—and I shall do it—at any rate, and meanwhile let my Milanese news go for what it is worth. You see I travel very deliberately, as I started for Rome six weeks ago, and I have only got thus far. My slowness has had various causes; among others my not being in a particular hurry to join the little nest of my compatriots (and yours) who cluster about the Piazza di Spagna. I have enjoyed the independence of lingering in places where I had no visits to pay—and this indeed has been the only charm of Milan, which has seemed prosaic and winterish, as if it were on the wrong side of the Alps. I have written a good deal (not letters), and seen that mouldering old fresco of Leonardo, which is so magnificent in its ruin, and the lovely young Raphael in the Brera (the Sposalizio) which is still so fresh and juvenile, and Lucrezia Borgia's straw-coloured lock of hair at the Ambrosian Library, and several other small and great curiosities. I have kept pretty well out of the Cathedral, as the chill of Dante's frozen circle abides within it, and I have had a sore throat ever since I left soft San Remo. On the other hand I have also been to the Scala, which is a mighty theatre, and where I heard *Der Frey-schütz* done *à l'Italienne,* and sat through about an hour and three quarters of a ballet which was to last three. The Italians, truly, are eternal children. They paid infinitely more attention to the ballet than to the opera, and followed with breathless attention, and an air of the most serious credulity, the interminable adventures of a danseuse who went through every possible alternation of human experience on the points of her toes. The more I see of them the more struck I am with their having no sense of the ridiculous.— It must have been at *Marseilles,* I think, that I wrote you before; so that there is an hiatus in my biography to fill up. I went from Marseilles to Nice, which I found more than usually detestable, and pervaded, to an intolerable pitch, with a bad French carnival, which set me on the road again till I reached San Remo, which you may know, and which if you don't you ought to. I spent more than a fortnight there, among the olives and oranges, between a

351

big yellow sun and a bright blue sea. The walks and drives are lovely, and in the course of one of them (a drive) I called upon our friends the George Howards, who have been wintering at Bordighera, a few miles away. But he was away in England getting himself elected to Parliament (you may have heard that he has just been returned for East Cumberland,) and she was away with him, helping him. The idea of leaving the oranges and olives for that! I saw, however, a most delightful little maid, their eldest daughter, of about 15, who had a mixture of shyness and frankness, the softness of the papa and the decision of the mother, with which I quite fell in love. I didn't fall in love with Mrs. William Morris, the strange, pale, livid, gaunt, silent, and yet in a manner graceful and picturesque, wife of the poet and paper-maker, who is spending the winter with the Howards; though doubtless she too has her merits. She has, for instance, wonderful aesthetic hair. From San Remo I came along the rest of the coast to Genoa, *not* by carriage however, as I might have done, for I was rather afraid of three days "on end" of my own society: that is, not on end, but sitting down. When I am tired of myself in common situations I can get up and walk away—; so, in a word, I came in the train, and the train came in a tunnel—for it was almost all one, for five or six hours. I have been going to Venice—but it is so cold and blustering that I think to-morrow, when I depart from this place, the idea of reaching the southernmost point will get the better of me, and I shall make straight for Rome. I will write you from there—where first I beheld you: that is, familiarly, (if I may be allowed the expression). Enough meanwhile about myself, my intentions and delays: let me hear, or at least let me ask, about your own circumstances and propensities. I believe you to be still in London—but I also believe you to have a prospect of going to Leamington; which I suppose will help you along toward your summer—or at least will help Mrs Leigh toward hers. You're capable of having had a very nasty March—but I hope it has used you mercifully. I trust Cavendish Square is a wholesome residence, if not a picturesque one. (I have an idea "wholesome" is American—so leave it—to please you.) I also hope they don't bleed you to death at your inn—but will leave you with a little pecuniary vitality. Do you ever go to the play? I'm afraid not, unless Aïdé is *de retour*. I am completely ignorant of his movements, and don't know whether he is still in Italy, though I should be very glad to find him in Rome. If he *has* come back, will you kindly mention I spoke of him, and give him my very friendly remembrances? I should like to send him also to Mrs. Procter—but on the whole to her I should have so much to say that I won't trouble you with so huge a package. I will put up one for her by itself. I trust the *entente cordiale* is completely re-established and that Miss Edith has no more hallucinations. If you were to see me—that is if I were to see you—you would give me some news of your daughter, and perhaps read me Mrs. Wister's last letter. As it is, I can only envy *you* the perusal of it. I gave your address, or rather your addresses, a few days ago, to a lady who wrote to me for them for her sons, the young Chapmans,[1] who are coming abroad this summer, and aspire to go to see you. I gave them so many that among them all they will find you somewhere. I am delighted to think there is a chance of your having the old one—i.e. the old address—back again. God speed the day.—You must have felt *splattered,* like all the world, with the blood of the poor Russian Czar![2] Aren't you glad you are not an Empress? But you are. God save your Majesty! —Mrs. Greville sent me Swinburne's complicated dirge upon her poor simple mother, and I thought it wanting in all the qualities that one liked in Mrs. T. I should like very much to send a tender message to Mrs. Gordon: indefinite—but *very* tender! To you I am both tender and definite (save when I cross). Ever very faithfully yours

H. James Jr.

1. One of these would have been John Jay Chapman, later critic and essayist, then twenty, whom HJ befriended in London.
2. Alexander III was assassinated on 13 March 1881.

To Grace Norton

Ms Harvard

My dear Grace.

I have no particular paper, and no particular pen and ink: but I *have* a particular wish to send you a greeting from this quiet corner of old Italy. It is a bright, hot Sunday morning; I have closed the shutters of my smartly-frescoed apartment, and only a stray sunbeam rests on the cool *scagliola* floor. I wish this rapid scrawl to carry a breath of the Italian summer, and of sweet Vicenza, into your New England hills (for I am taking for granted that by the time my note reaches you your annual migration to Ashfield will have been accomplished). I came back last evening to my inn with the intention of writing to you then and there; but being rather tired I lay down to rest first—and rested so well that it was near morning when I woke up. If I had written I should have told you that I had been sitting almost all the evening in the beautiful Square of this good little city, in a flood of moonlight and amid a host of memories. (I remembered among other things my first visit to this place, in 1869, and was pleased to find that on the whole I have not quite lost my "sensibility"—though it is far from being as hysterically keen as it was at that time.) The great Palazzo della Ragione was silvered by the moonshine, the tremendously tall and slim campanile seemed to lose itself in the brightness of the night. On the big smooth slabs of the piazza the gentle Vicentini strolled and conversed, while I sat before a *caffè* talking with a very pleasant, loquacious officer, whose acquaintance I had made by accident, and who treated me to all the gossip of the place, as well as to many lamentations over the hardness of his own lot. (He is a captain of cavalry, and his salary is $400 a year.)

Excuse me if I don't remember when I last wrote to you, and if I have not your own last letter before me. (I don't carry it about with me, but I have it safely at Venice.) I am tolerably sure, at any rate, that I haven't written to you since I went to Venice on the 25th March—where (bating a short excursion to Rome) I have been ever since, and where I shall remain till July 1st. I came away yesterday morning for a two or three days visit to this place and to Padua—taking advantage of a perverse high wind, which had prevailed for a week and blown much of the charm out of Venetian life. Of that life in general what shall I tell you? You know it for yourself—and if I am not mistaken you spent a number of weeks there before leaving Italy. I remember getting a letter from Jane from the little Pension Suisse—and I never pass that establishment without thinking of her, and of Susan, and of the irrecoverable past. The simplest thing to tell you of Venice is that I adore it—have fallen deeply and desperately in love with it; in spite of their having just begun to run an infamous *vaporino* on the Grand Canal. I had been there twice before but each time only for a few days. This time I have drunk deep, and the magic potion has entered into my blood. Tell Charles, whom I salute *caramente,* that I can tell him little good of St. Mark's. I know nothing of the necessities of what they are doing to the poor dear old beautiful building; but the effect produced is that of witnessing the forcible *maquillage* of one's grandmother! In a word, if it be a necessity, it is an abominable necessity, and the side of the church toward the Piazzetta, where the *maquillage* is now complete, is a sight to make the angels howl. But as to this, *basta così.*—I have enjoyed extremely this year being away from London during the Spring. I receive every now and then, forwarded from Bolton Street a memento of lost opportunities chiefly in the shape of invitations to dinner a month ahead; but they do nothing whatever to turn my heart against Venice. The rest, the leisure, the beauty, the sunsets, the pictures, are more than compensation. I go back to England, however, direct after July 1st, and it is PROBABLE that I go home in September. My sister has come out to spend the summer in England, and that may affect my plans a little, but I don't think it will seriously alter them. I can't tell, however, till I have seen her there. In view of my return I won't bother you with questions now; I will only give you blessings and greetings. Tell Charles I think a great deal of having some

355

good talks with him. I hope he is well, and that his summer's rest will make him better still. As for you, dear Grace, you know what I always hope for you. May it be with you now! I embrace all those big children—is Lily still abroad?—and I remember that I haven't yet had my breakfast and that I can't live by letter-writing alone. Farewell—*à bientôt.*

Ever most faithfully yours
H. James Jr.

To Houghton Mifflin and Co.

Ms Harvard

3 Bolton St.
July 13*th* [1881]

Dear Sirs.

On my return from the continent last night I find your note of June 23d. I was on the point of writing to you with reference to the eventual issue of the *Portrait.* I am afraid you will be a little alarmed to learn that I have had to ask from Messrs. Macmillan *one additional month* of their magazine, and I shall have therefore to beg the same favour of you. The story is to terminate in the NOVEMBER Macmillan, instead of the October, as first intended, and will have run therefore through *fourteen numbers!* The last three instalments, however, are to be considerably shorter than the others: September and October twenty pages, and November about fifteen. My story is so portentously long that I am very sorry to stretch it out further; but I have suffered myself to get overcrowded at the end. I hope this change will not make you, or the *Atlantic,* too uncomfortable. I do not think that as a book it will seem too long—that is, to be read with interest. It may be however impossible to put it into a single *readable* volume (let alone a handsome one), and I should think it would be: but of this I must leave you judges, acting on your discretion. The idea of a volume of seven or eight hundred pages *does* alarm me. I prefer that you should print the book from *revised* sheets of the *Atlantic,* which I will immediately send you. As the extension of the thing in Macmillan gives you more time, I don't suppose you will be inconvenienced by a slight delay. (The revisions are not numerous, but such as they are I should like them observed.) I must of course remind you that the book should not be issued in America before it is published here, as in that case I lose my English copyright. I am unable to say today just when it will appear in London, but I shall ascertain in a day or two, and will then let you know. But there is no probability that you will wish to be ready before my publishers here.

I beg to thank you for your cheque on London for $250 in payment for the July *portion* of my story—which I have just received. And I also beg to inquire whether a cheque for *June* was sent me in the usual course—or whether it was by accident overlooked? No cheque for June has reached me. I should have written about it sooner, but I thought it had perhaps been forgotten, and would be included in July. I now see there has been some accident and should like you to help me know *where* it has been. As you are very regular in your missives, I am afraid it has been lost on the way. Will you kindly let me know whether I thereby lose my cheque altogether, or whether there is any remedy? Don't you sometimes send duplicates? I should be thankful to have my mind relieved on this point at your earliest convenience. I send to Mr. Aldrich today the copy of my serial for October.

> Believe me very truly yours
> H. James Jr.

To Francis Parkman

Ms Mass. Historical

Reform Club
July 18*th* p.m. [†881]

Dear Parkman.

Are you to be in London some little time? If so I will put you down again at this place! I send you this inquiry by post, because it will be difficult to find you at home. I have, ever since my return, on the 12th, been (save for a few hours) out of town with my sister. Even if you are to be here very briefly I shall be glad to see that you come here.

Ever yours
H. James Jr.

To Katherine DeKay Bronson

Ms Private

3 Bolton St.
July 19th [1881]

Dear Mrs. Bronson.

I have been back in England a week, but until today it has been too hot even to write a letter. We have been gasping, panting, grilling; London society has been an *immense fritto misto, à la Vénitienne*. A little rain last night has cooled us off a little; but it was very scanty, and more is greatly needed. The country is parched and blighted with the drought; I have always heard of a green England and never expected to see a yellow one. I must not write to you about the weather, however, as if I had just been introduced to you at an evening party. My mind reverts, with a delicious pain, as the poets say, to Venice, and it serenades you every night beneath that balcony from which you waved me your last most friendly farewell. I am afraid you too have been *en nage,* without going to the Lido, but I hope the breezes of the Adriatic have not entirely failed you. I can't tell you with what affection I think of Venice, and how at this distance my whole stay there takes on the semblance of a beautiful dream. Happy you, to spend your life in such a dream.[1] Fortunately, however, I dream of going back as well as of having been there. To you I shall certainly go back as often as possible; and I chuckle over this thought a dozen times a day. Leaving Italy is always a heartbreak, but this time I bled more profusely than ever. If Italy looks lovely to you from the Grand Canal, you may fancy how it looks to me from Piccadilly. Do give me a little dear Venetian gossip: Has every one gone, and are you quite alone—with the Princess of Montenegro? How are the amiable duke and duchess? and your other sympathetic *habitués?* I am afraid your Thursdays are over—but will recommence *de plus belle* in September. How I regret to-day all those that I missed! The next time I won't miss any. How do these Curtises find their palatial experiment?[2] Please to give them my friendliest remembrance. Is Miss Edith with you, or has she fled to Alpine snows?[3] My blessings on her in either case. And the excellent Avignone—[4] tell him I salute him affectionately. And the little yellow dogs and the big brown gondoliers, and the stately balcony with its crimson cushions—I include them all in my embrace. I include even Miss Chapman if she will permit it—or rather, offer her, so to speak, another, *à part,* for herself. I kiss your hands, dear Mrs. Bronson, and remain

ever gratefully and faithfully yours
H. James Jr.

1. Mrs. Bronson's hospitable Casa Alvisi in Venice received many distinguished guests—among them Browning and HJ. It was during 1881 that she and HJ became close friends, a friendship that endured until her death early in the new century. HJ memorialized her in his essay "Ca Alvisi" in *Italian Hours.*
2. Daniel and Ariana Curtis, of Boston, were settling into the Palazzo Barbaro on the Grand Canal where they would reside for many years.
3. Miss Edith was Mrs. Bronson's only child, later the Contessa Rucellai.
4. Antonio Marcello Avignone, an Italian naval officer.

To William Dean Howells

Ms Harvard

The Reform Club
Oct. 4*th* [1881]

Dear Howells.

I expect to see you so soon (I embark for Quebec—on the 20th) that I could at a point forebear to write to you. But I won't forego the pleasure of letting you know a little in advance, what satisfaction the history of your Doctress gives me.[1] I came back last night from a month in Scotland, and found the October *Atlantic* on my table; whereupon, though weary with travel I waked early this morning on purpose to read your contribution in bed—

in my little London-dusky back bedroom, where I can never read at such hours without a pair of candles. They burned low while I said to myself that barring prehaps the *Foregone Conclusion,* this is your best thing. It is full of vivacity, of reality, of the feeling of life and human nature, of happy touches of all sorts; and the way you have put yourself into the petticoats of your heroine has an almost uncanny ability. I must confess to you that she affects me painfully, and so do the manners and customs of her companion, —but quite apart from this I have enjoyed the keenness and instinctive "naturalism" of the whole thing. I don't think you have done anything yet with so fine a point—I don't send you this as a bribe to be "attentive" to me after I arrive, but merely to express my satisfaction with you in instalments as I can't help reading you so—more shame to me!—I hope to be in Cambridge about Nov. 1st, and will lose no time in coming out to see you. You will find me fat and scant o'breath, and very middle-aged, but eminently amenable to kind treatment. One of the last impressions I shall carry from here is the remarkable interest and sympathy about poor Garfield's end. It made me feel as if I were already in the United States, and helps a little to bridge the dreadful sea. Don't be on the wharf but be at your door with Mrs. H. at the window.

Yours ever
H. James Jr.

1. *Dr. Breen's Practice*

To Frederick Macmillan
Ms BM

Adelphi Hotel, Liverpool,
Oct. 20*th* [1881]

Dear Macmillan.

I embark in half an hour; but I am literary to the last! I meant to have sent you before I left London a list of people to whom I should like author's copies of my book sent. As I already made it

out, I enclose it herewith. Please to make 'em send *me* a copy—
but I will write it on the list.—It is blowing stiffly, but bright, and
I have just performed the religious rite of buying a sea-chair from
that horribly dirty old woman opposite the hotel. Pray for me,
and don't let my fame die out. Many thanks for the draft. Be well
and happy (both of you)—and sell, you in particular, five thousand
copies of my works. I see them in *all* the shopwindows (book-
sellers' of course) here; which makes me feel as if I had not only
started but arrived. A tender farewell again to Mrs. Macmillan.

Yours ever, qualmishly,
H. James Jr.

To Mrs. Henry Adams

Ms Mass. Historical

Cambridge (20 Quincy St.)
Nov. *6th* 1881

Dear Mrs. Adams.

I wonder where I find courage (impudence you will perhaps
call it) to write to you now, after having never written to you
from the England you so cruelly deserted! I find it, I think, in the
exhilaration of the prospect of soon seeing you in the Washington
to which you so fondly cling—in the thought of the pleasant
hours we shall pass there together,—in the vision of the social
services which I know you will be so eager to render me! Your
gracious promises of this kind linger serenely in my memory, and
I find in them a pledge of delightful *intimate* weeks. I have been at
home but a few days (since the 1st) but I cannot longer delay to
let you know of my arrival—conscious as I am that it is fraught
with happy consequences for you. I returned by way of Canada
(in a ship of the Allen line) and getting off at a lonely village on
the banks of the St. Lawrence, stole into the country, as it were,
by the back-door. As therefore you may not have heard of my
advent, these few lines will come to you with all the force of a

delightful surprise. I am afraid, however, I shall not be with you —(*with* you—I like that phrase!) for a few weeks yet! When I do come, however, it will be to stay as long as possible. I remain another week or two at my father's—then go for a short time to Boston and New York—then take the train for the sunny South. I remember so well your last charming words to me: "it will be over there that we shall really meet *familiarly!*" I must tell you that I am prepared to be intensely familiar! America seems to me delightful: partly perhaps because I have kept my rooms in Bolton Street! I shall bring you plenty of anecdotes—if your store has got low.

English Gentlemen (in Paris, at a party). *An American Gentleman and H.J. Jr.* * * *

American Gentleman: Did you read that charming little anonymous novel *Equality?*[1] Have you any idea who it's by?

H.J. Jr. Not the smallest. But there are plenty of people over there—at least there are two or three—clever enough to have written it.

The A.G. No, it's not by an American—it can't be—from internal evidence.

H.J. Jr. Internal evidence? * *

The A.G. There's a single word that betrays the writer's nationality. The princess is said to have worn *mock-lace*. Now that's a phrase the English always use. The Americans always say "*imitation* lace." etc. etc.

I spent ten days at Tillypronie not long before sailing—where there is always an uneasy curiosity. * * * * *. I should be so glad to have a word from you letting me know that you count on me as I do on you! Love to Henry. Ever dear Mrs. Adams, impatiently and irrepressibly yours

H. James Jr.

1. HJ is humorously renaming the novel *Democracy*, published anonymously by Henry Adams the previous year.

To Miss Abby Alger

Ms Yale

Cambridge,
Nov. 21*st* [1881]

Dear Madam

I am extremely obliged to you for the honour you do me in inviting me to address an audience of seventy young women at the Saturday morning club; but hasten to assure you that the absence of a topic, the entire want of the habit of public speaking, the formidable character of the assembly, and an extremely personal diffidence, present themselves to me as cogent reasons for refusing myself the distinction you so kindly place within my reach. I remain, with many thanks, regrets and compliments, and the request that you will assure the ladies of the Saturday morning club of my extreme consideration,

Very respectfully yours
Henry James Jr.

To Isabella Stewart Gardner

Ms Gardner

New York
115 East 25*th* Street
Dec. 7*th* ['81]

Dear Mrs. Gardner

I didn't come in, after all, that last day, as perhaps you noticed; I was so hard pushed to get away that evening that I hadn't time even to ring your bell and run away and then, too, I thought it probable Mrs. Palfrey would be there, or if not Mrs. Palfrey, some other of *ces dames,* so that I shouldn't see you—to call it seeing you—after all. I therefore said to myself—"I will write her a little note; and that will make it up!" Here, accordingly, is the little note. You will say it has been a long time coming—and my only answer to that can be that time goes so fast in New York. I have stepped into a network of engagements made for me by my genial host (Godkin), and have rarely been able to lay my hand upon the fleeting hour and say "This is my own." New York seems to me very brilliant and beautiful, and the streets amuse me as much as if I had come from Hartford, Conn.—or Harrisburg, Penn.—instead of from London and Paris—and Boston! I have dined out every day for a week, and found the talk and the entrées equally good. Last night I was at a pleasant feast with three lovely ladies without their lords—Mrs. Butler Duncan, Mrs. Charles Post, and Mrs. Baldy Smith—the males being Charles Strong (the host), Godkin, and my susceptible self. These ladies were charming, but what made most impression on me was that we talked of you. They wanted to know about you—they had heard you were so original! I gave a sketch—with a few exquisite touches—and then they sighed and said to each other: "Ah, if we only knew how to be like that!" But they don't! I hope very much that your husband is doing well, and send him my hearty good-wishes. Have you found your ink-bottle yet? If so, I should greatly value a few drops from it. Or if you haven't, even a lead pencil might trace a few lines which though not indelible in themselves, would not easily be effaced from the memory of

yours very faithfully
H. James Jr.

To Grace Norton

Ms Harvard

115 East 25th Street
Dec. 13*th* [1881]

My dear Grace.

It seemed to me we had rather a ragged parting twelve days ago, and I have wished ever since to tell you that I had more to say to you than appeared on those occasions—for I include that complicated contract into which we were brought at Miss Curtis's lunch. Since then, however, New York and E.L. Godkin have marked me for their own, and the sense of what I had to say then has been a good deal merged in the impression of what I might say *now*, if you were only here to say it to! This is, first of all, that I was a great fool to leave Cambridge when I did, and that I should be a wise man to return thither tomorrow. Godkin is most friendly and hospitable and is doing his best to make me have a *"tempo assolutamente splendido,"* as we lately read somewhere that the Queen of Italy expresses herself after any occasion that she has enjoyed. But I have none the less a complication of homesicknesses—one of which is for London and the other for the banks of the Charles. The remedy for the latter is nearest at hand; but I foresee that I am to get a great deal worse before I shall get any better. My next two months are to be devoted to getting worse. I shall neglect no means of becoming so, as apparently that is the work cut out for me at present, and I have at all times a love of thoroughness. I am going from here to Washington and the South, and when I come back to you, you may flatter yourself that you will be appreciated. New York is very pleasant, and I am going to remain here till the 23d; then I depart, *never again to return!* (This is strictly confidential.) Godkin and I dine out a great deal, and we subject New York society to an exhaustive criticism. We laugh a great deal, but he more hearty than I. I envy him his laugh. I have seen many persons —but no personages; have heard much talk—but no conversation. Nevertheless the sense one gets here of the increase of the various arts of life is—almost oppressive; especially as one is so often reminded of it. The arts of life flourish—but the art of living, simply, isn't among them! I hope you are mastering them all, dear Grace, including that one. I think of you very often—with intense interest and wish you so well—so well! That is what I would say to you.

Ever yours
H. James Jr.

To Sir John Clark

Ms Barrett

Metropolitan Club
Washington. D.C.
Jan. 8*th* [1882]

My dear Sir John.

This is the fag-end of a rather busy morning, but I shall not let it pass without sending you a greeting. I meant to do so on New Year's day, but one isn't an American in America for nothing. It isn't the land of leisure, my dear Sir John, though it is doubtless to a certain extent that of pleasure. In the good old world one's mornings are sacred—and that is my letter-writing time. But here, as you know, we have abolished a good many of the sanctities, and the busy world marks you for its own before you have left the matutinal couch. It is not too late, however, to wish you a happy New Year, and a long continuity of the same. (By *you*, whenever I say anything pleasant, I always mean her Ladyship as well.) I want to give you a few *de mes nouvelles,* and to ask for as many as possible of your own. If, however, I should undertake to relate you my adventures and impressions in full, I should scarcely know where to begin. My adventures indeed have chiefly been impressions, for I have not been travelling extensively—I have only been seeing people and things in Boston and New York. I have spent a month in either place, and shall probably pass the rest of the winter here, which is probably the most entertaining (on the whole) of the three. I find here our good little friends the Adamses, whose extremely agrèeable house may be said to be one of the features of Washington. They receive a great deal and in their native air they bloom, expand, emit a genial fragrance. They don't pretend to conceal (as why should they?) their preference of America to Europe, and they rather rub it into me, as they think it a wholesome discipline for my demoralized spirit. One excellent reason for their liking Washington better than London is that they are, vulgarly speaking, "someone" here, and that they are nothing in your complicated Kingdom. They have the friendliest recollection of you and Lady Clark, and you were the first Europeans they asked me about when I arrived. I am spending my time very pleasantly, seeing a great many people and finding every one most genial and friendly. I too am "someone" here, and it will be at a terrible sacrifice of vanity that I return to England and walk in to dinner after every one, alone, instead of marching with the hostess or the prettiest woman present! But I love my London better than my vanity, and expect to turn up there about the month of May. I should like to put America into a nutshell for you; but like Carlyle's Mirabeau, it has "swallowed all formulas." Things go very fast here, and the change that has taken place in the last ten years is almost incredible. The increase of civilization, of wealth, luxury, knowledge, taste, of all the arts and usages of life, is extremely striking, and all this means the increase of the agreeable. I won't answer for what the country may have become in this way a hundred years hence. New York today is a very brilliant city—but it takes a great fortune to enjoy it, nothing under a million (sterling) is called a great fortune there now. On the other hand I believe that Washington is the place in the world where money—or the absence of it, matters least. It is very queer and yet extremely pleasant: informal, familiar, heterogeneous, good-natured, essentially social and conversational, enormously big and yet extremely provincial, indefinably ridiculous and yet eminently agreeable. It is the only place in America where there is no business, where an air of leisure hangs over the enormous streets, where every one walks slowly and doesn't look keen and preoccupied. The sky is blue, the sun is warm, the women are charming, and at dinners the talk is always general. Having been here but for a few days I haven't yet seen our British Minister, Sackville-West; but he appears to be much liked, and he has a most attractive little ingénue of a daughter, the *bâtarde* of a Spanish ballerina, brought up in a Paris convent, and presented to the world for the first time here.[1]—But while I sit scribbling here, where are you, my dear Laird? for I have not forgotten your dread scheme of sailing to the Cape. Are you rubbing shoulders with Kaffirs or tossing upon the Southern ocean? I won't take space in conjecture;

but shall send this to Tillypronie to be forwarded. I shall write my name on the outside, so that if it falls into Lady Clark's hands she may perhaps have the gracious impulse to open it and see in it a sign of my attachment. I trust, however, that she is not at Tillypronie, but at the more genial Bournemouth, where I remember it was a part of your plan that she should winter. Wherever either of you are I hope you are decently well and *vraisemblablement* happy. I am deadly homesick for the chimney-pots of London, and shall behold them again, I devoutly trust, about the middle of May; for after all, my sojourn here is an exile mitigated by optimism! Tell me about the Boers and the Kaffirs, and tell me too that poor Arthur Coltman, to whom I send my friendly remembrance, is the better for his rough remedy. I hope *you* are not the worse for it. *3 Bolton Street* will always reach me—or my father's—*Cambridge, Mass., United States*. But address rather Bolton Street, as the British mind has an indefeasable tendency to misdirect over here. It is the only fault I see in it.

Ever very affectionately yours
H. James Jr.

1. This was Victoria, illegitimate daughter of Sir Lionel Sackville-West and Pepita, a Spanish gypsy dancer. She married her half-cousin, who fell heir to the Sackville title, thus becoming Lady Sackville-West. Her daughter, Vita Sackville-West (Lady Nicolson), wrote a biography of Pepita.

To Grace Norton

Ms Harvard

Metropolitan Club
Washington. D.C.
Jan. 10th [1882]

My dear Grace.

What a coincidence that your note should have come in just as I was taking up my pen and invoking your name as my inspiration. When I say your note—I mean your generous and graceful letter. I am glad the little spice-vessels stand upright on your table; they were only intended to remind you of me at the dinner hour, the genial hour, the hour of conversation. There was to have been a mustard-pot to match, but this was not forthcoming in the press and scramble of the New Year's traffic, and shall be supplied later. When this trio of mementos is complete, I shall at least have the happy faith that you have a pungent impression of me! I am glad you are getting on, but sorry you are tired, though I should think you might be when people stay with you. I don't mean because the people you would naturally have are not the most agreeable mortals, but because your passionate urbanity must lead you to expend yourself too much for their entertainment. Try therefore to be—not less urbane, but less passionate! That is about what we are here—we combine amiability with discretion. You see I am already beginning to talk about *we;* though I confess that when I converse with myself I say only *they.* "They" are very pleasant, then, the people here; there seems to be a good many of them in one way and another, and I'm apparently in a fair way to see them all. I spent three days very agreeably at Mrs. Wister's; in spite of a certain painful impression that the lady takes life too tragically. But she is going to Jamaica, to see Lady Musgrave, and that, I hope (especially as she is going to Europe afterward), will interpose a little ease, as Milton says. She had one day a rather big Philadelphian dinner-party, and I liked her Philadelphians, in spite of their accent, very much; especially the ladies, who have something soft and sympathetic, expressive and effusive, that one doesn't find in the celebrated "New England temperament." I am comfortably settled here in a couple of sunny rooms, and shall probably do very well for five or six weeks. Washington seems queer, but genial, and I have no doubt that on acquaintance it grows interesting. I doubt whether social pleasure ever reaches the pitch of intensity, but I shouldn't wonder if the place were the most agreeable of our cities. The Henry Adamses, who are my principal friends here, have a commodious and genial house and have been very kind to me; it is *chez eux* that I have made most of my acquaintance. As yet (as I have been here but a few days) there are none among these that I need particularly mention. I will tell you about the mentionables later. The pleasant thing here is the absence of business—the economy empty streets, most of them rather pretty, with nothing going on in them. I am making the best of everything —so much so that I feel at moments as if I were rather holding my nose to the grindstone. It goes very well—but I will confide to you in strict privacy that in my heart of hearts I am woefully and wickedly *bored*! I am horribly homesick for the ancient world. *There* we needn't be always making the best of things. One may make the worst of them and they are still pretty good. The only thing I know here that I could afford to make the worst of is—you!

Ever most faithfully
H. James Jr.

To Mrs. Henry James Sr.
Ms Harvard

723 15th St. [Washington]
Jan. 22d [1882]

Dearest Mother.

I must thank you for your note, and father for one from him received two days since, and accompanying a packet of English letters: *although* I am not today in very good writing form. I have been having a rather bad time with my head—but it is the first since I have been in America, and very probably will be the last. It is passing away, but, having been pretty bad yesterday, has left me rather sore and seedy. Forgive therefore this inadequate scrawl, intended only to break silence a little, and don't be troubled about me, as on the whole I do very well. Any sort of emanation from home is always a refreshment to me. I am doing fairly enough here in spite of foul weather—and have dined out several times lately—though to one or two dinners I have had to drag myself (not to break the engagement) with a dreadfully aching brow. The chief of these was a big and gorgeous banquet at Mr. Blaine's,[1] to meet the President,[2] who pleased, if he didn't fascinate, me. He is an agreeable "personable" man, with an evident desire to please, and aspirations to culture. He has a more successful physical development than is common here (in the political world), and he talked for some time very genially with me—informing me that he assisted at the suicidal death-bed of Johnny James,[3] who was his intimate friend! He at one time knew Albany well, and descanted on Smith Van Buren etc; also evidently believed me to be the son of Uncle William, and wouldn't be disillusioned. This illusion was indeed apparently so dear to him, that I felt that if I had any smartness in me, I ought, striking while the iron was hot, to apply for a foreign mission, which I should doubtless promptly get. Gail Hamilton, who lives at Mr. Blaine's[4]—the latter I must wait to describe to you—and who was attired in pale blue satin, point lace and diamonds, I sat next to at the dinner, and she sent many messages and greetings to father. She told me I looked like him, and didn't I know it? I said I *felt* as if I sometimes looked like him: didn't she know what it was to feel that way—that one looked like some other person? She fixed me with her solitary eye, and replied: "No, I can truly say I have never had *that* on my conscience!" Repartee, for me, was difficult. I murmured something, not about her beauty, but about her conscience. The most amiable *families* here are the Bayards[5]—Bayard himself a regular dear fellow, and his two daughters such as one ought to marry, if one were marrying; girls intrinsically charming, and to whom Washington has given a sort of social education not obtainable elsewhere in this country; and the Frelinghuysens,[6] who have other desirable daughters etc. But I can't gossip—and I shouldn't be writing. I am very glad indeed to have good news of Bob, and wish I could see him. Give him my love and tell him I shall manage it somehow and somewhere. Thank William for his deaf and dumb document. I am delighted to know of his projected "lark." I embrace my father and sister, my mother and every one and will write better soon.

Ever your
H. James Jr.

1. Senator James G. Blaine.
2. Chester A. Arthur.
3. John James, whose uncle was William James of Albany, was born in

1793 in Ireland. The date of his death is not known, but his will was proved in Lockport, New York, 9 August 1866.

4. "Gail Hamilton," Mary Abigail Dodge, was related to Blaine.

5. Senator Thomas F. Bayard of Delaware was a brother of HJ's friend Mrs. Lockwood.

6. Frelinghuysen was the new Secretary of State.

To Isabella Stewart Gardner

Ms Gardner

Metropolitan Club
723 15th St.
Washington, D. C.
January 23rd [1882]

Dear Mrs. Gardner,

Why shouldn't I put into execution today that very definite intention of writing to you from Washington? I have been here nearly three weeks and I ought to have a good many impressions. I have indeed a certain number, but when I write to you these generalities somehow grow vague and pointless. Everything sifts itself down to *one* impression—which I leave to your delicate imagination. I shall not betray it if I can help it—but perhaps I shan't be able to help it.—Washington is on the whole as pleasant as you told me I should find it—or at least that you had found it. I try to find everything that you do, as that is a step toward being near you. I went last night to the Loring's where you told me you had flung down your *sortie de bal* in the dusky entry, where it looked like a bunch of hyacinths,—and found there the repulsive and fatuous Oscar Wilde, whom, I am happy to say, no one was looking at.[1]—Washington is really very good; too much of a village materially, but socially and conversationally bigger and more varied, I think, than anything we have. I shouldn't care to live here—it is too rustic and familiar; but I should certainly come here for a part of every winter if I lived in the United States. I have seen a good many people, dined out more or less, and tried to make

372

myself agreeable. The Adamses tell me I succeed—that I am better than I was in London. I don't know whether you would think that. I have not fallen in love nor contracted an eternal friendship, though the women, as a general thing, are pleasing. The most of a personage among them is Mrs. Robeson;[2] but she is fifty years old and fundamentally coarse. Very charming, however, with a *désinvolture* rather rare *chez nous*. There are also some charming girls— not rosebuds, e.g. Miss Bayard and Miss Frelinghuysen, who are happy specimens of the *finished* American girl—the American Girl who has profited by the sort of social education that Washington gives. Plenty of men, of course, more than elsewhere, and a good many energetic types; but few "accomplished gentlemen." I met the President the other day (at dinner at Mr. Blaine's) and thought him a good fellow—even attractive. He is a gentleman and evidently has that amiable quality, a desire to please; he also had a well-made coat and well-cut whiskers. But he told me none of the secrets of state and I couldn't judge of him as a ruler of men. He seemed so genial however that I was much disposed to ask him for a foreign mission. Where would you prefer to have me? I wish the States over here would send each other ambassadors—I should like so much to be at the head of a New York legation in Boston—I see a good deal of our excellent Adamses, who have a very pretty little life here. Mrs. A. has perennial afternoon tea—two or three times a day—and frequent dinners at a little round table.

I remain here till the middle of February, and after that I go back to New York for a fortnight. Then I go to make a little tour in the South, etc.; and *then*—and *then*—I should tell you if I were not afraid of betraying that emotion I spoke of in beginning. I hope you will be very amiable during the month of April, which I expect to spend in the neighborhood of Boston. I almost betray it there, and I must control myself. I hope you are having a genial winter—I should be delighted to hear a little about it. I venture to take for granted that your husband is completely recovered, and that you have never failed to be well. I remain

Very faithfully yours
H. James Jr.

1. Wilde had just begun his celebrated American tour.
2. The wife of Congressman George Maxwell Robeson of New Jersey.

To Robertson James

Ms Vaux

723 15th Street
Washington
Jan. 27*th*. [1882]

My dear Bob.

Your note has just arrived and I am filled with grief and horror at the news of poor Mother's illness. Give her my tender love and assure her of my liveliest sympathy. I cannot bear to think that she suffers, and would come on to see her if I believed it would help her through. But if Aunt Kate has come, and you are there, she has care enough (with what father and Alice can also give) and I should only be in the way. I earnestly hope moreover that she has seen the worst and I depend upon your writing to me again immediately to let me know how she prospers.—You don't tell me when she was taken ill—nor whether she had been ailing; but I hope that if her attack was sudden her recovery will be equally so. I was very glad to hear from you apart from this—as we have corresponded so little and particularly pleased that you are able to tell me that you are better in health and spirits and are you painting in Cambridge? That is a resource that I advise you to cultivate, the more things one can do the better.

I am amused at the impression my Washington life makes upon you for, seen from my own near standpoint, it is not at all fairy-like. I have learned no State secrets, nor obtained the inside view of anything, neither have I acquired any valuable familiarities. The number of persons here at present asking for consulates is I suppose about five thousand. I dined last night with Mr. De Biedt, Swedish secretary of Legation, and went afterwards to a ball at the British Legation; however, I remained but half an hour.

Do keep me informed about Mother and tell her that I embrace

her as firmly as she can endure. I trust father and Alice are equal to
the occasion and am happy at the advent of Aunt Kate. I am delighted those poor $250 have given you any obligation but don't
see how they can so long as they repose in the bank. An equal sum
is at your disposal as often as you need it.

Ever your affectionate
Henry James.

To Mrs. Henry James Sr.

Ms Harvard

Washington. Sunday a.m.
723 15th St. [Jan. 29, 1882]

Beloved mother.[1]

I must write to you and embrace you, though I am afraid it will
be sometime before you can return these attentions. I heard from
Bob of your illness, two days ago and immediately begged him to
give me more news. There is no post delivered today, so that I am
in suspense, even if a further bulletin has come from Cambridge,
which I doubt. But I hope indeed that you are better, dear mother,
and that you have ceased to suffer as you must have been doing.
It is impossible almost for me to think of you in this condition, as
I have only seen you hovering about the bed of pain, on which
others were stretched. May you have sprung up from it now,
restored to your precious activities, and breathing more freely than
ever. Asthma must be a terrible discomfort, and I hope the devotion
of the family has provided you with all possible mitigations. If it
hasn't, you have but to send for me, and I will nurse you night and
day. I shall be much disappointed if I don't get news of you tomorrow, and should be very glad if Aunt Kate had time to write
even a few words. (I am assuming perhaps gratuitously that Father
and Alice are somewhat fatigued by their ministrations.) Washington continues to be pleasant, in spite of most disappointing weather
and the fact that I haven't made any particularly interesting acquaintances. I shall probably be here a fortnight longer. The great

news of the moment is the exposure of Blaine with regard to South America—over which the little Adamses, who are (especially Mrs. A.) tremendously political—are beside themselves with excitement. I am afraid you have been suffering much with cold and trust you have had the worst. I should like very much to have something about William's journey to Chicago, but as I hardly expect him to write me about it, don't know to whom to apply. If father or Alice would only send me a line—or Bob would write again.

Ever your loving
H. James Jr.

1. Mrs. James died on the day this letter was mailed to her.

To Edwin L. Godkin

Ms Harvard

Cambridge,
Feb. 3d [1882]

My dear Godkin.

You will perhaps have already heard of the sorrow that has brought me back to my father's house and will keep me near him for some time to come. My dearest mother died last Sunday— suddenly and tranquilly, from an affection of the heart, just as she was apparently recovering happily and comfortably from a comparatively superficial fit of illness. We laid her to rest on Wednesday —I got back from Washington on Tuesday morning: in time to see her still looking unchanged and with much of life and—almost unendurably much—in her lifeless face. It has been a very acute pain to me.[1] You knew my mother and you know what she was to us—the sweetest, gentlest, most natural embodiment of maternity —and our protecting spirit, our household genius. But you know well the depth of deep sorrow, and I needn't talk to you of that. My father and sister are wonderfully tranquil, and in their intense conviction that even the most exquisite sense of loss has a divine order in it are even almost happy! My father however is very feeble and suffering and I must remain near him for the present.

My plans and intentions are all changed and for some time to come I must be within easy reach of Cambridge. I do not however share your appreciation of this place as a habitation, and I shall therefore settle myself for a while in Boston. I am full of regret at having to put off that pleasant plan of another fortnight at 115; but I can promise you that the pleasure is only deferred. A few weeks hence I shall be very glad to pay you a quiet visit, and as my return to Europe is *probably* suspended for this year, we have plenty of opportunity ahead. I know you will think of us all just now kindly and tenderly. Give my love to Lawrence and tell him I know how he will be able to do the same. We have all been together—save her who is so absent—for the first time in fifteen years. I hope the winter is going well with you.

Ever faithfully yours
H. James Jr.

P.S. The very clever review of my book in the *Post* has given me great pleasure.[2]

1. For a full account of HJ's emotions and sense of loss see his *Notebooks*, 39–41.

2. Godkin was editor of the *Nation* and the New York *Post*. Lawrence was Godkin's son.

To Isabella Stewart Gardner

Ms Gardner

Cambridge, Friday
[13 Feb. 1882]

Dear Mrs. Gardner.

I thank you kindly for your tender little note, and am much touched by it. I have *felt* my dear mother's death very deeply—I was passionately attached to her. She was sweet, gentle, wise, patient, precious—a pure and exquisite soul. But now she is a memory as beneficent as her presence; and I thank heaven that one can lose a mother but *once* in one's life. The loss of the love, how-ever, is a suffering absolutely apart—for it is the most absolutely unselfish affection any of us can know. Other forms of devotion seem to me comparatively interested; that of the being who went through nameless pain to bring one into the world and who has felt one's life in every fibre of her own being, is the purest essence of tenderness.

—I shall come to see you one of these days, not long hence; and shall see you often, a little later, as I shall settle myself for a while in Boston. I wish to be near my father.

Ever faithfully yours
H. James Jr.

To Mrs. Francis Mathews
Ms Harvard

Union Club, Boston
8 Park Street
Feb. 13*th* [1882]

My dear Mary.[1]

I have been intending to write to you ever since I came back to America, more than three months ago—I wished to give you news both of myself and my people, over here—whom I always consider a little as yours also. Today I have more reason than ever for sending you a friendly missive—but, I grieve to say, it is a very sad one. You will feel much sympathy for us when I tell you that my dear mother, for whom you were named, died a fortnight ago. It seems a great deal longer—her death has made the days move slowly! I am very happy to say that her death was tranquil and painless—she passed away—from one moment to another—as my father and sister were sitting with her in the twilight. She had had a rather sharp (but not at all alarming) attack of bronchial asthma, from which she was apparently happily convalescent—and in the midst of her cheerful sense of recovery she suddenly died. I was not at my father's house at the time—but in Washington, and I reached home but twenty-six hours after all was over. I didn't see my dear mother living—but I saw her with a tranquil, beautiful appearance of life. My three brothers had all arrived—it was the first time in fifteen years that we had been together—and we carried her to her rest on one of those splendid days of winter that are frequent here—when the snow is high and deep, but the sky as blue as the south, and the air brilliant and still. You will know for yourself that our loss is great. She was the perfection of a mother—the sweetest, gentlest, most beneficent human being I have ever known. I am extremely happy that I had come to America this year, after so long an absence—all my last recollections of her are inexpressibly tender. I thank heaven, however, that it is given to us to feel this particular pang but once. My father is infirm, but very tranquil; he has a way of his own of taking the sorrows of life—a way so perfect that one almost envies him his troubles. Alice, I am happy to say, after many years of ill health has been better for the last few months than for a long time; she is able to look after my father and take care of his house—and as she is a person of great ability it is an extreme good fortune that she is now able to exert herself. You were always interested in Wilky[2]—whom I lately saw for the first time in ten years. He is not particularly successful, as success is measured in this country; but he is always rotund and good-natured and delightful. Please tell your father and mother all this—I know they will think of us affectionately. My mother's death has changed my present plans. I was to have returned to England in May—but I have put off my departure till somewhat later, in order to be a while longer near my father. When I do go you shall soon see me; and as I expect to spend the remainder of my life in England I don't grudge my native land a few additional months. I greatly hope that you are all well, and I send you the very best wishes. Commend me kindly to your valiant husband, and to your father and mother, and believe me

ever faithfully yours
Henry James Jr.

1. Mrs. Mathews was the daughter of Dr. J.J. Garth Wilkinson, Swedenborgian friend of HJ Sr.
2. Wilky had been named for Dr. Wilkinson.

To Lord Rosebery

Ms Scotland

Boston,
February 27*th* 1882

My dear Rosebery.

Ever since I heard a few weeks ago that you had become the father of an heir to your greatness—and your goodness—I have wished to let you know that in this distant land I put candles into my window in honour of the event. This modest illumination was but the symbol of my sympathy and good wishes—fortunate father of a fortunate son! May the latter young man emulate your amiability and profit by your wisdom! He inherits at the outset a fund of good will which ought to make his little life a success even before other things arrive to confirm the tendency. I should have said this to you long ago, but that I have lately had a personal sorrow which has given me much occupation. My mother died suddenly a month ago, and the event has given me much to think of and to attend to. It will not however, probably, cause me to alter my original plan of returning to England in May. I spent the early part of the winter in seeing something of America— an extensive (and expansive) country, with many idiosyncrasies. It is not so much a country as a world—but you know all that better than I.—I am desperately homesick for London, and the intestinal convulsions of the British Empire only increase my tender interest in it, and my desire to be near the sick-room, as it were, to get the last news of the illustrious invalid. I am proud to think of the doctors—or nurses—I number among my friends— and I entreat you to use all your skill! I make my best obeisance to Lady Rosebery and I remain of your dear lordship, the very devoted

Henry James

To Frances Anne Kemble

Ts Lubbock

102 Mount Vernon St.
Boston.
April 5*th* 1882

Dear Mrs. Kemble,

I have before me your gracious letter of the last of February. Believe me that I thank you tenderly for your friendly sympathy in all that we have felt in regard to my dear mother's death. As the weeks have gone by they have made us at once miss her more and yet desire less that she should be back here again. There have been troubles and anxieties; and the sense that she is at rest forever from all these pains and pangs is on the whole the best sense we can have.—Suffer me to say that I smile with *derision*—absolute and unmitigated—when you speak of my getting "weaned" from my London loves and longings by remaining over here. If I were able to make it clear to you how little danger there is of that result, I should be almost ashamed to. The catastrophe won't happen now, at any rate, for I sail for old England on the *10th of May*. This is chiefly what I wish to tell you. I shall see you so soon that I can add other items at our leisure. My plan of spending the summer in America has evaporated—thanks to its appearing, as time goes on, that there is no need of it. My father is much better than he was a month ago, and will not listen to my making any "sacrifices" for his sake—amiably considering that I have made enough in spending three months in Boston, to be *à sa portée*. So I shall greet you face to face, most honoured friend, at a much earlier day than I a little while ago ventured to hope. I shall turn up in Bolton St. about May 21st or 22nd, and hope extremely that in spite of the convulsions of your domicile you will still be in town. Your picture of that domicile is most *lugubre,* and the image of your noble person seeking a precarious subsistence in the London eating-houses brings tears to my eyes. When I get back you must dine with me at my club! I have heard from Mrs. Wister on her return from the tropics, but of course you have heard more fully. I have also heard from Mrs. Procter, who writes as neatly as she talks, and from whose firm and brilliant surface the buffets of fate glance off! I am very sorry your new book is *indecent!* I shall risk the shock, on the first opportunity. I delight in your conversation whether printed or uttered, and I am thankful that the people who can't enjoy the latter may have a little compensation in the former. I am impatient to sail, and you are for a great deal in it.

Ever most faithfully—
Henry James Jr.

To Grace Norton

Ms Harvard

3 Bolton St. Piccadilly
May 25*th* [1882]

Dear Grace.

Only a word of greeting from *terra firma;* to tell you that I have arrived and survived. There wasn't much to survive, as I had the brightest and fairest, as well as the shortest, voyage in my numerous record. England looks green, and London looks black, and I am very glad to be here—though I doubt much if I could tell you just why I am glad—any better than I did that evening in Cambridge, when I remember that I made a very lame business of it. —I have been but three days in London and have already met three hundred and fifty people (to speak to). The whirlpool of the Season, however, doesn't draw me in and I shall keep out of it this year—even though I have already six engagements to dinner. The night I got back I found cards for three parties (for that night), to none of which I went. I left the ship at Queenstown, and tried to see something of Ireland and the Land League. But I saw little save some very green fields and dirty cabins, and perceived that to explore the subject would take more days than I had to give. So behold me settled, after a fashion, in London, where I have already spent an hour with J.R. Lowell, who seemed easy and happy, in spite of the suspects and his apparently probable recall.

Mrs. L. is better than I have heard her represented, and better than when I left.—How is Cambridge, and how are you? Is it summer—or is it winter!—For it certainly can't be spring!—I have a certain fear that you miss me—or shall I call it a certain hope? Whatever it is, the missing won't hurt you, and I rather like the idea. Excuse the apparent cynicism of this, which is only one of the multitudinous forms of the affection with which I remain, dear Grace,

very faithfully yours—
H. James Jr.

To Isabella Stewart Gardner

Ms Gardner

3 Bolton St
September 3*d* [1882]

Dear Mrs. Gardner,

I have an unanswered letter from you of almost two months (or rather of exactly that period) old! I have become the more fond of it as the weeks have gone by, and have been unwilling to *part* with it, as I may express myself, by answering it. It is only the thought that I may possibly get another in place of it that gives me this courage. I write you from the depths of this stale and empty London, and you will read my poor words on that wondrous piazza of yours, the haunt of breezes and perfumes and pretty women. Read them to the breezes, read them to the flowers, but *don't* read them to the pretty women! I don't know why I should give you this caution, however, as you are not in the habit of boring your visitors. There is nothing to tell you about London at this spacious and vacuous moment, except that it is very delightful. I have it absolutely to myself, and London to one's self is really a luxury. I have been paying certain country visits—but as few as possible, and even them I have now abandoned and I am spending this still, cool Sunday in the metropolis. The purpose of this proceeding is the ingenious effort to "make up for lost time"

—(I lost a great deal during June and July.) I really don't think lost time ever *is* made up—one can save a few hours out of the future but one never can out of the past! Fix your thoughts on your future then—and *forget* your past—if you can. It is very quiet—though a man has just come in, most unexpectedly, to propose that we shall dine together. So we shall repair to a hot and somewhat disreputable establishment at about the hour that you will have come out to listen to your creepers and tendrils rustle in the breath of the Atlantic. You have had a hot summer but I pray you have had a merry one. My sister writes me you kindly came to see her and were all freshness and grace. Your journey to Japan and India is a *coup de génie:* won't you take me with you as your special correspondent—and companion? (I mean special-companion.) Poor little Daisy Miller, in her comic form, has been blighted by cold theatrical breath, and will probably never be acted. She will in that case only be published. But she had two evenings' success, and that amply satisfies your very faithful friend—[1]

Henry James Jr.

I hope your health has been perfectly serene. I go to Paris for the autumn, on the 12th.

1. In the weeks after his mother's death HJ converted "Daisy Miller" into a play, and before sailing read it to Mrs. Gardner.

To Mrs. William James

Ms Harvard

Bordeaux,
Oct. 16*th* [1882]

My dear Alice.

I have long owed you a letter, but I shall always be in your debt for something or other, and you will be so used to thinking of me in this situation that habit will aid your natural generosity in forgiving my shortcomings. Why I should write to you from Bordeaux more than from another place I scarcely know; my best reason is that I am here today, and that tomorrow I shall be in Toulouse, which is perhaps even less natural. With your husband in Venice[1] and your eldest brother-in-law in these strange French cities, you must feel rather bewildered and abandoned. Your situation seems to me most unnatural, but I hope you bear up under it, and that you derive some assistance in doing so from your little Harry and William. I am afraid you don't from the ghastly Royce couple[2]—as the report of your impression of them which William has transmitted to me, seems to warrant me in calling them. What terrible people and above all what a terrible infliction! I hope you will not scruple to *pull them off*—as I had to do those fatal plasters with which I had saddled my chest last spring, when William and you sprang to my rescue! They must be really a couple of dreadful plasters! Abandoned by your husband who leaves you two Royces in his stead, you seem to me, dear Alice, very greatly to be pitied, and I assure you that I think of you with tender sympathy. I shall never, in future, embrace any man's philosophy till I have seen him—and above all till I have seen his wife. You see that William's own doctrines are by this system very well guaranteed! I hope that in spite of what you have lost and what you have acquired your winter begins (if it *has* begun, which, as yet, heaven forbid) with some promise of peace and comfort. I don't exactly understand in what house you are living, as the houses in Garden Street have, to me, a certain vagueness of identity; though probably when I see you in it, if you don't leave it before that, I shall find that it was impressed upon my brain, years ago, when I used to walk about the byways of Cambridge and endeavour to invest its habitations with a certain local color. I am afraid you miss the palatial proportions of Casa Peabody, but, if you have your children "on top of you" in your actual residence you will find some satisfaction in the pressure. I should like very much to feel that of the youthful William, in whom I take the greatest interest and beg to kiss wherever he is most kissable. Harry, with a younger brother, must be a great swell, but I hope this Glory doesn't make him forget his uncle. Does he remember me at all, or does he even, or only, pretend to? I expect to find him when I next go home, even if it be only a few months hence, in quite a different stage of development. I get every now and then a line from William, at Venice, where I fear he finds the wet weather which has cursed Europe this autumn everywhere. But he also finds James Bryce, and other consolations for the evening —including Mrs. Van Buren, the widow of the husband of one of our deceased aunts! I hope you see something of father and Alice, now that they are more nearly your neighbors again, and that they don't seem to you too lonely and disconsolate. I send very kind remembrances to your mother and sisters, who don't like Cambridge less, I trust, as they go on. You must have perpetual writing to William to do; but remember, whenever you have anything left over, as it were, what pleasure it will give to

yours ever affectionately
H. James Jr.

1. This was the second occasion on which WJ had taken off for Europe shortly after the birth of one of his children.

2. Josiah Royce (1855–1916), philosopher, was substituting for WJ at Harvard.

To Isabella Stewart Gardner

Ms Gardner

Paris, Grand Hotel,
Nov. 12*th* [1882]

Dear Mrs. Gardner.

Your gracious note of the end of last month, which came to me an hour ago (since when I have been reading and re-reading it), is almost as "crisp" as one of those "silver days" of winter (happy phrase—may I have it for my next article?). I wish it had been longer and regret extremely that, as you imply, the cultivation of virtue should have the effect of abbreviating your letters. If this is really the case I beg without delay to become vicious and diffuse! *Àpropos* of such matters you see that I am in the city of vice, where I am leading the same innocent and unagitated life that I drag about with me everywhere. I have been spending the last two months in France,[1] but six weeks of them have been passed—very agreeably—in wandering about the provinces—Touraine, Anjou, Poitiers, Gascony, Provence, Burgundy. I spent a fortnight on the banks of the Loire, examining the old chateaux of that region— Chenonceaux, Chambord, Amboise, Blois etc.—and having taken a fancy to such a manner of life, pushed my way farther and saw a hundred more castles and ruins, as well as cathedrals, old walled towns, Roman remains and curiosities of every sort. I have seen more of France than I had ever seen before, and on the whole liked it better. This has shortened my stay in Paris, for I return to my dear and dingy London on the 20th of the month. The autumn has been loathsomely wet; but since I have been here the weather has been rather shining and Paris has touched a certain place in my affections which only Paris touches. I don't imply by this that it is by any means the deepest place—that tender spot is like those compartments in a French railway carriage that are reserved for *dames seules!* But Paris has a little corner of my complicated organism and it has filled it fairly well on the present occasion. It filled it better, however, that time when you were here. I find the same rather threadbare little circle of our sweet compatriots, who dine with each other in every possible combination of the Alphabet— though none of their combinations spell the word satisfaction. That however is the most difficult word in the language—even I am not sure I get it right. I dined last night with Mrs. Strong—I dine tonight with Mrs. Von Hoffman; that is about the tenor of one's existence, though there are a few other things between. Did you ever meet Clarence King?[2] He is just below stairs (at this hotel) and I have been down to bid him good morning. He is a delightful creature, and is selling silver mines and buying water-colours and old stuff by the million. I believe I am to breakfast with him and the good John Hay (who is also very clever.) You see I am very national; do insist on that to people when you hear them abuse me—even when it's you yourself who have before. You don't abuse me however when you say such nice things as you have done about my article in the *Century*.[3] I am delighted it should have transported you a little, and that perhaps for a moment—your Beverly ocean looked like the flushing lagoon. The unhappy paper, however, like everything in American magazines when I don't see the proof, is full of odious misprints. Do kindly correct a few of them on the margin of your copy. On p. 19, at the top right "hardly" after *Europa,* should be *surely. Thrives* on the same page, below (left) should be *thrones.* "Loveliest", same page, first line on the left, should be *"loneliest* booth, and etc." On p. 12 on the left, "wavy-twinkling," which is idiotic, should be "many-twinkling," which is a shade less so. And just beside it, on the other column, the "bright sea light seems to flash" should be "seems to *flush"*—which is a very different thing. *Not,* on p. 10, left ("light is not in the great square") should be of course *hot!* Colours, p. 13 (left) should *colour,* which makes just the difference; and *streaked* ("the wrong way") on the column beside that, should be *stroked.* Furthermore, on the last page (left), the "beach at the Lido is lovely and beautiful" should be of course *"lonely* and beautiful." Excuse this horrid printers' letter, but it lacerates me to see my careful prose so disfigured. I have only mentioned some of the deformities. I agree with you that the portrait is one of these—and if you can accept the disagreeable photograph from which it is taken, I will send you the latter when I get back to London. Howell's charming article makes me *flush* not *flash* all over. It was about this time that I paid you that little visit last year—in the sweet sunny American autumn with just a little growl of approaching winter in it. I remember the sea, the woods, the colour of the rocks and the sound of the waves. Also the colour of your sofas and ottomans and the sound of your conversation. *Àpropos* of sound, what a hush must have fallen upon Beverly with that mutual silence of the Gordon Dexters! But it's better to be silent *que de se dire des bêtises.* "The Point of View" appears in the *January Century.* I *believe* I have an article on *Du Maurier* in the December—sure to be full of misprints. Please allow for them —you know, *mon écriture.* It is a shame to bother you with any more of this. I only hope it will be legible to you that I am ever

very faithfully yours

Henry James Jr.

1. The purpose of this journey was to write *A Little Tour in France*.
2. Geologist, head of the U.S. Geological Survey, and a close friend of Henry Adams and John Hay.
3. "Venice," *Century Magazine*, XXV (November 1882), 3–23.

To Charles H. Brookfield

Ms Colby

3 Bolton St. W
Nov. 22*d* [1882]

Dear Mr. Brookfield,[1]

It has come into my head to ask of you an opinion, and I will be as brief as possible in laying my case before you! Last winter, I being in America, the Manager of one of the New York theatres[2] asked me to write him a play. I agreed to do so, and took my subject from a little story which I had published some time before, and which had had great success in the United States. In a word I dramatised my story with large alterations. After the work was done, however, the Manager and I fell out; indeed, he didn't like the play (for which I am bound of course to hold him a jackass!) and I returned to England with my comedy in my pocket. I confess that I believe in it somewhat less as a good acting play than I did at the time I wrote it. Still, I cannot but think it has a certain value and is a rather pretty production; and I take the liberty of sending it to you to read. With this one special view— that you kindly tell me whether you *see yourself,* as the French say, in the part of Eugenio, the courier. That is mainly what I wish to learn from you; but there are two or three points besides. When I saw *Odette* last summer at the Haymarket and admired your remarkably accomplished acting of the major-domo at the gambling-saloon, I said to myself, "How well Brookfield would do my *Eugenio!*" The part is an important one—if you were to play it you might make it the most important one in the piece. My little reasoning is as follows: that if you *should* take a fancy to the part, and believe you might make a hit in it, it might be worth my while to make some overtures to Mr. and Mrs. Bancroft about

the play. I have no desire to do this without calculating proba-
bilities in advance; and one of them has sounded to me to be that
they may be influenced in some degree—perhaps in a large degree
—by seeing an opportunity for a good part for *you.* I learn moreover that they have lately engaged a young American actress—of
whom I know nothing. The heroine of my comedy can only be
played by an American (who should also be young and pretty)
and I have therefore made the further reflection that if the part of
Daisy Miller should appear to suit the young lady in question, and
the part of Eugenio strike you as good fit, these two facts, taken
together, may give me sufficient ground to address myself to Mr.
and Mrs. Bancroft. I must beg you in the meantime to *say nothing*
to them about my piece, if you will be so good, and indeed to say
nothing of the contents of this letter to any one at all—unless the
spirit should move you to impart it to your mother. If you have
the leisure, will you kindly read my comedy and meditate on it
in private only; for I wish this not in the least to be construed as an
appeal through you to the Bancrofts, but only as a request for
your *own personal* impression of the role of the courier—and also,
of the adaptability of the young lady just mentioned (if you know
anything about her) to the other part. I send you the play, in
another envelope: don't be frightened, I do not inflict upon you
the outrage of a manuscript. The piece has been printed—not, as
yet, published, and you will have no difficulty in deciphering it.[3]
I only venture to repeat my desire that no one else should see it.
—I have written you a long and somewhat complicated letter, but
I have no doubt that (with the assistance of your good-nature) you
will be able to make it out. There are two or three things more I
ought to say (one or two of them of importance); but I will keep
them till I see you. For, to close, I mean to ask of you to come
and see me after you have read my little book—assuming always
that you accomplish that feat. Will you meantime let me know
by a line that you have safely received it? I hope greatly that your
mother is well—I have only just returned from a long absence in
Paris, and shall soon ascertain for, myself.

Believe me very truly yours
Henry James Jr.

1. Brookfield, son of W. H. Brookfield, and his wife, the friend of Thackeray, was an actor with the Bancroft Company.

2. Daniel Frohman, of the Madison Square Theatre in New York.

3. HJ alludes to the now rare privately printed copy of the play. The dramatic version of "Daisy" appeared in the *Atlantic Monthly*, LI (April–June 1883), 433–456, 577–597, 721–740, and was published as a book during that year.

To William Dean Howells

Ms Harvard

3 Bolton St.
November 27*th* [1882]

My dear Howells,

It is not a "literary form" but a perfect verity that your letter this a.m. found me on the point of writing to you. Were you dissolved in Alpine torrents or frozen in Alpine snows—had you grown stiff over your current serial, or had you stealthily returned to a Boston suburb? These wonderments had passed through my mind, and I am delighted to have them answered. More seriously, I figured you fled to *Italia nostra*—I don't know however but that I envy you that pleasure the more as still impending. Of course you have been under the spout of heaven, as we all have been, but I am afraid it has been held more directly over your little corner of creation than over some others. May a sunny Italian winter make up for it.—I trust at least that the wetness of the world has only watered your ink—i.e. made it flow as freely as was necessary. Do you go to Italy with your novel finished? I wish you that joy. I hope the brevity of your mention of your wife's illness is the measure of its duration and gravity. May she be speedily as well as she likes! Please to give her my kind remembrances.—I came back from Paris (where after coming up from my six weeks in the provinces I had been since Nov. 1st) just a week ago—so that I missed the little breeze produced, as I am told, by the November *Century*. I see in the last *Academy* that you have never seen the magazine and of which I should long since have sent you a copy did I not suppose that the publishers had the civility to do so. I send you one today, that is as soon as I can procure it (having given all my own away)—with the hideous misprints in my *Venice* corrected. You are accused of having sacrificed—in your patriotic passion for the works of H.J. Jr.— *Vanity Fair* and *Henry Esmond* to *Daisy Miller* and *Poor Richard!*[1] The indictment is rubbish—all your text says is that the "confidential" manner of Thackeray would not be tolerable today in a younger school, which should attempt to reproduce it. Such at least is all I see in it and all you ever meant to put. When I say "you are accused" all I mean to allude to is a nasty little paragraph in the *World* which accuses Warner, you and me of being linked in the most drivelling mutual admiration, and which accuses me individually of a "tepid, invertebrate, captain's-biscuit" style! Of the articles in the *Saturday Review* and *Putnam's Monthly* I have seen only the former. Warner's article on England exposes him; I think it seems to me crude, boyish and not well written—especially for an editor of Men of Letters. But don't let the other matter bother you; it is infinitesimally small and the affair of three fourths of a minute. I don't know whether your Scotch publisher sends you (as he ought, if you wish them—I never do) notices of your *Modern Instance:* but there is no doubt that you are rapidly coming very distinctly before the British public. You have only to go on.—I saw a good deal of John Hay, and Clarence King in Paris, and got on beautifully, with them both. Hay is an excellent fellow, and King is a charmer. He charms all the bricabrac out of the shops. I made a goodly tour in France, to do it in *Harper,* and was informed on my return to Paris that Harper didn't want it! Laffan, who put me up to it, is much abashed. Write me as soon as you list, somewhere in Italy, and above all, GIVE ME YOUR GENERAL ADDRESS!! I embrace you all.

Ever yours
H. James Jr.

1. Howells had written an article in praise of HJ, and since HJ also wrote on Howells, the two were accused of "puffing" one another.

To Elizabeth Lewis

Ms Private

3 Bolton St. Sunday night.
[10 Dec. 1882]

Dear Mrs. Lewis,[1]

Many thanks for your sympathetic words. I sail for America on Tuesday (leaving London tomorrow), in the hope of seeing my poor Father once again before he passes away. I have only time to write you this hurried farewell (at 2 o'clock in the morning). I count on your good wishes following me on this sad errand across the wintry ocean. I am so tired I don't see what I write. Believe me

ever faithfully yours
H. James Jr.

P.S. When you next see Burne-Jones please to give him my love. Tell him I was on the point of going to see him when this sad news came—I shall do so as soon as I return.

1. Mrs. George Lewis (later Lady Lewis) was the wife of a prominent English lawyer. She was hostess to many figures in the London world of the arts.

To William James

Ms Harvard

131 Mt. Vernon St.,
[Boston]
Dec. 26*th* [1882]

My dear William.[1]

You will already have heard the circumstances under which I arrived at New York on Thursday 21st, at noon, after a very rapid and prosperous, but painful passage. Letters from Alice and Katharine Loring were awaiting me at the dock, telling me that dear Father was to be buried that morning. I reached Boston at 11 that night; there was so much delay in getting up-town. I found

Bob at the station here; he had come on for the funeral only, and returned to Milwaukee the next morning. Alice, who was in bed, was very quiet and Aunt Kate was perfect. They told me everything—or at least they told me a great deal—before we parted that night, and what they told me was deeply touching, and yet not at all literally painful. Father had been so tranquil, so painless, had died so easily and, as it were, deliberately, and there had been none—not the least—of that anguish and confusion which we imagined in London.—The next morning Alice was ill, and went to Beverly—for complete change, absence from the house etc.— with Miss Loring. Meanwhile I had become conscious of a very bad head, which was rapidly getting worse. I had disembarked with it, and hoped it would pass away, but on Friday p.m. I had to take to my bed, after having seen your Alice in the afternoon and definitely learned from her that you had *not* been telegraphed to. This had been judged best, but I regretted it so much that on Saturday a.m. which was the earliest time possible, I got Aunt Kate to go out and do it. Alice's letters will however already have explained to you this episode. Their not telegraphing you was not neglect, but simply a miscalculation of the advisable. My head got much worse, I sent for Dr. Beach, and have been for three days in bed, with one of the sharpest attacks of that damnable sort that I have ever had. Today, however, I am much better, but my still seedy condition must explain the poverty of this letter. Alice is still absent, and I have spent these days wholly with Aunt Kate who quite unexhausted by her devotion to Father, has been, as always, the perfection of a nurse. She has now told me much about all his last days—about everything that followed that news which was the last to come before I sailed. Your wife tells me that since then she has written to you every day or two —so that you will have had, by the time this reaches you, a sort of history, in detail, of his illness. It appears to have been most strange, most characteristic, above all, and as full of beauty as it was void of suffering. There was none of what we feared—no paralysis, no dementia, no violence. He simply after the "improvement," of which we were written before I sailed, had a sudden relapse—a series of swoons—after which he took to his bed not to rise again. He had no visible malady—strange as it may seem. The "softening of the brain" was simply a gradual refusal of food, because he *wished* to die. There was no dementia except a sort of exaltation of belief that he had entered into "the spiritual life." Nothing could persuade him to eat, and yet he never suffered, or gave the least sign of suffering, from inanition. All this will seem strange and incredible to you—but told with all the details, as Aunt Kate has told it to me, it becomes real—taking father as he was—almost natural. He prayed and longed to die. He ebbed and faded away—though in spite of his strength becoming continually less, he was able to see people and talk. He wished to see as many people as he could, and he talked with them without effort. He saw F. Boott, and talked much two or three days before he died. Alice says he said the most picturesque and humourous things! He knew I was coming and was glad, but not impatient. He was delighted when he was told that you would stay in my rooms in my absence, and seemed much interested in the idea. He had no belief apparently that he should live to see me, but was perfectly cheerful about it. He slept a great deal, and, as Aunt Kate says there was "so little of the sick-room" about him. He lay facing the windows, which he would never have darkened— never pained by the light. I sit writing this in his room upstairs, and a cast which Alice had taken from his head but which is very unsatisfactory and represents him as terribly emaciated stands behind me on that high chest of drawers. It is late in the evening, and I have been down into the parlour—I broke off half an hour ago—to talk again with Aunt Kate, who sits there alone. She and the nurse alone were with him at the last. Alice was in her room with your Alice and Katharine Loring, and had not seen him since the night before. She saw him very little for a good many days before his death—she was too ill, and Katharine Loring looked after her entirely. This left Father to Aunt Kate and the nurse, and the quiet simple character of his illness made them perfectly able to do everything—so that, as I said just now, there was no confusion, no embarrassment. He spoke of everything—

the disposition of his things, made all his arrangements of every kind. Aunt Kate repeats again and again, that he *yearned unspeakably* to die. I am too tired to write more, and my head is beginning to ache; I must either finish this in the morning, or send it as it is. In the latter case I will write again immediately, as I have many more things to say. The house is so *empty*—I scarcely know myself. Yesterday was such a Christmas as you may imagine—with Alice at K. Loring's, me ill in bed here, and Aunt Kate sitting alone downstairs, not only without a Christmas dinner but without any dinner, as she doesn't eat according to her wont!—27th a.m. Will send this now and write again tonight. All our wish here is that you should remain abroad the next six months.

Ever your
H. James Jr.

1. WJ had remained abroad (see HJ to Mrs. WJ, 16 October 1882), and was in Paris when word came of his father's serious illness. He went to London, but found that Henry had already sailed; a cable from Cambridge informed him his father seemed to be in no immediate danger, and he accordingly settled into his brother's rooms in Bolton Street to await further news. However, he wrote at once a letter to his father (14 December 1882) expressing his debt to him and saying farewell if he should not see him again.

To William James

Ms Harvard

131 Mount Vernon St.
Dec. 28*th* [1882]

Dear William.

I was not able yesterday to write you a second letter, as I hoped, as I was still suffering rather too much from my head; but this evening I am pretty well myself again, and shall endeavour to go on with my story. I have seen your wife yesterday and today, and she tells me again that she wrote you so minutely and so constantly during the progress of Father's illness that my very imperfect record gathered from hearsay will have little value for you. Mainly, I can only repeat that the whole thing was tranquil and happy—almost, as it were, comfortable. The wanderings of his mind which were never great, were always of a joyous description, and his determination not to eat was cheerful and reasonable. That is, he was always prepared to explain why he wouldn't eat—i.e. because he had entered upon the "spiritual life," and didn't wish to keep up the mere form of living in the body. During the last ten or fifteen hours only his speech became thick and inarticulate: he had an accumulation of phlegm in his throat which he was too weak to get rid of. The doctor gave him a little opium, to help him, as I understand Aunt Kate, to clear his larynx, which had to some extent this effect, but which also made him sink into a gentle unconsciousness, in which, however, he still continued vaguely to talk. He spoke then several times of mother—muttering (intelligibly) her name: "Mary—my Mary." Somewhat before this Aunt Kate says he murmured—"Oh, I have such good boys —*such* good boys!" The efforts that he made to speak toward the last were, the Dr. (Ahlborn) assured Aunt Kate quite mechanical and unconscious. I have had (with as little delay, myself, as possible) to learn as executor.[1] Father's property is roughly estimated at $95,000; of which $75,000 are in the three Syracuse houses, the rest in railway (B.C. and I.) bonds and shares.—I wish I could be assured that you have banished all thought of coming home, and that you find London habitable and profitable. If not, go back to Paris, but stay abroad and get all possible good, so long as I stay here, which will be till the summer. This is what we all wish. (Don't tell this to people in London, however,—or to Miss Balls,[2] to whom I shall soon be writing.) (If you are asked about my stay, say you don't know—it is uncertain.) Alice was here yesterday with the two children, whom she had been having photographed—all very lovely. Farewell, dear William.

Ever yours
H. James[3]

1. The second born, HJ, was named executor by his father—perhaps because he had been his mother's favorite son, but also probably because he alone of the four sons had earned his way in the world in the practical "money–sense."

2. HJ's London landlady.

3. Here, for almost the first time, HJ drops the "Jr." He occasionally from habit still signed a few letters in the old way, but from this point on removed as quickly as possible what he had called the "mere junior" from both his letters and the title pages of his books.

To William James

Ms Harvard

131 Mt. Vernon St.
Jan *1st* 1883

Dear William

I received this a.m. your note of the 20th, written after you had seen the news of Father's death in the *Standard*. I can imagine how sadly it must have presented itself, as you sit alone in those dark far-away rooms of mine. But it would have been sadder still if you also had arrived only to hear that after those miserable eight days at sea he was lost forever and ever to our eyes. Thank God we haven't another parent to lose; though all Aunt Kate's sweetness and devotion makes me feel, in advance, that it will be scarcely less a pang when *she* goes! Such is the consequence of cherishing our "natural ties!" After a little, Father's departure will begin to seem a simple and natural fact, however, as it has begun to appear to us here. I went out yesterday (Sunday) morning, to the Cambridge cemetery (I had not been able to start early enough on Saturday afternoon, as I wrote you I meant to do)—and stood beside his grave a long time and read him your letter of farewell[1]—which I am sure he heard somewhere out of the depths of the still, bright winter air. He lies extraordinarily close to Mother, and as I stood there and looked at this last expression of so many years of mortal union, it was difficult not to believe that they were not united again in some consciousness of my belief. On my way back I stopped to see Alice and sat with her for an hour and admired the lovely babe, who is a most loving little mortal. Then I went to see F.J. Child, because I had been told that he has been beyond every one full of kindness and sympathy since the first of father's illness, and had appeared to feel his death more than anyone outside the family. Every one, however, has been full of kindness—absolutely *tender* does this poor old Boston appear to have shown itself. Among others Wendell Holmes (who is now a Judge of the Supreme Court) has shone—perhaps a little unexpectedly, in this respect. Alice has been ill this last twenty four hours—but not with any nervousness; only from nausea produced apparently from the doses of salvic soda that Beach has been giving her. She is at present much better. Your letter makes me nervous in regard to your dispositions of coming home. *Don't for the world think of this, I beseech you*—it would be a very idle step. There is *nothing* here for you to do, not a place even for you to live, and there is every reason why you should remain abroad till the summer. Your wishing to come is a mere vague, uneasy sentiment, not unnatural under the circumstances, but corresponding to no real fitness. Let it subside as soon as possible, we all beg you. I wrote you two days ago everything that there is to be told you as yet as regards Father's will. Wait quietly till you hear more from me. I am going as soon as I can get away, to Milwaukee, and I will write you more as soon as I have been there. Aunt Kate is still here. Make the most of London.

Ever yours
H. James Jr.

1. The moving letter arrived too late to be read by his father. The full text is printed in Henry James, ed., *Letters of William James* (1920), I, 218–220.

To William James

Ms Harvard

131 Mt. Vernon St.
Jan 8*th* [1883]

Dear William.

I wrote you two days ago, and I add a few lines today to make that letter complete. It is simply to let you know that I spoke to Alice this a.m. on the subject of an equal re-division of the estate, and that she gives her complete and cordial assent to the plan.[1] It has not been possible for me to talk with her about it before, but I now find that the will has made her very unhappy from the first, and that she has placed her hopes on this arrangement. As soon as I hear from you, therefore, it will be made. I tell you this that you may know that your own voice alone is now wanting. I would tell you more (about the circumstances in which the will was made—the considerations which led Father to omit Wilky etc.) if I were not too pressed with writing at present. This must wait till we meet. There are such a multitude of letters here to be answered. I haven't seen your Alice for a week—and am therefore without any news I [she] may have received from you. I have been very busy (back at my work, thank heaven), and I can't leave Alice much. She is very much better, and I feel pretty sure will go on. I shall see your wife in a day or two. The redivision will be a perfectly simple transaction—not demanding in the faintest degree your presence, etc. I hope your situation is fair.

Ever faithfully yours
H. James [he writes half of "Jr.," and stops]

1. The elder HJ, with his impractical nature and abiding sense of Divine Justice, had arranged his will so as to leave less money to his third son, Garth Wilkinson James, who was improvident and had drained the family's resources. The father felt therefore that Wilky had had his share of the inheritance in advance. But Wilky had been wounded in the Civil War and suffered from a heart condition and rheumatic fever, and Henry, as executor, polled his sister Alice and the youngest brother Robertson on a compassionate redividing of the property. WJ, still abroad and outvoted in his absence, protested it was easy for bachelor Henry and spinster Alice to vote William's money away, but that they did not have children and his serious family responsibilities. The ensuing correspondence deals with this problem.

To William James

Ms Harvard

Globe Hotel
Syracuse [N.Y.]
Jan. 23d [1883]

Dear William.

I wrote you a long letter of a fortnight ago—and you will perhaps at the present moment be staggering under the receipt of it. I trust that the purity of my intentions may have served as an excuse for the exaggerated zeal—possibly—with which I entered into the question of your coming home. It seemed to me such a pity you should do so at this dreary season, and in the present situation of your wife, that, seeing she also thought it an equal pity, I couldn't restrain the violence of my feeling on the subject. It seemed to me—and it strikes me so still—very melancholy, and wanting in the proper dignity of your station, that you should come back to spend these next months in Cambridge without a home of your own and without your normal position in the College. However, I won't return to all that now, for by the time this reaches you, you will have made up your mind in pursuance of your own reasons. Perhaps—I certainly hope so— that the problem of life in London will have put on a fairer face. I hope at any rate that you are physically better, whether you come or stay. If you do come back the right place—i.e. habitation —for you will be the third bed-room in the Mt. Vernon Street house. That will be better than living at Mrs. Gibbens's. I occupy Father's room, and Alice her old room; but there is an excellent third story front bedroom, which used to be Aunt Kate's. I won't offer to give you up Father's room, because I lately made you a present of my rooms in London. But peace to all this—which is not *àpropos* as I sit at the window of the principal hotel at Syracuse, looking out at our "property" here, which returns my gaze from its eminently eligible position across the way.—I am on my way back from a visit of about four days to Wilky and Bob. We are in the midst of a period of terrific cold—the thermometer at Milwaukee was 20° below zero. This of course did not conduce to the cheerfulness of an episode intrinsically rather sad. The three letters I have written you as executor of the estate will have put you into possession of all that has lately passed with regard to it. It has been an immense load off my mind in seeing Wilky and Bob that before I did so I should have written you my proposal for your assent to an equal re-division of the estate. If I made you that proposal *then* with eagerness, I should have made it now with an even greater desire that it be realized. I wrote you last of Alice's entire assent to it—and Bob of course is only too glad.

That Father's will should have been made just as it was, has been a source of the greatest unhappiness to all of us here—an unhappiness but faintly reflected in the first letters I wrote you on the subject, for reasons which I shall be able to explain to you better some other day. Time—each succeeding day—has only made the thing more regrettable. I have so far presumed on your seeing it in this light that I asked Joe Warner, before leaving Boston, to send you a paper of agreement to a re-division, to sign—before waiting to hear from you definitely. I did this simply to save time—though I now see that it makes very little practical difference, as it will take three or four months longer to settle the estate. It will however be a great pleasure to me to write to Wilky and Bob on the earliest day that you *do* assent to the re-division. You probably will yourself have written to them to this effect. I staid with Wilky at Milwaukee, and found him, I am sorry to say, a sadly broken and changed person. I am afraid he is pretty well finished, for his spirits have gone a good deal, as well as his health, though all his old gentleness and softness remain. When I got there he was in the grip of a rheumatic attack, but it left him thirty six hours after my arrival, and then he was very much better. I think he might, in spite of his double malady, get on decently well in the future if he has some small idea of taking care of himself, or if his wife had some idea of taking care of him. But they have absolutely none—as is shown in their whole manner of life, and Carry's imbecility is especially deplorable. I lectured and preached them much; I hope with some effect. Bob strikes me as a good deal better than he used to be; he has become a landed proprietor. That is, he and Mary have by her father's advice, invested $7000 (of hers) in the purchase of a country residence or rural retreat about five miles from Milwaukee and about two from Holton's own residence. It is a small but solid brick house, with a Grecian portico, and a really very charming domain of thirty five acres. It needs to have a little money spent on it—but it is, says Holton, a very wise investment.—I have spent a large part of today with Munroe, our agent here. The "property" is very good; much better than I supposed—in the very best position in town, in good order, and occupied by prosperous first class tenants. It yields, after all charges are paid, $5,250. per annum—which makes for each of the four of us $1312 income. (As I told you, Alice's share is to be taken from the other property.) Munroe strongly advises its being kept together about four years longer, as it is constantly increasing in value. He is sure that at the end of that time the property would sell for about $87000. Of all this however I will write you later. I scribble this while I wait for the train which tonight bears me away—I reach Boston tomorrow night. Munroe drove me this afternoon, in spite of the cold, along *James Street*[1] the 5th Avenue of Syracuse, one of the handsomest American Streets I have ever seen—named after our poor Grandfather! I must close this, pack my bag, and eat my "supper." I shall probably find news from you in Boston.

Yours ever
H. James Jr.

1. Named for HJ's immigrant grandfather, William James of Albany.

To Helena De Kay Gilder

Ms N.Y. Public Library

131 Mt. Vernon St.
Boston. Jan. 26th [1883]

My dear Mrs. Gilder.[1]

Let me thank you with as little delay as possible for the great kindness of your note, which has a reference to the far-away past that touches me almost as much as its reference to the present. You are right in thinking that my dear Father had been a great source of happiness in the lives of his children and that it was a blessing to know him as we knew him. He pervaded and animated our collective and individual existence to an extraordinary degree —and his presence had the most generous, light-giving quality. There is nothing sad for me however in the death of a man who had so completely done with life and who longed so to die. He seems immensely absent—but he is absent from so many things that *we* are tied to in spite of ourselves! Alice tells me to thank you very cordially for your sympathetic thought of her. I remain with her for the present, and I hope that some day or other she will come abroad. I passed through New York on Wednesday and saw your husband, but saw almost no one else. It was a question of hours or I should have seen you. I shall still do so, for I am not without hope of spending a week or two in your neighborhood within a calculable period. Be well, and keep your children so.

Very faithfully yours
H. James Jr.

1. Wife of Richard Watson Gilder, the editor, and sister of Mrs. Bronson.

To William James

Ms Harvard

131 Mt. Vernon St.
Feb. 11<i>th</i> [1883]

Dear William.

I feel as if I ought to write to you again today on account of your letter of Jan. 22d (just received) although I have written you so much of late. My last, two or three days since, was a rather (perhaps) heated reply to the letter in which you acknowledged the arrival of mine (sent at the same time as the telegram) urging you not to return home. If this has seemed to you nasty or ill-tempered, please don't mind it. It *was* rather meddlesome in me to have so much to say about the question of your coming back—but I repeat that it was a case in which to meddle seemed the safest thing, and to trot out all the reasons against your return (leaving you to do justice to the others) seemed the only way to treat the subject from this side (if treated at all). I even persist in meddling, so far as to be glad that you have not yet come and that according to your last (of the 25th Jan.) to Alice you are probably now in Paris. (Alice reads me and sends me everything possible.) I write this with a clear understanding that you won't answer it, and that you will write to me after this as little and as briefly as possible. This is only to return very briefly on my side, to the question of the re-division of the estate with regard to Wilky, as to which I have already written you so much and to which you again return yourself, in this letter of Jan. 22d (I have just been for three days to Newport, and I find it on my return). I agree in all you say as to the *principle* of Father's holding Wilky responsible for the $5000 advanced to him before his failure, and I can only repeat that if the circumstances were now more favourable to our cutting down his allowance it should certainly be done. But they are as little so as possible. I have now decided to assent to his *own* request to accept $5000 from the amount I am to put into trust for him (*i.e.* the rest of his equal share), to enable him to pay his debt to Bob and two or three other "debts of honour." (His debt to Bob, it now appears, amounts, not as I told you last, to $1000 but to about $1500.) To cut off more than this would be rather grievous—and his state of mind and of health together are such that I shrink from carrying out such a plan. Just now both his children are ill with scarlet fever (it appears to be light) and in the midst of this addition to his other troubles I feel like letting him off easily. You may think that I am rather weak about this; and I am, I admit. But I put it all on the ground of Wilky's generally collapsed condition. If it were a palpable injury to any of us, I should not urge my own project in preference to yours. But as the difference between the two is so small, in favour of yourself, of Alice and of me, and as Bob moreover is to be paid in this way, as well as in yours, I think we had better abide by the fact that having Wilky equal with us and not insisting on the forfeit in order to justify Father, will be the thing which satisfies most of the proprieties of the case. The will was unfortunate, in its wholesale character, and the best way to justify Father is simply to assume that he expected us (as he *did* expect us) to rearrange equally. No need to go over all this though, as I believe that I said in my last, you will have assented to my way of doing this thing, before this reaches you. What I have, after all, mainly wished to tell you is that I have judged it best *not* to for-

ward him your letters recommending this modification of my
proposal. I shall let him suppose that you have simply assented to
it, and shall leave it to your confidence that I am acting for the
best as the circumstances appear to me here, to justify me.

Yours ever
H. James

Our Alice gets on very well.

To G. W. Smalley

Ms Yale

131 Mount Vernon St.
Feb. 21st [1883]

My dear Smalley.

I have just been reading in the *Tribune* your letter of Jan. 25, in
which you devote a few lines to the silly article in the Quarterly
on *American Novels,* etc. It occurs to me that as you apparently
have been misled by the author's insinuation that I had contributed
to *The Century* an article about Howells, preliminary to his ill-
starred amiabilities to me,[1] it is as well I should "just remark"
that I never in my life wrote a word about Howells in the *Century,*
and had not for years written about him anywhere. I once reviewed one of his early novels—eight years ago—anonymously,
in a New York paper. There was an article in the *Century* about
Howells written (and signed) by T. S. Perry. The *Quarterly* man
(it is interesting to hear it is the genial Jennings) doesn't say in so
many words I wrote it, but he evidently wishes to convey that
impression, by the way the phrase is turned and his talk about
mutual admiration, etc.; and the phrasing is disengenuous. Enough,
however, about this truly idiotic commotion.

—If I write you of this it will perhaps seem to you that I ought
to have much else to say. But alas, I have very little. Never have
I led a less suggestive life. I see myself fixed here till midsummer.
On the other hand, when I return to the banks of the Thames it
will probably be "for good." My thoughts, as usual, hover very

fondly about them; and my spirit doesn't in the least tread these abominably slippery pavements, though my overshoes (the consolation of my existence) do. I see no one to speak of, but live here very quietly with my sister and "take in" the English papers etc. Later in the winter I hope to go for a short time to New York and Washington, but just now my longest journey is to Cambridge. The walk out there and back (a violent measure) occasionally saves my life; it is my principal [illegible] diversion. I am not unhappy, however, I like the quiet, the repose from the feverish frenzy of London, and find time to read, to think and to wish I were back there! I greet your dear housefull and send you *mille amitiés*. I make you always my spokesman to Lady Rosebery and send her the most cordial regards. It is foretold me that I shall write to her.

Ever faithfully
Henry James

1. See HJ to Howells, 27 November 1882.

To Mrs. Henry Adams

Ms Mass. Historical

131 Mount Vernon St.
Feb. 28*th* [1883]

Dear Mrs. Adams.

It was very pleasant, the other day, to see your handwriting, and it would be pleasanter still to see something more of you. If I were at liberty to take the proper course for doing so, I should start tomorrow for your milder latitude. But I am tied rather tight to Boston just now—being unable to go away and leave my sister companionless. I don't despair however of spending a few days by the Potomac in April.—I see now the advantage, last winter, of having discovered the situation of that stream. I sent you my little volume the other day rather as a compliment than with the expectation that you would approve of many of my points of view. None of them, however, are my own—I can assure you of that. I am keeping my own for a grand ultimate work of fiction for which I expect the success in this country that *Democracy* has had in England. The latter work forms the favourite reading of Mr. Gladstone. Mrs. Sands told me last summer that she had sat next to him at dinner, one day, when he talked of it for an hour. "He said it was written in such a *handy* style, you know!" Trim your laurels, ye praised of prime ministers and professional beauties! You can imagine how I am enjoying my Boston winter, and what a charming series of New Letters I am preparing. I lunch almost every Sunday with your sister at Cambridge—but the intervals are as flat as the New Land! I miss immensely your little *douches* of last winter—they at least produced a healthy glow and kept me alive. I should like very much some Washington gossip, but I don't make bold to ask you for any— you will say come and gossip yourself! I write you at the hour when I should naturally be sitting at your fireside between Miss Beale and Miss Bayard possibly—if not between Miss Loring and the blonde widow who got me my rooms next [last] year and whose name I have forgotten. I find I am constantly much worse disappointed than Miss Beale disappointed me and have now learned to give another name to the sensation she produced. As for Miss Bayard, since seeing her last year I have sought her like in vain in the capitals of Europe. *Il n'y a qu'elle!*—and Miss West! You see in what a roseate vision Washington appears to me. I wonder whether you should be able to give me any news of Clarence King and of poor John Hay, of whom (both) I saw much last summer. If not, I should give you some. Clarence is a truly festive nature, and has more water-colours even than you. Hay is less festive, for good reasons I fear; but very pleasant to talk with in Paris after dining with King! I *do* count seriously upon getting on to Washington for a little about six weeks hence; I think that will be a cosy moment. Keep a place warm for me—or so late in the spring, perhaps, keep it cool, and with friendliest remembrances to Henry Adams believe me ever faithfully

Henry James

To George Du Maurier

Ms Harvard

115 East 25th Street,
New York.
April 17*th*, 1883

My dear Du Maurier,

I send you by this post the sheets of that little tribute to your genius which I spoke of to you so many months ago and which appears in the *Century* for May.[1] The magazine is not yet out, or I would send you that, and the long delay makes my article, so slight in itself, rather an impotent conclusion. Let me hasten to assure you that the "London Society," tacked to the title, is none of my doing, but that of the editors of the Magazine, who put in an urgent plea for it. Such as my poor remarks are, I hope you will find in them nothing disagreeable, but only the expression of an exceeding friendliness. May my blessing go with them and a multitude of good wishes!

I should have been to see you again long ago if I had not suddenly been called to America (by the death of my father) in December last. The autumn, before that, I spent altogether abroad, and have scarcely been in England since I bade you good-bye, after that very delightful walk and talk we had together last July —an episode of which I have the happiest, tenderest memory. Romantic Hampstead seems very far away from East 25th St: though East 25th St. has some good points. I have been spending the winter in Boston and am here only on a visit to a friend,[2] and though I am *New-Yorkais d'origine* I never return to this wonderful city without being entertained and impressed afresh. New York is full of types and figures and curious social idiosyncrasies, and I only wish we had some one here, to hold up the mirror, with a fifteenth part of your talent. It is altogether an extraordinary growing, swarming, glittering, pushing, chattering, good-natured, cosmopolitan place, and perhaps in some ways the best imitation of Paris that can be found (yet with a great originality of its own.) But I didn't mean to be so geographical; I only meant to shake hands, and to remind myself again that if my dear old London life is interrupted, it isn't, heaven be praised, finished, and that therefore there is a use—a delightful and superior use—in "keeping up" my relations. I am talking a good deal like Mrs. Ponsonby de Tomkyns, but when you reflect that you are not Sir Gorgius Midas, you will acquit me. I have a fair prospect of returning to England late in the summer, and that will be for a long day. I hope your winter has used you kindly and that Mrs. du Maurier is well, and also the other ornaments of your home, including the Great St. Bernard. I greet them all most kindly and am

ever very faithfully yours,
Henry James

P.S. I don't know whether your pen-and-ink is all for pictures; but if it ever takes the form of a short note, such a genial missive would find me at 131 Mount Vernon St. Boston, Mass. U.S.A.; or be punctually forwarded from my London rooms—3 Bolton Street, Piccadilly.

1. "Du Maurier and London Society," *Century*, XXVI (May 1883), 48–65.
2. E. L. Godkin.

To Frederick Macmillan
Ms BM

Washington. Wormley's Hotel
April 19th 1883

My dear Macmillan.

Your letter of the 6th comes to me here, where, after ten days in New York, I am spending a week. Let me immediately answer your inquiry about my views of the projected new edition of my stories.[1]

I like the idea very much, and only make the condition that the books be as pretty as possible. Can you make them really pretty for 18 pence a volume? I should like them to be *charming,* and beg you to spare no effort to make them so. Your specimen page will enlighten me as to this, and I will, after receiving it, lay out the arrangement into volumes as you suggest: though I shall not be sure whether you think it important that the old *grouping* (of the shorter things) be retained or may be departed from: i.e. whether for instance *The Madonna of the Future* might go with *Daisy Miller,* etc. I hope fortune will favour the enterprise. I should tell you, *àpropos* of this, that the property of Chatto and Windus in *Confidence* has expired; and that I have parted with the English copyright (prospective) in two books which I am to write as speedily as possible for my American publisher J. R. Osgood. One of these is to be a novel about half as long as the *Portrait;* the other a group of three tales, exactly corresponding to the *Siege of London* etc. which I sent you. I have sold him these things, to do what he pleases with for periodical and serial publication and otherwise, both in England and in this country. I mention this so that you may know in advance that there will ultimately be these several productions as to which, when the time shall come for your wishing to include them in the little "choice" edition, you will have to treat with him—not with me. I have no doubt he will be glad to arrange with you for the appearance of the shorter stories in the *Illustrated English.* One of these is to be another international episode, of exactly the length of the *Siege of London:* "Lady Barberina"—an earl's daughter who marries a New Yorker and comes to live in 39th St!—Of course I shall be at liberty to place the *Siege of London* and the *Point of View* in your 18 penny edition.—I suddenly remember, by the way, that the short tales abovementioned (to be supplied to Osgood) (as well as the novel) have by this time *probably* been disposed of by him in advance to the *Century*—with which my relations are apparently destined to become intimate, as I have been writing three or four essays which are to appear in its pages.

I spent ten delightful days in New York which decidedly is one of the pleasant cities of the world. Washington is also charming at present with the temperature of a Northern July, and great banks of pink and white blossom all over the place. It reminds me of Rome! The date of my return is I am sorry to say rather

411

more than less uncertain, and there is even a *possibility* of its not taking place till October next. I see however no reason to expect a longer detention than that. I shall then have been away eleven months. Thanks for your few items of London news, all of which I hold "precious." I am very glad to hear something of poor Mrs. Green,[2] to whom I lately wrote to your care. *Apropos* of the ventilation of your affairs with Julian Hawthorne, I can only say that the invasive impudence of the papers here is something unspeakable and horrible. I have suffered much from it myself. Many greetings to your wife and every one who remembers me.

Ever faithfully yours
Henry James

Please, in any more announcements or advertising (of things of mine) direct the dropping of the *Jr.*

1. This, the first uniform edition of HJ's writings, pleased him because of its pocket-size format, the opportunity to revise the text, and the chance to remove the "Jr." from his title pages.
2. Mrs. John Richard Green whose husband, the historian, had just died.

To James R. Osgood

Ms Colby

Washington, Wormley's Hotel
April 19*th*, 1883.

Dear Mr. Osgood,

I think I shall be willing to publish a volume of essays, *after* three or four which are latent in the *Century* shall have had time to appear. In fact I shall then have material for two volumes— different books, I mean—even without printing everything (that has appeared the last six years in magazines). To consider only one, however, to begin with, it would not be able to be a series of critical papers (on authors) simply—for I haven't enough of these; it would have to be essays and sketches (as you say) com- mingled. For instance (I don't set them in their absolute order):[1]

1 Sainte-Beuve (From *North American Review*)
2 Alph. Daudet.
3 Anthony Trollope.
4 Carlyle and Emerson. } *Century*
5 Du Maurier.
6 Eugène Delacroix—*N.A. Review*
7 Tommaso Salvini—*Atlantic*
8 Venice——*Century*
9 Washington in Spring (promised to *Century*)
10 Americans in Europe—*Nation*

As regards another possible volume, I have produced during the last six years a good many sketches of places and things (English, French and Italian) which are buried in old *Atlantics, Galaxys, Lippincotts, Nations* and New York *Tribunes*. A collection of these would be feasible and I think, entertaining. The trouble is that the best of these things are the sketches of England—which motives of delicacy absolutely prohibit my reprinting, *in toto,* at present. But I think I could reprint portions of them (the flattering ones!) and there would be more than enough of the other papers. This however we have time to discuss.

I should propose to call the *other* volume (contents enumerated) either *Studies and Sketches* or *Impressions of Art and Life*. There is a name I should like best of all, *i.e.* simply "Superficial Impressions." It would be so modest! My only hesitation about it is that it might possibly be too much so. But I think not.[2]

I enclose you part of a letter I have just received from Frederick Macmillan. My purpose in doing so is first to show you (*vide* the third page) that you may dispose to advantage of "Lady Barberina" in England if the *Century* doesn't want it (which however I think it does); and second to let you see that the arrangement I have made with you with regard to my two next books will be a source of profit to you in that country even greater than I believed when I last saw you: that is, of course, I mean, if you eventually arrange with the Macmillans to include the said two books in the 18 penny edition which Frederick Macmillan proposes. I have given my consent to their terms for what relates to my past production and notified F.M. that my two next ones are to be your property.

I am afraid I am not prepared to say definitely at present what the two short stories which are to go with *Lady Barberina* will consist of. I have the subjects of a couple of dozen tales of that length noted down—but I really can't declare which of them I shall some weeks hence feel most like working up. It seems to me that the Editor of any periodical ought to be ready to take a short story of mine not because it has been described to him, but because it is mine. However, on Gilder's[3] asking me the other day to specify (if convenient) these two short things, I related the plot of one I should *probably* write, which was to be called "The Impressions of a Cousin";[4] (I am afraid I haven't time to go over it here and now), and told him that the other would (also probably, but not certainly) be an episode in the lives of a group of contemporary "aesthetes," the former American, the other "international."

The latter, briefly, is the history of an American aesthete (or possibly an English one), who conceives a violent admiration for a French aesthete (a contemporary novelist), and goes to Paris to make his acquaintance; where he finds that his Frenchman is so much more thoroughgoing a specimen of the day than himself, that he is appalled and returns to Philistinism. Or else (I haven't settled it) he is to discover that the Frenchman who is so Swinburnian in his writings, is a regular quiet *bourgeois* in his life; which operates upon the aesthete as a terrible disillusionment. I may add that there will be a woman in the case. The idea of the thing is to show a contrast between the modern aesthete, who poses for artistic feelings, but is very hollow, and the real artist—who is immensely different. But I only mention this as a theme I *may* use: perhaps I shall take another.[5]

I go to New York (same address) on the 25th, and to Boston on the 30th.

Ever yours
H. James

[To this letter James added a leaf listing the "sketches of places and things" which would make an "entertaining" volume:]

1 Venice.
2 An Italian Autumn.
3 Paris Revisited.
4 From Normandy to the Pyrenees.
5 Chartres.
6 Rouen.
7 Etretat.
8 Rheims and Laon.
9 An English Easter.
10 The Suburbs of London.
11 London at Midsummer.
12 Abbeys and Castles.
13 Three Excursions.
14 In Warwickshire.
15 English Vignettes.
16 An English Winter Watering Place.
17 An English Christmas.
18x The British Soldier.
19 In Scotland.
20 Americans Abroad.
x Saratoga.
x Newport.
x Quebec.
x Niagara.

I propose to call the volume *Studies in Local Colour,*[6] until I think of something better: I put the Venice first, though the subject is rather threadbare, because the article is the best.

1. This volume never materialized in this form, but some of the essays were incorporated in *Partial Portraits,* 1888.
2. Published during 1883, titled *Portraits of Places.*
3. Richard Watson Gilder, now editor of the *Century.*
4. "The Impressions of a Cousin" and "A New England Winter," with "Lady Barberina," made up the volume *Tales of Three Cities* published during 1884.
5. James did not write this story. Instead, he wrote a social comedy, "A New England Winter," published in the *Century,* August–September 1884.
6. The title ultimately became *Portraits of Places,* whose table of contents is substantially as listed here.

To J. R. Osgood

Ms Yale

131 Mount Vernon St.
May 5*th* [1883]

Dear Mr. Osgood.

Should you think well of the idea of bringing out my little comedy of *Daisy Miller* in a small and pretty volume after its

termination (in the *June* number of the Atlantic)? You will probably remember that when I made last summer my agreement
with you to bring out my next production, I excepted the play
in question, as having been already promised to Messrs. Houghton
& Mifflin. I have now given them the opportunity to take hold
of it, and they have declined in the note which I enclose. This
absolves me from further consideration of them in the matter—
so that I may transfer the opportunity to you. I don't know what
you will think of it—but to myself it seems that the volume ought,
considering the success of the original story, to do well. I should
only make the condition that it be printed in the manner of French
comedies—that is, with the names of the characters *above* the
speeches, and not on a line with them. I enclose an example of
what I mean—and shall be glad to hear from you.

Yours very truly
H. James

To Frederick Macmillan

Ms BM

131 Mount Vernon St.
May 8*th* [1883]

Dear Macmillan.

I have arranged the short stories according to your request, to
the best of my ingenuity. (The specimen pages you send are charming.) The tales make four volumes of something less than two
hundred fifty pages each. The division I have made is arrived at
after various other attempted combinations, and appears to be the
one that satisfies most of the conditions—and the only one which
would make the volumes equal. They had better be issued, I
should say, in the order I have marked. I should think the little
series would be charming and I wish it all success.

I wrote you the other day from Washington—since when,
after another week in New York, I find myself back here. My
return to London has, alas, apparently quite definitely deferred

itself to the last days of the summer. Osgood, who is to publish some things of mine during the next year, tells me he has written to you—but to this correspondence I do not belong. In addition to the three or four new things (mostly short) that he is to bring out (they *are* all to appear in the *Century*), he will also put forth *two* volumes of essays (republished), a volume of short tales (early ones, collected from periodicals), and, in a small volume, the interminable dramatic *Daisy Miller*. I don't know what to say to you about the question of your bringing out a *portion* of this multifarious matter in London: e.g. the volumes of essays. If you don't they will probably be cribbed; yet on the other hand I am not very keen about their appearing there. (That is, with the exception of the first volume of the Essays, which will probably be called *Certain Impressions,* and contain articles on Ste. Beuve, A. Daudet, E. Delacroix, Carlyle and Emerson, Anthony Trollope, Du Maurier, Venice, Washington etc. Several of these things are yet to appear, in the *Century*.) The other volume of essays is to consist of sketches of travel and will possibly be named *Sketches and Studies in Local Colour.* But I will leave this till it seems more urgent. You are right: *Confidence* is now free. This letter is pure business—I will be sociable another time.—I am hideously homesick.

[sketch of hand pointing]—   Ever yours
Please make *that* now my name.   Henry James

To Emma Lazarus

Ms Columbia

131 Mt. Vernon Street
May 9*th* [1883]

Dear Miss Lazarus,[1]

I congratulate you heartily on your definite purpose of promising yourself of the other half (as it were) of our little world-ball, and send you with great pleasure a note to Mrs. Procter, who is a most delightful and wonderful old person, and a great friend of

417

mine. She doesn't "entertain" in the usual sense of the word—i.e. give dinners etc.; but she receives, eagerly, every Tuesday and every Sunday afternoons. She lives in a "flat," on the top of a high apartment-house, as her address. Send her my note by post, and send a word with it, saying that you will present yourself on the nearest Sunday or the nearest Tuesday, as the case may be, *without waiting to be* "asked." On Sunday afternoons you will be sure to find Browning there; go as often as you can. I will write to Mrs. P myself and ask her to make you acquainted with Lady Goldsmid, whom I think you will find it pleasant to know. Kindly send me your prospective London (bankers'?) address, that I may send you one or two notes more, in case I don't find time to do so before the 15th which I probably shall. Take everything "easy," amuse yourself largely and discreetly and believe me ever,

very truly yours
Henry James

1. Emma Lazarus (1849–1887), Jewish nationalist poet, had expressed to HJ a wish to meet certain poets abroad, notably Browning. HJ probably met her through her connections with the *Century*.

To Lady Rosebery

Ms Scotland

Boston, U.S.A.
131 Mount Vernon St.
June 16th [1883]

Dear Lady Rosebery.

I have just inflicted on you one of those injuries which require an instant apology. I have given a note of introduction to you— and I hasten to notify you of this audacious assault on your liberty and leisure. Perhaps you will forgive me when I tell you that the bearer is a very discreet, intelligent and amiable young man, who will neither bother you, nor bore you, and who is incapable of rash insistence. His name—rather an odd one—is Lawrence Godkin, and he is the son of one of my oldest and best friends, a man of much distinction here, and one of our first—or I should rather say our first—journalists, Edwin Lawrence Godkin, Editor of the *Nation,* New York. The youth goes to Europe for the summer, and when his father asked me the other day for a few introductions for him I bethought myself that I might perhaps appeal to your benevolence. I ought, I know, to minimize the crudity of this appeal by specifying something that you might do for him; but specifying is under the circumstances rather a delicate matter. However, I will risk the suggestion that if you should be spending a Sunday at Mentmore and should have an interstice for a very slender young New Yorker, he would drop into it gratefully and I should be very grateful for him. Perhaps this, after all, only makes my proceeding more crude—so, in my uncertainty, I will drop the question and leave my modest *protégé* to one of those happy accidents by which—when they are not still happier intuitions—your friends so often profit. This at any rate is another pretext for writing to you;—I had one already, but two are better (for my incorrigible modesty) than one. My letter has been hanging over your head for some weeks past, and if it has not descended it is because even from here I have seen you buried beneath those whitening drifts which the London heavens—if there be a heaven above London—discharge at this season of the year, and I was unwilling to contribute a particle of postal matter to the deluge. Then I reflect that it is very likely that after all you won't answer me (before I next have the honour of seeing you) and that my letter therefore will not greatly make you feel its weight. After many detentions I have at last the prospect of sailing for England toward the last of August. That is not immediate, but it is definite; and it is a great improvement in the prospects I have had all winter which were (on account of interminable family matters) a departure incalculably postponed. I must not however speak to even so sympathetic a Briton as yourself, as if my attitude toward my native land were that of constantly attempted flight! It isn't that I love it less, but that I love London more, and that being of a nature eminently constructed for homesickness my positive and negative poles have by a fatal (yet delightful) accident got turned upside-down. But I am (through my veil of my homesickness) enjoying our American summer, which is a revelation of light and heat such as I haven't had for ten years—upwards of that time having elapsed since I last spent these months here. Your English June is, like your roastbeef (I don't mean that of Mentmore, where the golden mean prevails), under-done; whereas ours is cooked beyond the possibility of any further cookery. I feel like a well-selected joint, slowly revolving on the spit, under the eye of the great chef who presides over our destinies—and our temperature. Excuse these irreverent pleasantries and remember that hot weather is relaxing. My sister, who is in the country, has lent me a little house which she has in this place, and I am leading an existence which I fondly try to flatter myself is productive. That is I am trying to scribble, and if I succeed I shall have the honour of sending you what I produce. Boston becomes about the 10th of June a social desolation; every one is in *villeggiatura* and remains so till the autumn. I am under various promises to various friends to participate with them in this mode of existence, but I relinquish with regret the lonely town, where I wear the minimum of clothing, take many baths a day and dine mainly on lemonade and ices. American life in summer is however very pleasant, and, given our climate, people understand it very well—people, that is, who cultivate the breezy verandah and dine as much as possible in the open air, where the viands can by no possibility grow cold. There are in this part of the country various centres of *villeggiatura*—Lenox, Beverly, Nahant, Newport etc.—of which the fame may in some degree have reached your ears, and which are very charming and original. Newport indeed is given up to billionaires and "dudes" (I will explain the dude when I see you next); but the others are a very pleasant mixture of carnal comfort and sweet simplicity. I won't however undertake to write the natural history of the American "summer resort"; perhaps some day your enlightened curiosity will lead you to come and look into the subject. Of topics I am afraid that we have none to speak of here just now—now that we have all read

Mrs. Carlyle, and "Mr. Isaacs,"[1] and even Ernest Renan's *Souvenirs de Jeunesse*.[2] We find Mrs. Carlyle rather squalid, but a great one for saying things well, and we thirst, generally, for the blood of J.A. Froude.[3] *Apropos* of saying things well, you will find some tremendously well said in the volume of Renan I just mentioned. "Des gens d'esprit vivent en Amerique, à la condition de n'être pas trop exigeants!" that is one of them, though of course it is insufferably impertinent. I won't bother you with vain conjectures about your family and your way of life—as I hope the former, and believe the latter, are all that can possibly be desired. I fix my eyes on your husband, through interposing newspapers, and the vision is always inspiring. Please to give him my friendliest —my very friendliest—regards. I feel very far away from English politics here, and I won't deny that there is a sweet repose in the feeling; all the more that I have them with such confidence in Rosebery, Smalley and Mr. Gladstone. I hope Rosebery is in good spirits and good health, and venture to believe in the former as I see he has been winning races—though I don't know that he does that for elation. Be so good, at any rate, as to congratulate him on anything that may have happened to him lately that he may happen to care about. I hope your little posterity flourishes, and shall return to England much agitated by conjecture as to whether your eldest daughter will remember me. I trust your season has been to your taste—neither too mild nor too wild! I have two excellent memories of about this moment—or a little later—of last summer. One is a breakfast—which I may perhaps be allowed to call *intime*—of which I partook in that dear little cylindrical room at Lansdowne House: the other is of a drive with Rosebery, the length of the Thames Embankment, late in the nocturnal hours. Each of these episodes, looked at across the Atlantic and from amid the vacancies of Boston, seems deeply romantic. I wish you a comfortable summer—many cylindrical breakfasts and also nocturnal drives, if you like them, and remain, dear Lady Rosebery,

very faithfully yours
Henry James

1. *Mr. Isaacs: A Tale of Modern India,* a novel by F. Marion Crawford.
2. Renan's *Souvenirs d'Enfance et de Jeunesse* (1883) contains his celebrated invocation to Athena on his first view of the Acropolis.
3. J. A. Froude had been publishing, as Carlyle's literary executor, the biographical materials of Carlyle and his wife; his frankness disturbed and outraged the Victorian traditions of privacy and of respectful homage to the dead.

To George Pellew

Ms Unknown[1]

131 Mt. Vernon St.
June 23*d*. [1883]

My dear Pellew:[2]

I found your thin red book on my table when I came in late last night. I read it this morning before I left my pillow—read it with much entertainment and profit. It contains many suggestive things very happily said, and I thank you much for your friendly thought in sending it to me. It is interesting as an attempt in scientific criticism of the delightful Jane—though when I read the first page or two I trembled lest you should overdo the science. But you don't overdo anything—you are indeed, I think, a little too discreet, too mild. I could have found it in me to speak more of her genius—of the extraordinary vividness with which she saw what she did see, and of her narrow unconcious perfection of form. But you point out very well all that she didn't see, and especially what I remember not to have seen indicated before, the want of moral illumination on the part of her heroines, who had undoubtedly small and second-rate minds and were perfect little she-Philistines. But I think that is partly what makes them interesting today. All that there was of them was feeling—a sort of simple undistracted concentrated feeling which we scarcely find any more. In of course an infinitely less explicit way, Emma Woodhouse and Anne Eliot give us as great an impression of "passion"—that celebrated quality—as the ladies of G. Sand and Balzac. Their small gentility and front parlour existence doesn't suppress it, but only modifies the outward form of it. You do very well when you allude to the narrowness of Miss Austen's social horizon—of the young Martin in *Emma* being kept at a distance, etc; all that is excellent. Also in what you say of her apparent want of consciousness of nature. A friend of mine in England went to see the "Cobb" at Lynn because in *Persuasion* it had inspired Miss A. with the unprecedented impulse of several lines of description. He said to himself that it must be wonderful, and he found it so, so that he bought a house there and remained. Do write another little red essay describing and tracing the growth of the estimate of local colour in fiction—the development of the realistic description of nature—the consciousness of places being part of the story, etc. You will do it excellently. The quotation (by "Mr. Murch") you mention on p. 26, is simply the closing sentence of Macaulay's essay on *Mme* d'Arblay!3—I shall be much interested in what you do next, and remain

Very faithfully yours,
Henry James.

1. The holograph letter was originally in the autograph collection of Captain F. L. Pleadwell in Honolulu, dispersed after his death.

2. George Pellew (1860–1892) received the Bowdoin Prize at Harvard in 1883 for his dissertation on Jane Austen's novels. The letter contains one of James's rare comments on Miss Austen, over and above his ironies in "The Lesson of Balzac" on the Austen cult.

3. The closing sentence of Macaulay's essay on Madame d' Arblay reads: "But the fact that she has been surpassed gives her additional claim to our respect and gratitude; for in truth, we owe to her not only Evelina, Cecilia and Camilla, but also *Mansfield Park* and the Absentee."

To Grace Norton

Ms Harvard

131 Mount Vernon St.,
Boston.
July 28th [1883].

My dear Grace,

Before the sufferings of others I am always utterly powerless, and the letter you gave me reveals such depths of suffering that I hardly know what to say to you. This indeed is not my last word —but it must be my first. You are not isolated, verily, in such states of feeling as this—that is, in the sense that you appear to make all the misery of mankind your own; only I have a terrible sense that you give all and receive nothing—that there is no reciprocity in your sympathy—that you have all the affliction of it and none of the returns. However—I am determined not to speak to you except with the voice of stoicism. I don't know *why* we live—the gift of life comes to us from I don't know what source or for what purpose; but I believe we can go on living for the reason that (always of course up to a certain point) life is the most valuable thing we know anything about and it is therefore presumptively a great mistake to surrender it while there is any yet left in the cup. In other words consciousness is an illimitable power, and though at times it may seem to be all consciousness of misery, yet in the way it propagates itself from wave to wave, so that we never cease to feel, though at moments we appear to, try to, pray to, there is something that holds one in one's place, makes it a standpoint in the universe which it is probably good not to forsake. You are right in your consciousness that we are all echoes and reverberations of the *same,* and you are noble when your interest and pity as to everything that surrounds you, appears to have a sustaining and harmonizing power. Only don't, I beseech you, *generalize* too much in these sympathies and tendernesses— remember that every life is a special problem which is not yours but another's and content yourself with the terrible algebra of your own. Don't melt too much into the universe, but be as solid and dense and fixed as you can. We all live together, and those of us who love and know, live so most. We help each other—even unconsciously, each in our own effort, we lighten the effort of others, we contribute to the sum of success, make it possible for others to live. Sorrow comes in great waves—no one can know that better than you—but it rolls over us, and though it may almost smother us it leaves us on the spot and we know that if it is strong we are stronger, inasmuch as it passes and we remain. It wears us, uses us, but we wear it and use it in return; and it is blind, whereas we after a manner see. My dear Grace, you are passing through a darkness in which I myself in my ignorance see nothing but that you have been made wretchedly ill by it; but it is only a darkness it is not an end, or *the* end. Don't think, don't feel, any more than you can help, don't conclude or decide— don't do anything but *wait*. Everything will pass, and serenity and *accepted* mysteries and disillusionments, and the tenderness of a few good people, and new opportunities and ever so much of life, in a word, will remain. You will do all sorts of things yet, and I will help you. The only thing is not to *melt* in the meanwhile. I insist upon the necessity of a sort of mechanical condensation— so that however fast the horse may run away there will, when he pulls up, be a somewhat agitated but perfectly identical G. N. left in the saddle. Try not to be ill—that is all; for in that there is a [failure].[1] You are marked out for success, and you must not fail. You have my tenderest affection and all my confidence.

Ever your faithful friend—
Henry James

1. HJ wrote "future" but fairly obviously meant "failure."

To Sarah W. Whitman

Ms Harvard

Albemarle Hotel
New York.
Aug. 21st [1883]

Dear Mrs. Whitman.

Please be duly sensible of the fact that the last words I address to any lady in this torrid zone, are addressed to the gracious hostess of the nameless cottage on the Beverly shore. This, however, is not the tone in which I ought to write you; for if I had been a truly systematic person I should have written to you weeks ago. I ought to have done so, and I am much ashamed of a silence, which though it was really but the dumbness of deep gratitude, was sadly wanting in the forms of civility. Had I written sooner, however (and this reflection mitigates my shame), I should not have been able to impart to my words the extreme tenderness of a farewell, which you must know it is my impulse to do at the present moment. I sail tomorrow for the ancient world. I am hot, I am tired, I am convinced I have forgotten most of the last things I have wished to do here. Therefore I am much distrought. But I don't forget, and shall never forget, the great kindness you heaped upon me the other month. If Miss Bayard is with (or near you) please say I kiss her hand. I wish you every desire of your heart, for they are all for the good of mankind, and am ever very faithfully yours

Henry James

INDEX

Conkling, Sen. Roscoe, 123–124
Conway, Moncure, D., 95, 119
Cookson, Mr. and Mrs. Montagu, 273
Cornhill Magazine, 166, 285
Cotman, John S., 111
Coulson, Mr., 4–5, 118
Couture, Thomas, 142, 173, 245
Crafts, James Mason, 10, 11, 74, 82
Crafts, Mrs. James Mason, 10, 20, 74, 82, 258
Craik, George Lillie, 168
Crawford, F. Marion, 422n
Crompton, Mr., 160
Crompton, Mrs., 157
Cross, John W., 94, 158, 234, 248, 337; letter to, 289
Cross, Mrs. John W., *See* Eliot, George
Cross, Miss, 332
Crossfield, Mr. and Mrs., 157
Cunliffe, Sir Robert, 94, 110
Cunliffe, Lady, 94, 110, 113
Curtis, Daniel and Ariana, 359
Curtis, George, 302, 307–308

Dalhousie, Mr. and Mrs., 336
Daly, Augustin, 53
Dante Alighieri, 351
Darlington–Johnson, Mr. and Mrs., 55–56
Darwin, William, 143, 150, 258, 316
Darwin, Mrs. William (Sara Sedgwick), 50, 112, 113, 116, 119–120, 130, 131, 133, 134, 143, 146, 148, 150, 158, 180, 210–211, 214, 258, 291, 316, 319
Daudet, Alphonse, xiii, 3, 20, 24, 29, 44, 165, 259, 417
Davout, Marshal Louis Nicolas, 34
Delacroix, Eugène, 417
Demidoff, Prince, 276–277
Dennett, John Richard, 262–263
Derby, Lord, 113

Dexter, Mr. and Mrs. Gordon, 388
Dicey, Albert, 99, 101, 119, 157
Dicey, Mrs. Albert, 99, 119, 157
Dicey, Edward, 124, 160
Dicey, Mrs. Edward, 94, 117, 124, 160
Dickens, Charles, 44, 221, 263, 272, 295, 296
Dilke, Sir Charles, 89, 175, 215, 218, 234, 248
Disraeli (Dizzy), Benjamin, 68, 163–164, 320, 339
Doré, Gustave, 37, 217
Dorr, Julia C. R., 15–16
Doudan, Ximénès, 55
Doyle, Sir Francis, 158, 200, 208
Droz, Gustave, 25, 44
Duchatel, Comte, 55
Duckworth, Mrs. (Julia née Jackson; Mrs. Leslie Stephen), 157, 177, 209
Duff, *see* Grant-Duff
Dugdale, Mr., 130
Dugdale, Mrs., 118, 185
Dumas, Alexandre *fils*, 29, 171, 343
Du Maurier, George, 113, 172, 388, 417; letter to, 409
Du Maurier, Mrs. George, 113, 172
Duncan, Mrs. Butler, 364
Durdan, Mr. and Mrs., 331
Duveneck, Frank, 245, 264, 277, 280, 349
Dysart, Lord, 5

Eastlake, Lady, 151
Effingham, Lady, 225
Eliot, Sir Frederick and Lady, 199
Eliot, George, 29, 30, 46–47, 55, 59, 60n, 70, 91, 94, 103, 172, 190, 194, 290n, 332, 337
Emerson, Ralph Waldo, 94, 417
Emmet, Bob, 297

Emmet, Miss "Posie," 93

Fiske, John, 244, 248, 249, 316
Flaubert, Gustave, x, xi, xiii,
3, 11, 14–15, 20–21, 23, 24,
26–27, 29, 33, 36, 38, 44, 52–53,
114, 164–165; letter to, 165
Ford, Mrs. Richard, 94–95
Forster, W. E., 223, 224
Forster, Mrs. W. E., 224
Frelinghuysen, Frederick T., 371
Frohman, Daniel, 391n
Fromentin, Eugène, 55
Froude, J. A., 93, 421

Gainsborough, Thomas, 330
Galaxy, 95–96, 155
Gallatin, Mrs. Albert (the former
Louisa Bedford Ewing), 21
Galway, Lady, 200
Gambetta, Léon, 41
Gardner, Isabella Stewart ("Mrs.
Jack"), 206, 266n; letters to,
265, 363, 372, 377, 383, 386
Garfield, President James A.,
320, 335, 360
Garrison, Wendell Phillips, 68,
120
Garrison, William Lloyd, 33
Gaskell, Lady Catherine, 123,
125–126, 128
Gaskell, Charles Milnes, 123, 125–
127, 158, 160, 180, 198, 199, 200,
208
Gaskell, Meta, 160
Gautier, Théophile, 15, 38, 69
Geoffrin, Mme., 39
Gérôme, Jean Léon, 27
Gibbens, Alice Howe, *see* James,
Mrs. William
Gide, André, 47n
Gilder, Helena De Kay, letter
to, 403
Gilder, Richard Watson, 277–
278, 404 and n, 414
Gilman, Daniel Coit, 213

Gladstone, William E., 339,
408, 421
Glück, C. W., 38
Godkin, Edwin L., 11, 57, 91,
146, 270, 364–365, 410n,
419; letter to, 376
Godkin, Lawrence, 377, 418–419
Godley, Mr. and Mrs. Arthur, 318
Goethe, Johann Wolfgang, 46
Gogol, Nikolai, 334
Goldsmid, Lady, 114, 418
Goncourt, Edmond de, xiii,
3, 15, 20, 23, 24, 165
Gordon, Mrs. Henry, 159–160,
223, 353
Gordon, Lady, *see* Hamilton-
Gordon, Lady
Gosse, Edmund, 255
Gourlay, Janet, 60
Gourlay, Margaret, 45
Gower, Lord Ronald, 99
Grant, Nelly, 233–234
Grant-Duff, Sir Mounstuart, 215, 234
Green, John Richard, 176, 412n
Green, Mrs. John Richard
(Alice Stopford), 176, 412
Greville, Mrs. Richard, 190,
194, 196, 241, 353
Grove, George, 167–168
Grymes, Nelly, 225
Guizot, Guillaume, 345
Gurney, Ephraim, 46, 73, 86, 92,
94, 186
Gurney, Mrs. Ephraim, 73, 94,
186, 215

Hamilton, Gail (Mary Abigail
Dodge), 371
Hamilton-Gordon, Lady, 89, 101–
102, 115, 152, 154, 184, 207
Hamley, General Edward Bruce,
211
Harcourt, Sir William, 167, 229,
338
Harcourt, Lady, 160, 167, 229,
237, 338

Van Buren, Smith, 371
Van Buren, Mrs., 119, 386
Van de Weyer, Mme., 113, 124
Van de Weyer, Misses, 124,
  160, 242
Verdi, Giuseppe, 48
Véron, Pierre, 44
Veronese, Paolo, 318
Viardot, Louis, 10, 346
Viardot, Pauline, 10, 16, 27,
  29, 37–38, 41, 46, 49
Villeneuve, Mme. de, 55
Vinci, Leonardo da, 351

Waddington, Mr. and Mrs., 288
Wade, Lady, 152
Wadsworth, Mrs., 41, 55
Wagner, Richard and Cosima,
  73 (R. only), 283, 287
Waldegrave, Lady, 247, 248–249
Wallace, Mackenzie, 99–100,
  108, 115, 123
Walsh, Catharine (Aunt Kate),
  5–6, 74, 293, 349–350, 394,
  395–396, 397, 398; letter to, 9
Walsh, Lawrence, 119
Warner, Charles Dudley, 36,
  38–39, 53, 392
Warner, Joe, 402
Watteau, Jean Antoine, 330
Webster, Daniel, 27
Wedderburn, Sir David, 170
Wedmore, Frederick, 120, 124

Westminster, Dean of, 223,
  224–225
Whistler, James Abbott McNeill,
  161, 167
Whitman, Sarah W., letter to,
  425
Wigan, Alfred, 115
Wigan, Mrs. Alfred, 118
Wilde, Oscar, 43, 372
Wilkinson, Florence, see Mathews,
  Mrs. Francis
Wilkinson, Mary, 169–170
Wilkinson, Dr. J. J. Garth, 228,
  294, 339
Wilson, E. D. J., 275
Wister, Sarah Butler, 23, 86,
  92, 99, 102, 353, 369, 381
Wolseley, Sir Garnet (later
  Viscount), 130, 151
Wolseley, Lady, 130, 151, 258,
  269
Woolner, Thomas, 94, 99,
  111, 117
Woolner, Mrs. Thomas, 94, 99,
  111
Woolson, Constance Fenimore,
  288
Wright, Chauncey, 149
Wyman, Charles, 117

Young, John Russell, 275

Zola, Émile, 3, 15, 24, 44, 53,
  165, 274n, 332, 341

438